Heroes and Martyrs of Pale

The history of the Palestinians over the last half century has been one of turmoil, a people living under occupation or exiled from their homeland. Theirs has been at times a tragic story, but also one of resistance, heroism, and nationalist aspiration. Laleh Khalili's fascinating and unsettling book is based on her experiences in the Lebanese refugee camps, where ceremonies and commemorations of key moments in the history of the struggle are a significant part of their political life. It is these commemorations of the past, according to Dr Khalili, that have helped to forge a sense of nationhood and strategies of struggle amongst the disenfranchised Palestinian people, both in Lebanon and beyond. She also analyzes how, in recent years, as discourses of liberation and rights have changed in the international community, and as the character of local institutions has evolved, there has been a shift in the representation of Palestinian nationalism from the heroic to the tragic mode. This trend is exemplified through the commemoration of martyrs and their elevation to tragic yet iconic figures in the Palestinian collective memory.

LALEH KHALILI is Lecturer in Politics at the School of Oriental and African Studies in London.

Cambridge Middle East Studies 27

Cambridge Middle East Studies has been established to publish books on the nineteenth- and twentieth-century Middle East and North Africa. The aim of the series is to provide new and original interpretations of aspects of Middle Eastern societies and their histories. To achieve disciplinary diversity, books will be solicited from authors writing in a wide range of fields, including history, sociology, anthropology, political science, and political economy. The emphasis will be on producing books offering an original approach along theoretical and empirical lines. The series is intended for students and academics, but the more accessible and wide-ranging studies will also appeal to the interested general reader.

A list of books in the series can be found after the index.

Heroes and Martyrs of Palestine

The Politics of National Commemoration

Laleh Khalili

University of London

CAMBRIDGE
UNIVERSITY PRESS

CAMBRIDGE UNIVERSITY PRESS
Cambridge, New York, Melbourne, Madrid, Cape Town, Singapore, São Paulo, Delhi

Cambridge University Press
The Edinburgh Building, Cambridge CB2 8RU, UK

Published in the United States of America by Cambridge University Press, New York

www.cambridge.org
Information on this title: www.cambridge.org/9780521106382

First published 2007
This digitally printed version 2009

A catalogue record for this publication is available from the British Library

Library of Congress Cataloguing in Publication data

Khalili, Laleh
  Heroes and martyrs of Palestine: the politics of national commemoration /
Laleh Khalili.
    p. cm. – (Cambridge Middl East studies; 26)
    Includes bibliographical references and index.

  ISBN-13 978-0-521-86512-8 (hardback : alk. paper)
  ISBN-10 0-521-86512-3 (hardback : alk. paper)

  1. Palestinian Arabs – History – 20th century. 2. National liberation
movements – Palestine. 3. Refugees, Palestinian Arab – Lebanon.
4. Arab-Israeli conflict. I. Title. II. Series.

DS113.6.K37 2007
956.9405–dc22   2006037412

ISBN 978-0-521-86512-8 hardback
ISBN 978-0-521-10638-2 paperback

For John

He who writes his story
inherits the land of that story

Mahmud Darwish

Contents

Acknowledgments

This book began as my doctoral dissertation, and I am grateful to my supervisors and mentors – Lisa Anderson, Ira Katznelson, Rashid Khalidi, Anthony Marx, and Charles Tilly – for the inspiration and support they provided and the difficult questions they asked. I thank As'ad AbuKhalil, Lori Allen, Frances Hasso, Roger Heacock, Isabelle Humphries, Laura Junka, Omar El-Khairy, Muhmmad Ali Khalidi, Peter Lagerquist, Adrienne Le Bas, Abeer Najjar, Shira Robinson, Wadie Said, Rosemary Sayigh, Yezid Sayigh, Jihane Sfeir, Gershon Shafir, Tamir Sorek, Linda Tabar, and Jennifer Zakaria who have read all or portions of the manuscript, made brilliant suggestions, caught embarrassing errors, and tightened the argument therein. John Chalcraft has read more versions of this study than anyone should have to, and each time, his incisive critiques have been crucial in making the book better. At some essential level, this work has been inspired by my parents, Dr. Khadijeh Tamaddon and the late Dr. Hedi Khalili, whose sense of justice and humanity I hope to pass on to their granddaughter, May.

In Ramallah, without Annemarie Jacir I would not have been able to see and experience what I did, or understand what I saw and experienced. In Beirut, Olfat Mahmoud helped me secure lodging and research permissions in the Burj al-Barajna camp, for which I am deeply indebted to her. I thank Ralph Bodenstein, Ruth Campbell, Mo'taz Dajani, Roula Al-Haj, Nasri Hajjaj, Jens Hanssen, Mona Harb, Bernhard Hillenkamp, Kirsten and Samah Idriss, Muhammad Ali Khalidi, Souheil al-Natour, Jim Quilty, Salah Salah, Jihane Sfeir, and Mayssoun Sukkarieh for their support in various stages of research. At the Institute for Palestine Studies, the patience and friendly assistance of the librarians – Mona Nsouli, Jihane Salhab, and Yusif Na'na' – allowed for a most pleasant and fruitful research experience. I am grateful to the Jafet Library Archives at the American University of Beirut and to Ambassador Afif Safieh for granting permission to use the poster that graces the cover of this book. My heartfelt thanks are also due to Marigold Acland at Cambridge University Press who has seen this book through various stages of publication. To all the Palestinian men, women, and children who contributed to this study and who cannot be named, I owe infinite gratitude. I would like to especially acknowledge my guide, comrade, and sister, Kholoud Hussein. Over the past five years, she has invited me to her house in Burj al-Barajna, helped me with my questionnaires, interviews, and interpretations, laughed and cried and gossiped with me, and become an aunt to my May. Kholoud, I am humbled by your strength, independence, intelligence, and good humor.

This book is dedicated to John for being the love of my life, the feminist father of our daughter, and my partner in intellectual debates, political activism, Mediterranean travels, and savouring silliness and laughter.

Abbreviations

AMB	al-Aqsa Martyrs' Brigade
ANM	Arab Nationalist Movement
ARCPA	Arab Resource Centre for Popular Arts
DFLP	Democratic Front for the Liberation of Palestine
Fatah-RC	Fatah-Revolutionary Council (Abu Nidal)
ICRC	International Commision of Red Cross
ISM	International Solidarity Movement
LF	Lebanese Forces
NGO	non-governmental organization
OPT	Occupied Palestine Territories
PA	Palestinian Authority
PFLP	Popular Front for the Liberation of Palestine
PFLP–GC	PFLP – General Command
PLO	Palestinian Liberation Organization
PNC	Palestinian National Charter
PRM	Palestinian Revolutionary Movement
SLA	South Lebanese Army
UN-ESCWA	United Nations Economic and Social Commission for West Asia
UNL	Unified National Leadership
UNRWA	United Nations Relief and Works Agency

1 Introduction

In a situation like that of the Palestinians and Israelis, hardly anyone can be expected to drop the quest for national identity and go straight to a history-transcending universal rationalism. Each of the two communities, misled though both may be, is interested in its origins, its history of suffering, its need to survive. To recognize these imperatives, as components of national identity, and to try to reconcile them, rather than dismiss them as so much non-factual ideology, strikes me as the task in hand.

Edward Said, "Permission to Narrate"

Discursive practices are not purely and simply ways of producing discourse. They are embodied in technical processes, in institutions, in patterns for general behaviour, in forms for transmission and diffusion, and in pedagogical forms which, at once, impose and maintain them.

Michel Foucault, "History of Systems of Thought"

By now, we know the images that flicker across the television screens during CNN or BBC or al-Jazeera news broadcasts about Palestinians: mournful or angry funerals of martyrs; walls papered with images of young dead men and, now and again, women; poignant or proud commemorations of collective death spoken in the idiom of battles and massacres; pasts that seem to linger; exile that is not forgotten; histories of suffering that are declared and compared. We hear about a surfeit of memory. Some claim that this mnemonic abundance is the final bulwark against capitulation – or compromise, depending on where you stand politically. Everyone may disagree about the causes and effects, but no one denies that the nationalist claims of Palestinians – and Israelis – are bolstered by stories about the past: memories and histories.

All nationalist commemoration is associated with iconic images, objects, and persons. These icons are part of a larger narrative about the nation, as the nation itself is often anthropomorphized and portrayed as having an identity, a "national character," and a biography. It is thought that the story of the nation, celebrated and commemorated in so many ways and venues, is passed from one generation to the next, forming the essential core of the nation and its character. French nationalism has *la Marseillaise*, the Bastille, and de Gaulle. US nationalism has the flag, Fourth of July, the Civil war, and Ground Zero. Massada, the *Sabra*, David Ben-Gurion, and "If I forget thee, Jerusalem" are the emblems of Zionist nationalism. Palestinian nationalism has the *Nakba*, the *Intifada*, the Dome of the Rock, Sabra and Shatila massacres, the chequered *keffiyeh* scarf, and martyrs' posters. But in listing these recognizable yet selective icons, these nationalisms and their pageantry of memory are reified: none of these icons are stable, historically unchanging, or uncontested. National(ist) narratives – and the crucial symbols at their core – are challenged from within and without.

This study is about performances of remembered Palestinian (hi)stories and transformations in national commemoration over the last few decades. I examine icons, events, and persons commemorated in ceremonies, calendars, schoolbooks, and history-telling, and by doing so, I shed light on transformations in the character, affinities, values, and mobilizing strategies of the Palestinian national movement. In order to understand nationalist commemoration, this book has posed and pursued an array of questions. Some concern the qualitative content of nationalist commemorations: in what ways are past heroisms and tragedies celebrated or mourned? Has Palestinianness always been about martyrdom – as both detractors of Palestinian nationalism and some proponents of an Islamist version of it (Abu-Faris 1990) claim? Or is it possible that at other times, martyrdom was not so central to Palestinian nationalist commemoration? Other questions examine the internal workings of commemorations. If, as I argue, nationalist narratives are not stable, and as such, commemorations are also fluid in their object, tone, and resonance, *how* do political and social transformations affect the way Palestinian refugees remember and commemorate their history of exile, and their lives and losses? In a deterritorialized nation, where the diasporic population has resided in camps and shantytowns rather than cosmopolitan metropolitan centers, and unlike nationalists cited by Gellner (1983: 101–109) who have not been prosperous and embourgeoised, what form does nationalist narrative-making take? A final series of questions interrogate sources and discursive boundaries of nationalist commemoration. Are nationalist commemorative forms and narratives borrowed transnationally or locally imagined and reproduced? How do seismic shifts in global politics – the end of the Cold War, the rise of human rights and humanitarian politics – affect local practices? Do transnational discourses, not all of which are Europe-centered, inform local vocabularies of mobilization? What roles do these discourses play in mediating the relationships between national communities and transnational institutions?

Ultimately, this study wants to know why representations of the past are so central to nationalist movements and sentiments.

Nationalist memories

Nationality requires us all to forget the boundaries between the living and the dead, the discrepancies between individual experience and the national history.

Anne Norton, "Ruling Memory"

In his seminal work on nationalism, Benedict Anderson (1991: 6) writes that imagined communities "are to be distinguished, not by their falsity/genuineness, but by the style in which they are imagined." Accordingly, in this study, I examine national narratives – or "stories of peoplehood" in Rogers Smith's evocative phrase (2003) – promulgated by commemorative acts, events, and objects. I argue that *what* is valorized, celebrated, and commemorated in different nationalisms reveals a great deal about *how* that nationalism is formed: I focus on the mechanics of production of national stories, rather than analyze them as "natural" by-products of an already existing national sentiment. My aim is to show that, contra Anthony D. Smith (1986), even the most intensely felt and fought-for nationalisms contain narratives of the past – "memories" – that are *not* (or not necessarily) ethnic, historically continuous, and unequivocally durable. I argue that while particular events are "remembered" as the shared basis of peoplehood, the construction and reconstruction of these events, the shifting mood of commemorative narratives, and ruptures in commemorative practices surrounding these events all point to a far less stable notion of historical or national memory – and consequently national sentiment – than some might think.

To make this argument, I contend that valorized national narratives – themselves so influential in shaping political strategies and aims – are often hotly contested and their reproduction often requires institutions whose power and resources affect what sorts of discursive modes are chosen, what types of narratives are promulgated, and which audiences are engaged. Furthermore, the affinity of local nationalisms with broader transnational discourses negates the idea that Palestinian nationalist practices are *sui generis* products of a static and unique Palestinian culture. By transnational discourses, I not only indicate global discursive trends but also those discourses borrowed from neighbors such as Iran and allies such as Hizbullah. As such, I challenge the notion of an "authentically" organic and unchanging nationalism nurtured by a prosperous bourgeoisie in the hermetically sealed greenhouse of a clearly bounded territory. I contend that in the crucial interface between the local and the transnational, nationalist commemorations, stories of peoplehood, and strategies of mobilisation are forged, reproduced, and transformed.

Histories, memories, stories

In this book, I have chosen to examine commemoration – *public* performances, rituals, and narratives – because I am concerned not with memories but with "mnemonic *practices*" (Olick 2003), not with images inside people's heads but with the *social* invocation of past events, persons, places, and symbols in variable social settings.

In his monumental work on *lieux de mémoire* in France, Pierre Nora (1996: 3) distinguishes memory from history:

Memory is always a phenomenon of the present, a bond tying us to the eternal present; history is a representation of the past. Memory, being a phenomenon of emotion and magic, accommodates only those facts that suit it … History, being an intellectual, nonreligious activity, calls for analysis and critical discourse. Memory situates remembrance in a sacred context. History ferrets it out; it turns whatever it touches into prose. Memory wells up from groups that it welds together, which is to say, as Maurice Halbwachs observed, that there are as many memories as there are groups, that memory is by nature multiple yet specific; collective and plural yet individual. By contrast, history belongs to everyone and to no one and therefore has a universal vocation … Memory is an absolute, while history is always relative.

Though certain aspects of Nora's definition of memory are suggestive – namely its selectiveness and polyvalence – his descriptions of historiography as universal and of memory as essential are problematic, and the distinctions made between history and memory are hyperbolic. This view of memory and history as respectively "popular" and intellectual stories about the past ignores the mutual imbrication of these two categories of narratives and dehistoricises and sanctifies an object called memory. In this view, memory bubbles up "naturally" from the collective experiences of a group and it is absolute, emotional, magical, and as such insusceptible to reason, dynamism, or change.

By contrast, I shift the focus of analysis from metaphysical or cognitive aspects of memory, to its effect and appearance in practice. This heuristic shift *externalizes* remembering (Olick and Robbins 1998), and allows us to look at processes of remembering and commemorating in a social setting, and in relation to particular audiences and contexts (Bruner 1984; Bruner and Gorfain 1984). I historicise commemorative practices and examine their multiple sites of production and reproduction. I consider commemoration to be constituted of *forms* – for example, history-telling (Portelli 1997), monument-building, ceremonies, – and narrative *contents*. The narrative content is of primary interest to me, because in articulating a vision of nationhood, commemorative narratives also proffer possible strategies of cohesion and struggle.

A large swathe of scholarship across disciplinary boundaries has viewed commemoration as either the site or instrument of contention. Throughout the world, different political actors have struggled over the form, meaning, and purpose of collective memory and national commemorations (Brubaker and Feischmidt 2002; Farmer 1999; Malkki 1995; Poletta 2003; Popular Memory Group 1982; Portelli 1997; Sayigh 1978; 1994; Slyomovics 1998; Swedenburg 1995; Tilly 1994; Trouillot 1995; Watson 1994; Yoneyama 1999; Zerubavel 1995).[1] Although this study is firmly located within this body of scholarship, I also hope to show the transnational affinities of nationalist commemorative practices and the profound influence of global politics on the production and reproduction of local memories. Furthermore, I emphasize the importance of narratives not only as a vehicle for transmission of memories but also as the core content of all commemorative practices. I argue that every commemoration, whether it is a ceremony, a monument, a mural, or commemorative naming, explicitly or implicitly contains a story. Much has been written about the importance of stories. Stories transform "the mere coexistence of experiences" (Turner 1980: 153) into meaningful narrative sequences, collate events, and organize them according not only to the actuality of the events that have passed but also on the basis of the exigencies of the present, the social and political context in which the narrative has developed, and according to the operational relations between the teller of the story and her audience. The teller of the stories "selectively appropriates" discrete events (Somers 1992: 601) and infuses them with meaning by sequencing, conjoining, or eliding them (Zerubavel 1995: 225). I look at the

---

[1] Collective memories are also said to be "moral practices" (Lambek 1996) that demand accountability not only in courts of law (Mamdani 2000; Osiel 1997) but also in the wider society (Tonkin 1992; Werbner 1995). Collective memories can form the basis of selfhoods (Connerton 1989) and affirm community (Winter 1995). National identities are said to be inseparable from the nation's memories (Gillis 1992; Halbwachs 1992; Le Goff 1992; Nora 1996, 1997, 1998; Smith 1986). Whether in Israel (Zerubavel 1995), revolutionary France (Ben-Amos 2000), post-Independence India (Amin 1995), Britain (Bommes and Wright 1982), or Germany (Mosse 1990), states use commemorative practices, holiday cycles, and especially textbooks "to establish a consensus view of both the past and the forms of personal experience which are significant and memorable" (Bommes and Wright 1982: 255–6). This shared – and crafted – memory forms the basis of communal feeling. Although this scholarship is very relevant to this project, I focus on the contentious element of commemoration and national memory narratives.

construction of these commemorative narratives, and by analyzing heroic, tragic, and *sumud* (steadfastness) stories embedded within Palestinian commemorative practices, I show the emergence of dominant narratives in particular contexts, their modes of reproduction, their subversion at other times, and their replacement by wholly dissimilar narratives when the context, institutions, and available transnational discourses have changed.

Approaching Palestinian nationalism

Palestinian commemorations are accessible openings through which transformations in Palestinian nationalism can be examined, since in the Palestinian refugee camps of Lebanon, as in the Occupied Palestinian Territories (OPT) these footprints of memory are easily visible. In both places, images of young martyred men stare out of posters pasted on alley walls alongside photographs and murals of Jerusalem. Interior walls of almost every house carry the picture of a young martyr, a son or daughter, a husband, a brother or sister. Schools, clinics, and even small shops are named after cities and villages left behind and destroyed in 1948. On the margins of most camps in Lebanon and throughout the OPT, pockmarked hulks of semi-destroyed buildings are left standing years, sometimes decades, after the bombings that rendered them uninhabitable; they are iconic objects reminding all of the violence of war. In Lebanon, grave markers in unexpected locations – mosques, schools, and nurseries – testify to urgent burials during sieges. In Beirut, sites of mass graves – even when unmarked – contain hints that render a history of carnage legible to attentive eyes: fifty-year-old olive and fig trees amidst ruins that were once camp houses in Tal al-Za'tar, flowerbeds that were once alleyways in Shatila. Stories of violence, catastrophe, and sorrow are made tangible through the constant and evolving practices of commemoration of the camp residents in Lebanon. In the OPT, stone-throwing children and political prisoners are celebrated alongside the heroic *shabab* (young men). There, martyrs' funerals are familiar commemorative events not only for the locals who participate in them but also for the international audiences who see broadcast images of the event.

Palestinians commemorate a broad range of events, objects, and persons. Some iconic objects of commemoration include olive trees, stone houses built in old villages, oranges, keys, and embroidered dresses. These objects are overwhelmingly associated with prelapsarian village life in Palestine, and were invoked as signifiers of Palestinianness once the nationalist movement re-emerged in the mid-1960s. Ghassan

Kanafani's fiction and Mahmud Darwish's poetry have been crucial in promulgating many of these icons, but so were other writers and poets, different political institutions, and the refugees themselves. In this study, I will not focus on the *Nakba* (the catastrophe of 1948) and its associated objects of memory, as a number of other studies have already examined the topic in great detail (Bardenstein 1998; 1999; Davis 2002, forthcoming; Khalili 2004, 2005a; Slyomovics 1998; Swedenburg 1990). Instead, I focus on those commemorative practices which specifically celebrate the heroisms of the nationalist movement and mourn the tragedies of endured losses since the start of the nationalist movement in the 1960s. In so doing, I investigate commemorations of iconic events such as battles and massacres, and of iconic persons such as martyrs or *fida'iyyin* guerrillas. I analyze narratives contained within commemorative practices, their production and promulgation, how some events have been retrospectively reinterpreted as heroic or tragic, the performative aspect of commemoration, and the way the Palestinians themselves sometimes subvert dominant commemorative narratives about important historic moments.

This study is based on ten months of continuous residence in the Burj al-Barajna refugee camp in Beirut (2001–2002) and several subsequent visits (lasting anywhere from two to eight weeks) to Lebanon and later to the OPT. Ethnographic work and hundreds of informal interviews and dozens of formal interviews were supplemented by extensive archival research through Palestinian factional and NGO publications. I have chosen to write about Palestinians for three distinct reasons. First and foremost, the Palestinian struggle for nationhood has been and continues to be a central question of Middle Eastern politics, especially as the Arab states were either defeated by or signed peace accords with Israel. For decades, the question of Palestine has animated discussions, passion, and contention throughout the Middle East, and the issues and concerns which arise out of it show no sign of abatement. Second, I have focused on Palestinians, especially those who have resided in Lebanon, because of their statelessness. Usually, the state is considered the basic unit of politics, yet in the twentieth century, the condition of statelessness has affected the lives of millions, among them the Palestinians, and especially the Palestinian refugees. Palestinian statelessness for much of the last few decades highlights both the mechanisms of nationalist struggle and the construction of nationalist narrative in the absence of state institutions, and it further emphasizes the importance of international political institutions and discourses to which Palestinians have appealed for support and sympathy. Third, the dramatic shifts in strategies and approaches within the Palestinian movement over time allow an important opportunity to understand changing nationalisms. During the period known as the *Thawra* (1965–1982), or the Revolution, Palestinian refugees in Lebanon sought the attainment of their rights through their struggle for a government of their own. But in the absence of a viable nationalist movement in Lebanon, before and after the *Thawra*, the refugees have turned to the international community, couching their struggle for rights in the lexicon of international rights and obligations. The range of their political and ideological discourse, of which commemoration is a significant element, clearly evinces their ideological and strategic shifts, and the transformations in the targets and audiences of their claim-making.

The bulk of this study focuses on the Palestinians in Lebanon because of their centrality to the Palestinian national project between 1969 and 1982. Among all Palestinian communities outside the boundaries of Mandate Palestine, those in Lebanon have experienced the greatest transformations in their political and social condition. Political mobilization in the late 1960s and 1970s placed them at the very heart of the Palestinian nationalist movement. Many of the commemorative narratives and practices that have become emblematic of Palestinian nationalism originated in the refugee camps of Lebanon during the *Thawra*. Furthermore, because Palestinian refugees in Lebanon have undergone the most drastic political transformations, the shifts in their commemorative practices have also been most perceptible and open to scrutiny.

In the course of the bloody Lebanese Civil war, and after the Israeli invasion of 1982, the leaders and fighters of the Palestinian Liberation Organization (PLO) were forced to abandon Lebanon, and with the start of the Intifada in the West Bank and Gaza, the PLO shifted its focus from the diasporan communities to the Palestinians living in the OPT. Since 1987, militant nationalist mobilization – of both secular and Islamist varieties – have flourished alongside exponentially growing non-governmental organizations (NGOs), which like their counterparts in Lebanon, play a decidedly political role. Crucially, however, what distinguishes the Palestinian community in the OPT from their counterparts in Lebanon or the rest of the diaspora is the nascent growth of a proto-state therein, with all the institutional and discursive transformations this emergence entails. This study appraises nationalist practices in the OPT in order to display the full range of available and utilized nationalist narratives. In the OPT, the role of states – or state-like institutions – in providing alternative nationalist biographies is highlighted. Furthermore, whereas in Lebanon, NGOs more or less succeeded militant factions chronologically, the co-existence of militant institutions (particularly Islamist ones) alongside NGOs in the OPT allows us to study the interplay and overlap between different nationalist narratives and practices.

The plan

To answer the questions posed at the beginning of this chapter, I first examine the transnational discourses and the local historical context of commemoration, then discuss the specific content of narratives in the refugee camps of Lebanon, and bring the study chronologically forward in a discussion of commemoration in the OPT. Chapter 2 focuses on transnational discourses that have been so crucial in shaping Palestinian commemorative narratives. I examine the Third Worldist discourse of the 1960s and 1970s, the rise of the human rights ethos in the late 1980s, and the concurrent rise of transnational Islamisms. Throughout, I weave in an analysis of gendered modes of representation in these discourses. To complement the examination of transnational factors, in Chapter 3, I provide a historical outline of the Palestinian presence in Lebanon between 1948 and 2005. While explaining the periodization I have used throughout the book and providing the local historical context, this chapter takes on a more analytical stance, interrogating the ways in which factions (1969–1982) and NGOs (from 1993 onwards) have penetrated the lives of Palestinian refugees in Lebanon and how they deploy their resources to act as conduits for tragic or heroic narratives.

Following the explication of local and international contexts, Chapter 4 describes various forms of commemoration: history-telling, pedagogy, paper and electronic media, naming, organization of time and space, and ceremonial gatherings. I then probe the contents of these forms. Chapter 5 lays out my analysis of heroic, tragic, and *sumud* (steadfastness) narratives in Lebanon and attempts to explain why and how in any given period, a particular narrative tends to dominate the discourse of the refugees.

The following two chapters illustrate how heroic, tragic, and steadfastness narratives inform the commemoration of heroes and of iconic events. Chapter 6 focuses on the shift from guerrillas to martyrs as the *commemorated heroic personae*. It analyzes the various forms taken by the commemoration of martyrs and seeks not only to find the local bases of the narratives of martyrdom, but also to show the available international discourses celebrating martyrdom. Chapter 7 similarly examines how tragic and heroic narratives are inflected in the *commemoration of iconic moments*. It critically examines the centrality of the battle as an icon of Palestinian nationalism during the *Thawra* and traces the shift in emphasis to massacres as iconic events. This chapter also interrogates the commemorative polyvalence surrounding the War of the Camps, once again outlining the historical and political bases of commemorative narratives.

Chapter 8 shifts the study of commemoration both temporally and spatially, through examining Palestinian nationalism as practiced in the OPT after 1987. Whereas in Lebanon, heroic, tragic, and *sumud* narratives appeared primarily in a diachronically sequential way, in the OPT, several different narratives coexist simultaneously and in hybrid form. These narratives are produced by the NGOs, the Palestinian Authority, and oppositional political organizations among others. The persistence of military occupation and the specificity of political relations within the OPT require that commemorative practices and narratives there appeal to *their* specific audiences.

The concluding chapter summarizes the impact and efficacy of commemorative narratives in shaping nationalist discourses and emphasizes the significance of this study in advancing our understanding not only of commemoration and commemorative practices, but also of the durable resonance of nationalist sentiments.

2 Transnational movements and discourses

> There is something paradoxical about the fact that nationalism should
> need *trans*nationalism to protect itself.
>
> Akhil Gupta, "The Song of the Non-Aligned World"

In July 1959, in the last throes of the Algerian revolutionary war, Frantz
Fanon (1963: 32), who had become one of the most eloquent spokes-
persons of that struggle, declared that:

> two-thirds of the world's population is ready to give to the Revolution as many
> heavy machine-guns as we need. And if the other third does not do so, it is by no
> means because it is out of sympathy with the cause of the Algerian people. Quite
> to the contrary, this other third misses no opportunity to make it known that this
> cause has its unqualified moral support. And it finds ways of expressing this
> concretely.

The awareness of a world whose sympathy can be mobilized in defense
of one's cause and the successful overcoming of national boundaries in
appealing to large audiences are distinguishing features of many political
movements of the post-Second World War era. Transnational networks
of solidarity and sympathy have come into being in universities, religious
institutions, solidarity organizations, battlefields, and conferences, and
different movements have provided one another with financial resources, volunteers – both militant and pacifist – and arms. But alongside the
more material manifestations of global affiliations, transnational discourses are forged in particular places which are then borrowed, nurtured, translated, and transformed across borders. By transnational
discourses I mean not only modes of representation of a particular time,
place, and political agenda, but the institutions and networks which
support this discourse. Discourses include symbols, songs, images, and,
most importantly, narratives articulating the history, meaning, and
strategies of struggle. These discourses emerge in specific contexts –
sometimes simultaneously across the globe – and then traverse national
boundaries. As they globalize, they lose some of their historical specificity and their concreteness and become more abstract, transportable,

11

and iconic. The portability of these discourses across national boundaries gives them legitimacy and authorizes them.

For my purposes, transnational discourses are broad – and therefore flexible – ways of imagining the world. Their broadness leaves much room for more textured adaptations and interpretations in more spatially restricted contexts, such as nations. Certain themes and figures dominate in each discourse, and these authorized themes give broad, transnational, and flexible discourses some coherence over time and space. A vivid example is the figure of Che Guevara, the flesh-and-blood revolutionary, the specificity of whose historical emergence and geographic plan of action was abstracted – especially after his death – and he became the single most recognizable iconic hero of national liberation during the 1960s and 1970s across the world. Che's call for "one, two, three, many Vietnams" was adopted as a call to action in the Third World. The famous slogan itself referred to yet another iconic transnational moment as the single most potent symbol of anti-colonial struggle: Vietnam in the 1960s.

Another iconic image, substantively and drastically different from those of the above, is that of a starving African child in need of international rescue. The quiet plea in his eyes seems to speak of an untold suffering which requires a humanitarian intervention. The evocative power of such transnational discourses and images rests in their ability to translate world-historical events into recognizable daily struggles and to create a sense of sympathy – if not kinship – and an imagined transnational community among people who, for the most part, had never met and would never meet.

The spread of transnational discourses has had less to do with technological advances that shorten distances and ease communication – although these have certainly facilitated boundary-crossings – and has more to do with the adoption of discourses by local institutions, and the subsequent interface between local institutions in transnational places. The latter are places that by virtue of their specific history have become the seedbed for a particular nascent discourse and a meeting place for its practitioners. The United Nations' General Assembly is such a place, wherein a seat authorizes a new nation-state's claim to independence and sovereignty. Gamal Abd al-Nasser's Cairo was another such place, becoming the home of the African and Asian People's Solidarity Organization (AAPSO) in 1957. Post-independence "Algeria welcomed representatives of South Africa's African National Congress and Pan-African Congress, of Mozambique's FRELIMO, Zimbabwe's ZAPU, and Arafat's PLO, which made its capital a 'veritable breeding ground of revolutionary movements'" (Malley 1996: 142). Tehran after the revolution of 1978/1979 similarly embraced revolutionary organizations, and radical students convened "the first worldwide gathering of liberation movements" (Ebtekar 2000: 179–184). Hasan al-Turabi of Sudan established the Popular Arab and Islamic Conference in Khartoum in 1991, which briefly brought together not only Islamist organizations, but also representatives from secular militant movements (such as the Palestinian PFLP). In later years, human rights conferences held in various world capitals – financed by European and North American governmental and non-governmental institutions – similarly encouraged the meeting of local NGO activists committed to the implementation of "universal" human rights/humanitarian agendas and the promotion of developmental policies in their own domestic environments.

In this chapter, I write of the primary transnational discourses that have been appropriated and adapted by various strands of the Palestinian national movement since the mid-1960s. Each of these discourses has emerged at a particular historical juncture and at the intersection of global and local politics. They all bear the stamp of their origins, and yet, their very traversing of national boundaries has transformed them in ways not originally intended or even imagined. The historical contingency of these discourses, along with their fluid movement across continents, lends them their dynamic character. The persistence of certain iconic aspects of these discourses and their evocative power over decades speaks of their appeal as frames through which the past is understood and future strategies are forged. All these discourses have a transnational audience in mind alongside the local one; they are all sustained by powerful institutions and networks; they all consider the past a compelling mobilizational resource; and they all deploy a particular narrative with specific moral and normative import, heroic or tragic protagonists, and a reserve of symbols and icons. In what follows, I analyze the heroic narratives of liberationist/nationalist movements, the nation-states, and Islamists, as well as the tragic discourse of human rights/humanitarian organizations, throughout drawing out the role of gender in the constitution of these discourses.

"A Brave Music": the celebration of nations and their heroes

> I do not deny the existence of the struggling "wretched of the earth", but maintain that they do not exist in isolation, as the "Third World." They are an integral part of the revolutionary world.
>
> Kwame Nkrumah, *The Struggle Continues*

> I am martyr Sana Yusif Muhaydli. I am 17 years old, from the South, from the occupied and oppressed Lebanese South, from the resisting,

resurgent South. I am not dead, but alive among you. Sing, dance, realise my dreams. Don't cry; don't be sad for me, but exult and laugh for a world in which there are heroes.

Sana Muhaydli, "Last Will and Testament"

When, in 1955, the leaders and representatives of "the despised, the insulted, the hurt, the dispossessed – in short, the underdogs of the human race" (Wright 1995 [1956]: 10) met in Bandung, Indonesia, as Richard Wright (1995 [1956]: 80) records in his fascinating report of the event, the response in the European and American continents was one of great anxiety:

Such was the atmosphere, brooding, bitter, apprehensive, which greeted the projected conference. Everybody read into it his own fears; the conference loomed like a long-buried ghost rising from a muddy grave.

Although the meeting of twenty-four African and Asian leaders continued a tradition of meetings by leaders of the Third World countries – the 1916 congress of colonized people organized by the Union of Nationalities in Lausanne was the earliest of such meetings (Young 2001: 118) – it was perhaps significant as the moment when commonality of struggles was recognized – if in the context of geostrategic struggles – by leaders of post-colonial states. "Most of the leaders of these nations had been political prisoners, men who had lived lonely lives in exile, men to whom secret political activity had been a routine matter, men to whom sacrifice and suffering had been daily companions" (Wright 1995[1956]: 10). These leaders had nurtured the heroic discourse of national liberation in a great many places and times, but for the first time, together, they found a global audience, when Egypt's Nasser, Sukarno of Indonesia, Nehru of India, and others addressed the conference. In his speech opening the conference, Sukarno proclaimed:

I recognise that we are gathered here today as a result of sacrifices. Sacrifices made by our forefathers and by the people of our own and younger generations. For me, this hall is filled not only by the leaders of the nations of Asia and Africa; it also contains within its walls the undying, the indomitable, the invincible spirit of those who went before us. Their struggle and sacrifice paved the way for this meeting of the highest representatives of independent and sovereign nations from two of the biggest continents of the globe. (Kahin 1956: 39–40)

Already the themes of heroic resistance, of sacrifice for the nation, and of a defiant pride in the sovereignty of former colonies informed narratives of anti-colonial struggle in the three continents. The heroic commemorative narrative sees the defiant rise of a central character out of the twilight of occasional and cyclical division, decay, and despondency. The heroic narrative claims that these temporary moments of decline and despair are ruptures in a continuously revolutionary/national past and that a decisive moment of heroism breaks the chain of past humiliation. Emphasis on the preceding degeneration and subsequent national awakening is a standard nationalist trope which underlines the necessity and inevitability of the nationalist movement. A classic nationalist work such as George Antonious's *The Arab Awakening*, similar to much of the subsequent repertoire of nationalist and liberationist literature, conveys "the narrative sense of human adventure" (Said 1994: 253) in its celebration of the emancipation of subjugated peoples.

The solidarity between nationalist movements, first displayed at Bandung, had such appeal that in 1960, the United Nations General Assembly issued resolution 1514 against colonialism. In the resolution, "welcoming the emergence in recent years of a large number of dependent territories into freedom and independence, and recognizing the increasingly powerful trends towards freedom in such territories which have not yet attained independence," it deplored the *colonizer's* armed action against liberation movements and declared that "all peoples have an inalienable right to complete freedom, the exercise of their sovereignty and the integrity of their national territory." But the newly decolonized states that met in Bandung, sponsored UNGA 1514, and formed the Non-Aligned Movement (NAM),[1] in fact, rode on a wave of popular – and far more radical – anti-colonial and anti-imperialist sentiment which found its expression in the liberationist writings of Frantz Fanon, Amilcar Cabral, Kwame Nkrumah, Regis Debray, Che Guevara, and their comrades. The liberationist discourse served the cause of anti-colonial nationalism and borrowed ideologically, tactically, and strategically from the Marxism of Lenin and Rosa Luxemburg. This radical discourse crossed continental boundaries and found a home among the ever-expanding rank of political activists and militants of the Third World. In fact, the Non-Aligned Movement would falter when it could not appeal to this "immense tyranny-destroying wave" (Fanon 1963: 97) and "revived when a majority [of its member states] were willing to link the question of the Middle East, Vietnam and Southern Africa in a single anti-colonial theme" (Willetts 1978: 44).

---

[1] The first meeting of the NAM – in which 25 heads of African, Asian, and Latin American nations participated – was held in Belgrade in 1961. Subsequent conferences were generally held every three years, and increasing numbers of states began to take part. In 2006, the NAM still exists and has some 77 members.

History and community were at the core of this discourse. In describing settler colonialism, Albert Memmi (1991: 91) wrote that "the most serious blow suffered by the colonized is being removed from history and community," and as such, the discourse of liberation envisioned both the restoration of history and the recuperation of community. But the recovered community was not simply "native" or local. The recognition of a transnational community of struggle was a central theme of the radical liberationist discourse, which found its institutional home at the Afro-Asian Solidarity Conference held in Algiers in 1965 or the Tricontinental Congress held in Cuba in 1967, or in the numerous political student unions which brought together radical student activists from the three continents. At the Afro-Asian Solidarity Conference, Che Guevara (1968: 386) embraced a tumultuous world of revolt:

Here and at all conferences, wherever they may be held, we should – along with our greeting to the heroic peoples of Vietnam, Laos, "Portuguese" Guinea, South Africa, or Palestine – extend to all exploited countries struggling for emancipation our friendly voice, our hand, and our encouragement; to our brothers in Venezuela, Guatemala, Colombia who, having taken up arms today, are saying a final "No!" to the imperialist enemy.

Later, addressing the Tricontinental Congress, he (1968: 413) invited his global audience to "create two, three, many Vietnams," a slogan taken up even by radicals in Europe and the United States (Varon 2004). Fanon (1963: 97) thanked this transnational community when he wrote of "the 'Week of Solidarity with Algeria,' organised by Chinese people, or the resolution of the Congress of African Peoples on the Algerian war." Amilcar Cabral (1969: 66–7) of Guinea-Bissau declared his solidarity with the Palestinian refugees and announced his "whole-hearted" support for "all that the sons of Palestine are doing to liberate their country." Different Palestinian political organizations showed solidarity with other anti-colonial and guerrilla movements by printing posters celebrating their emergence or victories.[2] The liberationist discourse in fact celebrated a legacy of struggle transferred across not only spatial boundaries, but also temporal ones. Vietnam's Ho Chi-minh saw in the nineteenth-century anti-colonialist Algerian warrior Abd al-Qadir a "national hero, the forerunner of people's war [in Vietnam]"

---

[2] A non-exhaustive list of the international movements and revolutionaries in solidarity with whom the Palestinian parties printed posters in the 1960s and 1970s includes Castro (Fatah), Polisario (PFLP), Vietnam (Fatah, PFLP, and DFLP), and Che Guevara (PFLP) (Ridhwan 1992; The Special Collection of Posters, American University in Beirut).

(Davidson 1981: 54). The poetry, films, novels, and texts of liberationist movements were readily translated into Third World languages – as well as European ones – and an intellectual community of resistance "played a pivotal role in chronicling revolution wherever they believe it might be" (Malley 1996: 81–82):

There were ... individual folk heroes: Wilfred Burchett in Asia, Regis Debray in Latin America, René Dumont in Africa, Jean Ziegler practically everywhere, to mention but a few. They included historians (Basil Davidson, Abdallah Laroui, Jacques Berque), economists (Pierre Jalée, André Gunder Frank, Samir Amin, Aghiri Emmanuel, Françoise Perroux), political scientists (Anwar Abdel-Malek), philosophers (Jean-Paul Sartre), sociologists (Pierre Bourdieu), anthropologists (Georges Balandier), poets and fiction writers (Pablo Neruda, Gabriel Garcia Marquez, Kateb Yacine, Jean Genet), even movie directors (Costa-Gavras).

To this list, one might add the songster Victor Jara – tortured and executed after the 1973 coup in Chile, the Palestinian poet Mahmud Darwish and Turkish poet Nazim Hikmat, the analyst and polemicist of Algerian anti-colonial struggle Frantz Fanon, and of course the *guerrilleros* Mao Tse-tung, Ho Chi-minh, V. N. Giap, and Che Guevara. If conferences were a place where the practitioners of the liberationist discourse met one another, Patrice Lumumba University in Moscow was another such meeting place for radical students from Asia, Africa, and Latin America; so too were Paris, London, Berlin, and even US campuses, where many Third World students and future revolutionaries rubbed shoulders.

The awareness of narratives about the past – history or memory – as a domain of resistance is a prominent element of the liberationist discourse. Fanon (1963: 169), the eloquent theoretician of liberation, wrote in his *Wretched of the Earth* that:

colonialism is not satisfied merely with holding a people in its grip and emptying the native's head of all form and content. By a kind of perverted logic, it turns to the past of the oppressed people, and distorts, disfigures and destroys it. This work of devaluing pre-colonial history takes on a dialectical significance today.

Thus, if the colonized are to be liberated, it is imperative for them to decide "to put an end to the history of colonization – the history of pillage – and to bring into existence the history of the nation – the history of decolonization" (1963: 51). Cabral (1973: 43) similarly saw the conquest of the past as a primary task of the liberation movements: "the foundation for national liberation rests in the inalienable right of every people to have their own history." This conquest includes an appropriation of past heroes in the cause of present struggle and a weaving of historical stories of dissent as originary moments into contemporary narratives of insurgency. There is an attempt to recover from the ruins and exclusions of colonialism "narratives of wholeness and continuity" (Norton 1993: 460). Thus, in the liberationist discourse, the nineteenth-century struggle of Abd al-Qadir begets the twentieth-century Algerian war of independence (or the people's war of Vietnam, as Ho claimed). The uprising of José Marti begets Fidelismo or Guevara's guerrilla insurrections, and Toussaint L'Ouverture's revolt begets Nkrumah's rebellion. A past appropriated in the course of struggle leads to the creation of a new man, and of a new "political and social consciousness" which even supersedes nationalist identities (Fanon 1963: 203). In turn, the "constant and eternal rebirth" of the new man (Guevara 1968: 363) guarantees national liberty and transnational solidarity.

The heroic narrative in the writing of the liberationists has brought into focus not only the reclaiming of history, but also the idea of violent political struggle and the possibility of self-sacrifice. Armed struggle is considered the only possible path to liberation, and theorists of guerrilla warfare – foremost among them Mao, Giap, Guevara, and Debray – see political violence as a necessary mobilizing action. Guerrilla warfare is theorized as the opening salvo of a war of liberation which would eventually generate mass action. The celebration of violent struggle contains within it not only the promise of liberation, but also the making of the new man. Fanon, in writing about the redemptive and unifying force of violence (1963: 93–94), provided a justification for armed struggle and for the blood-sacrifice in the cause of national liberation.[3] Within liberationist movements, however, some thinkers and activists contemplated the problematic aspects of emancipatory violence. They argued that political violence – once an instrument of becoming the author of one's own future – can generate institutions and logics that prove far more durable than originally imagined and intended (Feldman 1991; Sayigh 1997). The presence and institutionalization of militant groups – imagining themselves as the vanguard of the revolution – come at the expense of mass mobilization and exclude a public which may not choose armed struggle as its modus operandi (Jallul 1994). Militarist resistance replaces political struggle as the primary virtue.

Another deeply valorized theme in the heroic narrative is that of martyrdom. Political sacrifice can be adopted as a basic strategy for a number of reasons and in a variety of circumstances; for example, "when valued others will clearly benefit from the sacrifice; when not to

---

[3] Said (1994: 270–7), however, cautions against a simplistic reading of Fanon as solely glorifying violence.

sacrifice would betray weakness, fear, or disloyalty; when visible suffering has a chance of attracting third-party intervention; and when inconspicuous exit is difficult" (Tilly 2003: 174). Even if the notion of martyrdom in transnational liberationist discourses co-opts the religious cosmology which justifies sacrifice,[4] the act itself is performed in the cause of the nation – this new and "pure" object of veneration (Anderson 1991: 144) – rather than the glory of religion.[5] Guevara (1968: 363) celebrates "the ones who fell early and those still to come [as] the ... most complete expression of the heights that can be reached by a nation fighting to defend its purest ideas and ... its noblest goals." In his speech to the Tricontinental Congress in 1967, and shortly before his execution in Bolivia, Guevara (1968: 424) again extols self-sacrifice:

Wherever death may surprise us, let it be welcome, provided that this, our battle cry [against imperialism], may have reached receptive ears and another hand may be extended to wield our weapon and other men may be ready to intone the funeral dirge with the staccato singing of the machine guns and new battle cries of war and victory.

For Guevara, martyrdom was an invitation to action and the starting moment of a larger revolt. Cabral (1973: 55) similarly saw patriotism as "the spirit of sacrifice and devotion to the cause of independence, of justice, and of progress."

Martyrdom in the liberationist discourse is not considered a celebration of death. The seventeen-year-old Lebanese suicide bomber, Sana Muhaydli, invites her mourners to celebrate, "sing and dance" (Nasrallah 1985: 123). Self-sacrifice is not necessarily sought as an end, but is deemed necessary by those who resist oppression in the cause of the nation. Nkrumah (1973: 33) speaks of the fallen when he says, "we could mourn them but they don't want our tears. We scorn death knowing that we cannot be defeated." Rebirth, renewal, and ultimate victory are seen as immanent to self-sacrifice. Often martyrdom is deemed the only route to a meaningful life. In the opening to his memoir, the American Black Panther Huey Newton (1995: v) thanks his

---

[4] Juergensmeyer, for example, sees martyrdom as a religious act in a cosmic battle (2000: 161).
[5] Axel (2001: 139–140), Farmer (1999: 110), Feldman (1991: 237–263), Leys and Saul (1995), Marvin and Ingle (1999: *passim*); Mosse (1990: ch. 5), and Zerubavel (1994: 75–78) all describe how the nationalist idiom of self-sacrifice borrows religious themes, symbols, and vocabulary to justify martyrdom in the cause of the (putative or existing) nations of Khalistan, France, Ireland, Namibia, USA, Germany, and Israel, respectively. Self-sacrifice can also occur for an entirely secular cause that is not the nation, as Ramphele writes about the death of anti-apartheid activists (1997).

parents for making him "unafraid of death and therefore unafraid of life." At a large rally in support of the Palestinians under Israeli military siege in the OPT, held in the Beirut Stadium on 14 April 2002, the Palestinian national poet (and an avowed secularist) Mahmud Darwish told an anecdote about a young fighter of Jenin – then under Israeli siege: "When someone spoke to him on their mobile phone, he was smiling. The person asked, why are you happy? Don't you love life? You are about to lose your life! The fighter said, I am happy because I love life. If I will be martyred it is because of my love of life that I am becoming martyred." Though the anecdote could be apocryphal or allegorical, it conveys the liberationist interpretation of the act of self-sacrifice as a life-generating moment of agency. Palestinian novelist Ghassan Kanafani (1973: 30) writes:

Self-sacrifice, within the context of revolutionary action, is an expression of the very highest understanding of life, and of the struggle to make life worthy of a human being. The love of life for a person becomes a love for the life of his people's masses and his rejection that their life persists in being full of continuous misery, suffering and hardship. Hence, his understanding of life becomes a social virtue, capable of convincing the militant fighter that self-sacrifice is a redemption of his people's life. This is a maximum expression of attachment to life.

Similarly, in his Rivonia defense, Nelson Mandela (1965[1963]: 170) declares, "I have cherished the ideal of a democratic and safe society in which all persons live together in harmony and with equal opportunities. It is an idea which I hope to live for and to achieve. But if needs be, it is an ideal for which I am prepared to die."

A persistent element of the liberationist heroic narrative is its emphasis on hyper-masculine heroism. Though all liberationist movements attest to the importance of female warriors (and Palestinian Leila Khaled became a heroine and iconic figure far beyond the confines of Palestinian nationalist iconography), ultimately the virtues through which heroism is defined are those often considered masculine: courage under fire, the ability to deploy political violence in a cool and effective manner, and regenerating the nation through self-sacrifice, rather than birth-giving which is the domain of women (Hasso 2000; Massad 1995). Even the regenerative element of the heroic discourse refers to the creation of new "men" free from fear. The unspoken corollary of this new man is a more liberated woman who nevertheless embodies "womanhood." For example, Amilcar Cabral celebrates "Lebete Na N'Kanha – this time not the party militant but the woman, the young rebel as fine as a gazelle, the mother of a family, the wife whose husband listens to her, the producer of rice" (Davidson 1969: 12). Cabral follows the list of characteristics) of a complete woman with the praise of her smile and her eyes. Although a great many liberationist discourses have the progressive freedoms of women as their mantra, nevertheless in their commemorative discourses, the warrior virtues are most instrumental in making the world over (Braidotti 1997).

The extraordinary coherence of the heroic liberationist narrative across boundaries – the themes of a new man reclaiming and renewing his history through the force of arms – was in a sense "inspired by a vivid hope of change, scarcely present before, certainly never before felt with any such intensity or wide appeal" and as Basil Davidson (1978: 200) has written about Africa, this liberationist discourse was "spoken by men and women whose hearts beat to a brave music." A sense of hope animates the liberationist movements, and in the conjuncture of historical inevitability and human agency (Malley 1996: 95), despair and immobility are conquered and the nation is realized. Coming chapters will discuss how militant Palestinian organizations used the heroic narrative to frame their commemoration of the past. As the following section will suggest, however, heroic narratives can also be harnessed by both nation-states and by Islamist movements.

"Preserved in anthems, in flags and at the bank": domestication of heroes in states

Shall we fight?
What matter,
Since the Arab revolution
Remains preserved in anthems,
In flags and at the bank.
In your wounds' name they speak their speech.
        Mahmud Darwish, "Sirhan Drinks his Coffee in the Cafeteria"

What had once been the imaginative liberation of a people and the audacious metaphoric charting of spiritual territory usurped by the colonial masters were quickly translated into and accommodated by a world system of barriers, maps, frontiers, police forces, customs and exchange controls.
        Edward Said, *Culture and Imperialism*

When a revolutionary movement is domesticated and institutionalized in the apparatus of a state – as it happened so often towards the end of revolutionary or anti-colonial struggles in the Third World – the heroic liberationist discourse metamorphoses into the heroic narrative of nationhood. Transnational solidarity and the universal human struggle for liberation are exchanged for "national security and a separatist identity" (Said 1994: 307). The celebration of the nation-*state* as the preordained telos of the struggle co-opts the narrative of heroic insurgency, and where once the revolutionary underdogs were valorized for their tenacious battle against despotic establishments, today the nation-state, embodied in the statesman, takes center stage.[6] No longer does a new nation-state emphasize bloody wars of inception against collaborators and traitors, except to forget them as fratricide (Anderson 1991: 199–201). Histories of struggle come to focus on the glorious moment at which the state is recognized and seated at the table of nations. The contingent emergence of the new nation-state gives way to a linear narrative about its birth where only one ending – a valorized, sovereign, independent state – is allowed. In the stories that state institutions tell about the nation, the new man has been transformed into the citizen of the new state, who more often than not has obligations rather than rights (Malley 1996: 109). The revolution is cloaked in the ancient finery of the dynastic state (Anderson 1991: 160). History, rather then being the transformative legacy of and call to struggle, becomes a legitimating instrument for the state, and a tool of citizen-making pedagogy.

Gender imagery is also prevalent in nation-statist discourses. The nation itself is often portrayed as a woman (Baron 2005), the homeland is imagined as a fertile female body that can be subjected to rape by invaders and occupiers (Humphries and Khalili forthcoming), and women regenerate the state through fulfilling their biological functions (Mosse 1985; Yuval-Davis 1997). Men on the other hand are founding fathers, benevolent patriarchs, and protectors of the nation's honor which often dovetails with the honor of its women (Warnock 1990). Their fraternity is the basis of the imagined community (Anderson 1991: 7). Female bodies bring to the world the citizens and in both senses reproduce the nation (Kanaaneh 2002). Mothers and widows carry the banner that has fallen out of the hands of their heroic sons and husbands (Ramphele 1997; Shamgar-Handelman 1986), and gender symbols and, more specifically, the bodies, dress, and comportment of women become the primary markers of national or communal cultures (Yuval-Davis 1997). While national citizenship laws reproduce gender difference and disparity, the founding documents of most nations reinforce this disparity in the domain of nationalist discourse. The Palestinian

---

[6] See Connell 2002 for a comparison of the Eritrean, Nicaraguan, Palestinian, and South African revolutionary movements' transformation into states.

Declaration of Independence and the Palestinian National Charter both imagine the nation as a male body and, more important, masculinize political agency (Massad 1995).

In the nation-statist discourse, celebration of armed struggle gives way to obeisance to the "legitimate use of force" enshrined in the new state's coercive apparatus. Where once political violence was intended to bring about radical change, sacrifice is now only authorized in the cause of the nation. The nation *and* those who struggle for it come to be narrativized in heroic epics. In the nation-state's telling of the national narrative, the national hero casts off the yoke of passivity and victimhood, and surges *forward* – national narratives are always progressive – towards a glorious future of national sovereignty and unity.[7] If he is martyred in the process, his blood "waters the tree of the nation." The nation is not only an ideal, but also an institution concretely manifested in the bureaucracy, the cabinet, the courts, the army, and banks. Martyrdom is seen as regenerating the nation's political form and guaranteeing its survival.

The telling of heroic narratives of martyrdom is not solely the forte of radical nationalist movements. Blood-sacrifice for the nation is embedded in the patriotic rhetoric of all nations, including European and American countries where historical references to founding moments and contemporary discourses of patriotism include abundant allusions to selfless sacrifice.[8] Though martyrdom is allowed only through venues authorized by the state – such as the military in wars waged by the state – the centrality of the sacrificial discourse is striking. A frequently heard American patriotic song, *America the Beautiful*, contains the following lyrics:

> O beautiful for heroes proved
> In liberating strife
> Who more than self the country loved
> And mercy more than life!

Similarly, after the US invasion of Iraq in 2003, American soldiers killed in action were said to have made "the ultimate sacrifice for our freedom" (Rahimi 2003). Though opponents and proponents of that war interpret these sacrifices differently – as a waste of America's youth, or as a necessary guarantor of liberty – both groups nevertheless deploy symbols associated with blood-sacrifice as potent evidence of their

---

[7] See Bilu and Witzum 2000 for the Israeli version, and Bellah 1967 for the American one.
[8] Marvin and Ingle in fact claim that "violent blood sacrifice makes enduring groups cohere" and that the "sacrificial system that binds American citizens has a sacred flag at its center" (1991: *passim*).

arguments. More generally, American nationalism is replete with sacrificial symbolism, where the death of soldiers for "freedom" and the flag (Billig 1995; Lieven 2004; Marvin and Ingle 1999) and self-sacrifice for the nation in such pop-culture artefacts as the films *Red Dawn* and *Independence Day* attest to the continuing resonance of patriotic martyrdom. Furthermore, institutions established by the state aim to ensure that those willing to sacrifice themselves have peace of mind about the future and well-being of their families, by providing welfare assistance to the families of soldiers and veterans. This is as true of liberal democracies with their veterans' programmes as it is of – for example – the Islamic Republic of Iran's Martyrs' Foundation.

One nation-state distinguishes itself from others by its symbols and icons; hence, the emergence of new nation-states is accompanied by a flurry of symbolic activity, all of which reproduces the heroic story of the nation's birth. The national flag is raised above government buildings, the national bank opens its doors, national stamps are issued celebrating founding fathers, the national army and national police don their special uniforms, the new anthem and the new map are introduced in schools, city streets are renamed after heroes of national independence, new monuments and museums are inaugurated that embody the national narrative, holiday cycles are established, national colors are donned at the Olympic Games, and, perhaps most important, the new nation seeks a seat in the United Nations.[9] As East Timor's Xanana Gusmão (2005) states, "For small countries like East Timor, the United Nations is a very good thing. It's somewhere we can make our voice heard and defend our interests alongside the major powers. Obviously we have no real power at the UN, our weight is limited. But we are a recognised nation, our vote counts and that is very important."

International recognition of the state's right to be – through its acquisition of a vote at the UN and its signature on international treaties and laws – authorizes the new state, gives it prestige, and grants it formal equality among nations. Because the nation depends on the certification of international institutions – such as the UN – to consider itself independent, it turns intensively to international representations of sovereignty, rather than transnational revolutionary narratives of struggle. In those instances where the nation emerges from a colonial war, the subjection of the new nation-state to external norms and logics further

---

[9] On maps and museums see Anderson 1991; on recognition by the United Nations, see Willetts 1978; on holiday cycles, see Zerubavel 1995 and Zerubavel 2003; on street names, see Azaryahu and Kook 2002; on monuments, see Farmer 1999, Mosse 1990, Winter 1995, and Young 1993; and on Olympics garb, see Billig 1995: 86.

intensifies the domestication and mainstreaming of liberationist national narratives. The nation-state as a political form and "nation-statist" narratives as authorizing discourses are special features of modernity (Anderson 1991; Gellner 1983). But the worldwide spread of the discourse of national sovereignty and the existence of an international institution, membership of which certifies the authenticity of a nation-state's claim to independence, are more recent phenomena arising from the blood and fury of two world wars and many wars of decolonization. While the nation-state form was universalized along with the spread of capitalism and new forms of communication (whether print or electronic), international institutions standardized and legitimated this form. The United Nations was created to ensure that nations would "live together in peace with one another as good neighbours,"[10] and as the various UN documents made it clear, what made good neighbors were good fences.

It is at the intersection of local practices (an internal way of constituting the nation-state) and transnational discourses (world recognition of the nation-state) that a nation-state's story is told and its associated symbols are established. All these anthropomorphize the nation and narrate its biography as if it were a human protagonist at the center of a recognizable drama.[11] In this drama, the nation, long ago glorious, powerful, and triumphant, falls into a state of decay – often brought about by foreign intervention. The great men (and far less frequently women) of the nation awaken it from its slumber of ruin and silence, often through blood-sacrifice, and found a new, progressive, triumphant state. The Roman Empire, in this narrative, becomes the progenitor of modern Italy after the dark ages of division and decline. Aztec and Inca empires bring forth Mexico and Peru. Ancient Athens gives birth to modern Greece, once the Greeks are liberated from the Ottomans. Biblical Israel legitimates the modern state founded in the aftermath of the Jewish exile. The pharaonic and Persian pasts of Egypt and Iran become the precursor of the modern states once the liberators of Egypt and Iran have thrown off the foreign yoke. Modern Arab nations find their ancestors in the caliphate or Andalucia or the victory against Crusaders, and Pheonicia and Babylon are invoked as direct ancestors by modern nation-states. Although they mark the glory of the past, nevertheless, new nation-states require the kind of legitimacy granted to them internationally. The new nation-state needs the approval of the "community" of states, or the "family of nations," as the

---

[10] See the Preamble to the Charter of the United Nations at http://www.un.org.
[11] See the debate about the state as person in the *Review of International Studies* 30 (2004).

UN is frequently called. In this family of nations, each member then commemorates its genealogy and propagates it through national holidays, schoolbooks, and visual commemorative icons. The Palestinian Authority, notwithstanding its limited sovereignty, enthusiastically promulgated such heroic nation-statist discourse, as subsequent chapters will show.

"Permanent battles of history": transnational Islamist Heroism

> In the permanent battle of history – everywhere and every place, all fields are Karbala, all months are moharram, all days are Ashura.
> Ali Shariati, *Martyrdom: Arise and Bear Witness*

It is now an article of faith that the defeat of the Arab nation by Israel in 1967 had given birth to Islamist politics, and for this birth to happen, Arab nationalism had to die (Ajami 1978/79). This piece of received wisdom does not acknowledge the continuities between nationalist and Islamist discourses in the Middle East and their intimate family resemblance. The heroic nationalist and liberationist discourse did not die in 1967 in the Middle East. While its original variety still has some purchase in mobilizing Arab publics, a popular version of it persists as the kernel of Middle Eastern Islamist discourses (AbuKhalil 1992; Gelvin 1999). I do not intend to cover the wide range of Islamist discourses which vary a great deal in different social and political contexts. Aside from basic differences between Sunni and Shi'a practices and beliefs, the different historical, socio-economic, and political experiences of adherents to political Islam have meant that there is no essential, monolithic, and coherent "Islamism" which can be summarized in a few words, paragraphs, or even monographs. Despite their firmly rooted origins and the specificities of their emergence, however, Islamist movements are not *sui generis*, even if their particular characteristics owe a great deal to the social and historical context of their emergence. Here I choose the broadest possible meaning for Islamism: the utilization of religious practices, discourses, and symbols to achieve concrete political goals, almost always within the territorialized nation-state. Islamist discourses share characteristics across borders that bear striking similarities to one another and to other – liberationist, Marxist, or nationalist – discourses alongside which they have emerged. Examination of the larger, even global, context for the emergence of Islamist discourses is an imperative not always undertaken by those who analyze Islamism.

Nikki Keddie (1998: 697) has argued that the rise of Islamism in the latter decades of the twentieth century was part of a global nascence of what she calls new religious politics and which she defines as "populist movements that aim at gaining political power," through appealing "to a reinterpreted, homogenized religious tradition."[12] While she emphasizes the specificity of particular cases, she, nevertheless, recognizes broad global trends underwriting the new religious politics. These trends include uneven capitalist development, urbanization and migration, the spread of mass education, the backlash against the widening entry of women into public social spaces, the reaction to secular and oppressive states, and the rise of identity politics (Keddie 1998: 699–700). With regard to political Islam, she cites three watershed events as turning points in the history of religious politics in the Middle East: 1928 – the year in which the Muslim Brotherhood emerged, 1967 – when Israel defeated Arab states and occupied vast swathes of their territory, and especially 1979 and the victory of Iran's Islamic revolution (Keddie 1998: 713). These events are significant because, viewed in their larger historical context, one can see the relationship and similarities of the Islamist movements with nationalist ones of their time, and the resultant mutual imbrication of nationalist and Islamist discourses. One also might add to this list the Afghan "jihad" against the Soviet Union, where the mujahidin and their Pakistani, Saudi, and US sponsors effectively borrowed and transformed the language of liberationist movements and fused them to their Islamist discourse (Mamdani 2004).[13]

Olivier Roy (2004: 50) argues that many transnational Islamist movements – those which claim that they are not rooted in and their aims are broader than nation-states – are heirs to the radical liberationist movements before them, because "the fault-line between Europe and the Third World [previously, the home of the liberationist movements] goes through Muslim countries, and former spaces of social exclusion in Western Europe are partly inhabited by Muslims at a time when the radical Marxist Left has disappeared from them." Though Roy's argument that these spaces of social exclusion in European capitals are often the fountainheads of transnational Islamist radicalism is perhaps too

---

[12] Also see Karner and Aldridge 2004 on the recent rise of religious politics.

[13] An examination of the CIA's manual on *Psychological Operations in Guerrilla Warfare* shows the CIA's liberal borrowing of guerrilla warfare and propaganda tactics from liberationist movements. This includes the use of "local and national history," the insistence on suffering which "acquire[s] meaning in the cause of the struggle," the emphasis on peasantry as the soul of the "revolution," and recourse to religion as a liberating discourse (http://www.cnn.com/SPECIALS/cold.war/episodes/18/documents/cia.ops/accessed 7 September 2005).

broad, nevertheless the mobilizing role of interchange between Europe and the Third World cannot be denied. A striking resemblance between Islamist and nationalist/liberationist movements is the frequency of border-crossings by the leaders and ideologues of these movements. It was often in traveling between European capitals and the "home" country that the revolutionary ideas of these intellectuals and warriors was formed. Robert Malley (1996) details the importance of Paris as a central node in the Third Worldist networks, while Wiktorowicz (2005) documents the centrality of London mosques in the radicalization of Muslim youth. Many Islamist theoreticians also became radicalized in this process of migration and return, most prominent among them being Sayyid Qutb of Egypt and Ali Shari'ati of Iran in their respective journeys to the United States and France.

In many instances, Islamist leaders are former liberationist or nationalist ideologues who – disappointed with the failures of nationalism or Marxism – turned to Islam as a mobilizing force. Iran's Jalal Al-Ahmad, who once belonged to the communist Tudeh Party, turned to Islam towards the end of his life, articulating a vision of mobilization against Occidentosis and the mechanization of social life in his famous book *Gharbzadegi* (Dabashi 1993: 39–101). More than a few sympathizers and members of the Lebanese Hizbullah were also former communists. In his early years, Sayyid Qutb was dedicated to social justice as a "Muslim secularist and Arab nationalist" (Shepard 1996: xv); the Palestinian ideologue Munir Shafiq similarly traversed the political spectrum from Maoism to Islamism (Sayigh 1997: 630). Where such conversion did not occur, the extent to which Islamist ideologues borrowed from their nationalist and liberationist kin is nevertheless significant. The leader of the Iranian revolution, Khomeini, was influenced by the Third Worldist ideology of revolution (Keddie 1988: 311), and Muhammad Baqir al-Sadr of Iraq argued that Islam could incorporate Marxism's emphasis on social justice and political commitment without compromising its principles or identity (Mallat 1993: 28–58). When celebrating resistance against the monarchy, Khomeini used the language of class and valorized the "working classes" as "the ones who rose during the revolution [and] the ones who really care about humanity" (Khomeini 1981: 270). All Islamists liberally spoke about imperialism as the ultimate adversary; this included the Afghan mujahidin, who saw their struggle as a battle against Soviet imperialism.

Perhaps the most striking example of this cross-fertilization is Ali Shari'ati, the ideologue of Islamist revolution in Iran and beyond, who forged the Karbala paradigm, where the martyrdom of the Prophet Muhammad's grandson in 680 AD was transformed from an originary myth of Shi'ism into a mobilizing narrative of political struggle and self-sacrifice (Fischer 1980; Muttahari 1978: 84–86). Shari'ati, who had translated into Persian Che Guevara's *Guerrilla Warfare* and had begun a translation of Fanon's *The Wretched of the Earth* and *A Dying Colonialism*, had been in correspondence with Fanon, challenging his secular vision for a liberated post-colonial world and insisting that "the countries of the Third World had to rediscover their religious roots before they could challenge the West" (Abrahamian 1988: 291; Rahnema 1998: 117–130).

In their national homes, Islamist movements were clearly entangled with the nationalist movements, alongside or in opposition to which they often declared their being. Pan-Islamism and pan-Arabism both emerged in the last few decades of the Ottoman Empire. The Muslim Brothers became politically active following the Egyptian nationalist revolution of 1919 and radicalized in the 1950s as a response to the Arab nationalism of Gamal Abd al-Nasser. Post-1967 Islamists in the Arab states saw themselves as an alternative to the "failed" Arab nationalist project even as they borrowed its discourses, goals, and strategies. And the Iranian revolution, nurtured on the memory of the anti-nationalist coup of 1953, successfully combined Islamist, Marxist, and nationalist ideologies and strategies, while after coming to power, annihilating these secular alternatives. Despite their rhetorical appeal to a transnational public, Islamists basically accepted the nation as the fundamental unit of politics. Khomeini of Iran declared that the "*ulama* of Islam … desire the welfare of the nation, the welfare of the country" (Khomeini 1981: 179). Though Sayyid Qutb (1990: 59) derided the homeland except as the territorial basis of an Islamic utopia, earlier editions of his *Social Justice in Islam* contained traces of nationalist arguments and specific references to his Egyptian context (1990.: xxix). Furthermore, the practices of Egyptian Islamist organizations that profess to following Qutb's ideologies indicate that their political focus, their mobilizing discourse, and their politics are all shaped by and targeted towards the Egyptian political context (Hafez 2003). In mobilizing publics, furthermore, it is often difficult to tell whether nationalism borrows tropes and transcendence of religion to appeal to a larger public (Anderson 1991: 12–19; Johnson 1982; Zubaida 2004: 409), or Islamism the symbols and narrative of nationhood (Abrahamian 1993; Gelvin 1999; Zubaida 2004: 411).[14]

---

[14] Shaykh Fadlallah of Lebanon himself borrows the anti-imperialist language of the Arab nationalists, but argues that "most positive values of Arab nationalism had been derived from Islam in the first place" (Kramer 1997: 93).

The gender differences, so familiar from the nationalist heroic discourse, are often reproduced in the Islamist context. Shari'ati, for example, placed great emphasis on women's political engagement, and one of his manifestos re-casting Islamic history as a blueprint for radical politics is named after Fatima, the daughter of the Prophet Muhammad. Shari'ati advocated women's resistance through both the semiotics of bodily practice (e.g. dressing modestly) and political organisation alongside men. Khomeini's position was much more ambivalent about women's engagement in politics: he had in 1963 stridently objected to women's suffrage in Iran, but during the revolution in 1978–1979 had praised women's active presence in politics. Khomeini's view of women in fact was very close to nationalist positions: women were envisioned as reproducers of nation and culture and as supporters of the national heroes of revolution. Originally, Hamas's position *vis-à-vis* women was far less ambiguous. Women were seen as national agents only insofar as they literally reproduced national citizens. According to the Hamas charter, "Muslim women have a role in the liberation struggle which is no less than the role of men; for woman is the maker of men, and her role in guiding and educating the generations is a major role" (quoted in Hroub 2000: 278). Hamas also saw the astringent (and sometimes coerced) adoption of codes of modesty, veiling practices, and domestication of women (i.e. their forced absence from streets and their relegation to homes) as manifestations of nationalist practice (Hamas Charter quoted in Hroub 2000: 278–9; Hammami 1990, 1997). However, when faced with its political rivals' mobilization of women in politics, Hamas also reluctantly allowed for affiliated women warriors and female electoral candidates (Hasso 2005).

In Islamist discourses, similar to nationalist and liberationist ones, history is a legitimating instrument which shows the force and persistence of Islam as a political program. Whether invoking Muhammad's just rule some 1,400 years ago, the triumphant conquest of vast swathes of land in the wake of his death, or the victories of Muslims against the Crusaders centuries later, the past becomes a linear progenitor of the present.[15] Qutb celebrates "that throng of amazing personalities whose memory the history of Islam has preserved from its beginning" whose "spiritual purity, psychological courage, moving sacrifice ... and living heroism" illuminate the profundity and power of Islam (Shepard 1996: 184–5). Shi'a Islamists also see in Ali and Husayn, in the conquest of empires by the force of faith, and in the legends of self-sacrifice, models of emulation, bases of belief, and sources of legitimacy (Aghaie 2004).

---

[15] See Ismail 2003: 41–2.

Similar to nationalist narratives, current struggle is aimed at subverting popular torpor and inaction, and is as important in achieving collective identities as it is in reaching strategic ends. For example, following the footsteps of the Nahda movement[16] and Antonius's *The Arab Awakening*, Sayyid Qutb's writings charts the same sort of path that nationalist discourses map. If the nationalist discourse is one of awakening from the slumber of decay and weakness, Qutb sees a *jahiliyya* – an era of darkness and ignorance – out of which the heroic *mujahid* awakens, and through his insurgency redeems his time and place (Qutb 1990: 8–9; Mouassali 1999: 149–152). Sharia'ti (1981: 67), in telling the story of Husayn's revolt as a model of emulation, also speaks of the struggle to overcome "despair, obscurity, deterioration, deviation, silence, fear." The Islamist narrative can lead to a telos of an Islamist utopia or to a constant and permanent revolution, and what determines the attenuation or calibration of these discourses are the specificities of local politics.

Heroic resistance which redeems suffering and overcomes tyranny is a persistent theme of both Shi'a and Sunni Islamism. Jihad, as armed battle against the adversary, plays a central role in all the writings of Sayyid Qutb. Shari'ati (ND: 61) writes of the first Shi'a Imam, Ali, as a heroic myth, in the sense that he is "bold and courageous in battle, and a symbol of purity" as well, and he "belongs to the rank of those humans who must be [to redeem humanity], but who are not, and whom humanity has always constructed as mythical figures. But Ali is historical and real." Shari'ati has a sophisticated awareness of the utility of iconic figures as models to be emulated. The act of redemption itself requires heroic martyrdom and self-sacrifice. Much of the rhetoric here is the same, although the figure of the "hero" is replaced by that of the "mujahid," the epic battles are fought under the sign of "jihad" – when interpreted as political struggle, itself a modern innovation (Roy 2004: 41–2) – and, most important, the meaning and significance of self-sacrifice is modified to some degree. Hizbullah of Lebanon, for example, considers martyrdom "not merely valued as a means to an end, but as an end in itself" (Saad-Ghorayeb 2002: 129). Nevertheless, borrowing the language of Arab solidarity and resistance, as well as Fanon's redemptive violence (Norton 1987: 105), Hizbullah celebrates "the Islamic Resistance martyrs and fighters who both lose and risk their lives in order to *liberate national territory*" (Saad-Ghorayeb 2002: 83;

---

[16] The Nahda – or the Awakening – was a late nineteenth-century intellectual movement in which the revival and modernization of the Arabic language was to lead to a nationalist movement of cultural renewal.

emphasis added). Shari'ati (1981: 74) similarly sees the value of martyrdom in its "guarantee[ing] the life of the *nation*."

As in the nationalist and liberationist movements before them, seeking martyrdom is not seen as a desire for death, but as a struggle for life. In his *Encyclopedia of Religion* entry on martyrdom, Samuel Klausner (1987: 235) states that "a martyr's ideology centers on the meaning of life in relation to death. It does not aim simply to attenuate the pain of martyrdom through a fantasy of a future life but provides a meaning for dying continuous with the meaning of the martyr's life." Islamists refer to the Qur'an's Al-i-Imran Sura (3:169), which declares, "Think not of those who are slain in the way of Allah as dead. Nay, they are living." Martyrdom gives life meaning and belongs to a different genus than death. Shari'ati declares that "death chooses those who are not brave enough to choose" martyrdom (Taleqani *et al.*, 1986: 193). In the aftermath of a bloody demonstration in Tehran during which the Shah's army killed many protesters, Khomeini (1981: 216) commemorated the martyrs and spoke of their martyrdom as a sign of them being "fully alive." Khomeini (1981: 242) also referred to the martyrdom of Husayn not as a story of suffering, but as a moment of "epic heroism" and of "struggle against tyrants" where "blood triumphed over the sword." Shari'ati (1981: 15) explains martyrdom very specifically not as death, but as life, as witnessing.

Even the symbols and ceremonies associated with martyrdom have traveled between nationalists and Islamists. Various Iranian Islamists, for example, borrowed the practice of covering walls in the pictures of martyrs from Palestinian nationalist movements, while the use of headbands with revolutionary slogans – often in praise of martyrdom – traveled from Iran to Lebanon and Palestine. The taping of video "wills and testaments" by those seeking martyrdom – which is today associated with Palestinian secular *and* Islamist suicide bombers – was in fact first practised by communist and nationalist suicide bombers in Lebanon (Nasrallah 1985; Toufic 2002). To bury the martyr in her bloodied clothes (for she has been purified in martyrdom and does not need to be cleansed), to speak of martyrdom for the young as a "wedding" to be celebrated, and to congratulate the family of martyrs are all ritual elements shared by Iranians, Lebanese, and Palestinians. Some elements of the rituals can be traced back to particular teachings and texts (e.g. the purity of the martyr's blood), but others have traveled across borders as Islamists from different nations have interacted with one another. Lebanon, with its military training camps, first belonging to the PLO and later to Amal and Hizbullah, acted as a node of exchange of rituals between Sunni and Shi'a Muslims (Paknejad 1970).

Like nationalist discourses, Islamism also imagines a transnational community of solidarity and sympathy. If nation-statist discourses celebrate the family of nations and the liberationists lionize the community of armed struggle across the globe, Islamist discourse appeals to a "community of belief" (Qutb 1990: 41) and a transnational *umma* (Mouassalli 1999: 57–60) which – over the past few decades – has come to bear an uncanny resemblance to Fanon's wretched of the earth. The public to which most Islamist organizations appeal is one which would fit into histories of the colonized and the exploited. Qutb's community of faith does not recognize race or class (1990: 40). Shari'ati's radical Islam is "the Islam of the people, of the exploited, and of the poor" (Abrahamian 1988: 295). Interestingly, sometimes, Islamist discourses aim to appeal to the losers in the war against capitalism (Roy 2004: 46–7). The sentiment of injustice and the possibility of solidarity across borders create bonds among the publics to which the Islamists appeal. Advocacy for these bonds of cross-border concord is what gives the Iranian revolution much of its revolutionary appeal – despite its Iranian and Shi'a specificities – in the Sunni Arab Middle East. It is in recognition of the transnational heroism of revolutionary Islam that Palestinian Fathi al-Shiqaqi writes a book – *Al-Khomeini: Al-Hall al-Islami wa al-Badil* (*Khomeini: the Islamic Solution and the Alternative*) – in which he declares Khomeinist Islamism to be the only possible strategy of liberation. The liberation, however, that Shiqaqi has in mind is still *national* liberation, as his plan of action is decidedly defined by national allegiances.

The family resemblance of the nation-statist, liberationist, and Islamist discourses should not be surprising, as they are all products of modern social and political conditions, and a form of understanding and a response to global arrangements of power. That they all deploy heroic narratives to reclaim history, appeal to a transnational audience, and celebrate political violence and heroism as not only a route to victory but as a forge of collective identity speaks of an ever more intimate global imaginary and of the ease with which narratives and institutions travel across borders.

Trauma drama: the human rights/humanitarian victim subject

Where nation-statist, liberationist, and Islamist discourses are variations on the theme of heroism, in the past few decades, another transnational discourse has emerged that does not represent the world in epic images, instead performing a drama of suffering for an audience whose sympathy is sought. The emergence of the tragic discourse is profoundly entangled with the ascendancy of the humanitarian and human rights ethos which seeks to redress distant suffering through transnational juridical means, and through appealing to the widest possible audience's sense of pity and sympathy.[17] Although the language of human rights was already present at the French Revolution, its enshrining in international law first emerged in the wake of the First World War and, later, in the charters signed by members of the UN. However, both human rights and humanitarianism have taken the international center stage in the wake of the collapse of the Soviet Union and the transformation of the United States into the sole world hyperpower. Some proponents even consider it "the new standard of civilization" (Donnelly 1998). Along with development NGOs, organizations which seek to redress political and social malaise through the application of ostensibly "non-political" expertise and a discourse of redemption from suffering have multiplied exponentially: the number of international NGOs worldwide has gone from fewer than 1,000 in 1948 to tens of thousands today. While on the one hand, the UN and ever-multiplying legions of NGOs have been instrumental in disseminating this discourse along with funds, norms, and world-views, the United States has also taken on the mantle of defender of "freedom" and "human rights" in distant corners of the world.

In the Middle East, many local NGOs are viewed with some suspicion by the publics they are supposed to serve. They are considered elitist, reliant on foreign support, and disconnected from politics. The prominent Sudanese human rights activist Abdullahi an-Naim, for example, critiques local Egyptian NGOs for their total dependency on foreign resources (which makes them accountable to their foreign donors), for their use of inaccessible and legalistic language, and for their method of "generating pressures in the North to persuade governments in the South to protect the rights of their people," rather than mobilizing internal grassroots support for rights (an-Naim 2000: 22). In the Palestinian setting, after Oslo, the flood of foreign aide and the glare of international attention transformed most local NGOs from "mass mobilisers" into "development centres" populated by professionals the focus of whose agenda was commensurably altered from the politics of occupation and resistance to the depoliticized program of

---

[17] Achille Mbembe (2002) claims that the victimization narrative is in fact a residue – nay, a continuation – of anti-colonial and liberationist discourses, what he calls *Afro-radicalism*, when wed to the nativist discourse of new nation-states. What his polemic chooses to ignore is the profound discursive differences between narratives of suffering and heroic stories, where the former abdicate agency, and the latter reclaim it.

development, humanitarian relief, and legalistic protection of human rights (Hammami 1995: 53).

The discourse deployed by NGOs bears the marks of its historical origins and subsequent transformations. It originally enshrines historically particular narratives of rights (derived from the French and American revolutions) as universal norms. It increasingly borrows the American prophetic language of redemption, which sees in human rights and development of the possibility of salvation from misery and prosecution (Asad 2000), a civilizational paradigm which promises freedom from "barbarism of a pristine sovereignty" and "international neglect" of entire peoples (Donnelly 1998: 16). Meanwhile, humanitarian organizations increasingly have recourse to representations of extreme suffering in order to mobilize sympathy and support (Boltanski 1999; Rieff 2002; Kennedy 2004). As Jeffrey Alexander (2002: 30) argues, the presence of suffering as a central theme of the discourse of human rights and humanitarianism has also another source: the universalization of narratives and symbols of trauma related to the Holocaust. Alexander argues that over several decades, and through the agency of activists, the Nazi genocide of Jews was transformed from a war crime committed against a particular group of people into a "world historical" or universal event signifying untold suffering. By becoming a universal event, the trauma is stripped of its social moorings and made transcendental, providing the basis of "identification on an unprecedented scale." The basic mood of this drama is one of anguish, and it forces "the audience to identify with the story's character, compelling them to experience their suffering with them" (2002: 31). Alexander then traces the institutionalization of the trauma drama, and how its routinization imbues all recent discourses of humanitarian intervention. This universalization of the trauma drama in the human rights and humanitarian discourse focuses on victims of injustice in such a way that suffering and tragedy are made immanent to their being, sometimes to the exclusion of their political struggle for justice. Sometimes, the narrative of victimization and suffering directly replaces justice-seeking liberationist discourses (Meister 2002). Thus, for example, an American NGO called the Population Crisis Committee (PCC) in the 1980s creates an International Human Suffering Index which measures patently political and socioeconomic factors – such as freedom from government terror, or the ability to own property – and ties them to unchecked population growth in the Third World. In so doing, the PCC transforms politics into a function of biology and reproduction, and the suffering of the Third World, recorded on a color-coded map of the world, is proffered for measurement, observation, and *political action* by an American – rather than local – audience.[18] While the tragic discourse still seeks a transnational audience, it does so by mobilizing histories of pain and neglect. The more heartbreakingly human rights and humanitarian organizations can portray suffering, the more they can appeal to their transnational publics for "sympathy, attention and money" (Bob 2002: 36), or what Daniel Bensaid has called *capital victimaire*. This results in a "politics of pity," the fetishization of the spectacle of distant suffering, and an exaggerated emphasis on tragedy (Boltanski 1999: 3).

The tragic discourse narrates a story of abjection and suffering with an "authentic victim subject" (Kapur 2002) as the narrative's central protagonist. Being a victim subject deserving of rights or humanitarian assistance is dependent on suffering, which rather than a measurable "natural phenomenon" is a social status that can be extended or withheld (D. Morris 1997: 40). The experience of suffering begins with a moment of loss, violence, or defeat, and developments subsequent to the suffering can intensify, alleviate, or redeem it. In the intervening stretch between the originary moment and the resolution of suffering – which can be imagined as lasting for generations – nothing affirmative can happen, and all events are significant in that they replay and reconfirm the original moment of defeat. The end point of suffering, however, is often a vague sense of redemption, brought about through the agency of international actors moved to action through their spectatorship of suffering and sense of sympathy with it.

The social construction of suffering lends humanitarian discourse its multivalence and utility for a number of different actors, for as Talal Asad (2000) points out, "as instruments human rights are available to the powerful as well as to the weak." Furthermore, the paradox of the human rights and humanitarian discourse is that ultimately, despite its appeal to a transnational community, it leaves the task of securing rights primarily to the state, or – all too frequently – to military or political intervention by powerful actors who choose to enter the fray on the basis of narrowly defined national interests. The primacy of state power in the language of rights makes the adoption and use of this language by the powerless a complex undertaking (Arendt 1968). In a sense, the discourse of human rights and humanitarianism already assumes a public in need of assistance, but denuded of agency, and it sees the possibility

---

[18] "'We released the International Human Suffering Index in 1987,' writes Kathleen Mazzocco of the Population Crisis Committee in Washington, D.C., 'and the response from the public has been overwhelming. We estimate a U.S. audience of 100 million to date.' The Index is presented as a colour poster, with all the countries ranked in order, and showing the close linkage between high suffering and high rates of population increase" (GIB ND).

of transformative action as vested in the bodies of states or more powerful actors. Thus, a narrative which emphasizes suffering and powerlessness as scourges to be eradicated perpetuates that same suffering and
powerlessness, and instead of addressing the man-made causes of suffering, the palliative quality of humanitarianism de-politicizes suffering
and transforms it into a case for charity (Ferguson 1990; Kennedy 2004;
Rackley 2002; Rieff 2002). The human rights discourse then honors the
suffering of victims "as a claim to moral victory precisely insofar as they
are willing to accept moral victory as victory enough, and to forgo the
demands of revolutionary justice" (Meister 2002: 95) of the sort liberationist movements sought. The institutional character of NGOs,
their competition for scarce resources, and the marketization of the
process through which they secure funding and mandates all exacerbate
these characteristics by mainstreaming the agenda of NGOs in order to
make them palatable not only to their donors, but also to the states
within whose jurisdiction they have to operate (Cooley and Ron 2002;
Bob 2002).

Gender plays an interesting role in NGO politics and in the construction of the language of suffering. In the interest of mobilizing the
feelings of sympathy, "innocent victims" are often imagined as worthy
objects of international attention. These "innocent victims" are habitually "women and children" (Kapur 2002). If the central character of
the heroic narrative is a strong man valiantly forging ahead, in the
trauma drama, the protagonist is a suffering woman carrying a limp
child. Furthermore, appeals to politics of sympathy, pity, and intimacy
are increasingly conceptualized as a feminization of politics (Braidotti
1997). This feminisation indicates a move beyond contentious political
encounters considered masculine, to a more affective politics driven by
sentiment and consensus-seeking. Whether celebrated or denigrated,
the feminization of politics is seen as a shift from the muscular politics of
collective violence (whether it be the "national security culture" of
political conservatives or the revolutionary armed struggle of leftist
radicals) to an ethos of care. What is often forgotten is that this ethos of
humanitarian care or economic development – with its focus on bet-
tering the lot of "women and children" within extant social–political
frameworks – in fact smuggles in a depoliticization of action and agency,
itself a corollary of neo-liberalism (Ferguson 1990). The ostensible
feminization of politics leaves the structures of power – both local and
international – more or less intact, though the modes of mobilizing
resources, the language of legitimation, and the audience for political
performances have now expanded to include ostensibly "womanly"
forms of politics. In addition to the gendered transformation of political

discourse, gender also plays a role in the more mundane aspects of NGO (anti-)politics. NGOs are often inviting and hospitable working places for women, and, especially in the Middle East, happen to be prestigious places of work for women who hail from the middle – or more affluent – classes. These NGOs "represent" women, children, and the powerless of their nation-states in the struggle for international sympathy, recognition, and resources. In so doing, they also become the conduit for the transnational discourse of care, humanitarianism, economic development, and universal human rights.[19]

What cannot be forgotten, however, is that the local adoption of the language of rights and development can intrude upon the transnational depoliticizing logic, and can modify the meaning and intent of the language through domesticating it. For example, the Palestinian prisoner rights NGO, al-Dameer, uses the idiom of human rights in order to challenge the Israeli occupation – and the NGO itself is populated with former leftist political activists (Allen 2005; Hajjar 2005). In more than a few instances, the discourse of rights, pity, and victimhood is deployed within the nationalist framework to advance deeply political causes. With an increasing production of refugee populations through wars, and the communitarian clamor for national rights resulting from colonization of much of the Middle East, various collectives appeal increasingly to an international audience for sovereignty and legitimacy. In more recent decades, however, it is no longer the heroic warriors for the nation who secure its legitimacy but the abject victims who can garner pity and sympathy, and whose suffering legitimates the larger collective's claims to nationhood (Brog 2003; Zertal 2005). Palestinian refugees similarly use the tragic language of suffering as an authorizing discourse which legitimates a stateless and "powerless" public's persistent nationalist claims.

Conclusions

Karl Marx famously remarked that "men make their own history, but they do not make it as they please; they do not make it under self-selected circumstances, but under circumstances existing already, given and transmitted from the past." One can add that people also create mobilizing discourses, but they do so within the social and political

---

[19] Gender also plays a more mundane role in Middle Eastern NGO politics. Even if the number of NGOs voluntarily organized by women for women is quite low in the Middle East (Chatty and Rabo 1997: 1), nevertheless, their visibility both locally and internationally is quite high.

constraints of their time and place, and in mutual interaction with existing institutions and extant histories. The creation of discourses is not solely the work of an intellectual elite; nor is the movement of discourses across national boundaries simply a transmission of language. For discourses to emerge and to travel, for them to take root and flourish, they have to emerge in a hospitable environment, they have to speak to a particular human condition, they have to have resonances in the local setting, and the weight and legitimacy that transnational appeal lends them are also of great importance. Discourses need resources, institutions, and technologies to emerge and travel. They also need to be performed for receptive audiences who can reproduce these resources, institutions, and techniques.

The nation-statist discourse, with its heroic celebration of icons, commemorations, and rhetoric found its legitimacy in the halls of international institutions which certified the state form as the most legitimate form of political organization in a transnational setting. The grafting of nationalist discourse to the liberationist ethos emerged in the decolonizing world, where now nationalism had come to mean the right to self-determination, and the liberationist movements saw this right as best secured through armed struggle. Self-sacrifice for a greater cause – the nation or the revolution – was a central element of both the nation-statist and the liberationist discourses, as was a gendered perception of heroism, in which masculine warrior virtues were the necessary instruments by which liberation was secured and/or the sovereign nation-state was founded. The Islamist movements emerging often concurrently with or following closely on the heels of the nationalist/liberationist movements shared much of the same rhetoric of self-sacrifice – if now justified additionally by divine sanction – and though varying slightly across the spectrum, reproduced the gender division of labor necessary for political contention.

The most significant rupture in transnational discourses, then, was not the appearance of Islamist movements, but rather the ascension of the liberal discourse of rights and development at the end of the Cold War. Not only was the masculine celebration of political violence replaced with a politics of pity for the "women and children" victims of such violence, but also the locus of political mobilization and the audience for such mobilizing discourses shifted. If in the 1960s and 1970s, the liberationist movements spoke to other tricontinental states and peoples – in solidarity or recognition – and where once revolutionary transformation of society was the celebrated mode of politics, in the 1990s, non-governmental organizations formed a network of action along with their donors and cohorts in the North. Despite real divisions between Northern and Southern NGOs, politics was now conducted with an international audience – especially in Europe and North America – in mind. Revolutionary armed struggle ceded to the gradual alleviation of "suffering" and the heroic narrative gave way to the tragedy of abject victims in need of transnational sympathy and support.

3   Palestinian lives and local institutions
     in the camps of Lebanon

Beirut is our tent
Beirut is our star

Mahmud Darwish, "Beirut"

Transformations in transnational discourses, outlined in the previous chapter, were accompanied with local political changes that crucially provided the indigenous terrain for appropriation of transnational discourses. Local institutions – whether nationalist political parties or humanitarian and human rights NGOs – became the conduits for these discourses, but they did not leave them unchanged. While Palestinian refugees in Lebanon have been restricted by the severely circumscribed borders of their camps and by the repressive control of the Lebanese state, nevertheless, world events and regional conflicts have profoundly influenced their lives, and their political contention in turn has been incisive in shaping the broader contours of Palestinian nationalism and political developments in the region.

To understand the politics of Palestinian nationalist commemoration, one has to look at the confluence between these transnational discourses and local political institutions, and to best understand the latter, a brief study of the historical background of Palestinian refugees' presence in Lebanon is necessary. Palestinian history in Lebanon is punctuated by the transformative events which led to the refugees reorganizing their social relations within the camps, choosing new modes of political mobilization, or articulating their demands for political participation in new ways. The exile from Palestine has been an originary cause of all subsequent conflicts in which they have found themselves. Rapid and sweeping upheavals that came with the Zionist colonization of Palestine and the subsequent establishment of the state of Israel transformed the Palestinians into comprehensively dispossessed *and* stateless refugees with little or no access to political or economic power. The significance of this moment is such that the *Nakba* (or Catastrophe) still plays a crucial role in Palestinian narratives of themselves and in their mobilizing practices.

While the Palestinian refugees in Jordan received Jordanian citizenship and those in Syria enjoyed the same rights and privileges (and suffered the same restrictions) as Syrian citizens, from the very outset, poorer Palestinian refugees in Lebanon were prevented from social and economic integration into the Lebanese society and were spatially and judicially ghettoized and monitored. Furthermore, Palestinians in Lebanon have since 1948 been the focus of and actors in the ongoing drama of sectarian and politico-economic conflict in Lebanon which has been further exacerbated by the intervention of foreign states such as Israel, Syria, and the United States. Throughout the Palestinian refugees' presence in Lebanon, different nationalisms have held appeal and promise for them: the pan-Arabism of the early years was supplanted by liberationist Palestinian nationalism in the 1960s, which itself gave way to the nation-statist movement of the last two decades. After the signing of the Oslo Accords, Palestinian refugees in Lebanon have demanded inclusion in the national polity as transnational citizens, and to make this claim, they have addressed not only their elite and other Palestinians, but also international audiences.

What has been extraordinary throughout the Palestinian history of exile and struggle has been the extent of difficulties they have faced in their attempts to establish archives, collect documents pertaining to their condition, and tell their own histories and stories. The final section of this chapter will discuss how Palestinian memorialization and history-telling has been silenced, in order to give a sense of the constraints on their commemorative practices.

The *Nakba* (1948)

The Palestinian refugees who reside in the camps of Lebanon are primarily from the Galilee, Tiberias, and Safad provinces of Mandatory Palestine. Galilee had been a largely Arab region of Palestine, rich in water and sparsely colonized by new Jewish immigrants; whereas Safad had a slightly higher concentration of Jews. The primary economic engine of this northernmost part of Palestine had been agriculture and the villages were by and large self-sufficient in production of fruits and vegetables. Most of the villages had a mixture of Muslim and Christian residents, with religious institutions and village *mukhtar*s (headmen) who governed their respective confessional groups.

Between December 1947 and May 1948, an event known by Palestinians as *al-Nakba*, the Catastrophe, destroyed entirely the Palestinian polity and dispersed the community (Zurayq 1948). At the beginning of 1948, the population of Palestinian Arabs and Jews in Palestine had been 1.3 million and 600,000 respectively, and Jews held 7 percent of the land. By the end of that year, the Arab population had halved, and the state of Israel came to hold 77 percent of the Palestinian territory (Khalidi 2001 12). The superior military capabilities of the Zionist forces, the collusion of some Arab leaders, Palestinian institutional failures, and the lack of unified and capable military leadership and organization all contributed to the Palestinian defeat (Shlaim 2001, 1998; Khalidi 2001). The Arab Rescue Army organized by the Arab League seems to have been largely ineffective, if not downright helpful to the Zionist forces. Many refugees recalled the lack of any backing from the Army and its active role in *disarming* the Palestinian peasants during the hostilities (Nazzal 1974: 71).

By the time the war had ended, its violence, not to mention the overt or implicit "transfer" policies of the Zionists, resulted in the uprooting of some 726,000 Palestinians, around 110,000 of whom ended up in Lebanon (Finkelstein 1995: 51–87; Khalidi 1988; Masalha 1992; Morris 1987: 297, 2004; Pappé 1992; Sayigh 1994: 17). The first wave of refugees had included the affluent urban professionals and merchants who resettled in Arab capitals. The majority of the peasants who were abandoned or expelled from their villages began leaving in the early spring of 1948. Many fled after hearing rumors about Zionist forces' rapes and massacres of Palestinians in villages near and far – most significant among them Dayr Yasin (Kana'ana and Zaytawi 1987; Khalidi 1999; Morris 2004). Many others were forcibly expelled, in direct attacks on the villages. A major wave of mass expulsion followed in July 1948, when in a ten-day period, Israeli commandos drove more than 100,000 peasants to Arab-held areas or to the borders with Lebanon and "ordered them to run as fast as possible to the other side of the border and not to look back" (Najib Sa'd quoted in Nazzal 1974: 76). Another major wave of expulsions and massacres of civilians occurred in October and November 1948 (Morris 1988: 233–239; Pappé 1992: 97). Many of those who fled or were expelled thought that they would eventually be able to return to their homes.

For the first few months after the exodus, the borders were still porous. More than a few refugees who had left thinking they would return after a day or two, returned – often at great risk – to retrieve buried gold, cash, and other valuables, should the war last longer. Many of the refugees attempted to return to the villages from their place of temporary refuge, to water their fields or orchards, or feed their farm animals with the expectation of eventual return for harvesting the crops (Anonymous 1988: 161; Morris 1997: ch. 2; Nazzal 1974, 1978; Shoufani 1972: 116–117). Thousands were shot dead as "infiltrators" by the Israeli forces (Morris 1993: 147). To bar the eventual return of the refugees, in the coming months and years, the Israeli state confiscated Palestinian properties and turned them into "national land," and implemented draconian measures to ensure "infiltrators" – frequently peasants attempting to return to their harvest and homes – could not enter the country (Kimmerling 1983: 134–146; Morris 1997; Shafir and Peled 2002: 112–120). Furthermore, in dealing with the remaining villages, Joseph Weitz, the head of the Jewish Agency's Land Department, ordered the "destruction, renovation and settlement by Jews" of Palestinian villages (Pappé 1992: 98). In all, the nascent Israeli state destroyed more than 350 villages and incorporated or transformed others into Jewish settlements/villages (Khalidi 1992).

After the exodus (1948–1969)

Between 1947 and 1949, the peasant refugees walked or were trucked by the Haganah – and after 1948 by the Israeli military – to the Lebanese border. Many spent their first few nights – and some, their first few weeks – under olive trees. Others were fortunate enough to be helped by Lebanese villagers:

We lived in poverty; the men who were finding work were only getting 2 livres, and the women were getting only 75 'irshes and sometimes one livre. The people in Qana were as poor as the Palestinians, so life was hard. My father who was used to tending trees and farming wanted to find this kind of job. We were renting our home from this family, but they stopped taking rent from us and we stayed in their house as if we were their family; but my father stopped taking his wages from them [in return for the lodging]. The people of the south were kind people, unlike other people now. (Um Jamal, Burj al-Barajna, 4 March 2002)

Some of the Palestinians who ended up in Lebanon had been urban professionals and merchants who had minimal financial problems resettling in Lebanon,[1] but the majority of the refugees who became camp residents in Lebanon were originally rural laborers, small-holders, and village artisans. Their uprooting and resettlement resulted in

---

[1] Even the well-to-do, however, were not exempt from Lebanese discrimination, as the engineered collapse of the Palestinian-owned Intra Bank reveals (Brynen 1990: 28).

simultaneous, radical and traumatic processes of urbanization,[2] prole-
tarianization and loss of whatever political rights they may have held in
Palestine. Though ordinary Lebanese men and women provided food
and shelter for many of the refugees, the Palestinians' presence exacerbated Lebanon's internal sectarian and class frictions from the very
beginning. The refugees constituted 10 percent of the Lebanese population, and the confessional adherence of a majority of Palestinians to
Sunni Islam was said to endanger the fragile sectarian balance of power
in Lebanon. Ironically, the vitriol many local elite had used in their
rhetorical attacks against Palestinian refugees did not prevent them from
exploiting the Palestinians as a source of cheap labour, forcing them to
relocate at the pleasure of the Lebanese state and businessmen (Sayigh
1997: 45–46).

Between 1948 and 1950, the International Committee of the Red
Cross (ICRC) served the refugees, providing them with tents and
humanitarian assistance. In 1949–1950, the United Nations Relief and
Works Agency (UNRWA) was established and given the mandate of
assisting the refugees. Though UNRWA provided some financial relief
and health and education services to the refugees, it was considered
by the Palestinians to be "part of the machinery of dismemberment
and dispersion" (Sayigh 1979: 109), intent on settling the refugees in
host countries rather than finding a political solution to their dispossession.[3] By the late 1960s, the tents originally given to the refugees
by the ICRC and UNRWA had given way to cement-block houses with
corrugated tin roofs. In 1971, "less than twelve per cent of homes [in the
camps] had toilets; sixty percent had no running water. Most camps
lacked either garbage collection or adequate sewer systems" (Brynen
1990: 28). Only in the mid- to late 1970s did the camps receive proper
electricity, water and sewerage services. The transience of life in the
camps was partially reinforced by the Lebanese state's refusal to allow
any construction which could indicate permanent settlement. The
Lebanese state considered roofs on houses to be a sign of permanence,

---

[2] Even in instances where the refugee camps were located in more rural areas, the high
congestion of inhabitants in the camps created a quasi-urban spatial and social context.
[3] Evidence of this has been the difficulties the refugees have faced in trying to influence
UNRWA's administration of their lives. Weighill (1999) compares the ability of
Palestinians and southern African and Tibetan exile organizations in shaping the policies
of UN agencies concerned with their welfare. UN agencies acted in partnership with the
South-West Africa People's Organization (SWAPO), the Pan-Africanist Congress
(PAC) and the African National Congress (ANC), and in providing services to Tibetan
refugees, deferred to their government in exile. In contrast, Palestinians have – except for
the 1969–1982 period – been vehemently excluded from UNRWA planning.

and as such the Palestinian addition of corrugated zinc to keep out the weather could be construed as illegal.

Throughout this period, if the refugees mobilized political dissent, this often occurred using the idiom of Nasserist pan-Arabism, itself considered subversive by the Lebanese regime. Though Nasser belonged to the ever-growing ranks of Arab leaders who wished to dominate Palestinian politics, and despite the fact that many of his more fiery statements in support of the Palestinians only remained within the realm of rhetoric, he was nevertheless revered by many as an anti-colonial hero and the only Arab leader who could realistically challenge Israeli hegemony in the region.[4] Leila Khaled (1973: 44–45) recalls:

The 1956 invasion of Egypt ceased on November 6. That day a new baby was born in the Khaled family. We called him Nasser in honour of President Nasser, to symbolise our first hour of victory since the defeat of 1948. That autumn was the most exciting period of my childhood. It seemed as if the whole school was one family, the whole of [the city of] Sour was one tribe, the whole of the Arab world was one nation-state. It was a time to remember and enjoy, a time of pride and self-confidence.

The first Lebanese civil war in 1958 began as a result of a political deadlock between President Camille Chamoun who was supported by the United States and a coalition that opposed Chamoun's suggested changes to the constitution. This coalition included prominent Arab nationalists. Since Palestinians were numerously represented in the pan-Arab ranks, the state placed greater control over the camps in the aftermath of the civil war. Throughout the 1950s and '60s, the Lebanese *Sureté Generale* and the later *Deuxième Bureau* virtually controlled the camps and monitored all resident activities, including the usage of water, bathing hours, and building activities. The day-to-day harassments of Palestinians and prevention of their free movements (Abu Iyad 1981: 38–39; Sayigh 1997: 41) were accompanied by imprisonment, torture (Jallul 1994: 35) and deportation of Palestinian men (Al-Hut 1986: 52), and in a few instances even execution of a number of the youth thought to be politically active (Sayigh 1994: 68).

The Israeli defeat of the Arab armies in the June 1967 war, and the gradual transformation of the (mostly Palestinian) Arab National Movement (ANM) from a pan-Arab political organization to the precursor for the Popular Front for the Liberation of Palestine (PFLP) and Democratic Front for the Liberation of Palestine (DFLP) all contributed to the

---

[4] Rosemary Sayigh points out that the largest number of Palestinian supporters of pan-Arabism came from within the ranks of the bourgeoisie, whereas poorer Palestinians were less sympathetic to pan-Arabism (1979: 101–103).

mobilization of the camps. Most importantly, Fatah – which was established years earlier but came to the fore after 1967 – was a broad-based nationalist organization which pointedly refused to adopt a Marxist line and defined its roots in regional politics, signalled the emergence of *Palestinian* – as opposed to pan-Arab – liberationist nationalism. Starting in the mid-1960s, the aforementioned Palestinian organizations began publishing magazines, pamphlets, and newspapers in earnest, targeting the camps for recruitment, and mobilizing the young teachers and professionals in the camps (a majority of whom were themselves children of the camps). Fatah ran its first cross-border military operation against Israel in 1965. By 1969, the Palestinian and Lebanese left-wing resistance regularly planned meetings and demonstrations in the streets of Beirut, and the Lebanese state used force on more than one occasion to suppress the demonstrations, but the mobilization did not cease. By August 1969, most of the camps were "boiling" (Sayigh 1994: 87), and some camps even saw armed battles between Palestinian militant organisations and the Lebanese military.

The *Thawra* in the Palestinian camps (1969–1982)

The emergence and consolidation of the national movement in the Palestinian refugee camps of Lebanon was the result of protracted political and military maneuvering of the armed groups against the Lebanese state. The state at the time was more or less dominated by Maronite Christian parties who were less sympathetic to Palestinians than the majority of the Lebanese population may have been (Brynen 1990: 37–52; Khalidi 1979: 113). Additionally, the social forces in Lebanon that wanted to transform the sectarian social system saw the *fida'iyyin* guerrillas as harbingers of social change, beneficially upsetting the extant balance of social forces (Brynen 1990: 48).

With the Cairo Accords of 2 November 1969 between the PLO and the Lebanese state, the camp residents gained control over the administration of the camps, and established popular committees to take care of the management of the day-to-day affairs of the camp. Various Palestinian political factions all had representatives on the committees, thus enacting a quasi-representative pluralism in the camps. Until trained Palestinian military forces arrived to take over the camp defense, "everyone took turns on guard duty, even women. There was a mood of total identification with the Resistance; fighters from outside [the camps] were treated as honoured guests: 'It was felt to be shameful not to be the first to give the fighters food, water, shelter'" (Sayigh 1994: 91). The guerrillas took on the role of protectors of the camp, social mediators, and even camp police. Joining a political organization and taking up arms in service of the Palestinian cause were considered to bestow maturity and wisdom on the *shabab* (the youth), and becoming a protector was also a sign of manly courage. Armed Palestinian militiamen came to control the neighborhoods in which the camps were located as well as their training grounds and bases in southern Lebanon, from where they ran operations against Israel.

After the expulsion of Palestinian political leaders from Jordan in 1970–1971, Palestinian political organizations moved to West Beirut, and located their bureaucratic offices near the Shatila camp. By 1969, the ideological shift from pan-Arabism to Palestinian nationalism within the Palestinian political organizations was perceptible, causing clashes and power struggles with those Arab leaders, such as Syria's Hafiz al-Asad, who had pretensions to the leadership of a united Arab *mashriq*. As the 1970s proceeded, the Palestinian national movement became more bureaucratized, increasingly resembling parastatal institutions rather than grassroots revolutionary movements. Although liberationist/Marxist factions such as PFLP still spoke about social revolution and resistance against reactionary Arab regimes, the ambitions of the more centrist PLO/Fatah eventually became wholly statist (Sayigh 1997: 202). The extent of the shift was such that by the end of the 1970s, the PLO headquarters in West Beirut was labelled "the Fakihani Republic" after the neighborhood which hosted the buildings and offices of the PLO. The PLO poured money into education and health services in the camps. Jobs in the slowly bureaucratizing political organizations were plentiful, and the PLO's social service organizations raised the standard of living in the camps considerably. Often, the institutional structures which provided services to many of the poorest families of the camp were originally established to support the families of the guerrillas who were maimed and killed in action. The aims of these institutions were:

(a) financial and 'identity' support for the families of the martyrs; (b) provision of special schools for their children; (c) provision of cultural institutions for the children and for the incapacitated and the elderly belonging to the family of martyrs; (d) establishing social support institutions for the children and for the incapacitated and the elderly belonging to the family of martyrs; and (e) provision of health services for them. (Khurshid 1972: 107)

These aims were accomplished through the allocation of cash payments and foodstuffs, health services, education, vocational training, and cultural programs for the families of martyrs and maimed guerrillas.

Whether explicitly or not, the celebration of heroic figures – the *fida'iyyin* and martyrs – was woven into the infrastructure of service-provision.

Weekly visits to the families of martyred guerrillas and hospitalized fighters, ceremonies honoring the martyrs immediately after their martyrdom and on the fortieth day of their death, and establishing at least one martyrs' cemetery in each host country were intended to "allow for the perpetuation of the revolution, as a fighter's certainty about the fate of his family eases the burden of his self-sacrifice" (Khurshid 1972: 106). The valorization of the guerrillas' self-sacrifice was incorporated into the routines of the PLO leadership. Arafat often visited martyrs' families, and supporting them had become such a part of his rhetorical repertoire that in 1993 Suha Arafat claimed that the PLO's financial inability to support the wives and children of the martyrs deeply depressed him (Hart 1994: 530). Arafat also adopted a number of orphaned children of guerrillas.

Any evaluation of this period has to grapple with the complexities of the situation. On the one hand, the refugees in the camps became the emblem of the *Thawra* or the revolution. Peasants who were once transformed into refugees now reversed the ignominy of defeat by becoming *fida'iyyin*, the foot-soldiers of the guerrilla warfare against Israel. The ranks of political leadership, however, only somewhat reflected the complexion of Palestinian refugee society, as most of the leadership were middle class or upper middle class Palestinian professionals who in time came to bolster their power through networks of patronage within the community. While on the one hand, there were substantial changes in the social relations in the camps, with women becoming far more active and taking on new roles and responsibilities (Peteet 1991), the former village social structures and hierarchies (which were encouraged and utilized by Fatah as an alternative network of control within the camps) nevertheless proved durable (Roberts 1999; Sayigh 1994: 98–9).

Palestinian political organizations had different agendas and alliances. While they all identified themselves with the revolutionary anti-colonial struggle, their models and allies differed depending on their political ideologies and agendas. For example, while the Marxist–Leninist PFLP and DFLP had identified themselves with Che Guevara, Vietnam, and Cuba, nationalist Fatah (which had genealogical affiliations with the Muslim Brotherhood) spoke of Palestinian solidarity with Algeria. The military camps of the various political organizations came to host and train fighters from around the world. Marxist Palestinian factions had relations with radical Japanese and European militants, as well as with Marxist Iranian guerrilla groups, while Fatah trained and accepted volunteers from the leftist-Islamist Mojahedin-e-Khalq of Iran as well as dissident groups from across the Third World (Çandar 2000). Fatah was most successful in mobilizing and recruiting refugees for training as guerrillas (Cobban 1984: 42), but other organizations (especially PFLP, DFLP, and even Syrian-supported al-Sa'iqa) had significant constituencies within the refugee community. The competition and imperfect coordination between political factions – who all had somewhat differing strategies and tactics – resulted in several political crises, the most devastating being the events of Black September 1970 in Jordan, where the escalation of tensions around the PFLP's aeroplane hijackings led to the brutal suppression of Palestinians by the Jordanian state and the massacre of thousands of Palestinian civilians. However, after Black September and through most of the PLO's ascendancy in Lebanon, co-operation between political factions was far more significant than any conflict. This changed with the Syrian intervention in the nascent civil war in the mid-1970s (Khalidi 1979: 80).

The relations of the PLO with Lebanese political actors were similarly complex. On the one hand, the movement's revolutionary organization and rhetorics resonated with Lebanese leftists and Muslims who had grievances against the institutional domination of Lebanon by Maronite Christians. On the other hand, Palestinians were demonized by right-wing representatives of the Maronite community, and particularly by the Kata'ib (Phalange) party, led by the Jummayil family, who over time had developed close relations with Israel, and whose cadre received military training there. Finally, in southern Lebanon, many farmers and villagers came to resent the Palestinian militias based among them not only because they were unruly and arrogant, but also because their raids against Israel invited Israeli attacks on and collective punishment of the civilian population. After their experience of expulsion from Jordan, the PLO leadership came to view the Cairo Agreement of 1969 "as an acquired extraterritorial right never to be abandoned but rather to be consolidated and expanded where possible" resulting in tensions with even allies within the Lebanese community (Khalidi 1979: 80).

Foreign intervention in Lebanon exacerbated such tensions. The Israeli state assassinated a number of Palestinian leaders, intellectuals, and artists in Lebanon in the 1970s, and punished Palestinian military activities by targeting both Lebanese and Palestinian civilians. Between 1968 and 1974, this amounted to some 30,000 Israeli violations of Lebanese territory (Picard 2002: 83). Israeli bombing raids against Beirut airport in 1968, against southern villages and all refugee camps throughout the 1970s, and their invasion of Lebanese territory in 1978, all resulted in thousands of civilian deaths, millions of dollars in damages to properties, displacement of hundreds of thousands of civilians, and the enflaming of Lebanese resentments against *both* Israel and the

Palestinians. The Israeli state found sectarian discord and even the possible partition of Lebanon to its benefit and tried to hasten this conclusion by providing as much as $100 million in financial and military aid to various Maronite parties – and principally the Kata'ib – before 1976 (Khalidi 1979: 90–91.). Syria was also deeply interested in Lebanon, as on the one hand, it considered the country part of its "strategic backyard" and on the other hand, Hafiz al-Asad had long wanted to control the Palestinian national movement now based in Lebanon.

In 1975 several clashes – including the raid by Lebanese Forces (LF) on a bus carrying twenty-six Palestinians at Ain al-Rummana, and the massacre of 200 Muslims in response to the assassination of three LF militiamen – led to a full-scale civil war, and foreign actors quickly took sides. In order to prevent the partition of Lebanon, Syria deployed its military in Lebanon, in support of the Lebanese Forces, who were also receiving training and aid from Israel. In three years of protracted and intense violence between the bus massacre at Ain al-Rummana in April 1975 and the Israeli invasion of southern Lebanon in 1978, thousands of Palestinians (as well as Lebanese citizens and Syrian workers) were massacred in Nabatiyya, Maslakh-Karantina, Tal al-Za'tar and Jisr al-Basha, and thousands more were expelled from Maronite neighborhoods. The Lebanese infrastructure was devastated, over 30,000 were killed, twice as many were wounded, and 600,000 were internally displaced (Khalidi 1979: 104; Picard 2002). During the siege and fall of the Tal al-Za'tar camp alone, over 4,000 Palestinians perished.

Regionally, the Camp David Accords of 17 September 1979 between Egypt and Israel, though devastating the dream of a united Arab front against Israel, had invoked unified opposition within the PLO ranks, thus – at least for a while – papering over factional disputes within the organization. The Iranian revolution – with its slogan of "Iran today, Palestine tomorrow" – had raised Palestinian hopes of a revolutionary resolution to their struggles (Cobban 1984: 104). In Lebanon, the Palestinian parastatal infrastructure was still in place, and, in fact, reacting against political interference from Arab states and the USSR, it further centralized, consolidated its bureaucracy, and more or less transformed into a fully statist organization (Sayigh 1997: 446). Aided by a massive influx of Arab funds, by the time the devastating war with Israel came about in 1982, the PLO leadership was using patronage in order to maintain cohesion among the rank-and-file members (Sayigh 1997: 446). This meant an extension of the PLO's social services, and provision of support for not only the thousands of displaced Palestinian families, widows, and orphans but also ordinary camp residents.

The years of war and destruction (1982–1993)

On 3 June 1982, gunmen belonging to the Abu Nidal splinter group shot and wounded the Israeli ambassador in London. Despite Israeli intelligence's knowledge about the culpability of Abu Nidal and its hostility towards the PLO, the Likud government of Menachem Begin with Ariel Sharon at the helm of the Defense Ministry used the assassination attempt as a pretext to invade Lebanon on 6 June 1982. The Israeli state mobilized 75,000–78,000 Israeli troops (eventually to be increased to 100,000), 1,240 tanks, 1,520 armored personnel carriers, and massive airborne attacks against civilian and military targets (using napalm and phosphorus bombs) to defeat the PLO whose armed personnel in Lebanon numbered 15,000, and who possessed sixty decrepit tanks and no air power (Sayigh 1997: 524). Sharon had stated that the goal of the mission was nothing short of the obliteration of the refugee camps in Lebanon and the mass expulsion of all 200,000 refugees (Schiff and Ya'ari 1984: 211). The Israeli invasion of southern Lebanon and heavy bombing of Muslim West Beirut and PLO positions was greeted with joy by the Lebanese Forces, who only seven years earlier had greeted Syrian troops with equal delight. For three months Beirut and southern Lebanon – and especially Palestinian refugee camps in that area – were pounded by missiles, artillery, and bombs. Beirut's water and electricity supplies were severed and the Lebanese police reported 17,825 dead and 30,203 wounded (over 80 percent of whom were civilians). UNRWA estimated that Ain al-Hilwa refugee camp, home to over 40,000 refugees, was 100 per cent destroyed, while other camps in and around Beirut and further to the south sustained damage to 20–50 per cent of their buildings (Sayigh 1997: 540). By the beginning of September, in order to stop the carnage and under heavy pressure from foes and allies alike, the PLO evacuated from Lebanon in return for an international guarantee of safety for the refugees remaining behind in the camps (Khalidi 1986: 180). When on 14 September 1982, Bashir Jumayyil, the newly elected Lebanese president and head of the Lebanese Forces was assassinated by a Lebanese member of the Syrian Social Nationalist Party, the Israeli military seized the opportunity, fully occupied West Beirut, and voiced their intention to "flush out '2,000 terrorists' who had remained in Beirut after the PLO evacuation" (Sayigh 1997: 539). What followed was the occupation of several embassies (including those of the USSR and Kuwait) by the Israeli military, confiscation of the contents of PLO offices (including the PLO Research Centre's extensive academic library), seizure of bank files (Sayigh 1997: 540) and, most notoriously, the massacre of at least 1,200 Palestinian refugees in Sabra and Shatila at the hands of LF and South Lebanese Army (SLA) militiamen supported logistically by the Israeli military (MacBride *et al.* 1983: 162–186).

The exile of the PLO leadership from Lebanon was followed by the reinstatement of Lebanese military control over what remained of the camps and the installation of draconian measures to control men in those camps. Though there was a strong Palestinian desire for investigation of the conduct of the PLO and other political factions in the war, such investigations if ever held were muted and their records were placed "under strict embargo" (Sayigh 1997: 541). Instead, political organizations and the camps were beset with internal strife and discontent, and grievances resulted in widespread cleavages within the militant groups (Brynen 1990: 184). Oppositionist factions were opposed to the possibility of diplomatic settlements considered by Fatah, while, within Fatah, many cadres were clamoring for reform and the eradication of corruption and incompetence (Sayigh 1997: 559). Internal disagreements culminated in the first War of the Camps, in northern Lebanon in 1983, between Palestinian factions loyal to Yasir Arafat and opposition groups, backed and incited by Syria. Syrian support for the opposition and their brutal siege of Tripoli in 1983 had the converse effect of solidifying Palestinian support behind Yasir Arafat in both the refugee camps of Syria and in the OPT (Sayigh 1997: 571–573). In southern Lebanon, the Palestinian population was far too dispersed, devastated, and harassed by the LF and the Israeli military to be able to mobilize a unified response to the conflict, while in the northern camps – which were the site of conflict – Palestinians eventually rallied against Syrian attempts to encourage internecine fighting.

In the end, after Arafat, who had returned to northern Lebanon from Tunis, agreed to a second withdrawal from Lebanon, 4,700 Palestinians (including women and children) sailed away from Tripoli to a second or third exile in PLO camps in Algeria, Sudan, and other Arab nations (Sayigh 1997: 573). After this moment, the core of the Palestinian national struggle and its state-in-exile shifted away from Lebanon, and Palestinian refugees in Lebanon found themselves – in the words of one refugee woman – "on the outside." The war had devastated much of the institutional infrastructure the PLO had built in Lebanon and "hospitals, social services, mass organisations, offices, and administration had been uprooted or destroyed" (Brynen 1990: 181). In the years following the PLO evacuation, the Lebanese military and Maronite militias, and even the Palestinians' former ally, the Shi'a Amal party, harassed and persecuted the refugees, and forced many families to move back into the ruins of the camps for the protection that large numbers afforded. Syria and its allies in Amal were concerned about the "gradual reestablishment of a

Palestinian armed presence in the camps" as a result of both deliberate planning by the PLO and the desire of the camp residents to defend themselves (Brynen 1990: 188). To disarm the camps and consolidate its power, between 1985 and 1988, Amal waged a brutal war against the camps in Beirut and the south, placing them under siege for months on end, while the Israeli Air Force bombed Palestinian camps and bases in the Biqa' Valley and around Saida. This second War of the Camps left an indelible mark on the refugees who were on the brink of starvation, and resulted in the death of yet other thousands of refugees. By 1987, though the camps of Lebanon were receiving support in communiqués issued by the Unified National Leadership of the Intifada in the OPT, the refugees in Lebanon felt themselves cut off from the rest of the Palestinian community and unsupported by their leadership (Giannou 1991). The PLO leadership, desperate to assert its relevance, had shifted its focus to the OPT and the nascent popular uprising there, and Palestinians in Lebanon felt that their suffering in the camps were cynically used by this leadership to bolster its credentials in the OPT (Sayigh 1997: 589, 592).

When in 1988, the PLO recognized the state of Israel in its Declaration of Independence and became fully engaged in the Intifada in the OPT, Lebanon had ceased being "the heart of the Palestinian resistance" and had become a marginal battleground within which political conflicts generated by the leadership's position could be fought. With the cessation of the Lebanese civil war in 1990, and the declaration of a general amnesty in Lebanon in 1991, Palestinians found former architects of war crimes and massacres against them "parading through the corridors of power in civilian clothes" (Picard 2002: 167). Among these was the perpetrator of the Sabra and Shatila massacres, Elie Hobeika, who, in a grotesque twist, became the Minister of the Displaced after the war. Meanwhile, multilateral negotiations which began in Madrid in October 1991 said little about a comprehensive return of the refugees to their original homes. Consequently, many of the younger and educated workers in the camps of Lebanon emigrated to Europe or North America. The remainder became the primary scapegoats by the Lebanese, and their rights were severely circumscribed by the Lebanese state.

After the Oslo Accords (1993)

The level of violence against Palestinians in Lebanon has dropped substantially since the end of the civil war. Despite occasional internecine fighting in Ain al-Hilwa camp, the Palestinian armed forces are more or less invisible, until recently because of tight Syrian control over the camps and since the Syrian withdrawal in 2005, due to Lebanese military cordons around the camps. Some Syrian-backed militant groups – such as the PFLP–General Command – have a handful of small military camps in the Biqa' Valley, but have come under increasing scrutiny as the state of Lebanon attempts to rid itself of Syrian influence and proxies. The position of Palestinians in Lebanon has been further complicated by events in the OPT. After the death of Yasir Arafat who frequently oscillated on the question of the refugees, Mahmud Abbas (Abu Mazin) has become the president in Palestine, and has on several occasions made remarks interpreted as the abdication of the right of return. He has even suggested that Palestinian refugees should accept the citizenship of the countries in which they reside. Though ostensibly this is a good idea which will protect the civil rights of Palestinians in exile, refugees in Lebanon see this as a further proof that they are going to be either forcibly resettled in Lebanon or expelled from there to anywhere but Israel/Palestine where the Israelis consider them a demographic threat. The refugees are thus faced with a stark choice: further impoverishment and marginalization or legal or illegal emigration to European or North American countries (which after 11 September 2001 has become nearly impossible). The state of Israel is vehemently opposed to any return of refugees to their homes and occasional debates about mass *tawtin* (resettlement) in Lebanon meet with refusal from Palestinians. Polls conducted by political magazines indicate that the Lebanese public are strongly averse to the idea of Palestinian resettlement (Sayigh 1998a, 2000, 2001). Since the declaration of general amnesty at the end of the Lebanese civil war, various confessional groups have found it easier to apportion blame for the civil war and for any political domestic disturbances on Palestinians, casting them as provocateurs or a proverbial "fifth column." Labor strikes, attacks against American fast-food restaurants, and assassination attempts against political figures – especially former prime minister Rafiq Hariri – are blamed on Palestinians.

The deteriorating socio-economic conditions of the Palestinians in Lebanon in the post-Oslo period attest to their increasing marginalization. With an ever-diminishing budget, the UNRWA offices in Lebanon attempt to provide hundreds of thousands of refugees with free education until the age of sixteen, relatively inexpensive health-care until the age of sixty, and some assistance in housing construction and repair. Around 200,000 of Palestinian refugees registered with UNRWA live in twelve official camps (UNRWA 2001) and in unrecognized settlements in several villages in the south (Hajjaj 2000a: 21).[5] The camps are tightly packed spaces with narrow winding alleys separating houses that have been vertically – and often illegally – expanded to accommodate natural population growth within strictly circumscribed spaces. Individual camps do not have access to telephone lines, but camp health clinics and telephone "centrals" as well as most political party and NGO offices can afford the necessary costs of installing a telephone line connected to the Cypriot or Lebanese telephone networks. Mobile phones are rare and expensive symbols of prestige. Electricity supplies to the camps are highly erratic, especially during the winter, when daily power outages of at least four hours are typical. Camp water supplies, especially in and around Beirut, are polluted and non-potable. Camp residents purchase water for consumption from water-dealers who have access to unpolluted wells and taps outside the camp. Those families whose breadwinner has secured employment can afford televisions, and almost all families with televisions have affordable satellite connections which give them access to a wide range of Arabic-, English-, and French-language channels. Because of hardware expenses, the irregularity of electricity supplies, and the absence of telephone lines, very few families have home computers. Public spaces in the camps are scarce and young Palestinians, who constitute 60 percent of the camp population, have few gathering places within the camps themselves. Under Lebanese law, until recently Palestinians were unable to find employment in over seventy occupations, and even today after gains made in this area, Palestinian professionals are still barred from holding jobs outside the camps (Khalili 2005a). The refugees cannot legally own or inherit property (al-Natour 2001), and cannot petition to gain Lebanese citizenship (al-Natour 1997).[6] Those who through Lebanese demographic calculations were granted citizenship in the 1950s and later in the 1990s, may have their citizenship revoked.[7] The refugees

---

[5] In 2002, unofficial sources placed the total number of refugees in all of Lebanon around 250,000, with around 150,000 refugees remaining in the camps and the difference made up by Palestinian residents of Lebanon working in the Gulf or Europe. However, as Rosemary Sayigh points out, the Lebanese government estimates the number of refugees in Lebanon to be as high as 400,000, for the purposes of any future resettlement negotiations (2001: 101).

[6] In 1994, a deal between Nabih Berri (leader of Amal) and Sunni political notables facilitated the naturalization of around 15,000–20,000 Palestinians (Peteet 1996: 29), some of whom were Shi'a, and most of whom belonged to seven villages in Galilee near the border between Israel and Lebanon to which Lebanon lays historic claims.

[7] A recent court ruling in Lebanon has declared the 1994 deal illegal, and the Lebanese government has seized on this ruling to declare a "review" of the naturalization of the Palestinians.

have to endure a difficult process to obtain housing repair or construction permits, cannot establish NGOs dedicated solely to Palestinians, and since 2002, have to pay a substantial fee to attend Lebanese universities which were previously open to them with little or no restrictions. Furthermore, Lebanese post-war reconstruction plans have included the destruction of parts of some camps in Beirut, in order to accommodate highways and expansion of Lebanese neighborhoods (Abbas *et al.* 1997). Although these plans are yet to be implemented, they are still officially on the table.

Since before 1993, heated debates in Palestinian factional periodicals have centered on naturalization and out-migration of Palestinian refugees. At a meeting in 1994, "PA delegate Nabil Shaath stated emphatically that Palestinians in Lebanon were not the PA's responsibility but UNRWA's" (Sayigh 1995: 41), hinting at a permanent separation between the diaspora and the OPT. Opposition factions within the PLO angrily denounced attempts at settling Palestinians in their respective host countries, and did so by quoting the voices of the Palestinian refugees themselves. For example, in June 1992, the PFLP's *al-Hadaf* published an article compiling short excerpts of Palestinians' accounts of their life in Ain al-Hilwah camp, and while most of the accounts referred back to the life in the camp since its early days, the headline of the article boldly asserted, "We will not exchange Palestine for another homeland and we will fight against naturalisation [in Lebanon]" (*al-Hadaf*, June 1992: 9–11). When in 1994, Lebanese Interior Minister (and former PLO ally), Walid Junblat, proposed the construction of permanent housing for Palestinian survivors of camp massacres, now being displaced out of their squat residences by returning Lebanese property-owners, a great outcry arose not only from the Lebanese citizens (in particular, the representatives of Maronite and Shi'a sects), but also from the local Palestinian factions who saw this proposal as the work of Arafat and the PA and part of a larger plan for the settlement of Palestinians in Lebanon. For example, in October that year, Hamas's *Filastin al-Muslima* (October 1994) wrote that in fact:

three months ago, in a meeting with Assistant Secretary of State Robert Pelletreau and the American Ambassador in Tunisia, John McCarthy, Arafat pointed out that on the basis of the Gaza–Jericho agreement, the door of return for the refugees of 1948 is closed and that the majority of [the Palestinians in Lebanon and Syria] are to live in the aforementioned countries.

Whether or not Arafat had officially given up the right of Palestinians to return to their pre-1948 homes, most Palestinians in Lebanon felt that after Oslo their fate *vis-à-vis* the PA was far more uncertain than it had ever been. The exclusion of the issue of refugees from the negotiations signaled that Palestinians in Lebanon (and other diaspora locations) did not belong to the national body. Until the al-Aqsa Intifada in 2000, most Palestinians in Lebanon felt abandoned by the PA and considered their predicament, opinions and demands overlooked in the 'peace' negotiations.[8] The al-Aqsa Intifada, however, has spelled the end of the Oslo Accords, therefore reassuring the refugees and rekindling their hopes. The refugees in Lebanon see the al-Aqsa Intifada not only as a struggle for statehood but also – and perhaps more importantly – as a mobilization in support of *refugee* rights, wherever they may be. As long as a final settlement is not reached which finalizes the exclusion of refugees, they imagine there to be a possibility – however remote – for their participation in Palestinian political decision-making.

Today, the primary institutions shaping political life in the camps, and greatly influencing the everyday life of refugees, are the NGOs. Palestinian NGOs filled the service gap left by UNRWA and replaced lost social services previously provided by the factions and the PLO. The dizzying expansion in the number of international NGOs and development/relief funding in the 1990s similarly encouraged the rise of the third sector in the camps. In recent years, numerous local Palestinian NGOs have emerged which have had to register as Lebanese civil society organizations, but which are based on or near the camps and provide supplementary services especially for Palestinians in the camps. These local NGOs finance their activities by applying to international funding agencies, foundations, and international NGOs, and are managed and operated by local activists with ties to various political factions. Less than 20 percent of all their funds comes from local sources (Suleiman 1997b: 401), but their foreign funding is also dwindling. With the establishment of the PA in the OPT, most humanitarian aid from donor nations and organizations has been re-routed to the OPT, encouraging competition between the diaspora and home communities for scarce funds.

Situated somewhere between an organization with a political mission, and a local extension of the transnational NGO community, local Palestinian NGOs are crucial in sustaining the basic operation of the camps, as they provide child-care services for working mothers, after-school tutoring for children who attend the over-burdened UNRWA schools, supplementary health services for the elderly, vocational training, and

[8] On 28 September 2000, Ariel Sharon, accompanied by hundreds of armed soldiers visited the Haram al-Sharif/Temple Mount complex, setting off demonstrations and protests which in the first few days resulted in the death of tens of unarmed Palestinian civilians and which set off the al-Aqsa Intifada.

legal rights training. These NGOs are connected through a web of interactions, resource allocations, and loyalties to both international and local political actors. Some of these NGOs began as extensions of political factions, but as the power of these factions has diminished in Lebanon, the NGOs have become increasingly independent and more powerful. They also have long-standing and hard-fought connections to Northern NGOs and donors.

In many instances, local NGOs have acted both as conduits for transnational liberal discourses of rights and pity, and as a welcoming terrain for creative transformations and adaptations in these discourses into instruments of claims-making. Since the end of the civil war, many Palestinian youth have regarded their condition as refugees pathological and humiliating, and have often preferred to mask their identities as Palestinians when in a Lebanese context. In challenging exclusion, they have appealed to those identities that could provide a forum for voicing their grievances. As Randa Farah (1997: 262) points out, in the aftermath of Oslo, the divergence of interests between different trans-border communities, and the fragmentation of the *national* polity, attachments to both sub-national (such as village, camp, and kinship networks) and supra-national (such as Islamist ideologies) relations have grown. One can add the appeal to international sympathy and solidarity as another instance of supra-national mobilizing discourses. Perceiving the global importance of transnational NGO networks, Palestinian refugees also attempt to overcome their political/national isolation by focusing on *international* norms, human rights and institutions. Aside from NGO activism, Palestinian appeals to the international community take the shape of demonstrations that often end at the Beirut headquarters of international organizations (UNRWA or the offices of the UN Economic and Social Commission for West Asia, UN-ESCWA). They erect symbolically potent "refugee tents," slung with slogans in front of UNRWA to demand attention for the plight of the refugees. On International Women's Day (8 March) they gather in front of UN-ESCWA, with their placards calling for the recognition of "the rights of Palestinian women and children" (*al-Safir*, 9 March 2002). During the Israeli re-invasion of the West Bank in 2002, the refugees and their local allies demonstrated in support of Palestinians under occupation, marched through the city and their final destination was almost always UN-ESCWA (*al-Nahar*, 30 March 2002: 12). Whereas protesters inside the camps carried placards bearing slogans about "the Intifada, and resistance, and the right of return" in Arabic (*al-Safir*, 28 March 2002: 15), in front of UN-ESCWA, the English-language signs frequently referred to human rights; for example, one asked, "USA, Human Rights

Defender?"(*Daily Star*, 2 April 2002: 3). Occasionally, the US embassy was also chosen as a destination for protests. In such instances, the slogans also referred to human rights: "Are massacres on the USA human rights agenda?" (*Daily Star*, 11 April 2002: 3). The bifurcated appeal to both national and supra-national regimes of rights not only speaks of the refugees' strategic decision to pursue their goals in multiple arenas, but also points to the multivalent performances of claim-making deployed for different audiences and contexts.

The NGOs' work, despite providing much-needed relief and a language of protest, however, is not unproblematic. As an astute foreign observer wrote, "there [have been] few attempts to involve the people in party programs – any party, any program – except as objects of charity" (Connell 2002: 74), and the NGOs have often acted as the charity-allocating arm of many political factions, while having little or no influence on the political programs of the factions. Other problems are more endemic to Southern NGOs. Their reliance on foreign funding sources, or "NGO rent-seeking" (Carapico 2000: 14) not only makes local NGOs vulnerable to external political changes (Suleiman 1997b: 408), encourages intense competition between them over scarce resources (Roy 2000; Hammami 2000), and subjects their project planning to the foreign development and foreign aid fads and fashions, it also introduces a discourse of victimization into the mix, which is something I will discuss in greater length in subsequent chapters.

Silencing Palestinian pasts

For years I sought out traces of my history, looking up maps and directories and piles of archives. I found nothing, and it sometimes seemed as though I had dreamt, that there had been only an unforgettable nightmare.
George Perec, *W or The Memory of Childhood*

Whether in the heyday of the *Thawra*, or in the post-civil-war era, Palestinian attempts to constitute a coherent story of their past have been challenged, contested, and sometimes silenced. In *Silencing the Past*, Michel-Rolph Trouillot (1995: 26) writes:

Silences enter the process of historical production at four crucial moments: the moment of fact creation (the making of *sources*); the moment of fact assembly (the making of *archives*); the moment of fact retrieval (the making of *narratives*); and the moment of retrospective significance (the making of *history* in the final instance).

The ordinary refugees who left Palestine in 1948 did not publish their experiences, write memoirs, or produce visual accounts of their exile.[9] The artefacts of their everyday lives were lost, and the very villages that could have attested to their eviction were destroyed (Khalidi 1992). In subsequent years, violent dispersion and displacement, and the well-founded fear of authorities have prevented the "making of sources and archives." Massacres and destruction of the camps have dispersed people who experienced historical events. The layering of experienced atrocities and the strategic choice of commemoration have also silenced older memories and narratives.

At the point of the creation of archives, there has been a great deal of internal silencing. As Ted Swedenburg (1990: 152–3) writes:

> Perhaps the sensitive nature of the subject of infighting during the [Arab] revolt [1936–1939] is one of the reasons why PLO, which funded numerous projects in Lebanon during the seventies and early eighties, never supported a study of the [Revolt] based on the testimony of the refugees living in Lebanon. Maybe the resistance movement was hesitant to allow any details about the internal struggle of the thirties to be brought to light because bad feelings persisted in the diaspora community.

During the *Thawra*, the PLO seems not to have been interested in commemorating pre-1948 Palestinian lives, or archiving their experiences of the *Nakba*.

While various political factions created many holidays and produced numerous symbolic events, their efforts at recording ordinary refugees' memories were at best dismal. In factional organs, commemoration of village life was maintained at a highly abstract level, even by those Palestinian factions that ostensibly spoke for the "workers and peasants." For example, articles about villages in *al-Hadaf*, a factional organ of the PFLP, were either theoretical essays about pre-capitalist modes of production, or about the lives of peasants in Vietnam, rather than life-stories of Palestinian villagers. The journals of the PLO Research Centre (then in Beirut) published a handful of memoirs of the 1948 exodus during the 1970s, but these were mostly written by urban and urbane Palestinians now living outside the camps in Arab or European capitals. When in the late 1990s, the Arab Resource Centre for Popular Arts (ARCPA) undertook an oral history project in the camps, elderly Palestinians greeted the interviewers by saying "It's good that you're doing this. The political organisations and leaders before you should have paid some attention ... but if you are doing it, well bravo" (ARCPA 1998: 43).

---

[9] Palestinian elite and intellectuals, on the other hand, produced a number of memoirs which were subsequently published. See Davis 2002; Fleischmann 2003; Tamari 2002, 2003.

The lack of interest in more textured – and perhaps fractious – histories of smaller locales went hand-in-hand with the imperatives of the nationalist movement which demanded a more homogenous and harmonious history. Scholars performing oral history research during this period tried to secure institutional support for their research and were refused: "I recall clearly that before the invasion of 1982, I and a number of comrades tried our hardest to convince leading academic institutions, any of which would have been able to start collecting oral history testimonies, even if only from certain camps or in a limited number. However, our attempts … failed" (Al-Hout 1998: 11). Others recall that Palestinian national research institutions – and even PLO activists – "weren't convinced that [oral history] research could help the national struggle, or the aims of their *tanzim*" (Sayigh 1998: 6). The lack of institutional support for oral history projects could also have been explained by the potential of such history to reveal lines of fissure in the nation, local betrayals by notables, and Palestinian collaboration with the colonizing forces, and much bottom-up history was suppressed in favor of heroic narratives which form the basis of all nationalist histories.

More devastating, however, has been the deliberate intervention in and repression of the archives, as Palestinian documentary collections – both in exile and in the OPT – have been the target of Israeli aggression. The PLO Research Centre in Beirut was ransacked in 1982 (during the Israeli invasion of Lebanon) and its entire contents were taken away to Israel. After the Sabra and Shatila massacre, twenty Lebanese and Palestinian female volunteers collected some 300 eyewitness accounts of the massacres under extreme duress.

After going through the motions in October [1982] of appointing a [Lebanese] commission of inquiry, whose findings were never released, the subject of the massacre was virtually dropped. Any effort to collect names became virtually taboo, to the point that the ICRC has never published the names it did collect, and those conducting field work on the subject had to do with extreme discretion. Such was the climate that even death certificates became impossible to obtain. (Linda Butler's introduction to Shahid 2002: 44; also see Anonymous 1983: 101–2)

Nevertheless, some of the clandestinely collected eyewitness accounts were published in *Shu'un Filastiniyya* (Anonymous 1982, 1983; Al-Sheikh 1983), and they are detailed, raw, and painful to read. Not only the eyewitnesses, but also the researchers chose to remain anonymous in order to prevent retaliation. However,

on February 5, 1983, a car bomb [presumably left by the Israeli military or its local allies] gutted six stories of the Research Centre building killing 18 people and wounding 95 ... Among the dead was Hannah Shaheen, the wife of the Research Centre director, Sabri Jiryis. At the time of the blast she was working on the Sabra–Shatila eyewitness interviews. In the final terror campaign against the Research Centre, most of the interviews were lost or destroyed. (Garfield 1984: 102)

The silencing of Palestinian history through suppression of its archives has continued. Ellen Fleischmann records the holdings of various Israeli libraries and archives which include the papers of George Antonius, documents of the supreme Muslim Council and almost all Arabic-language Palestinian newspapers from the Mandate era and before. She (2003: 225–6 fn. 51) also attests to the inaccessibility of these documents to Palestinians without European or North American passports:

When Hala and Dumya Sakakini visited the Hebrew University Library after 1967, they saw their father's extensive collection of books, which had been confiscated after the family's flight to Egypt during the fighting in Jerusalem in 1948. They even recognized his handwriting on the margins of the pages, but were not allowed to recover the books.

In August 2001, the Israeli government confiscated Orient House, the unofficial seat of the Palestinian Authority in Jerusalem, and seized all documentation therein. The expropriated archives included land ownership documents going back to Ottoman times. Also in 2001, the contents of the Palestinian Office of Statistics which included data on all aspects of Palestinian society were confiscated. Between 29 March and 12 April 2002, during the Israeli re-occupation of the West Bank, "scores of NGO offices, radio and television stations, banks, schools, hospitals, and cultural centres were wrecked, looted and most importantly, robbed of their documents and computers' hard disks where all kinds of vital information was stored" (Karmi 2002). These included the Land Registry Office, the Education Ministry, the Health Ministry, the entire collection of laws and human rights legislation belonging to the human rights NGO al-Haq, banks, private commercial enterprises, infirmaries, and supermarkets (Hass 2002; Twiss 2003). Also during 2002, the entire archives of several Palestinian literary magazines, including *al-Karmel*, was looted (*al-Sharq al-Awsat*, 21 May 2002: 14).

At the point of production of narratives about the past, the Syrian, Lebanese, and Israeli states have also attempted to silence Palestinian commemoration. In her memoir of Sabra and Shatila, Ang recalls that even laying flowers at the massacre site could result in the Lebanese state punishing the Palestinian Red Crescent Society (Ang 1989). While the Syrian military was present in Lebanon, the Syrian intelligence services' intimidation tactics not only suppressed political criticisms of their actions, but also silenced commemoration of and stories about Tal al-Za'tar massacre and to a lesser extent the War of the Camps. There has never been a commission of inquiry to examine the massacres of 1975–6, especially Tal al-Za'tar, and the Lebanese general amnesty granted in 1991 has meant that those culpable of the worst atrocities have escaped unquestioned.

Though the massacre at Sabra and Shatila resulted in massive demonstrations in Israel which pressured the government to appoint the Kahan Commission of Inquiry, the conduct and conclusions of the Commission were both problematic. Members of the Commission did not visit the massacre site, interviewed only a handful of "non-Israelis among the 221 witnesses who testified before the Commission," and excluded any testimony about important elements of the assault, such as the massacres at the Acca Hospital in Shatila (Kapeliouk 1983: 81). Attempts at silencing of the story of Sabra and Shatila have continued with a general amnesty declared subsequent to the civil war (which has allowed former militiamen to boast about their bloody exploits with impunity), with the assassination of Elie Hobeika (the LF militiaman directing the massacres), and with the failure of the Belgian court case against Ariel Sharon to go forward (see Chapter 7).

Challenging the silencing of the past requires resources, stamina, and concerted effort. Although many local activists and ordinary refugees have tried to overcome barriers to commemoration, history-telling, archiving, and the recording of local histories (Khalili 2004, 2005b), nevertheless, institutional access, power, and financial backing is often needed to engage the tellers of history secure spaces – however small or ephemeral – for storage of artefacts and stories having to do with the past, and for dissemination of these stories and histories. Most important is the manner in which pasts are made to sing: people who have been tossed to and fro by forces of war, exile, and dispossession have to trust the collectors of these histories, and the pasts thus salvaged – from bulldozers, theft, looting, and forgetting – have to have some local meaning or resonance, or they become obscure museum arcana. Political institutions that have the necessary resources for production and reproduction of these stories provide the necessary venues and resources for the transformation of commemorative narratives into instruments of mobilization.

4 Forms of commemoration

> Because my voice is barren as a flagpole
> and my hand empty as a national anthem
> and because my shadow is vast as a festival
> and the lines of my face go for a ride in an ambulance
> because of all of this
> I am a citizen of an unborn kingdom.
>
> Mahmud Darwish, *Psalm Eleven*

A political demonstration ends at the Shatila Martyrs' Cemetery, where orators point to the grave of Ghassan Kanafani and remind the demonstrators of the obligation the martyrs have placed on their shoulders. An elderly woman wearing an embroidered dress waves a large old-fashioned key in the air. A young girl receives via email a digital image of the remnants of the destroyed village her grandparents inhabited. A calendar published by a political faction chronicles battles and massacres on every page. The image of a young martyr stares out from a large and colorful mural on the walls of a camp alongside ubiquitous posters commemorating Abu Jihad. During a tour of Burj al-Shamali camp's monument to unsung martyrs, a young NGO activist pleads for international sympathy.

In the realm of commemorations, Palestinian political institutions and the refugees themselves have a mutual relationship. The refugees' lives, language, and experiences provide the raw materials co-opted by the institutions and transformed into the narrative content of their commemorations. On the other hand, the manner in which the refugees engage in or reject these practices indicates the extent to which these commemorations resonate with them – or not. The forms commemorations can take are important means of taking "memories" into the lives of refugees. Most commemorative forms require institutional resources, although there are some, such as history-telling, that need no such resources. Commemorative forms have remained fairly constant over time, while their content has changed – as we shall see in subsequent chapters. Both political factions and NGOs use the following forms of commemoration to promulgate commemorative narratives: history-telling, commemorative images, pedagogy, publishing and electronic media, naming, organization of time and spaces, and ceremonial gatherings. In this chapter, I will examine these commemorative forms in greater detail and illustrate their workings by providing examples.

History-telling

One of the most significant and recurrent forms of commemoration has been "history-telling," where a narrator weds her personal biography to historical events in a public performance. Alessandro Portelli's history-telling (1997: 6) is a medium where "the combination of the prevalence of narrative form on the one hand, and the search for a connection between biography and history, between individual experience and the transformation of society on the other" allow for an examination of the effects of large-scale social transformations on individual lives, ideas, and strategies. History-telling occurs in a variety of contexts, including memorial ceremonies, political gatherings, televisions serials, and through intergenerational and public enactment of narratives about the past, but it always includes a person – often with a certain authority acquired through age or office – telling the personal narrative of a particular moment in time, through which the larger (hi)story of the nation is illuminated.[1]

Although one of the primary tropes of Palestinian commemoration is the insistence on intergenerational transmission of memory through *spontaneous* telling of stories to children and grandchildren by the elders, the telling of histories can be instigated by researchers, journalists and film-makers. With the emergence of oral history as a legitimate source of historiographic data, researchers, writers, and artists all engage with those Palestinians who have a story to tell. Multiple projects in the OPT and the diaspora have focused on gathering the memories of pre-exilic life in Palestine, as well as the narratives of 1948 – and to a lesser extent 1967 – expulsions and exiles.[2] These projects provide the impetus for the kind of public history-telling made legendary in Palestinian

---

[1] Transformations in style and content of history-telling is incredibly difficult to trace over time, as recorded or documented oral narratives of Palestinian lives have only emerged in the last few decades, and as such, recorded stories told by the Palestinian camp refugees themselves in the years prior to 1970 are rare.

[2] For a full bibliographic listing of these projects and other bibliographic citations, see Sayigh 2002. Since 2002, several new publications and projects have focused on Palestinian memories of 1948, but also of collective memories of other periods. Some of the most notable are Allen 2005; Collins 2004; Robinson 2003; and Rosenfeld 2004.

self-imaginings, yet stimulated and invited forth more readily by external intervention. Because so much of the focus of this type of mediated history-telling has been in response to projects aiming to preserve memories of 1948, with few notable exceptions, history-telling in a public setting has focused on the *Nakba*, rather than on the ascent and transformation of the nationalist movement.[3]

History-telling is often the forte of the less affluent and less powerful Palestinian refugees. On the one hand, narrating stories requires scant resources and hence can be more easily deployed in variable settings (though often the media on which these stories are recorded are indeed expensive). On the other hand, a kind of authority has accrued to the narratives of former peasants – "sons and daughters of the land" – whom nationalist discourse sees as having a more intimate relationship with the lost homeland and as such better able to tell its stories.[4]

The Palestinian literary elite were also important in producing and reproducing commemorations by transferring history-telling onto printed pages. Scholars have analyzed the representations of *fida'iyyin* and martyrs in Palestinian poetry (Slyomovics 1998: ch. 5), or the role of poetry as an important mechanism for the transmission of memory (Cooley 1973: ch. 4). Ghassan Kanafani extended the domain of symbolic exchange to prose. The image of "sad oranges" or the "axe-shaped key" all borrowed from his own experience of exile, have been re-disseminated and become central in the Palestinian national semiotics. Kanafani's own illustrations for many of his stories have become iconic and are familiar images for those who may not even know that Kanafani has drawn them. Postcards and posters printed by various political organizations (during the *Thawra*) and by the Palestinian NGOs (in recent years) all unselfconsciously borrow elements of the symbolic language Kanafani perfected. Factional posters, ubiquitous throughout refugee camps, have been crucial in spreading these iconic images beyond the bounds of a particular organization's publications, or a given writer's books. The poetry of Mahmud Darwish, similarly transmits icons and images to a much larger audience when they are sung by popular singers. Darwish lived in Beirut during the latter years of the *Thawra*, edited the PLO journal, *Shu'un Filastiniyya*, and wrote voluminous and influential poetry whose images of life in Galilee, of exile,

---

[3] These exceptions include Allen 2005; Collins 2004; Rosenfeld 2004, and Sayigh 1979; 1985, 1994.

[4] Narratives of exile written by middle-class urbanites have emerged in more recent years, for example on the fiftieth anniversary of the *Nakba* in 1998. See Tamari 2003 for analysis and critique.

and of the subsequent devastation in Beirut have made their ways into the camp vernacular imagery through popular songs.

While the literary language of poetry can introduce new symbols into commemorative semiotics, memory can also move in the other direction: literature can incorporate mnemonic narratives told by the refugees, in some ways concretizing, perhaps even *authorizing* them (White 1981: 13). The poetry of Mahmud Darwish freely borrows "popular cultural heritage," imagery, and even popular rhymes within them (Khoury 1973: 151). Liana Badr's *The Eye of the Mirror* (1994) and Elias Khoury's *Gate of the Sun* (2005) are two novels similarly containing "memories" of Palestinians. *The Eye of the Mirror* tells the story of the siege and fall of Tal al-Za'tar camp in 1975 and 1976 through the eyes of the women who lived through the siege and many of whom were slaughtered thereafter. Badr conducted extensive interviews ("7 years of oral research") with survivors of the siege and the subsequent massacre, and the resultant document reads as both testimony and fiction (Salaita 2001: 11). The novel elucidates many of the quotidian aspects of life under siege, including resorting to lentils as the only possible edible, and incorporates frequently repeated elements of massacre narratives – e.g. the death at the water taps – in its story-telling. Badr herself states that she insisted on preserving "the stories, tales, songs, quotidian lives and feelings, the vernacular, the colloquial accent, spoken cadences and multiplicity of voices" because she believes that her book "belongs to oral history rather than literature" (Yunis 2001: 52).

Khoury also successfully deploys the same fragmentary and non-linear method of story-telling in his enormously powerful *Gate of the Sun* which was published to great acclaim in Beirut in 1998. The novel's narrator-protagonist, Dr. Khalil, sits at the bedside of a forgotten national hero in a hospital in Shatila, telling stories to his comatose patient in the hope that he shall awaken. The stories Khalil/Khoury tell aim to preserve and reproduce memory. In telling stories of characters who cross temporal and spatial boundaries in their multiple exiles, the novel – also researched for some seven years – builds from its hundreds of fragmentary narratives a powerful story about 1948, Palestinian lives in the refugee camps, and the stories of Sabra and Shatila and Tal al-Za'tar massacres. Khoury writes of exodus, exile, and civil war, but because Khalil, his main protagonist, is speaking to himself (or at most to a comatose audience), the stories are told reflexively, even critically. The novel deals directly with the memory *work* needed to sustain the community, the polity, and the nation. It also addresses the multivalence of mnemonic narratives. As Khoury (2005: 275) himself writes, "I am scared of a history that has only one version. History has dozens of versions, and for it to ossify into one leads only to death." Khoury's novel, as such, recreates multiple lives of suffering and joy, of victimhood and heroism, of victory and defeat, neither of which are predominant but all of which together create a tapestry that is a polyvalent national history.

The audience for both Badr and Khoury are primarily middle class and intellectually inclined readers. But there are other forms of published history-telling which are written and read by the refugees. Village memorial books written by elderly camp residents – and often as a result of cooperation between elders belonging to the same village – and self-published are examples of concretization of memories and its dissemination (Khalili 2004; 2005b). Memoirs of the civil war are another such media. In my interviews, I encountered more than a few Palestinian men (and they were always men) in the camps who had written their memoirs for their children and families. Many could not publish these documents because they could not afford to do so; others had recorded such controversial issues that they were afraid of the consequences of publishing their works (mostly from Syrian retribution, but also from those in the camp who may not have been portrayed in a kind light). Abu Mustafa told me:

I wrote my memories of the War of the Camps in the form of diaries; something personal and general about what life was like. The War of the Camps created lots of memories. I have more memories about that than anything else. I was fighting both as a fighter and as a human being. For a fighter there is a difference between fighting on bases against the enemy and fighting on a front that is his home. At that time, the war was just about defending our people. And sometimes things happened during this war which negatively influenced my people. So I had to write about it all. (Burj al-Barajna, 6 February 2002)

Though unpublished, these accounts, nevertheless, tell the history of seminal events in the lives of the camp through Abu Mustafa's personal experience, and when recounted in public settings, as Abu Mustafa did in my presence, reproduce commemorative narratives.

Images

Images are powerful and evocative commemorative forms. Whether they appear in murals, cartoons, photographs, posters, postcards, or in digital form on the internet they are important mechanisms for iconizing familiar objects of memory. The most popular use of images as commemorative forms is the martyrs' posters and murals which I discuss at greater length in Chapter 6, but other images are also used for public and private commemorations.

Most camp houses have photographs or paintings of the Dome of the Rock prominently displayed alongside images of their martyred relatives. Camp walls often act as canvases for murals celebrating Jerusalem, martyrs of Palestine, or important moments in the Palestinian refugees' history, often rendered allegorically (with flowers, for example, standing in for martyrs). Postcards sold cheaply in camp shops often have images of women in embroidered Palestinian dresses, or images of keys and horses, Palestinian villages and cities, or stylized photographs of olive trees and stone houses. These postcards have in recent years been digitized and now are available not only in paper form, but also electronically.

Allegorical paintings of Isma'il Shammut, who hailed from Gazan refugee camps have appeared on such postcards as well as PLO posters. These paintings often portray Palestine as a woman and set her image within other symbolic objects of memory (Boullata 1993). Shammut's image of a Palestinian peasant carrying Jerusalem upon his bent back is one of the most familiar renderings of the idea of a peasant as signifier of nationalist resilience. The best-known producer of memory images, however, must be Naji al-Ali whose incisive political cartoons sharply critiqued the mendacity and cruelty of adversaries and the Palestinian leadership alike. Al-Ali produced some of the most scathing caricatures of Arab military and business men, corrupt Arab leaders, and brutal American and Israeli powers. But he is also known for his loving cartoons of refugees, allegorical female Palestine in tears and defiant suffering, and for his reproduction of important mnemonic symbols such as barbed wire, *keffiyeh*s, and stonethrowing children. I discuss his famous creation, Hanzala, in greater detail in Chapter 6.

Pedagogy

Formal pedagogy is one of the most important forms promulgating commemorative narratives. Stories of peoplehood are often first learned in a formal pedagogic setting (Ben-Amos and Bet-El 1999; Resnik 2003; Zerubavel 1995: 79–83). The pantheon of national heroes is often first populated in the future citizens' imaginations in schools (Sheffi 2002). Education is crucial in defining those events that constitute the collective self and the boundaries that exclude the Other (Gur-Ze'ev 2001). Images that eventually become symbolic representations of the nation are often images perpetuated through school textbooks. Many of the ceremonial elements which dramatize representations of the nation are taught and learned in schools (Zerubavel 1995: 93–94).

Since its inception, UNRWA – along with UNESCO – has been responsible for the education of Palestinian children, especially in the camps (Buehrig 1971; Sayigh 1952). Originally, the educational program was intended to supplement UN economic measures aimed at the integration of refugees in their host countries. In the 1960s, however, the educational program supplanted those economic measures in order to "[cultivate] individual capabilities [of the refugees] through basic education and vocational, technical, and professional training" (Buehrig 1971: 147). After the 1967 War, UNRWA had to reach an accommodation with the state of Israel in order to continue to teach Palestinian refugees in the OPT (Buehrig 1971: 158). As such, UNRWA agreed to modify textbooks throughout the UNRWA network to exclude hostile references to Israel. In Lebanon, this meant that if there were any institutionalized instruction on Palestinian history, it had to be done through the initiative of individual teachers. This resulted in unofficial commemorations of the Palestinian past in ceremonies or informal lessons, rather than through textbooks.

In an essay written in 1973, Basim Sarhan (1973: 107) outlined the learning of Palestinian history and geography, songs, clothing, and culture alongside the "firm rooting of the image of the *fida'yi*" as important components of "Palestinian Revolutionary Education" (also Bowker 2003: 137). UNRWA's photo archives similarly provided an institutional mechanism for commemorating the lives of the refugees (Bowker 2003). By 1974, a new book of history was introduced and Palestinian history and geography was being taught (Graham-Brown 1984 quoted in al-Ali 1999: 135). As Abu Mustafa recalls, "During the *Thawra*, the teachers did teach the kids Palestinian history to some degree. But, the teachers were giving these lessons on their own, not because of the UNRWA school [curriculum]. At that time, the *Thawra* was controlling the situation, and so they were behind the teachers" (Burj al-Barajna, 6 February 2002).

UNRWA teachers – especially in the 1960s and 1970s – were crucially important in propagation of nationalist narratives and icons so prevalent during that period. They were themselves children of the camps. Most were born in pre-1948 Palestine, and many became grassroots organizers and activists forming the core of nascent political organizations in the 1960s (Sayigh 1997: 74). When UNRWA was pressured to delete or replace the words Palestine, *tahrir* (liberation), or *fida'yi* in the textbooks, cancel Palestinian history courses, and replace Arabic place-names on maps with their Hebrew counterparts, UNRWA teachers in Lebanon called a strike (Bashur 1971: 240; Brand 1988: 208). Their mobilization led to the threat of a general strike by all diaspora teachers, the support of the Arab Teachers' Federation, Arab newspapers, and the official complaint of the Syrian government which resulted in a review of some 127 textbooks by an independent UN commission (Brand 1988: 208–9; Buehrig 1971: 159–161). Though this review affected textbooks in Syria, Jordan, Egypt and the OPT, in Lebanon, the school textbooks remained relatively unaffected (Buehirg 1971: 165). The teachers' political activism often transformed school classrooms and youth activities centers into "places where a collective Palestinian exile identity, based on the memory of the land of Palestine and the claim of return was constantly reactivated and transmitted to the younger generations" (al-Husseini 2000: 53). It is also noteworthy that the great majority of local historians who have written memorial books about pre-1948 Palestine and the founders of the only Palestinian ethnographic museum in Lebanon are former UNRWA teachers (Khalili 2004; 2005b).

Palestinian children have not been the sole recipients of nationalist pedagogy. In adult literacy classes held during the *Thawra*, Palestinian history and geography were taught through narratives about signal events and places such as the Balfour Declaration, the Great Revolt of 1936–39, or Jerusalem as the capital of Palestine (Peteet 1991: 122). Textbooks and oral discussions used a military/nationalist vocabulary and focused on " 'weapons,' 'ambush,' 'struggle,' 'organizations,' 'mobilization,' 'bullets,' 'committees,' 'revolution,' 'martyrs', etc." (Peteet 1991: 122).

However, since the exodus of the Palestinian leadership from Lebanon in 1982, the salience of UNRWA as a source of nationalist pedagogy has drastically decreased. As Afaf Younis, the head of UNRWA's education services in Lebanon has clearly stated, "within the frameworks of UNRWA Field and Agency requirements, the school teachers and principals have little autonomy and they have to follow UNRWA guidelines extensively. The same norms and the same mandate govern the running of the schools" (Beirut, 25 January 2002). Homogenisation of norms and guidelines has meant an increasing inflexibility *vis-à-vis* teachers initiating Palestinian nationalist pedagogy. Burj al-Barajna's Abu Mustafa recounts:

It was the *Nakba* day (15th May) and I went to a school to ask the kids if they knew what the day was. Some students thought that it was the Lebanese national day, and some thought it was *Ashura*.[5] Then I started to talk to the kids about how our people had lived in Palestine and how they left it. The teacher became embarrassed; she turned red, because her students didn't know about this day.

---

[5] *Ashura* is the tenth day of the lunar month of *Muharram*, during which Shi'a Muslims commemorate the martyrdom of the third Shi'a Imam, Husayn in 680 AC.

Then I went to the principal of the school. I wanted to tell him that these children, these students should know about this day. (Burj al-Barajna camp, 6 February 2002)

Even in the absence of direct and formal teaching of commemorative narratives, however, school holidays and even schools' names are mnemonic devices. In addition to Lebanese holidays, UNRWA in Lebanon has designated 7 January as Palestine Martyrs' Day and, additionally, set aside three dates as "Dates of Remembrance, which should be dedicated for explaining to the pupils the meaning and significance of the occasion" (UNRWA document). These three dates are Balfour Declaration Day (2 November), Palestine Partition Day (29 November), and Palestine Remembrance Day (15 May). All UNRWA schools in Lebanon are named after Palestinian towns and villages (many destroyed in 1948) and all contain "detailed maps of those villages and towns and information about them" (Afaf Younis, Beirut, 25 January 2002).

The current absence of Palestinian historical or geographical education in UNRWA schools has led to Palestinian NGOs taking on this pedagogic role. To the extent that an NGO considers itself a "political" organization, the pedagogic function often converges with nationalist commemoration, but not always. In recent years, a number of local NGOs have chosen to move away from an obviously nationalistic program of instruction. Throughout Lebanon, the Kanafani Children's Centres (founded by Anni Kanafani, and named after her husband, Ghassan), for example, have used drawing classes to teach children about the post-nationalist imagination of communities, where a universal human community is privileged. At the Najda after-school program in Shatila, volunteer teachers have used their classes to focus on international regimes of rights and their influence on children's lives (Sukarieh 1999). These approaches, however, tend to take the back seat to pedagogy which commemorates the nation. In their after-school programs, nurseries, and summer camps, NGOs teach nationalist songs, tell nationalist stories, and promulgate symbolic narratives imbued with olive trees and oranges. NGO schools commemorate historical dates on their walls and in their buildings. Children are taught the *dabke* line-dance, claimed as the Palestinian national dance. In drawing classes, iconized images of keys, flags, doves, barbed-wire fences, and stone-throwing children are drawn alongside scenes of children's everyday lives. In some NGO programs, children perform skits based on iconized events, moments, and persons, learn about the heroic personae of the time – guerrillas or martyrs – and learn to revere them.

In order to provide a more uniform teaching resource for other NGOs, the Arab Resource Centre for Popular Arts (ARCPA) has created the *Ahmad and Maryam Learning Package*. The textbook draws from a variety of sources, including oral histories collected by ARCPA and interviews conducted by children who work with ARCPA. It tells the story of two small Palestinian children, Ahmad and Maryam from the town of Saffuriyya near Nazareth, and their exodus to Lebanon in 1948. The book includes beautiful illustrations by Sa'ad Haju and Sahar Burhan, which combine cartoon imagery of children with stylized iconic images, including that of the Key to lost Palestinian houses, the Dome of the Rock, and patterns drawn from Palestinian embroidery. The 1948 conflict is graphically rendered in cartoons, and violence is not whitewashed. The package does not show Palestinian villagers fighting back, arms are only in the hands of the Zionist characters (who can be distinguished by their European looks and a Star of David), and Palestinians are represented as resilient and long-suffering. Though the package is inexpensive ($15), I am not certain how widespread its use has been. Nevertheless, it contains a great deal of mnemonic narratives, and reproduces more than a few iconic objects.

Paper and electronic media

Because of the relatively high degree of literacy in the camps of Lebanon, especially among the generation that came of age in Lebanon, published material, circulars, factional periodicals, and leaflets are of some importance in disseminating Palestinian stories of the past.

At least during the *Thawra* period, Palestinian party periodicals were crucial in setting the agenda for commemoration.[6] They advertised the dates that were to be commemorated, reproduced iconic images (especially that of the gun), and included memorial sections about massacres, battles, lost villages, and heroic personae – both guerrillas and martyrs. Having a publication in effect consolidated and legitimated the position of a particular faction.[7] These periodicals disseminated

---

[6] For a complete list of these publications, see Kurayyam 1995.

[7] As Khalid al-Hassan, one of the founders of Fatah recalled, between 1958 and 1962, young Palestinian activists were forming groups throughout the Arab world. "But we [the Kuwait group] were the only ones who managed to have a magazine called *Falastinuna [Our Palestine]* ... So though this magazine – and there was a P.O. box at the magazine – so we became known before the others. So the others started to talk to us, to write to us ... So we became the core through the P.O. Box of this magazine. And then we managed to see each other and finally, in '62, we had a conference in Kuwait, and the whole were united in Al-Fateh" (Cobban 1984: 24). See also the critical discussion in Sayigh (1997: 84–5).

information about commemorative calendars: through their special issues, editorials, and commemorative sections, dates of important battles and massacres were remembered. Throughout the 1970s, the inside cover of the periodicals were almost wholly dedicated to commemoration, often of the "on this date in ... twenty years ago" variety.

The latter pages of the periodicals contained images and short biographies of martyred activists, especially in times of intense conflict. Most periodicals had – and some continue to have – sections titled "Lest We Forget" (*Hatta la-Nansa*) which include brief and formalized biographies of martyrs or descriptions of lost and destroyed villages. The last page of the PLO's *Filastin al-Thawra* often contained images which explicitly or implicitly commemorated past events. For example, on the fifth anniversary of the Israeli invasion of Lebanon, *Filastin al-Thawra* included images from the war in Lebanon, but the article title spoke of the "Lessons of the Two Junes" – June of 1967 and of 1982 – weaving a coherent historical narrative from the accumulation of two major defeats which coincidentally occurred in the month of June (*Filastin al-Thawra*, 31 May 1987: back cover).

When commemorating the Balfour Declaration, the Partition, or the 1948 war, short pedagogic essays accompanied historic images. But commemoration was not limited to these explicit articles. In 1975, *Filastin al-Thawra* began publishing revolutionary song lyrics containing mnemonic markers, and other factions followed suit. Even mundane amusements such as word puzzles in factional periodicals included iconic words, reinforcing their importance as mnemonic devices. For example, a word puzzle in *Filastin al-Thawra* (15 March 1986: 57) required the puzzle-solver to find in a jumble of letters the words Kafr Qasim, Qibya, Dayr Yasin, Tal al-Za'tar, Sabra, and Shatila, among others. A palimpsest of massacres was not so subtly reproduced through puzzle-solving.

Old and new electronic media have been immensely influential in reaching across borders to various segments of the diasporic community, in an attempt to "[keep] alive their hopes for a return to their homelands" (Browne 1975: 133). Since the Palestine Service of Radio Cairo came on air in 1954, Palestinians have had some sort of broadcasting presence in Arab capitals. As Rashid Khalidi has written, in the absence of a commemorative infrastructure, the PLO could reinforce its version of history only through publications – discussed above – "and especially its radio station *Sawt Filastin*, 'The Voice of Palestine,' which was much listened to by Palestinians, for many of whom it soon took the place of Egypt's *Sawt al-'Arab*" (Khalidi 1997: 199–200). In the late 1960s and 1970s, all broadcasts of the multiple "voices of Palestine" included the segments devoted to the *fida'iyyin*, and celebrated momentous battles (e.g. Karama) regularly (Browne 1975: 139), thus contributing to the iconization of those heroes and transformative moments. The broadcasts were largely devoted to inter-state politics, reports on donors and revolutionary songs. "Radio plays and documentaries [were] rare, perhaps because they [required] more elaborate preparation, and educational broadcasts (Palestinian children fortunate enough to be in school learn little of their own heritage) [were] almost non-existent" (Browne 1975: 147). In the 1980s, the oppositionist al-Quds radio, operated by PFLP-GC and broadcast from Syria, challenged the PLO's policy of *sumud* or steadfastness, and encouraged Palestinians in the OPT to expend "blood, efforts, sweat and pain" in their heroic resistances (Bookmiller and Bookmiller 1990: 101).

Local broadcasts by independent activists alleviated the dearth of educational material in schools by propagating commemorations on air:

At the radio station where I worked as a journalist there was a regular report on Palestine. In the period given to me during this broadcast, I would do special reports. At first I did a program on the Intifada. Then I did a second program on the history of Palestine – for example, how the Zionists came to Palestine, the developments up to the Balfour Declaration. Now this second section became quite diverse and came to include something like oral history ... There was a section called 'Lest We Forget'. I would talk in it about a certain village each time. I tried, as much as possible, to host someone from that village and get them to talk about the daily life, customs, and traditional ways there ... The show was well-heard and well-liked by people who would wait for it and for the nationalistic songs in it – it had an attractive presentation. (Bushra al-Moghrabi 1997, Sidon; ARCPA 1998: 41–2)

Moghrabi's area of broadcast, Saida, includes the Ain al-Hilwa camp, which is the largest Palestinian camp in Lebanon, as well as the city of Saida itself, which after Beirut has the highest number of Palestinian residents.

Television in recent years may have supplanted radio as the primary means of access to news and information. By installing cheap satellite dishes, many houses in the camp have access to ever-multiplying Arabic-language channels, broadcast from Arab and European capitals. During the period of my fieldwork, the most popular television channels for listening to news and programs were al-Jazeera (Qatar), Abu-Dhabi (UAE), Filastin (the OPT), and al-Manar (Beirut). Listening to news of the OPT is itself an important way of confirming one's belonging to and solidarity with the larger Palestinian polity. The al-Aqsa Intifada was followed assiduously in every household I visited. This was in some contrast with the events of the first Intifada which had been far from the minds of the Palestinian refugees in Lebanon who were themselves undergoing sieges, a brutal civil war and devastation. As Abu Mustafa recounted for me:

> During the first Intifada, we weren't talking about it much [in Lebanon], but the second one, people are talking about it very much now. The first time, there were no media. But now, there are lots of media. Also then, we were under siege. [During the first Intifada], there were no satellites and no internet communication. Now, we have plenty of time, so we can actually focus on the Intifada. The communication is much better now. For example, we all saw the martyrdom of Muhammad Durra[8] in every house. (Interview with author, Burj al-Barajna camp, 6 February 2002)

Abu Mustafa points to the transmission of iconized images – in this instance of a well-known martyr – on electronic media across borders. These transmissions are crucial in propagating narratives of sacrifice and suffering to wide populations (Allen 2005: ch. 2). Broadcasting funerals, ceremonies, and commemorative events, as well as the background songs and symbolic imagery which frame news transmission provide means of convergence between practices of Palestinians across borders. The news broadcasts also reinforce a particular commemorative narrative, as for example, the multivalent ways in which the Israeli military's invasion of Jenin and the War of the Camps were felt, represented, and connected to one another by camp residents as both battles and massacres (see Chapter 8).

Television has also been profoundly important in shaping Palestinian collective memory. For example, Hizbullah's al-Manar television channel produced *al-A'idun* (*The Returnees*), a docudrama series based in the various Palestinian camps which highlighted the history of the camps, the conditions of their emergence, and their current political and social landscape. Throughout the months when the series was being filmed and broadcast, many camp residents in Beirut spoke proudly of having participated in the series, even if their only appearance was in the background of a short scene. Camp residents watched the series assiduously, glued to the television set in order to see their own living spaces validated and certified in this way, looking out for relatives and acquaintances, and in the process learning much about the history of the camp which may not have been taught to them by previous generations. Another al-Manar series, *Yatzakkirun* (*They Remember*), brought

---

[8] Muhammad al-Durra was a 12-year-old Gazan boy whose killing by Israeli sniper fire in 2001 – despite his father's futile efforts to protect him – was captured on film and caused an outcry against Israel.

together elders from different villages and asked them to tell the story of Palestine and of their exodus during the *Nakba*.

While at night, camp residents continuously watched news programs (especially at times of crisis), during the day, the news had to compete with Arabic music videos, which are immensely popular with the youth and women. In fact, these video channels, which play popular songs by Arab singers often acted as the background for many of the women engaged in housework, and even to some of the interviews I had conducted. Songs can become vehicles of transmission of particular iconic images which are crucial elements of commemorative narratives. For example, the appearance of guns in the songs of Fayruz ("The Bridge of Return," 1969) and Umm Kulthum ("I Have Now Got Me a Rifle," 1969) after armed resistance had begun in the 1960s promulgated *bunduqiyya* or armed struggle (Massad 2003: 28).[9] Similarly, images of returning flocks of birds and steadfast trees, and of a land longing for its exiled peasants reinforced particular commemorative constructs. In addition to the more generally popular Arab – rather than Palestinian – singers, beginning in the late 1960s, diasporan singers took to forming bands, often affiliated with particular PLO factions, and performed throughout the diaspora. Their songs combined folkloric tunes with European martial rhythms and lyrics sung in rural accents (Massad 2003: 31). These bands were and continue to be popular in the camps. Many of the songs memorized by Palestinian children in the camps are songs popularized by these bands. During my interviews and visits to schools and NGO after-school programs, on more than a dozen occasions, both children and adults sang for me songs written by such bands (most prominent among them, the band *al-'Ashighun*). During my fieldwork, an ode to Jerusalem sung by Iraqi Kazim al-Sahir and Tunisian Latifa, "O Jerusalem, The City of Sorrows" ("Ya Qods, ya madina al-ahzan"), was played constantly throughout the camps.[10] A respectful hush would fall on conversations when their video would appear on the television screen, and the bootleg tapes of the song would exchange hands at awesome speeds. Pop music

---

[9] The Lebanese Fayruz and Egyptian Umm Kulthum are perhaps two of the best-known female singers in the Middle East, whose music has been the soundtrack of decolonization, nationalism, and war in their respective countries and in the region as a whole.

[10] Interestingly, the popularity of certain pop singers in the camps is very much related to the political position they take *vis-à-vis* Palestinians. More than once I was told the story of Lebanese Raghib 'Allama who had allegedly claimed that he would cut his little finger off if he found out that the little finger was Palestinian. When one of 'Allama's videos appeared in the music television station's rotation, my friends would usually utter an obscenity and change the channel. Popular singing was not considered innocent or neutral in the camps.

videos containing idealized images of Palestine alongside footage of Muhammad al-Durra were other means of establishing a widely accepted frame of understanding for the political situation, and along with other music videos, it commemorated martyrs and promulgated memory images.

New electronic media are also used extensively for mnemonic purposes. When in the April 2002, the Israeli army invaded and re-occupied a number of West Bank towns, villages, and camps, the text-messaging service of mobile phones was used to coordinate a grassroots commemorative gesture in honor of the victims of the re-occupation. On the days leading to Friday 26 April 2002, almost everyone I knew received messages – from as far as Amman, Jordan – inviting them to wear black on the following Friday. The effort was more or less successful, as that Friday, many people on the streets of West Beirut and in the camps were in fact dressed in black. The Internet has also been crucial in facilitating not only the flow of information, symbols, narratives, images, and commemorative information across borders, but also encouraging friendships and even love affairs between Palestinians of the OPT and the diaspora. Whether through the infrastructure provided by the Across Borders Project – which attempts to connect the refugee camps throughout the Arab world – or through the grassroots efforts of cyber-savvy young Palestinians of the camps, many of the camps now have websites, on which Palestinian mnemonic symbols (such as images of Keys, or of the pre-1948 life, or of revered martyrs) and narratives (of the 1948 exodus, of massacres and battles, and of life in the camps) appear alongside histories of the camps and of the pre-exile home villages and towns (Khalili 2005d). Even more importantly, exchange of cyber-graphics and cyber-texts through emails has provided a medium for symbolic discourse, and propagating particular narratives about martyrdom, for example, or the rights of refugees. This new version of "print capitalism" (Anderson 1991) has the added advantage of easy travel across borders, and can be a significant medium for reproducing the Palestinian national past and identity transnationally.

Naming

Town maps registered the street as Mains Avenue, but the only coloured doctor in the city had lived and died on that street, and when he moved there in 1896 his patients took to calling the street, which none of them lived in or near, Doctor Street ... Some of the city legislators whose concerns for appropriate names and the maintenance of the city's landmarks was the principal part of their political life, saw to it that "Doctor Street" was never used in any official capacity. And

> since they knew that only Southside residents kept it up, they had
> notices posted in the stores, barbershops, and restaurants in that part of
> the city saying that the avenue ... had always been and would always
> be known as Mains Avenue and not Doctor street. It was a genuinely
> clarifying public notice because it gave Southside residents a way to
> keep their memories alive and please the city legislators as well. They
> called [the street] Not Doctor Street
>
> Toni Morrison, *Song of Solomon*

Naming places and people after "objects of memory" (Slyomovics
1998) brings representations of the past into people's quotidian lives. A
name can become a text of memory, encapsulating a lost object or place,
or celebrating a moment or event. In repeating a name, the object of
memory is invoked again and again in conversation, weaving memory
into everyday practices (Slyomovics 1998: 201–3). Laurie King-Irani
(2000) writes about how in 1982 internal refugees in Israel named two
streets of their neighborhood in Nazareth after Sabra and Shatila,
emphasizing their links to the diaspora through their common ancestry
in Saffuriyya. In the camps of Lebanon, performance groups are named
after Muhammad al-Durra or local martyrs. Throughout my fieldwork,
I met both male and female Palestinians whose name meant "something" relevant to the Palestinian predicament. Aside from names such
as *Jihad* (Holy War), *Yasar* (Left), and *Tha'ir* (Revolutionary), more
than a few women in the camps of Lebanon are named after the cities of
Jaffa, and Haifa, or after villages. A baby girl born in April 2002 was
named after the camp of Jenin, which was being invaded at that moment
by the Israeli military. Self-naming also allows such conscious acts of
commemoration. Many camp youth have chosen cyber-monikers which
remember their ancestors' hometowns (Safuriya@aaa.com), or the
camp's martyrs (MartyrShadi2000@aaa.com).

Naming, however, is not simply a private act. Institutions promulgate
particular names, and with those names, particular narratives and identities. Names implicitly tell the stories and histories of persons and events,
and as such, can be contentious. The Hebraization of place names in
Palestine (Slyomovics 1998: 60), the struggle over the "symbolic construction" of the identity of Palestinian citizens of Israel through the
commemorative naming of streets in Israel (Azaryahu and Kook 2002),
and the naming of archeological artefacts in such a way as to legitimate
political entities and institutions (Abu El-Haj 2001: 118–23), all replay
struggles over power and identity in a physical space. In Lebanon, camp
quarters, schools, nurseries, and clubs are named after the villages
from which camp residents hailed (Khalili 2004, 2005b), while in
Damascus, camp neighborhoods are named after the decisive battles of

Yarmuk (636 CE), Hittin (1187 CE), Qastal (1948 CE), and Karama (1968 CE). In spanning several centuries of history, historical battles are incorporated into a modern nationalist discourse, in effect retrospectively placing the birth-date of the nation in the ancient past, and vivifying the "memory" of those ancient battles through their present-day invocations.

Organization of time

> calendars do not measure time as clocks do; they are monuments of ...
> historical consciousness
> > Walter Benjamin, "Theses on the Philosophy of History"

Calendars and holiday cycles are vital vehicles of commemoration. Holidays provide an occasion for pedagogy, storytelling and ceremonial gatherings. They structure lived time in such a way as to incorporate significant political events into the refugees' daily lives. National calendars even co-opt natural/agricultural holidays. For example, throughout the first Intifada, the communiqués would list commemorative holidays which became the focus of demonstrations. The "day of harvesting olives" was celebrated alongside the "day of national independence" and "Balfour Declaration day," and Palestinians in the OPT were invited to show their symbolic and material solidarity by helping in the harvest (Lockman and Beinin 1989: 390–1). National holidays far outnumber religious ones in the Fatah and PA calendars for the year 2002 (and other years). The physical calendar itself can be a container of commemoration: the document itself often contains flags, images of the checkered *keffiyeh*, of the Dome of the Rock, or the map of Palestine (Kuttab 1988: 15). On a national calendar, each day contains individual narratives about the nation's past. As Zerubavel (1995: 219) has shown *vis-à-vis* Zionist holidays, cyclical and decontextualized holidays enhance overarching nationalist narratives. Iconization of particular events such as the Dayr Yasin massacre (also see Lindhom Schulz 1999: 66–7) allows for that day to stand for *all* massacre days. Local variations on holidays serve to enhance local connections to a larger Palestinian narrative while at the same time challenging the central official narrative. As outlined in Chapter 7, while a PA calendar in the OPT emphasizes the Oslo Accords and Palestinian state-building, the Fatah calendar in Lebanon does not even mention Oslo or any of the days significant in the history of the emergence of the PA. After all, while Oslo may have been a milestone for those in the OPT, refugees in Lebanon believe that it marked the divergence of interests and goals between Palestinians in the OPT and diaspora. Similarly, the Fatah calendar in Lebanon has only one entry for 17 September: remembering 1970 when the Jordanian military effectively wiped out Palestinian militancy in Jordan and massacred thousands of camp residents. The calendar is in Arabic and its audiences are Fatah members and sympathizers. By contrast, the PA calendar for 17 September includes two entries: one commemorates the assassination of Count Folke Bernadotte by Irgun (*sic*) militants in 1948,[11] the other, the Sabra and Shatila massacre in 1982. The PA calendar is in both Arabic and English and its audience is almost certainly as likely to be "foreign" as to be Palestinian or Arab. After all, to celebrate Bernadotte and commemorate his death is to appeal to a European audience, to draw parallels between "acts of terror," and to create solidarities with foreigners across borders. The narratives that the calendars tell thus differ depending on the audience of the commemorative event.

Organization of spaces

> Historical memory is a mass-produced commodity in Belfast's political culture, written into the built environment – by place names, memorials, bullet pockmarks, and home debris – into people's choice of residence and spouse, into almost every calendrical observance and march.
>
> Allen Feldman, "Political Terror and the Technologies of Memory"

Spaces provide a stage for commemoration, but they can also act as mnemonic markers, sources of commemorative narratives, and a focus of contention over meanings of history. Marshaling spaces in the service of commemoration, and building museums, monuments, and memorials all require institutional resources (Khalili 2005c). In Chapters 6 and 7, I will discuss the role of memorials, massacre and martyrdom sites, and cemeteries in commemorating violent pasts. I have also written of grassroots museums that attempt to salvage destroyed and fragmentary pasts from the oblivion that comes with dispersion and exile (Khalili 2004, 2005b). More recently, the PA has announced plans for an official state museum which will commemorate the life of Yasir Arafat, and through him, the history of the Palestinian national movement. But here, I want to focus on how various institutions utilize the refugee camps as instruments of reproducing memory. The refugee camps themselves become iconized spaces whose name and history

---

[11] Folke Bernadotte, a Swedish UN mediator, was assassinated not by the *Irgun Zvai Leumi* (Irgun), but by *Lohamei Herut Yisrael* (Lehi). However, the Fatah calendar lists Irgun as the culprits.

evokes a particular commemorative and interpretative political discourse (Peteet 2005).

The walls of the camps act as billboards for graffiti – that "major channel of communication between political groups" (Hunter 1993: 273). Murals, posters and slogans – sometimes defaced or challenged, at other times enhanced – become a barometer for gauging the moods and agendas of various political organizations. Most significantly, political organizations use camp walls as spaces for displaying photographs of martyrs and for commemoration of battles, massacres, the *Nakba*, or guerrillas in murals. Camp mosques not only serve as places of prayer and gathering, they also become the site of commemorative ceremonies. Mosque loudspeakers announce deaths, the time and place of funerals, the dates of demonstrations and ceremonies, and significant events. The camps have been the only places outside the OPT where Palestinian institutions have had some control – however episodic, nominal, or contested – over the naming and arrangement of the space. This allows the space of the camps itself to become a place of commemoration and contention: streets and alleyways have been named after fallen fighters; and those names have been overlaid by names of more recent martyrs. After its establishment, Burj al-Barajna neighborhoods were named after Palestinian villages the refugees had left behind. After the *Thawra*, the neighborhoods were re-named for the offices of the political parties located in that particular quarter. Once the Palestinian political parties left Lebanon behind, the names of many of these quarters reverted to their village origins (Roberts 1999), but directions are still given using the offices of political parties as markers. The camps' cartographies often act as a document of Palestinian political transformations, and as a means of subtly remembering the history of this transformation.

During the Lebanese civil war, the concentration of Palestinians in the camps, the safety they felt therein, and the very spatial arrangement of the camps – labyrinths difficult to navigate for those unfamiliar with them – all protected the Palestinian community and provided the necessary communal density for the perpetuation of commemorative practices and nationalist sentiment. Spatial proximity between people can facilitate commemoration by allowing people to gather and reminisce about shared events. It eases the organization of commemorative ceremonies. Frequently, the spatial density of a particular community in a locale results in the creation of specific memory-places (often cemeteries) therein which themselves provide foci for group gatherings. The dispersion of the victims of Tal al-Za'tar massacre, for example, has made difficult the widespread reproduction of the memories of that massacre.

But the camps are not simply sites of commemorative events. The very spaces tell commemorative narratives. In the early years of the *Thawra*, militant factions equated the refugee camp (*mukhayyam*) to a military training camp (*ma'askar*). Weeks after the Cairo Accords, Ghassan Kanafani – in his role as the ideologue and spokesperson for the PFLP – asked rhetorically whether the camps in Lebanon were to remain "concentration camps or [become] revolutionary bases" and responded that of course they were to become the latter, thus achieving an important step on the revolutionary path (*al-Hadaf*, 8 November 1969). The entry of armed guerrillas into the camps and the transformation of the camps into "the essence of resistance" (*al-Hadaf*, 15 November 1969: 5) or the "incubators of the *Thawra*" (*Filastin al-Thawra*, 9 October 1982: 12) were celebrated throughout the *Thawra* even if the activists who formed the core of armed resistance did not necessarily hail from the camps. Years after the evacuation of PLO leaders from Lebanon, and subsequent to the devastation of the camps, official narratives began to celebrate the camps differently. In a commemoration of the Tal al-Za'tar camp, a*l-Hadaf* wrote that the essence of the camp was its centrality in the Palestinian "collective memory and identity" (*al-Hadaf*, 22 August 1992: 42), thus affirming the importance of the refugees as an important constituency in the intra-PLO struggles in the wake of the Madrid talks. After the Oslo Accords, intra-PLO political contention over compromises with Israel and future PLO strategy intensified. At that time, in opposition to PA policies, the PFLP asserted that the camps were the only means of enabling refugees in the diaspora to obtain justice through their "peaceful civilian" activities. These included the establishment of popular clubs, committees, and cultural groups whose aim was to be the reproduction of Palestinian identity and social rejuvenation (*al-Hadaf*, January 1998: 43).[12]

Particular camps came to be iconized as *archetypal* camps. Shatila was one such camp. After the War of the Camps which had devastated Shatila, the PLO executive committee labelled Shatila "a luminous

---

[12] Regardless of how the political elite of various parties viewed the role of the camps as military bases, consciousness-raising locales, or the site of the reproduction of Palestinian culture, the refugees who resided in the camps in fact viewed the camps as safe havens where they were protected from Lebanese harassment and violent assaults. Again and again in my interviews with residents of Beirut's camps, they recalled how throughout the war they often returned to the camps from their squats and/or rented apartments in times of increased instability or uncertainty. The one exception was after the heavy bombardments of all the camps in southern Lebanon during the Israeli invasion of 1982 and after the Sabra and Shatila massacres, when the refugees in fact stayed away from the camps for fear of being specifically targeted for bombing, harassment, arrests, or another massacre.

symbol among the symbols of our long national struggle" (*Filastin al-Thawra*, 3 July 1988: 12). During the *Thawra*, the camp was known – along with the Sabra and Fakihani neighborhoods – as the headquarters of Palestinian resistance (Sayigh 1994: 3). Among the refugees themselves it was seen as the place where Palestinian dialect could be used unmolested, Palestinians could be Palestinian without fear of harassment or ridicule, as heroic locales and "fountainheads of fighters" (Abu Husayn, Burj al-Barajna, 14 February 2002).

However, Shatila's and other camps' symbolic value as icons of nationalism has not been fixedly heroic. In the last decade, the camps have been celebrated as definitive symbols of Palestinian suffering. The residents at Shatila, prompted by NGOs, have themselves strategically deployed an iconized Shatila in their self-representation to foreign audiences. "Misery tours" (as one disillusioned Palestinian activist has called them) often take foreign volunteers, visitors, and activists on a circuitous route through Shatila – and other camps – which pass by buildings collapsed like a "house of cards." "Those are the effect of Israeli bombings" – says the fifteen-year-old chosen as a tour guide by his after-school tutor. The tour includes the mosque where many victims of the War of the Camps are buried, and those alleyways in the camp which are not paved, are rubbish-strewn, or which have open sewers and exposed pipes. This same style of touring is also used by UNRWA officers who often take foreign visitors to the Burj al-Shamali camp or the Ouzo neighborhood of Ain al-Hilwa camp. What distinguishes these two locales is the open sewers, tin-and-plastic-sheeting shacks, and their devastating poverty. Though all camps have exposed pipes and dangerous wiring, undrinkable water, large populations of rodents, and narrow shoulder-wide alleyways, they are in fact maintained lovingly by their residents. The extreme poverty of those two neighborhoods is then often paraded for foreign visitors, both as a plea for financial assistance, and as the proof of the necessity of UNRWA or NGO charity.

The self-conscious use of Shatila as a representative symbol of victimhood has even prompted teenagers affiliated with a local NGO, the Shatila Children and Youth Centre, to establish a backpackers' hostel in Shatila. They explained their decision by enumerating the costs of hosting volunteers who come to work in the camps during the summer and the possibility that travelers could "get a personalized look at life in a refugee camp and learn a great deal about grassroots initiatives in the refugee community" (Sundstrom 2003: 10):

The scores of people who come here to do humanitarian work are not to be denied. And foreign travelers to the Middle East are inevitably intrigued by life in the camps. The center's hostel in Shatila will give them the opportunity to experience it firsthand.

The refugees' awareness and mobilization of foreigners' "interest in the life we live" not only generates a source of income, but also – and more importantly – opens a space of interaction with foreign youth in which NGO-affiliated refugees represent themselves. This strategic appropriation of Shatila's bloody history and devastated space is one way in which commemorative practices tell a story about the nation to local and foreign audiences.

Ceremonial gatherings

When I heard that the DFLP was going to hold a ceremony commemorating the thirty-third anniversary of its establishment on 3 March 2002, I asked various friends in the camp to secure an invitation for me. When I had the invitation in hand, I asked a friend from the camp whose family had been active in the DFLP whether she was going, and if so, whether I could accompany her. At first she wasn't certain about going; "these things are so boring," she said. Once she realized I was eager to go, she dressed in her more formal clothes and came with me. As we were walking to the ceremony, I asked her, "why do you think people go to these things?" She responded absent-mindedly, "these ceremonies, these gatherings, lift our spirits!" When I asked her how the ceremonies can be uplifting yet boring, she looked at me uncomprehendingly. Upon further prodding I learned that she found the ceremonies uplifting because they were occasions on which the existence and unity of the Palestinian people were affirmed and their story and cause was narrated, performed, and commemorated. Yet, they could also be "boring" because as she explained, "since the end of the war, we can get together so many times – but nothing happens. No one listens to us." For her, the ceremonies were affirmative experiences which reinforced community bonds and boundaries, yet she was ambivalent about their efficacy in reaching the ears of Palestinian leadership.

The ceremony itself was highly stylized and contained many ritual elements. It was held in the Palestinian Centre (a community room) on the edge of the Burj al-Barajna camp. In the meeting room, a platform was staged where various "responsible" men of different camps sat in a semi-circle behind a podium from which a handful spoke. The room was thick with cigarette smoke and festooned with flags and banners and photographs of Nayif Hawatma, the Chairman of the DFLP (not present at the ceremonies). Separate seating for men and women was not strictly enforced and men outnumbered women by one third. A group of young DFLP activists in party T-shirts stood at the back of the room around a loudspeaker and loudly applauded when applause was called for. When we walked in, the speaker – who was speaking in authoritative modern standard Arabic – was giving a speech steeped in oratory rhetoric and style. In his speech, he spoke of Palestine (and clarified that he meant the West Bank, Gaza, and East Jerusalem), but also referred to the inalienable right of the Palestinian refugees to return. His major statements were applauded by the crowd and by the young men on loudspeakers. When speaking about the right of refugees, he significantly never used the words *biladuna* (our villages/country) or *ardhuna* (our land) and instead focused on returning to "Palestine." At the end of the speeches (which all resembled one another), the last speaker invited the people to visit the martyrs in the cemetery. The visit to the martyrs entailed a tour of the memory-places in the camp, including the hospital, an important landmark from the War of the Camps. Upon arriving at the Burj al-Barajna cemetery, the chief of the camp's branch of the DFLP gave a quick speech (by then, the other leaders had already left), while no one from the procession, with the exception of two elderly women, actually visited the graves of the dead. After a few minutes, the crowd returned to the space in front of the Palestine Centre, where young men brought out the Palestinian bagpipe and drums, beat out rhythms accompanied with clapping by those gathered, and began a genuinely joyous *dabke* circle. Elderly women dressed in embroidered Palestinian clothes joined in and after ten minutes of vigorous dancing and clapping, the crowd dispersed.

I followed up this event by researching similar events during the *Thawra*. Interestingly, photographs from the ceremonies of the 1970s and 1980s showed mostly middle-aged men in attendance. But at almost all the commemorative events and ceremonies I attended, younger men and women dominated the proceedings. It seemed that when the *Thawra* had a presence in the camps, such events tended to be highly male-oriented. In the era of the dominance of the NGOs, by contrast, women and youth are more directly involved in ceremonial proceedings. In a way, one could see the transformation of gender politics in the make-up of such events. Yet, certain ritual elements have persisted: speeches, symbolic demonstrations (the embroidered dress, the keys worn and waved in the air, etc.), playing Palestinian folk music, dancing the *dabke*, and visits to memory-places.

These ritual elements have been prominent elements of many Palestinian *mihrajanat* (festivals), *ihtifalat* (ceremonies), and *ijtima'at* (gatherings) sponsored by factions through the years, and NGOs more recently. Theatrical performances by children trained in NGO after-school programs occur quite frequently at such events. Other elements are more "tailor-made," as for example the performance of "traditional" coffee grinding and coffee-making and the "traditional" making of bulghur wheat by an elderly woman during the NGO-sponsored Land Day Celebrations in 2002 at Beirut's Arab University. The performance was intended to evoke the tasks performed in the village setting by former peasants. Among the most important – and most politicized – rituals are of course the funerals of martyrs, which I will discuss at some length in Chapter 6.

In Palestinian settings, institutions use ceremonies to encourage re-enactment of stories and histories, proffer semiotically rich performances which powerfully evoke the nation (*dabke*, wearing of embroidered dresses, music), disseminate pedagogic materials, and invoke the sacrificial dead as legitimation for the cause. However, rituals do not always have to be utilized instrumentally or functionally to reinforce particular memories. The unintended consequence of top-down or coercive ceremonies can be reinforcement of oppositional memories. After the death of Hafiz al-Asad, the president of Syria, whose military had a repressive and large-scale presence in Lebanon in the last decade, a number of Palestinian organizations attempted to hold ceremonies in his honor. Their desire to pay their respects to the man came out of necessity and pragmatic calculations rather than any genuine political allegiances, especially since Palestinians had been so comprehensively targets of Syrian military violence. One of these Palestinian organizations ran an orphanage for children whose parents had been killed in the War of the Camps. Syria had openly supported the Amal militia during the War of the Camps, and was as such held responsible by many of the Palestinians for the atrocities committed at that time. Nevertheless, the said organization forced the children to come out to the symbolic funeral and perform in the pageantry of grief. I spoke to one of the children – now a teenager – in 2002. When I asked him about the event and how he had felt, he simply said to me, "with every tear that I cried, I remembered the War of the Camps."

Conclusions

Different forms of commemoration all show the very concreteness and materiality of the practice of remembering. That "memory" is sub-stantiated in places, paper, and pixels, and in stories recounted and recorded, shows that far from being a wholly ideal construct, narratives that commemorate the past are produced and reproduced through the practices of institutions and persons. History-telling, pedagogic text and practice, school holidays, the naming of persons and places after "objects of memory," songs and videos, calendars, monuments, cemeteries, memorials and memory-places, books and electronic media, and ceremonial gatherings of various sorts have all commemorated some aspect of the Palestinian past in a particular way.

Political institutions are the primary commemorators, and borrowing transnational discourses they tell particular stories about the Palestinian past. Despite dwindling institutional resources required for ceremonies, monuments and the like, commemoration continues apace and constantly reproduces nationalist pasts. Even those acts of memorialization that require very little resources, such as history-telling or the naming of persons, however, are *not* natural phenomena. Even such intimate acts require work and sometimes the mediation of external actors. These commemorative forms all contain narratives, whose contents will be discussed in Chapter 5.

5   Contents of commemoration: narratives of heroism, suffering, and *sumud*

Don't tell them only about our suffering. Tell them that we are strong; that we are still resisting.

Mahir Yamani, former PFLP guerrilla, November 2001

The Palestinian refugees' commemorative narratives have at various times and in specific historical contexts exhibited moods which can be categorized as tragic, heroic or *sumud* (steadfastness).[1] Most schematically, heroic narratives of the past are mobilizing elements of nationalist discourse, while tragic narratives – reinforced by the victimisation discourse of aid agencies and NGOs – use past suffering as the legitimating basis of claims made on an international audience and against the Palestinian leadership. Finally, *sumud* narratives appear in liminal times, and see the past as moments of passive resistance. Here, I will analyze different Palestinian narratives in turn, tracing the political milieu and

---

[1] Tragic and heroic narratives do not solely occur within the Palestinian national context. For example, Ratna Kapur (2002: 1) writes eloquently and critically about Western human rights activists' promulgation of the victimization rhetoric *vis-à-vis* Third World subjects. In the African context, Achille Mbembe (2002: 251) derides a "conception of politics as pain and sacrifice," and he also locates this narrative form in political conflict. In reference to Israel in Jewish history, some write of "heroism [as] a central and recurrent motif in the fostering of the Jewish historic patrimony" (Tzahor 1995: 69), while others decry "the lachrymose view of Jewish history" which presents "Jewish history as a long series of trials and tribulations culminating in the Holocaust" (Salo Baron quoted in Shlaim 2001: 79). Writing about a state funeral for Jewish Second World War heroine, Hannah Szenes, Baumel (2002:683) conceptualizes two commemorative frames, the Holocaust frame and the heroic national frame, and claims that the funeral ceremonies held for Szenes years after her death removed her from the former and placed her in the latter frame. Most suggestively, in her analysis of the construction of Israeli collective memories, Yael Zerubavel refers to "tragic" and "activist" Israeli national narratives which have intriguing parallels to my own conception of Palestinian commemorative narratives, though the different political contexts result in different sources and aims in the two cases. In Zerubavel's work (1994: 87–89), the activist narrative "creates a model to emulate" whereas the tragic narrative emphasizes the "national trauma that should be avoided by all means."

social relations out of which they emerge. This chapter lays the groundwork for analyzing specific commemorative themes such as martyrs, *fida'iyyin*, battles and massacres.

Contents of commemoration

Commemoration is almost always staged or "performed" for a public or an audience and demands reactions from this audience, whether that reaction is a compulsion to political action (Polletta 1998a, 1998b), an engagement in a critique of the present (Williams 1985), a demand for "moral accountability" (Werbner 1995: 102), spurring political choices (Werbner 2002: 81), or charting a map of the future (Tonkin 1992:1). That commemoration is dialogic and shaped by the constant interaction with its audience allows for ambiguity and polyvalence. Hence, particular commemorative practices can be interpreted as engaging a nationalist audience in one setting, and as appealing to international human rights in another. The same story can mean different things to a member of the Palestinian political elite and to a refugee living in a camp.

The narrative content of commemoration is used by local and transnational Palestinian elite, political institutions and organizations, Palestinian NGOs, and the ordinary refugees themselves to explain the past and frame the present and future. Tracing the originary inception of each narrative is perhaps futile, because as Gramsci writes, these narratives are "a product of the historical process to date which has deposited [therein] an infinity of traces, without leaving an inventory" (quoted in Popular Memory Group 1982: 211). Particular narratives have become predominant in a given period due to the extant social relations between Palestinians and their hosts, allies, enemies, their external international audience, and one another, but also importantly, because the mood of particular narratives is authorized by the transnational preponderance of that type of narrative beyond the borders of the camp and the host country.

Concurrent with a dominant nationalist narrative, competing accounts survive in popular practice, but the prevalence of one particular narrative does make access to these opposite views more difficult. Nor do competing narratives necessarily subvert the prevalent narrative, and can sometimes even be complementary. The analytic and heuristic significance of this categorization of narratives is in the way their specific social and historical usage elucidates the web of social relations out of which these narratives emerge and which they in turn influence.

Heroic narratives

> The international community's sympathy goes to revolutionaries rather
> than to beggars.
>
> *Filastinuna*, April 1964

The triumphant narrative of an awakening giant emerged in the Lebanese camps contemporaneously with the emergence of the militant men
and women who took on the protection of the camp and who embodied
the political mobilization of Palestinian refugees:

> We saw our young men eager to go to training camps in the Ghor, and take part
> in operations. They would come back with stories of the war; so, instead of
> telling the old stories, people began to tell these new stories, about how our
> young men were fighting. The whole nature of talk changed, as if there had been
> a deep psychological change among our people. Because the Arab states were
> defeated, we Palestinians had a chance to be active, and we felt we had to use it
> to the ultimate extent. (Quoted in Sayigh 1979: 151)

To valorize the mobilised "new men" of the revolution, the former state
of abjection out of which he had arisen had to be highlighted. Thus,
during the period of mobilization (1969–1982), a Palestinian newspaper
described the preceding period of exile (1948–1969) as "the years of
wandering and silence" (*Filastin* No. 8, 1965: 6). The writings of
Ghassan Kanafani, the pre-eminent novelist of the Palestinian *Thawra*,
bespeak of "loss, death and impotence" (Siddiq 1984), and in his *Men
in the Sun*, of Palestinians suffocating in silence prior to the national
awakening. A Fatah leader similarly describes the previous period as a
time of squalor and devastation:

> Palestinians were divided between the residents of the [refugee] camps, eaten by
> diseases of laziness, dependency and indifference and young people who
> [obtained education] and went off to seek [ways of] improving their personal
> condition. (Anonymous Fatah leader speaking in 1968; quoted in Sayigh
> 1997: 92)

For this Fatah official, Palestinian armed resistance – or Revolution
(*Thawra*) as it was called – was legitimated by the suffering that pre-
ceded it.[2] The memoirs of Palestinian writers and activists who hailed
from the refugee camps in Lebanon (e.g. Turki 1972, 1988, 1994), and
the contemporaneous literary work of prominent Palestinian writers
obscure the hope, the steadfastness (*sumud*), and the sheer resilience of

---

[2] This retrospective narrative, however, overlooks Palestinian political resistance in the
camps, engagement in regional politics, and the emergence in the 1960s of a core of
dedicated activists – mostly UNRWA teachers – mobilizing the refugees.

the refugees in the years immediately following the Nakba, and instead point to these years as the years of humiliation, stasis, and nihilism.

The heroic narrative counters its *Doppelgänger*, existential stasis, by invoking an ancient history of heroism and a glory lost to the intervening degeneration and decay.[3] Thus, the Palestinian claim to a national ancestry of revolt and heroism reaches into ancient times and traverses deep into ancient/mythico-history, to the time of the Canaanites, in order to counter the equivalent Israeli claim to the land on the basis of quasi-biblical history (Abu el Haj 2001). The stories that form the corpus of heroic nationalist mythmaking are those that allow uncanny allegorical parallels between the historical past and the current struggle.

The heroic narrative insists on interpreting all past events teleologically as the epic progress of revolutionary courage and envisions nationalist history hurtling towards an inevitable victory, the establishment of the nation-state in the statist narrative or the liberation of society in the liberationist one. For example, Fatah leader, Abu Iyad (1981: 30–33), mentions the "uprisings of 1919, 1922, 1928, 1933, and 1936–1939" as the precursor of the armed resistance of the 1960s, while *Filastinuna* (No. 16, 1971: 5) names "the revolution of April 4 1920 in al-Quds; and the revolution of 1 May 1921 in Yaffa, and the revolution of 23 August 1929 in al-Quds during which a great number were martyred" as the insurrectionary inheritance of the Palestinian guerrillas.[4] The Palestinian Declaration of Independence, in fact, reinterprets all prior rebellions in the land of Palestine as part of the perpetual national movement: "For what has been the unbroken chain of our people's rebellions but the heroic embodiment of our will for national independence?" (Palestinian National Council 1988).

The audience for this narrative is not only the members of the community, who are thus encased within the clearly bounded borders of the nationalist movement, but also an external audience which is to be convinced that a continuous history of revolt legitimates the nationalist claims of the political factions and underscores their revolutionary commitment. Commemoration thus becomes a performance of self-assertion, and streamlines a cacophonous and eventful history into a unified nationalist narrative. Once claiming an inheritance of revolt, political organizations celebrate and commemorate all wars and revolts

[3] A parallel process occurs in Zionist commemoration, where "Zionist memorial literature ... attached its martyrs to a different historical narrative – that which began in Masada, skipping nineteen hundred years of diaspora Jewish history" (Baumel 1995: 150–1).
[4] The actual dates of insurrections were 1918, 1920, 1921, 1923, 1929, 1933 and 1936–1939 (Hadawi 1989: 192).

against the enemy of the nation as moments in which the existence and resilience of the nation is affirmed. By producing continuity between these distinct historical events, an essentialist identity of "us" and "them" is created, reinforcing the boundaries of the nation, while the nationalist ideology obscures class differences, gender disparities and potential religious discords *within* the nation. The constructed continuities in turn allow comparisons to be made between leaders of the present movement and the victorious leaders of the past: thus, Arafat can be compared to Caliph Umar or Salah al-Din al-Ayyubi (Çandar 2000: 77).[5] These comparisons implicitly certify the authority of the leadership through analogy rather than a detailed evaluation of the leader's activities.

Heroic narratives take battles as their turning-points, and see steadfastness not simply in the resilience of a beleaguered population, but in their violent defiance. It is by this logic that on the anniversary of the Karama battle between Palestinian guerrillas and the Israeli military, the DFLP's *al-Hurriya* can call the battle the "beginning of the *real* steadfastness" (21 March 1969: 5; emphasis added), belittling the daily struggles of ordinary refugees in favor of the exploits of a militant organization. Heroic narratives replace grief or doubt. They impel the wife of a *fida'yi* to set aside possible anxiety for her fighter husband and dismiss social norms concerning women's roles and say, "I am prepared to join a [military] base, any base, not just my husband's. Because the PLO represents us and supports our revolution" (*al-Hurriya*, 9 June 1975: 7). In heroic narratives, the camps are no longer miserable refuges, but militant – if not military – bases. The camp, in fact, during this period becomes a potent nationalist symbol, and the refugee (imagined as fully mobilized and armed) becomes the valorized archetypal Palestinian national. The heroic narrative – in its Palestinian context – has armed resistance as its central motif, the *fida'yi* guerrilla fighter and his gun (a Russian Kalashnikov) as its primary symbol, and military bearing as the virtue it adulates.[6] Complex past events are disassembled into

---

[5] Posters attesting to the heroic stature of Arafat by comparing him to Salah al-Din or to Caliph Umar were abundant during the April 2002 demonstrations of the Palestinians and Lebanese in Beirut against Israeli aggression in the West Bank and Gaza. Caliph Umar won Jerusalem from the Byzantine Empire in the seventh century AD, and Salah al-Din al-Ayyubi, known as Saladin in European accounts, was a Kurdish Muslim warrior who won Jerusalem from the Crusaders in the twelfth century AD.

[6] Even in the narratives written by outsiders about the Palestinians, this heroic mood is apparent. In his "Affirmation of Existence through Rebellion," Jean Genet (1987: 70) – who was a sympathetic supporter of the PLO, also deploys the epic mood in describing Palestinians during this period: "I wonder if this beauty [of the Palestinian people] ... does not come from the fact that rebels have recovered a freedom they had lost ... [In 1970] I was immediately, or almost immediately, struck by the weight, by the truth of their gestures ... What I found in Jordan in 1970 was people whose every

their constitutive elements, and those events that may speak of suffering or quotidian lives are pushed to the background, while heroism in battle is foregrounded. The heroic narrative is complex enough to accommodate interim defeats and losses in the process of hurtling towards the final victory, but nonetheless, finds dynamic standards which allow reinterpretation of these defeats as victories.

The predominance of heroic narratives is closely associated with the establishment and rise to prominence of political factions that took over the administration of Palestinian affairs in the camps in Lebanon. This process began in the mid-1960s and lasted until 1982. During this time, since the diaspora community had become the institutional core of Palestinian nationalism, the *local* story of Palestinians in Lebanon converged with the *national* Palestinian narrative promulgated by the PLO. The prominence of the heroic narratives in the Palestinian political publications, the transcripts of the political festivals, the mood and content of political and community meetings, and the text of demonstration slogans attest to this convergence.

The predominance of nationalist institutions and discourses has encouraged Palestinians in Lebanon, whether in the camps or in the city, whether belonging to the elite or to the subaltern classes, to overwhelmingly consider the period between 1969 and 1982 as a time of heroism both contemporaneously and to a lesser extent in retrospective commemoration. The social and political transformations wrought by the PLO in the camps partially account for the appeal to and acceptance by the Palestinian refugees of the heroic nationalist narrative. The expansion of the political infrastructure (such as party offices) in the camps, proliferation of factional and community gatherings, festivals, and ceremonies, the development of printed materials – from party circulars to novels and poetry – among the camp refugees, as well as extra-curricular political, militaristic, artistic, and social education for younger children, all helped in not only the mobilization of the refugees, but also in the spread of the heroic nationalist narrative. In the 1960s and 1970s, the heroic discourse had had wide appeal in the camps, but also among middle-class Palestinians. Violent nationalist struggle in a sense recuperated the dignity of humiliated refugees, by portraying the peasant (Swedenburg 1990), the worker (Mandas 1974), and the refugee (Sayigh 1979) as agents of revolutionary nationalist history. In the feverish years of the *Thawra*, the heroic narrative of guerrilla warfare also appealed to middle-class Palestinians, living in Beirut and often assimilated. In fact, for

gesture had a density, a real weight. There was the weight of reality, of the real. No cigarette was lighted or smoked casually."

many who had until then adopted the Lebanese way of life, accent, and demeanor, Palestinianness became a badge of pride. The peasant *keffiyeh* became as much a sartorial emblem among middle-class Palestinians as it was among the refugees and guerrillas. Celebration of the Palestinian cause, and more specifically *bunduqiyya*, was as recurrent in Beirut's fashionable circles as they had been in the camps.

During this period, UNRWA history books were found to be deficient in depicting "popular resistance to the British occupation and to Zionism" (Sayigh 1979: 173), and as such PLO institutions produced supplementary histories for use in schools. History became a story of armed struggle.

A contemporaneous narrative of the camps claiming their control from the Lebanese captures the heroic nationalist mood:

> [The Lebanese state] brought tanks and the army tried to enter the camps. That day, we can remember with pride, we brought out the few guns that we had – they were eleven. We did well at first, but then we ran out of ammunition. A rumour ran around the camp that the ammunition was finished and we tried to calm the people by telling them that rescue would come from the Resistance. But we didn't really know whether it would come. But what was amazing was that *people returned to what they had been in 1948*, preferring to die rather than to live in humiliation. Women were hollering because it was the first time a gun had been seen defending the camp. It was the first battle that we didn't lose. The children were between the fighters, collecting the empty cartridges although the bullets were like rain. It was the first time that people held knives and sticks and stood in front of their homes, ready to fight. (Nahr al-Bared resident quoted in Sayigh 1979: 161; emphasis added)

The elision between the fighting of 1948 and the effort to liberate the camp not only creates an equivalence between the battle against the Lebanese army in 1969 and resistance against Zionist forces in 1948, but also creates a coherent narrative of heroic resistance over the span of decades. More important, it transforms the *communal* history (of the camp residents defending themselves) into an event of *national* historical significance (by reference to the 1948 war). In this narrative, 1948 is remembered as the year of heroic Palestinian defiance, rather than as the year in which the Zionist national project resulted in the expulsion and flight of these same Palestinians from their villages.[7]

The linchpin of the heroic narrative of the time is the *Thawra*, the Revolution. The discourse of revolution and armed struggle was familiar from other Third Worldist contexts. The Palestinian struggle against Israel was considered a central node of this worldwide liberationist wave. In a

---

[7] Also see Shoufani 1972; Barghuti 1973; and al-'Azm 1974.

report on guerrilla training camps for *Le Monde Diplomatique*, Gerard
Chaliand (1969: 4) wrote that he saw books by Mao, Guevara, Fanon
and Debray among Palestinians:

From Fanon they take the description of the psychology of the colonised and the
need to resort to violence; from Guevara, the texts advocating the need for
armed conflict; from Mao, the concept of the prolonged war; from Debray,
whose works are extensively translated into Arabic, the idea that the party is
useless, for "the guerrilla nucleus is the party in gestation."

The PFLP and DFLP alluded to their solidarity with the Vietnamese
peasants and with Che Guevara, to whom many of the leftist Palestinian
parties felt a deep allegiance. Palestinian guerrillas were in turn celebrated by other Arabs as the rightful heirs of "Mao, Guevara, Fanon,
and the French Maquis of World War II . . . testifying to the universality
and human vitality of the movement" and as the "prototypes of *the new
Arab man*, mainly defined in terms of freedom from all the traditional
faults that it now became fashionable for Arabs to deplore in themselves" (Kerr 1971: 135; emphasis added).

It is not surprising then that the word *Thawra* – already present in
Palestinian political language – was grafted onto the vocabulary of other
tiersmondiste and Marxist movements, especially those of Vietnam,
Algeria and Cuba (*Filastin al-Thawra*, 11 May 1975: 3). Though the
word *Thawra* primarily meant the war of national liberation, when used
by leftist political factions, it also implied the movement of armed
vanguards that was to spark a wider social revolution among "Arab
masses" inspired by and in solidarity with other liberationist movements. While the official usage of the word saw it as a euphemism for
guerrilla warfare, in 1979 Sayigh (1979: 146) showed that in everyday
usage, the word:

contains multiple layers of meaning. It can mean the present P.R.M. [Palesti-
nian Revolutionary Movement] and its cadres (as in 'So-and-so is working with
the Revolution'), but more often it is used as a synonym for armed struggle, or
the return to Palestine, or rejection of the *status quo*. Often it appears as a symbol
of the life and destiny of the Palestinian people, reaching back into the past to
cast new light on uprisings in Palestine, and pointing out a path into the future.

Sayigh (1979: 146) went on to claim timelessness for the concept of
Thawra and to state that the resonance of the word:

go[es] far beyond the situation of the moment to the core of permanent identification, built around the ideas of fidelity to the land, to [pan-]Arabism, to
struggle, and to sacrifice: a powerful amalgam that requires little organisation to
sustain it, for its foundations lie in the collective experience of 50 years of
oppression and betrayal.

But the polyvalence of the word *Thawra* and the transformation of its meaning, especially after 1993 (and the conversion of some members of the PLO leadership into a "National Authority"), attest to the efforts that were in fact needed to naturalize "Revolution" as an ordinary mode of existence. In a commemorative account of the revolt of 1936–1939, *Filastin al-Thawra* (2 July 1979: 28l; emphasis added) writes:

While editing this magazine, it is possible for us to call upon any participant in the nationalist revolution of our time, the era of sophisticated weapons and well-trained and organised revolutionary forces. *And this is now an ordinary event.* But today, we hear from one of the participants in the great Palestinian revolution of 1936, during one of whose great battles, the men possessed neither the newest arms nor sufficient provisions. Undoubtedly there are special meanings and lessons to be gleaned from the heroism of these true revolutionaries.

For the *Thawra* to be considered "an ordinary event" a great deal of activism was required. The notion of revolutionary action had to be incorporated in both quotidian and particular practices of the camp residents. During the time that I conducted my interviews, the word *Thawra* had ceased to mean "revolution" itself and no longer automatically evoked the possibility of return to Palestine. *Thawra* almost uniformly had come to mean *a period of time in the past* when Palestinians had power over their lives in the camp, armed resistance was ascendant, and during which the Lebanese civil war began. Many of my interlocutors in fact looked upon this time critically and their retrospection no longer saw this period as a time of unqualified heroism, though those who sacrificed during this time are commemorated – depending on the context – using heroic narratives.

Though the nationalist heroic narrative was dominant throughout the 1970s, there were significant ruptures in this narrative, most notably during the siege and massacres of Tal Za'tar in 1975–1976 and in the years of low-intensity conflict between 1976 and 1982, cleaved by an Israeli invasion in 1978. During this latter period, voices of complaint about hardships appeared with frequency on the pages of *al-Hadaf, al-Hurriya, Il al-Amam* and other journals belonging to different PLO factions, but even these critical voices insisted on recognizing the importance of the *Thawra*, the PLO, armed struggle, and resistance. The gun was so important that one *al-Hadaf* headline (25 December 1976) claimed that "Palestinian workers in Lebanon say our unionist work is part of armed struggle for reaching our land." Voices that critiqued this stance could not find an outlet during this period: for example, Faysal Jallul's *Critique of Palestinian Arms* – which argues that

PLO factionalism and armed resistance distorted social relations within the Burj al-Barajna camp – was refused publication for seventeen years and did not appear in print until 1994. In my study of massacres and battles in Chapter 6, I will discuss these moments of rupture in greater detail.

Narratives of *sumud*

> I'm calling for steadfastness. The important thing is to hold on. Holding on is a victory in itself.
>
> Mahmud Darwish, *Memory for Forgetfulness*

Sumud, or steadfastness, has gone far beyond a rhetorical embellishment and has become a strategy of survival and even an organizational policy (Lindholm-Schultz 1999). Raja Shehadeh (1982: vii) has written about the usage of the term in the OPT: "*Samid* means 'the steadfast', 'the persevering' ... We, who had been living under occupation for ten years, were now called on to be *samidin* and urged to adopt the stance of *sumud*: to stay put, to cling to our homes and land by all means available." Though s*umud* did not necessitate active or armed resistance, it "*was not submission*. It was keeping open all options, enduring without giving up anything, and waiting to understand" (Shehadeh 1992: 6; emphasis in the original). *Sumud* can be categorized as a kind of *infra-politics* mobilized quietly and unobtrusively (Scott 1990: 183). It is the only strategy of struggle when all other avenues are closed, when organizational infrastructures are destroyed, and when complete anni-hilation – not only of political institutions, but of every person – is a real possibility. It is this fear of obliteration and the possibility of resistance to it, which Peteet (2000: 196) considers the core of *sumud* in Lebanon:

Steadfastness takes on connotations of survival for Palestinians, who see them-selves as victims of a neocolonial movement in which their displacement defined the possibility of the project. *Sumud* registers a refusal to acquiesce ... *Sumud*, as an act of resistance, is only meaningful in the context of an exceedingly powerful, well-equipped Other in possession of and willing to unleash the means of mass destruction.

After the Israeli invasion of southern Lebanon, the summer-long siege of Beirut, and the evacuation of PLO fighters from Lebanon in August 1982, a period of massive transition began for Palestinians in Lebanon. Foreign experts had considered the evacuation and scattering of the *fida'iyyin* the death-knell of the PLO and the end of Arafat's political career. Palestinians in Lebanon meanwhile had undergone a second (and in some instances third) dispersion: the camps in the south – among them the most populous one, Ain al-Hilwa – had been entirely destroyed by Israeli bombardment. Beirut itself was devastated, and many camp families had scattered throughout the city and squatted in half-destroyed buildings. In his influential "Permission to Narrate," written during this period, Edward Said (1984: 31) regretted the disintegration of the Palestinian nationalist narrative: "Having made a strong impression regionally and internationally during the years 1970 to 1982, the Palestinian narrative ... is now barely in evidence." While between 1969 and 1982, the history and story of the Palestinians in Lebanon had overwhelmingly converged with that of the deterritorialized Palestinian nation, with the exile of the PLO leadership in Tunisia and subsequent internecine violence in the camps of northern Lebanon, the Palestinian community in Lebanon found itself violently disassociated from the national community and isolated by the continuing civil war. Ellen Siegel (1983: 69) recalls that in the immediate aftermath of the Sabra and Shatila massacres:

[s]lowly, the Red Crescent workers were returning, and the portrait of Yasser Arafat was still hanging in the [Gaza] Hospital lobby. But the PLO posters and magazines, calling each other "comrade" or "sister," that's just disappeared. What strikes anybody who knows Beirut is how can a revolution suddenly disappear? The PLO as an organizational structure is visibly gone. The only thing that remains is the Red Crescent, and that only barely remains. It was not wise to talk about SAMED or the General Union. You could tell that people were just hanging on and nobody wants to talk about politics. People's spirits are low: somebody in the family is in Yemen, one in Sudan, one in Damascus. They are not in the mood to raise their fists. They are deeply grateful and appreciative of the people who are there in solidarity, they love their struggle and they still love their homeland, but at the moment it's a matter of day-to-day survival.

Throughout 1982–1993, the devastation of Palestinian camps and community life continued not only at the hands of the Lebanese army and the Maronite-led Lebanese Forces (LF), but also through the destructive War of the Camps, waged by Amal and its sponsor, Syria. The centrifugal forces of fragmentation at both national and communal level was exacerbated by organized violence against Palestinians, which paradoxically pushed them back into the camps in search of communal protection, forced them to rely on one another for survival and tested their organizational capacity in the camps to its limits.

The contemporaneous rise of *sumud* in the OPT as a policy of resistance against the occupying Israeli military may also account for the prevalence of this concept across borders (Lindholm-Schultz 1999). As *sumud* entered Palestinian politics in Lebanon, it colored commemorative practices and narratives. Before this period, of course, references to *sumud* had been common. After the fall of Tal al-Za'tar in

1975, to support the orphans of the battle, the PLO even established a welfare organization, *Bayt Atfal Sumud* (The House of Children of *Sumud*) under the wing of its economic "ministry," which was itself called *Samid* (or steadfast), but only after the evacuation of 1982 did *sumud* became the dominant discourse. Writing about Palestinian political strategies in the Occupied Territories, Lindholm Schultz (1999: 55) shows that *sumud* was a concrete policy materialized and embodied in specific educational and welfare programs and even bank accounts and funds. In Lebanon, however, *sumud* was not concretized in policies and bank accounts as in the OPT, but rather became an everyday act. To remain in the camps, to prevent dispersion, to conduct the daily affairs of life – provisioning of food, protecting the peripheries of the camp, even speaking in a Palestinian accent which may mark the speaker out for harassment at checkpoints – all became acts of political resistance against the Lebanese army and militias.

Sumud narratives differ from tragic narratives in their inclusion of an explicit hopefulness. A narrative of *sumud* recognizes and valorizes the teller's (and by extension the nation's) agency, ability, and capacity in dire circumstances, but it differs from the heroic narrative in that it does not aspire to super-human audacity, and consciously values daily survival rather than glorious battles. The archetypal *sumud* narrative commemorates women's quiet work of holding the family together and providing sustenance and protection for the family (Peteet 1991: 153), or remembers the collective defence of the camp:

When we came out of the shelters, they [various Lebanese militias] were there to arrest our men; so the children and the women returned to the camp. We had *nothing*. Not even milk for the children. We were sleeping on tenterhooks. Some of us were helped by our neighbours and relatives. We slowly repaired the buildings and in the absence of all of our men too! The burden was all on the wives and children. The doors of UNRWA were shut in Tyre and so we couldn't even get help from them. (Hajja Amna in *Filastin al-Thawra*, 25 May 1985: 32)

The camps during this time were (and were commemorated as) destroyed ruins under siege and attack, yet going through cycles of reconstruction and destruction:

We stayed here in the [Al Bass] camp during the Israeli invasion as it was not possible to leave Tyre. We were here in this camp which we built house by house, and all of it was destroyed during the summer of 1982. So we stayed behind to find solutions, especially since many of our friends and relatives had lost their houses, and lots of them were missing family members, or their young men were imprisoned. So we just helped them to hang on. (Abu Said Yasin in *Filastin al-Thawra*, 25 May 1985: 31)

The ruins housed resilient families, and this image of survival amidst the chaos of war concretizes the notion of *sumud*:

You see they destroy us and we rebuild. They chase us away and we come back. That's how it's been since 1948. I don't know if I'll be allowed to stay here. It doesn't matter. If they move us to the Beqa', to the South, to heaven, I'll take my wheelbarrow and my tools and I'll rebuild a decent home for my family. (AFP interview with a Palestinian in August 1982, quoted in Sayigh 1994: 196)

Sumud narratives are perhaps the least lachrymose and the least confrontational framing of a coherent past. During 1985–1987, in the numerous interviews conducted by Rosemary Sayigh in which people told the (recent) history of the siege of Shatila and its defense by its inhabitants, the narrative again and again is of survival. Neither resigned, nor heroic (with the exception of one or two accounts by the leadership of various political factions), these accounts of surviving blockades, sniper attacks, and internal divisions are reported matter-of-factly and with a muted wonder at the refugees' endurance (Sayigh 1994: 231–319). Sayigh's interlocutors recount everyday practices that could have been fatal and in many instances were: "We began cooking for the *shabab* ... It encouraged the fighters a lot when they saw us bringing them food under bombardment" (1994: 238). "After this, attack followed attack, continual shelling, night and day. Some of the sisters here cut up blankets and bed-covers and sewed them to make sandbags. We got the sand for them by digging under the floors of houses" (1994: 243). "At the beginning I was very frightened but it was a hidden fear ... I really wanted to take some steps forward. When I was afraid of something but managed to do it, this increased my confidence" (1994: 246). "Morale sank in the last ten days. Food stocks were getting low and more important, ammunition was short again. In those ten days everyone expected to die, we were waiting for death from moment to moment. But no one thought of surrender" (1994: 254). "Cigarettes gave out after the first two weeks, there was a 'cigarette crisis.' Whoever had one passed it round to four or five other people. Many people smoked tea, others smoked dried grasses, or filters, or cigarette ends they had picked up off the ground. Smokeable, unsmokeable, they smoked it" (1994: 255).

Palestinians in the OPT were aware of the predicaments of the Palestinians in Lebanon. During the first Intifada, the communiqués of the Unified National Leadership of the Uprising recognized the uncertainty of life under siege and the destruction of the Palestinian camps in Lebanon. Communiqué No. 22, dated 21 July 1988 states:

We call on Syria to immediately stop the scheme of liquidation and spare the Sidon area from what happened in the valiant *Burj al Barjina* [*sic*] and *Shatila* camps. We call on all the revolution factions and the friendly Lebanese forces to stand up like one man to defend our people's rights in the *camps of steadfastness* in Lebanon. (Quoted in Lockman and Beinin 1989: 369; emphasis added)[8]

Steadfastness as a daily strategy of survival and as a mode of commemorating past events carried Palestinian refugees through the Lebanese civil war (which ended in 1990) to the negotiations of Oslo. With the end of the civil war, the Palestinian community was marked as a convenient scapegoat for war-blame in Lebanon. The lack of institutional power, the considerable deterioration in Palestinian organizational infrastructure, and a serious decline of the refugees' material resources exacerbated this marginalization. The seismic events of the 1990s led to yet another type of nationalist commemorative narrative.

Tragic narratives

It is necessary to reverse the common opinion and acknowledge that it is not the harshness of a situation or the sufferings it imposes that lead people to conceive of another state of affairs in which things would be better for everybody. It is on the day that we are able to conceive of another state of affairs, that a new light is cast on our trouble and our suffering and we decide that they are unbearable.

Jean-Paul Sartre, *Being and Nothingness*

The narrative of heroism has long been replaced by one in which the refugees' suffering takes center stage. A young woman told me, "we know we are Palestinians because we suffer so much" (Fatin I., Burj al-Barajna, 22 January 2002). Fatin sees tragedy as not only the central theme of the national past, but as an inseparable part of Palestinian identity. Tragic narratives obscure small victories or moments of individual and collective resistance and eclipse the survival – much less achievements – of the community *despite* their suffering. The refugees' commemoration takes on a tragic cast when considering the post-Oslo era.

Since the 1980s, but especially after the Oslo Accords (1993), Palestinian refugees and the NGOs that represent them perform tragic narratives of the Palestinian past for international audiences whose sympathy and support are requested. In almost all my interviews, Palestinian camp residents voiced their despair with their life of

---

[8] Many of my interviewees in the camps, however, did not remember the first Intifada in the OPT. To my naïve incredulousness they responded that they had been without radio or televisions, in half-destroyed houses and under siege for nearly the whole of the first year of the Intifada. They were barely surviving, they said, how could they be expected to pay attention to what was going on elsewhere?

humiliation and anguish. Their narratives of pain and suffering contain rhythmic repetition of a litany of grievances, some explicitly political, others having to do with physical pain and deterioration of their health, as if the literal embodiment of pain was a symbolic manifestation of the appalling conditions in which they have had to live. Time and again, regardless of generation or gender, I found narratives articulating the despair and suffering of the community as a whole woven in with detailed anecdotes of bodily pain. In a different context, Bourdieu writes of how "the forms supplied by politics, law, psychology and literature" are considered "legitimate forms of expressions of suffering" (Bourdieu 1999: 615). These refugees authorize their tragic narratives by borrowing the legitimacy of that most legitimate of all discourses of suffering: the medical discourse of pain. Interestingly, many refugees claimed that speaking about the past, commemorating it, made them feel better:

And even though normally, with my health, I get a bit dizzy or uncomfortable, with this [talking about her memories], I felt my chest expand – do you understand, sweetheart – and my spirit and life opened. ... And even though now I've been talking to you, and for a month I've been sick with a bit of nausea and dizziness in my head, but today I'm not, praise be to God. (Fatima Abd al-Salam Hanafi, 1997, Tyre, ARCPA 1998: 31)

For the refugees, speaking about bodily pain was an entry point into a discussion of their claims to justice. For example, the elderly though animated Umm Faruq began her history-telling with an explanation of the pain in her knee. After she had spoken with me for an hour about her memories of the *Nakba* and subsequent life in the camps, I asked her what her best memories were. She threw her head back and said that she had none: "Our life is difficult since Israel started fighting us. My whole life is hard. First, we lost Palestine, and in addition, we lost our things and were dispersed." I asked her whether she spoke about her memories to her children and grandchildren, and she gave me the standard response: "always." When I asked why, she responded:

Because we have been so tormented. We have suffered. I want my sons and my grandsons to know what happened, what the world and the Arabs have done to us; how they betrayed us. They all opened their borders to us, and the Arab Rescue Army betrayed us. They said that they were going to defend us but they betrayed us. They gave us damaged weapons, and we weren't able to fight the Israelis who had heavy weapons. Arab leaders made the Arab Rescue Army leave Palestine, and the Jews took over Palestine. All the borders were opened to make us leave. They are all betrayers; this was a plot against the Palestinians.

When I asked her if there was any way that she could improve her situation, she said,

Like what? We can't do anything. We can't change anything. Palestinians even can't record their names for an apartment ... There isn't anything for us to do. You can't have a job even if you are a doctor. We have no protectors ... Syria is much better. In Syria, the government allows everything.[9]

I persisted, by asking her whether things would be better if there were to be another *Thawra*. She threw her head back:

Probably not. We don't have any security in the camp. I have three sons, but they are unemployed, and they can barely give me a little money to live. I have a son in Denmark, and without him I couldn't survive. And you know Sa'id worked outside [in Saudi] for 5 years. Palestinians can't do anything. There is nothing they can do, and the Lebanese won't allow them to have another revolution. Israel and America are strong. They may even kick out the Palestinians in the Palestinian lands, and unless we have another strong government on the field to force Israel, we won't be able to go back. God knows. It is said in the Qur'an that this shall happen. We hit them with stones and they call us terrorists, and the Jews hit us with tanks and aeroplanes and missiles and guns and everybody watches and says nothing. (Umm Faruq, Burj al-Barajna, 6 February 2002)

Though Umm Faruq spoke about the beauty of Palestine, and the "sweetness" of her memories there, it was about the "black" memories of torment which she spoke to her children. For Umm Faruq the pain in her knee and the suffering of her body were inseparable from the larger communal suffering ("You can't have a job even if you are a doctor"), and the national one ("They may even kick out the Palestinians in the Palestinian lands"). In her narrative, the bleakness of the situation could not be mitigated by Palestinian agency ("We can't do anything; we can't change anything") and she explicitly wished for international intervention. The extensive interviews Rosemary Sayigh (2001: 104) has conducted in the camps during the 1990s confirm this view: "The camps ... [have become] a shadowy terrain of victimisation, shorn of the revolutionary message that attracted so many Lebanese in the 1970s."

For others, there was a keen awareness that the tragic narrative was political and inseparable from the power relations within Lebanon and across national boundaries. For example, Abu Husayn saw suffering as the basis of action. When I asked him, "Do you want your children to know the story of your life [rather than the history of Palestine]?" his response

---

[9] In almost all the interviews, Palestinians claimed that life is Syria was much easier for Palestinians, as refugees can obtain work permits, housing, educational and health services, and other material amenities much more easily than the Palestinians in Lebanon. However, in a few instances, and in particular when my interlocutors had come to trust me, and once they were certain they were not being overheard by the Syrian *Mukhabirat*, they mentioned that in Syria and Jordan, "you can get jobs, but you can't speak."

was unequivocal, "Absolutely. I suffered a lot and they should know and they have to do something about it" (Burj al-Barajna, 14 February 2002). For Abu Said, a gentle 43-year-old father of three young children and the loving husband of an after-school teacher at an NGO, the Palestinian despair in Lebanon was inflicted by outside powers who wanted to keep Palestinians busy to ensure their submission and obedience:

Here you can't do anything. Any official workplace, any centre, as soon as they know you are Palestinian, they make your life difficult. You can't make financial transactions, you can't work, you can't do anything. You can't even register your car, you can't even carry a proper identity. They constantly create obstacles. People here stop thinking that they can go and do anything with the Lebanese, because they know how many obstacles there will be. That is why I feel depressed about life in this country. Part of it is the foreign powers, especially America who exercises its power over all Arabs. If America tells them don't let the Palestinians come in, they obey. If the Palestinians are kept suffering, they won't think of their land. Anyone who wants to work here, to register their children, get them healthcare, they just can't do it. That is how our mind is kept distracted from Palestine, so that we can't even dream about Palestine, plan about it. The Arab leaders don't help either. (Abu Said, Burj-al Barajna, 10 February 2002)

Since we had been talking about "return," being "let in" to a country in fact meant return to Palestine. Abu Said, without naming him, saw Arafat as a puppet of the United States, and yet another Arab *leader* who had betrayed the cause of the Palestinians.[10] The references to the leaders who betrayed the Palestinian people occurred consistently throughout the interviews. Much the same way as the Palestinian history could be seen as a *continuity* of suffering, or resistance, or *sumud*, the role of the Arab leadership was also seen as continuous betrayal. Abu Said differed from Umm Faruq in that he did not see Palestinians in Lebanon as utterly helpless, only distracted by the quotidian struggle from a revolutionary one. Nor did he conflate his individual stories and memories with that of the community, or nation, though he gave priority to the national narrative. In response to my question about his best memories, Abu Said claimed:

Nothing. The best memories of mine are personal memories, memories of love. That's it. After that, memories of my having kids. As for my worst memories,

---

[10] In a great number of interviews, but only after having known me for a while, my interlocutors openly criticized Arafat. That was until his compound in Ramallah was placed under siege in Spring 2002. From that point forward, only my closest friend in the camp, an independent and rebellious thinker in more ways than one, continued to criticize Arafat openly to me, an "outsider." The new PA president, Abu Mazin, was not afforded this status and was openly and contemptuously criticized.

they are many. For example, the fact that I didn't have a childhood. My whole childhood was wars. . . . And now, we can't get any financial help. We want to think about our children and their education and healthcare, but our money is insufficient, and we need insurance etc. The economic situation is very difficult.

When I asked him whether he spoke to his friends or children about this, he responded that his children were still too young and his friends had all emigrated (Abu Said, Burj al-Barajna, 10 February 2002).

In talking to me, the conduit to the outside world, Abu Said privileged national memories. While initially he claimed that he had no good memories, he was immediately considering *national* memories as those appropriate enough to mention, though after some reflection, he saw his marriage and his children as bright spots in his life. The conscious separation of his affirmative family life from public or national memories (while the painful childhood *is* subsumed within the national narrative) exposes the fragmentation of the nationalist narrative. When during the *Thawra* or *sumud*, the story of a life was told – whether the story referred to the space of the family, neighborhood, camp, the city, or host state – it was colored by the nationalist narratives of heroism or of steadfastness, respectively. In the post-Oslo period, however, despite the ever-present traces of factional politics in the architecture of the houses, the posters on the camp walls, and the daily lives of the refugees, in moments of conscious reflection the family was abstracted from the national narrative. This separation of the person and family from the nation is a familiar trope within the liberal discourse of human rights and humanitarianism. After all, to guarantee the equal application of human rights, persons have to be abstracted from their communities and have to become individuals.

Abu Said also consciously defied a nationalist ritual of commemoration: he denied that he spoke to his children spontaneously about his memories. One of the persistent tropes of commemoration – according to camp Palestinians, activists, social scientists, and political elite – has been the transmission of Palestinian memories of its existence in pre-1948 Palestine, and as a community in Lebanon, to the next generation by a deliberate process of history-telling. A resident of the Burj al-Shamali camp declares that "every Palestinian generation memorizes its sufferings by heart and hands it down to the next generation" (Muhammad Mustafa 'Abdallah quoted in Suleiman 1997a: 76). Another resident of Burj al-Shamali, Fayiz Hasan Yunis, who lost his wife and eight children (the eldest of whom was thirteen years old) in the shelter bombing in 1982, says that he takes his eldest son with him to the site of the massacre "so that we don't forget from generation to generation" (Suleiman 1997a: 84). This intergenerational transmission of histories and memories is considered by both the practitioners and social scientists as the glue that binds the Palestinian essence, whether that is their "collective memory," "identity" or "the nation." But like Abu Said, Na'ma Mustafa Abdallah who also lost two children and his wife in the aforementioned bombing of the Burj al-Shamali shelter, locked the photographs of his dead children away and doesn't talk about the massacre with his children. "I still get a headache when I remember the catastrophes. I can't watch images of massacres on television and I wasn't capable of watching the images from the recent Qana massacres. It strangled all expression out of me. That is why my inner thoughts remain a locked trunk and I don't say a word" (Suleiman 1997a: 78–79). For Abu Said and Na'ma Mustafa Abdallah to disavow this transmission ("my children are still too young, and my friends have all emigrated"; "my inner thoughts remain a locked trunk and I don't say a word") is to challenge nationalist obligations.

However consequential "national" fragmentation, political exclusion from the broader Palestinian polity, and material hardship in a hostile and inhospitable post-war environment may be in shaping the tragic narratives of this period, another important factor is crucial in understanding these tragic narratives: the emergence of human rights and humanitarian NGOs. In Lebanon, to provide necessary and urgent social and economic relief for the Palestinian refugees in the camps, local NGOs have had to complement the work of UNRWA, and take the place of the factions. In order to ensure the continuity of their work, NGO managers have to write proposals, host visiting delegations, give these delegations tours of the camps and NGO facilities, hire foreign volunteers or monitors, and provide them with reports of their progress. This process requires them to "tell the story" of their aid constituency for their foreign audiences. These stories have to be affecting, effective, and mobilizing. Hence, suffering takes the center-stage in NGO narratives. In turn, NGOs translate the language of their funding appeals into their day-to-day operations and in their interactions with the refugees whom they serve. As part of their work, they conduct "misery tours" of the camps for foreign donors and sympathizers, where the refugees are "gazed upon" and the squalid conditions of the camps are emphasized.[11] The refugees are expected to confirm NGO narratives of misery in their interaction with these touring foreigners. The NGOs' language of victimization spills into their quotidian practices and interaction with

---

[11] Many younger Palestinians in the camps strongly dislike these "poverty" or "misery tours" and consider themselves to be watched by foreigners "like zoo animals on display" (personal conversations with Shatila youth, November 2001).

their camp constituency through ceremonies and pedagogic functions, thus encouraging and reinforcing the narrative of pain and suffering to the exclusion of any others. Their primary audience is not the PA, but rather the international community represented by foreign visitors and their performances of Palestinians pain and suffering extends to the commemorative practices they encourage in their ceremonies, after-school programmes, and nurseries.

The NGO narrative often entails painting a dire picture of Palestinians as a helpless community of victims, whose lives are entirely defined by trauma, and who are devoid of human agency. One NGO activist says in an interview, "our group survives on international aid. We are refugees, and it is virtually impossible to sustain any projects on our own because in Lebanon we cannot work, we have no government of our own, and we have few guaranteed rights" (Short 2003). A critic of the NGO practices, who herself has been a volunteer teacher in camp schools, claims that:

The traumatic recounting of Palestinian history is pretty bad, but everyone does it: NGOs, the *Tanzimat* (political organisations) ... All the students learn is the *Nakba* and the Balfour Agreement, and 1982 and the Black September ... This becomes a burden on the kids. In a way, they think they are the only refugees in the world. They think their exile is the most traumatic one. They don't accept that they are not alone in the world. NGOs use the children as props for international fund-raising. The children have a victimised mentality. It is a passivity that is reinforced by the NGOs, because should they be engaged, the NGOs would be out of business ... (Beirut, 15 November 2001)

In my own experience, one particularly active NGO manager would introduce all the refugee women I met through her by telling me their stories of dire suffering and would portray them as helpless, passive, hyper-feminized creatures subject to the whims of their husbands, employers, and fate. As I got to know these women, I found them all to be anything but passive and helpless. They had all found mechanisms for successfully responding to and managing their husbands' demands, and had created niches for themselves in the camp. Many of them earned extra income through clever informal means and retained this income for themselves, thus earning a measure of independence from their families. I also found that women who were not directly supported by these NGOs tended to view my interviews less as a platform for political declamations than their NGO-supported peers. For example, Umm Husayn did not automatically interpret my question about her memories as an inquiry into her *political* memories – like most other interlocutors did. Umm Husayn had survived the Tal al-Za'tar massacre but had lost her husband, two children and several male relatives in that massacre, and now supported herself through small contributions from a son in Europe, but mostly through backbreaking work at the age of sixty as a house-cleaner in affluent Beirut neighborhoods. When at the end of our interview I asked her how she could have survived all she had, she simply responded, "If we cried for everything, we would die. If we started crying, what could we do? How would we stop?" (Burj al-Barajna, 29 January 2002).

Throughout various conversations, the NGO activists with whom I spoke had insisted that providing "charity" was their most important mandate. One complained about the fashionable discourse of sustainability espoused by international funders, and asked, "How can we give vocational training to the people in the camps when they can't find jobs? What we need is charity!" When I asked them whether there could be any efficacy in grassroots *political* organization around demands for civil rights, all voiced concerns about their hosts' reactions: "What if they think we are making trouble?" or even: "What if they think we want civil rights so we could stay here rather than return to our homelands?" Lebanese opposition to Palestinian settlement is so strong[12] that both NGO activists and ordinary Palestinians in the camps are wary of visibility in Lebanon's political arenas[13] and wary of resettlement in a country where they have known several large-scale massacres, sieges, and betrayals by former allies.

The work of NGOs in reproducing a history of suffering is most visible in their commemorations of 1948, where the stories celebrated efface histories of resistance and focus on dispossession, abjection and helplessness. Similarly, their stories of Palestinian refugees' lives in Lebanon erase the history of nationalist mobilization and armed struggle in Lebanon in favor of those transformative events – mostly massacres – which are recognizable markers of Palestinian suffering far beyond the Middle East.

[12] In 1999, 72 percent of the Lebanese rejected Palestinian settlement in Lebanon, down from 88 percent in 1994. In 1994, 40 percent of all respondents threatened military action if settlement was undertaken (see Sayigh 2001: 103). A slogan voiced by the Guardians of Cedars (a violent Maronite militia) in 2000 was "There will not remain one Palestinian on Lebanese soil" (Sayigh 2001: 94).

[13] During spring 2002, several large demonstrations against Israeli military aggression in the OPT took place. Palestinian and left-wing Lebanese youth held small demonstrations near the American embassy, which was made inaccessible by barricades set up within a one-kilometre radius from the remote embassy building. As the youth threw stones at the Lebanese security forces, the police shot back with tear-gas and water-cannons. Many of the camp women I interviewed looked at the young men's stone-throwing with disapproval. One said, "The Lebanese are our hosts. What will they think of us if we are violent?"

Conclusions

In the nearly six decades that have passed since Palestinians sought refuge in Lebanon, Palestinian commemoration has transformed in fascinating ways. When nationalist militancy shaped the contours of Palestinian life in Lebanon, heroic narratives predominated in practices of commemoration. These narratives legitimate present-day activism by locating it in a family of other movements, whether they are the Vietnamese resistance against the USA, or past Palestinian revolutions. These other heroic moments are either similar or are made similar through narrative elisions and attentions. Furthermore, heroic narratives help create a community centered on acts of bravery and self-sacrifice by creating essentialized adversarial characters (the heroic nation and its villainous enemies), thus reinforcing the boundaries of the "imagined community" of the nation. Palestinian heroic narratives during 1969–1982 in Lebanon assimilated armed resistance, the glory of the gun, and the *fida'yi* guerrilla fighter as their symbols and motifs, and thus forced the definition of heroism in militant terms.

Heroic narratives often deliberately counter tragic narratives which have been prominent in the Palestinian camps during periods of political fragmentation and perceived exclusion from the national imaginary. Since the Oslo Accords (1993), Palestinians in Lebanon have felt themselves excluded from the national polity, which is now being constituted mainly as Palestinians residing in the OPT. In this context, suffering legitimates claims of belonging to the nation. Tragic narratives, furthermore, appeal to international audiences, predominant among whom are transnational activists, NGOs, and the international community of the United Nations. Tragic narratives construe all past events as an accumulation of unmitigated disaster, and deny the agency of the refugees themselves, thus demanding from other political actors – the supra-national agencies, the PA, or the regional states – a solution for their plight.

Finally, narratives of *sumud* or steadfastness are those which commemorate and valorize quotidian acts of resistance necessary for survival during the harshest times. Most predominant in the transitional periods when the fate of the Palestinians as a community was uncertain (but whose "national" membership was unquestioned), these narratives personify the "infrapolitics" of dispossessed communities.

Each of these narratives that inhabit ceremonies, monuments, and history-telling has been dominant during a particular period and as a consequence of particular institutional conjunctures. Militant political factions during 1969–1982, and NGOs since 1993 have been instrumental in perpetuating the narratives of heroism and of suffering, respectively. In the chapters that follow, I will delve in greater detail into the institutions, audiences, and contexts that generate different commemorative practices and the narratives of heroism, tragedy or *sumud* enshrined therein.

6   Guerrillas and martyrs: the evolution of national "heroes"

> why talk of beauty what could be more beaut-
> iful than these heroic happy dead
> who rushed like lions to the roaring slaughter
> > e.e. cummings, "next to of course god america i love you"

During May 2002, a "Memorial Exhibition" titled *100 Shaheeds, 100 Lives* was held at the UNESCO Palace in Beirut. The exhibition was planned to coincide with the fifty-fourth anniversary of the *Nakba* on 15 May. Despite severe restrictions on leaving the OPT and entering Lebanon, exhibition organizers had brought the artefacts – which consisted of objects belonging to and photographs of the first 100 martyrs of the second Intifada – from Ramallah to Beirut. The Ramallah organizer of the exhibition was the Khalil Sakakini Cultural Centre; its Beiruti counterparts included the Arab Resource Centre for Popular Arts. The 100 martyrs were the first 100 casualties of the al-Aqsa Intifada killed by Israeli gunfire during protests, stone-throwing, in suspicious circumstances, or as bystanders.

The exhibition of quotidian objects belonging to the deceased was accompanied by a sophisticated modern arts exhibition, a concert, and a film festival. The attendees – particularly on the opening night when a Palestinian singer from Ramallah was set to appear – represented a wide social spectrum: Lebanese leftists of all sectarian backgrounds, Lebanese Islamists, middle- and upper-class assimilated Palestinians, Lebanese and Palestinian intellectuals and artists, international activists, and last but certainly not least in numbers, Palestinians from the camps in Beirut and further afield. Before the opening night concert was to begin, and while the art exhibition room was fairly empty, the salon in which the items belonging to the 100 martyrs were on display was so crowded that moving through the crowds was nearly impossible. The spectators were almost all camp Palestinians, who – as they moved from one discreetly-lit display case showing the martyrs' belongings to another – commented knowingly and with great emotion on the accompanying short biographies of each deceased Palestinian, and confidently pointed to the familiarity of the objects whose very ordinariness evoked empathy, sorrow, and on occasion sobs of recognition.

Perhaps the only thing that was unfamiliar to the sympathetic foreign viewers of the exhibition was the publicly and *institutionally* acknowledged juxtaposition of "martyrdom" with the "banality and fragility" (Laidi 2001, p. 204) of the non-heroic objects such as work trousers, a trowel, stone-throwing slings, family photos, favorite items of clothing, a much used and chipped coffee cup, worn boxing gloves, empty birdcages, or school copybooks covered in daydream doodles. The exhibition broadly targeted both Palestinians and foreign audiences, and was funded by a combination of local and international NGOs and groups. It implicitly stated that martyrdom was *sought* by none of the 100 martyrs (none were suicide bombers), and that they were killed in an asymmetry of violence perpetrated by a powerful state upon unarmed bodies.

Martyrdom, however, is more frequently portrayed as intentionally sought by believers in faith or nation. Affinities between self-sacrifice and a political cause have always been present within the nationalist, liberationist, or Islamist movements in general, and in the Palestinian nationalist movement specifically. Sakakini's representation of martyrdom as the sorrowful lot of unwilling martyrs shows that there are multiple ways in which martyrdom is commemorated in public or institutional narratives. During the ascendance of Palestinian nationalism as a revolutionary project (rather than a statist one), martyrdom was subordinated to the heroic figure of the *fida'yi* (the guerrilla fighter, and literally, the redeemer or the person who chooses sacrifice). Since 1982 and the rupture in the nationalist politics of Palestinian refugees in Lebanon, the figure of the martyr has also fragmented: while factional commemorative practices see martyrdom as an embodiment of heroism, NGOs which also include foreigners in their audiences tend to commemorate the unintentional martyr as the archetypal Palestinian victim.

By examining the historical processes by which the heroic archetype is transferred from the body of the *fida'yi* onto the body of the martyr, and by analyzing the multiple narratives of martyrdom, this chapter aims to show the performative aspect of commemoration, its institutional bases, and the transformation of heroic and tragic narratives over time. To do so, I examine various forms of commemoration of martyrs such as funerals, commemorative murals, naming of places and people after martyrs, commemoration of martyrs by their mothers, and iconization of archetypal martyrs. I then analyze the multivalence of martyrdom which can be read from different and sometimes overlapping commemorative practices. I end the chapter by examining the shift in the embodiment of the celebrated national hero from the figure of *fida'yi* to that of the martyr. The aim of this chapter is not only to show the dynamism and polyvalence of commemorative practices, but also to show the effect of local performances on forms that are celebrated worldwide.

Commemorating martyrs for international audiences

I opened this chapter with the description of an event specially designed to commemorate martyrs. The sophisticated and polyvalent exhibition held to commemorate the first 100 martyrs of the Intifada differed from most events celebrating martyrs in several aspects, namely the transnational and cross-class nature of the event and the absence of heroic narratives therein.

That the exhibition was brought to Lebanon from the OPT for the consumption of Palestinians in Lebanon explicitly emphasized the transnationality of the Palestinian public. Periodic and commonplace gatherings and assemblies held in the camps for the purpose of commemoration often implicitly suggest or celebrate the fraternal relation of Palestinians everywhere, but the Sakakini exhibition went beyond rhetoric and logistically connected the diaspora to the Palestinian homeland. Further, the event was not only targeted towards Palestinians, but it also spoke to the Lebanese and foreigners in Beirut, encouraging the meeting and creation of transnational advocacy networks around human rights issues. Another significant characteristic of the exhibition was that it brought together camp residents, local activists, and middle-class Palestinians into contact in a single locale. That the original exhibitor itself was located *outside* Lebanon, and therefore outside the realm of ordinary class and political divides at play in the Palestinian community of Lebanon was perhaps one reason underlying such an in-gathering of different social groups. But such an admixture of social classes was also authorized by the very character of the commemorative narrative on display. While the *form* of the exhibition emphasized the lot of dispossessed Palestinians in the OPT (thus invoking a visceral solidarity and recognition from Palestinian refugees in the camps), the *content* of the exhibition appealed to the cosmopolitan tastes and pretension of the middle-class assimilated Palestinians by its subtle rejection of violent resistance, and its marriage of visual arts and historical exhibit.

The most significant characteristic of the exhibition was its intentional rejection of heroic narratives which valorize wilful self-sacrifice. The

NGOs which brought the exhibition together wanted to speak about Palestinian victimization, and they wanted to do so by subverting what they thought was the prevalent representation of martyrdom in "the West" as an irrational act of irredeemably violent Palestinians. By highlighting the martyrdom that was *not* sought by the martyrs in the exhibit, the organizers shifted the focus to Palestinian suffering and commemorated their past as tragic. In addition to the prosaic objects which made these dead men, women and children ordinary and familiar, the blurbs accompanying each image were entirely constructed from interviews with the deceased's family members. These short biographies of the martyrs contained fragments of raw oral testimonies, maintaining their colloquial oddities which made them far more effective than the standard heroic tropes often deployed in such situations, but which nonetheless conveyed a shared narrative of suffering.

The exhibition, however, was significant in other ways as well. The primary local sponsor of the commemorative event was the Arab Resource Centre for Popular Arts (ARCPA) whose main activity has been the collection and preservation of folk arts and oral histories of Palestinians in Lebanon. By sponsoring an exhibition which commemorated Palestinian martyrs, ARCPA in effect reaffirmed the significance of martyrdom as an element of the Palestinian collective experience.

Sometimes, other ceremonies in which martyrs are commemorated similarly appeal to international audiences. During public demonstrations, martyrs' photographs are frequently displayed by demonstrators from the camps. For example, during the demonstration held in front of the United Nations Economic and Social Commission of Western Asia (UN-ESCWA) on the occasion of International Women's Day (8 March 2002), women and girls carried photographs of two female suicide bombers, Wafa Idriss and Daryan Abu Aysh, and of Fayza Mufarija, who was killed by the Israeli military during the first Intifada. In addition, several small girls accompanying their mothers carried a blurry photograph of the twelve-year-old Muhammad al-Durra – who has become the archetypal Palestinian child martyr.

Martyrs' photographs do not often cohere into a singular immutable narrative; their multiple nuances, meanings, and valences are very much defined by the particular situation in which they are mustered. However, ostensibly fragmentary photographs often tell a narrative which draws upon familiar memories, histories, and icons. Celebrating Idriss, Abu Aysh and Mufarija creates a feminine connection between the two Intifadas. It also implicitly says that if Fayza was killed by the military, Idriss and Abu Aysh have taken revenge through their suicide bombing.

Photographs and effects of martyred children contain two narratives: on the one hand they remind the national(ist) audience of the heroic *ashbal*, the young PLO "lion cubs" of the *Thawra* era fighting alongside their adult cohorts, while simultaneously invoking for a foreign audience the suffering of innocent children. Other commemorative forms and the multiple narratives they contain are discussed later in this chapter.

Commemoration of martyrs

Commemorating martyrdom has taken a number of forms among Palestinian refugees in Lebanon; but martyrs' photographs, their funerals, commemorative naming and memorials, and cemeteries and quotidian memory-places have been some of the most potent and familiar forms of commemoration. Furthermore, the canonization of certain martyrs as archetypal ones, and the emergence of martyrs' mothers as iconic figures in commemorative practices have all been crucial elements in the promotion of martyrs as heroes.

Commemorative photographs and murals

> Faces on the walls – martyrs freshly emerging from life and the printing presses, a death which is a remake of itself. One martyr replacing the face of another, taking his place on the wall, until displaced by yet another or by rain.
>
> Mahmud Darwish, *Memory for Forgetfulness*

The most recurrent institutional artefacts commemorating Palestinian martyrs have been the mass-produced martyrs' photographs pasted on the camp walls. During the Lebanese Civil War, palimpsests of martyrs' posters proliferated throughout the beleaguered cities, sometimes hundreds of them pasted next to one another, forming a black and white wallpaper of blood sacrifice. During the War of the Camps,

> an epidemic of white T-shirts with photos imprinted on them broke out. As after each round of fighting, Shatila's inhabitants had the workshops of West Beirut make shirts with the likeness of the camp's dead martyrs printed on the front. This time was no exception; soon it seemed that the entire camp, including many men from factions other than Fatah, was wearing the photo of Ali Abu Toq. Ali belonged to them all. He had led them all in the struggle for survival; in death he was cherished by all. (Giannou 1990: 189–190)

At the time of my field research, commemorative T-shirts or walls entirely covered with photos were little in evidence, partially because the conditions were relatively peaceful, and also because of the scarcity of material resources required to produce them in large quantities. Rather, in 2002, most photo posters commemorating the dead on the walls of the camp were higher-quality photographs of a few recent martyrs of suicide bombings and political leaders such as Abu Jihad (Fatah founder Khalil Wazir), Mustafa al-Zibri (head of PFLP), and Faysal Husayni (late PA minister), none of whom had died in Lebanon. In 2004, images of Hamas leaders Shaykh Ahmad Yasin and Abd al-Aziz Rantisi were hung in great numbers alongside these. After Arafat's death in November 2004, his image – adorned with the national colors and the black band of mourning – was also added to the lot, with Arafat also receiving the honorary moniker of *shahid* or martyr. Wazir's assassination by Israeli commandos in 1988 in Tunis, Mustafa's assassination in an Israeli missile attack on his office in the West Bank in 2001, Yasin's assassination by gunship-fire in Gaza in 2004, and the murder of Rantisi by missile a few weeks later bestowed upon them the status of martyrs. However, Husayni and Arafat had not died violent deaths, yet they were considered martyrs for the cause. Their commemoration as *shuhada al-wajib* (obligatory martyrs) was guaranteed by a life dedicated to national struggle and their deaths were not considered ordinary events, but rather honored and blessed instances of martyrdom.

Alongside the images of the political elite in the Burj al-Barajna refugee camp, several murals and photographs of handsome young Palestinian men also appeared. One such young man was Shadi Anas. On 7 October 2000, in the first week of the al-Aqsa Intifada, a protest visit at the Lebanon–Israel border was organized by various political factions in the Beirut camps.[1] The visit was intended to show the solidarity of diaspora Palestinians with Palestinians in the OPT. On this particular occasion, the usual curses and stones thrown across the border by Palestinians (and answered by tear-gas from the other side) escalated into the throwing of Molotov Cocktails. In response, Israeli troops shot and killed two young men, Shadi Anas of Burj al-Barajna and Hasan Hasanayn of Shatila. The *shabab*'s death gave Palestinians in the Lebanese camps *their* first al-Aqsa Intifada martyrs. The smiling

[1] After the evacuation of occupying Israeli forces and their allies from southern Lebanon, such protest visits were frequent. Several such trips were organized by political leaders of various factions in the camp, who used the emotionally charged and politically symbolic journeys as means to recruit activist youth. The degree to which the recruiting was successful is indeterminate, but eyewitness accounts allude to the fact that many of the youth treated the political "bosses" with some derision. A fifteen-year-old son of the Shatila camp says about that day: "[w]e continued throwing stones. The bosses were telling us to throw stone while they were sitting up the hill, each with his camera and some of them with video-cameras. For a while I thought it would be good to throw stones at them, but this was not the time. I had the Israelis in front of me" (Walid Balkis quoted in Sukarieh 2001b: 288).

photographs of the martyrs were on display throughout their camps of origin and in Burj al-Barajna, Shadi Anas's home at the heart of the camp bore a mural portrait of him with the al-Aqsa mosque and Palestinian flags in the background bearing the slogan "Martyr of al-Aqsa" flanked by two tulips.[2] The mural had been commissioned by the local branch of the PLO's Martyrs' Affairs Bureau which provides welfare services to the families of martyrs and organizes commemorative events in their honor. Such murals appeared quickly and frequently on camp walls, commissioned by factions or NGOs, and often contained an image of the martyr (taken from an identity card or group photo) placed within a context of heroic symbols, words, and imagery. Bloodied doves and bleeding oranges, flags fluttering in the wind, carefully rendered maps of the homeland painted in the red, black, white and green of the Palestinian flag, galloping horses, a solitary stone-throwing child pictured against a tank, barbed wires, and rising suns are some examples of such imagery. That the portrait of the martyr is accompanied by a familiar heroic repertoire of nationalist and/or religious symbols and words as well as the ever-increasing presence of Quranic verses, reinforces the interconnectedness of sacrificial death with more abstract concepts such as "the nation," increasingly "religious salvation," and, nowadays far less frequently, "the revolution."

For a few months in 2002, on the well-traversed thoroughfare from Haifa Hospital to the Burj al-Barajna cemetery, a large mural of Wafa Idriss – the first female suicide bomber of the al-Aqsa Intifada – adorned a long wall. In the mural, Idriss wore her *keffiyeh* around her neck and was flanked by the requisite Quranic verses and national symbols. This mural, which appeared only days after Idriss's suicide operation, was itself commissioned by the Martyrs' Affairs Bureau and its highly visible position and composition performed several tasks: first and foremost, it declared the solidarity of the Palestinians in Lebanon with the Palestinians in the OPT. By highlighting a woman's self-sacrifice – considered to be the duty of men – it pointed to the extremity of Palestinian despair under occupation and how this despair had driven women to self-sacrifice; but it also, and paradoxically, highlighted the gender egalitarianism achieved in performing a suicide operation (see Hasso 2005). The mural of Wafa Idriss included the usual heroic symbols – but as the violence in the OPT took a turn for the worse, and as more young women carried out

---

[2] Tulips and poppies are symbols of martyrdom and memorial flowers not only in the Middle East (where, for example, in pre-Revolution Iranian political poetry, tulips symbolized fallen guerrillas fighting against the Shah's regime), but also in Europe. In Britain, red poppies symbolize fallen soldiers of the First World War, in reference to Wilfred Owen's poem, "In Flanders Fields the Poppies Blow."

suicide operations, Idriss's mural was replaced by other commemorative images. The ephemeral commemoration, nevertheless, had its intended effect of valorizing heroism, now embodied in a woman's much-debated violent act, intended for the local camp audience.

Images of martyrs also appear in the private spaces of their families' homes. Even when these houses have undergone successive waves of destruction, reconstruction, and re-destruction, and even when they are starkly devoid of any adornment or furnishings, photographs of lost sons, husbands, or beloved relatives stubbornly declare their presence. In one of the poorest camp residences I visited, the room in which I was entertained and which had an attached toilet and a sink in the corner, was the sole room in the house of an old woman and her daughter. The only furnishings of the room were meagre beddings, dented pots and pans, a handful of dishes, and a transistor radio. Nonetheless, professional – and paid – work had gone into reproduction of the photographs of the family's martyrs. Images of the three sons the woman had lost in the war were obviously modified in a studio which had produced a pastel-tinted collage of the their portrait against a background of Mecca. These photos are hung on the wall of the most "public" room of the house, the room in which visitors are received, which, as often occurs in the poorer families, is also the sole room in the house. The portraits are almost always accompanied by an emblematic image (i.e. an image of the Dome of the Rock, or a map of Mandatory Palestine, or in more religious households, an image of Mecca), and in a hierarchy determined by prevalent social norms (i.e. the eldest members of the family in higher and more central positions). These personal photographs are not simply the commemorative artefacts of martyrdom. Quite often, they are indices of personal or familial loss and mourning, as heads of household who may have died of old age, or younger family members whose deaths were not for "the cause" are also celebrated. It is, however, an indication of the degree to which political violence has affected the lives of Palestinians in Lebanon and more often than not, these photographs are images of martyrs in the family. In telling their stories to a foreign interviewer, the constant gestural reference to the martyrs' photos is both a recounting of a narrative of loss, and an insistent claim of honor and dignity redeemed through the sacrifice of a son.

In addition to the personal and familial photographs, some of the households I visited also contained photos of archetypal or heroic martyrs. Significantly, in none of these households did I ever see a photograph of a dead or living party leader. Households affiliated with the PFLP sometimes prominently displayed a photograph of the eminent Palestinian writer and PFLP spokesman, Ghassan Kanafani (assassinated by an Israeli car bomb in 1972 in Beirut), whereas in several households with Fatah leanings, photographs of famous guerrillas who had lost their lives in attacks against Israel were on display. In one such household where I had been a frequent visitor, a few days after Wafa Idriss's suicide bombing, the only child of the family, a precocious sixteen-year-old girl, brought out a carefully framed photograph – obviously reproduced from a newspaper image – of the freshly dead body of Dalal Mughrabi.[3] Nura retrieved the photograph from a desk drawer, dusted it and proudly showed it to me, while giving me a history lesson on Mughrabi's death. The image showed a younger Ehud Barak, pistol in one hand, lifting Mughrabi's dead body off the ground by the hair. Her photo was not prominently on display, because her shirt had been ripped off her dead body and she was in her brassière. Nura, who had on a previous occasion told me that she wished she could die for Palestine "like *shahid* Shadi [Anas]," commented that women had always sacrificed themselves for Palestine.

Mughrabi had obviously been elevated to heroic status through her gruesome death, and her heroic martyrdom erased the potential loss of honor due to her nakedness in death, or her questionable "reputation" in life (Peteet 1991: 151). In the early 1980s, Mughrabi had had a multivalent image. While she was represented to foreigners as a symbol of heroic resistance by women, among Palestinians themselves, she was considered a "subject of gossip" (Peteet 1991: 151). By the time I was conducting my fieldwork, Mughrabi's (perceived) transgressions were forgotten, and the Fatah-affiliated family celebrated Mughrabi by keeping a framed photograph of her bloodied martyred body. By then, Mughrabi seemed to be a progenitor to the young women from the OPT who were with alarming frequency blowing themselves up in the early months of 2002. She was also considered an indispensable link in the chain that bound Palestinians in Lebanon to their brethren and cousins in the OPT. By remembering her, the family was insisting that their history and their fate could not be easily unwound from that of the Palestinians across the borders, and their plight and problems could not be easily forgotten in the interest of political concessions made by the PA.

Usage of photographs in commemoration of the dead – and particularly martyrs – is not solely the domain of Palestinians, but bringing the martyrs into the public domain in immense numbers, to plaster entire walls with their posters, is an innovative mode of commemoration, at

---

[3] In March 1978, the eighteen-year-old Mughrabi led eight guerrillas to Israel, hijacked a bus, and in the ensuing shoot-out, 37 people, including 6 guerrillas were shot dead (Cobban 1984: 94). Three days later, Israel invaded Lebanon in retaliation, killing 700 Lebanese and Palestinian civilians.

least in its Middle Eastern political context. Personal, familial, and institutional commemorative photographs all testify that the persons whose bodies are no longer around, are still extant in the memories, lives, and communities of the survivors. This testimony of permanence is frequently performed for foreign audiences who may question the viability of Palestinian nationalism in exile. Importantly, the photographs – whether as posters on city streets, or as private memorials inside homes – are the opening points of narratives, prompting conversations and encouraging the active practices of remembrance through history-telling. If one asks about the identity of the person in the photo, a conversation is begun, which in the presence of a tape-recorder will be politico-historical, and in its absence will be colored with the nuances of a life lived in many dimensions, with loves, defeats, and losses fleshing out the heroism. The performative aspect of commemoration is important. While these images are indices of personal and familial loss, when performed for the sake of the nation, they act as conduits of nationalist feeling and the proof of fidelity to the cause.

At the height of Palestinian armed mobilization in Lebanon, these images were tools of recruitment (Sayigh 1997: 111 and 122), enkindling "feelings of militancy" (Peteet 1991: 151), inspiring "communal defiance in the face of destruction" (Slyomovics 1998: 183), and forming "strands in the web of affiliations [that] Palestinians use to tie [them]selves to [their] identity and to each other" (Said and Mohr 1986: 14). The story of the person who is thus remembered is always embedded in (violent) historical events, even if the deceased died a natural or accidental death, and the narrative of his life includes anecdotes about love and beauty and kindness. Commemoration of the martyr through the ever-present visual memorial invites questioning by visiting foreigners, provides a pedagogic response (often unconsciously so), and weaves the community of the dead into the daily lives of the living. Institutionally, the photographs of Abu Jihad, Ghassan Kanafani, and Shaykh Yasin have emplotted a narrative of Israeli assassinations of Palestinian political leaders. Shadi Anas's mural speaks of the ongoing violence of the Israeli military against Palestinians in Lebanon; and along with the mural commemorating Wafa Idriss – like the photograph of Dalal Mughrabi – it implicitly declares the interconnectedness of the fates of Palestinians across borders.

Naming of people, institutions, and events after martyrs

Another prominent form of commemoration of Palestinian martyrs is the naming of people, organizations, institutions, places, and events after martyrs. The primary Palestinian cemetery in Lebanon functioning as a quasi-national cemetery is named the "Cemetery of Martyrs." The tenth of April of every year is commemorated by Fatah as Martyrs' Day; commemorating the assassination of three Fatah officials by Israeli commandos in 1973. During the Civil War, camp quarters were named after martyrs; those names where erased and replaced as new martyrs fell (Sayigh 1992: 687). Their impermanence reflected the ever-accumulating roll-call of martyrs. However, there are also more specific naming practices honoring those who are considered to have sacrificed themselves (or been sacrificed) for the nation. For example, one PFLP sympathizer had named his daughter Lamis, after Ghassan Kanafani's seventeen-year-old niece who was killed in the car bomb which also killed Kanafani. Several young men born shortly after 1973 were all named Ghassan, all of whom claimed to have been named after Kanafani himself (also Abu Shawar 1992: 611). A baby girl born to a fervent young woman at the Nahr al-Barid camp at the beginning of 2002 was named Wafa after Wafa Idriss. The child's name acted as a mnemonic association between a new-born child and a national narrative, thus literally embedding the new child into the national history.[4] In addition to legal names given at birth, the *nom de guerre* of many Palestinian activists honor past martyrs: Leila Khaled chose to call herself Shadiah Abu Ghazaleh after a PFLP woman killed in the mid-1960s (Khaled 1973: 142).

Commemorating martyrs through honorific naming extends to organizations and events as well. The military wing of Hamas is called Martyr Izz al-Din al-Qassam Brigade.[5] An NGO originally affiliated with the PFLP – and promoting art education among Palestinian camp children – is named The Ghassan Kanafani Centre. Some commando operations against Israel were named after assassinated leaders, one of the most prominent being the operation led by Dalal Mughrabi, which was named Martyr Kamal 'Udwan Operation, to honor the Fatah Central Committee member assassinated in an Israeli commando raid on Beirut in 1973 (Brynen 1990: 62). Interestingly, despite the official name of the operation, it became known as Operation Dalal Mughrabi in both the oral recall of the Palestinians in the camp and in the official

---

[4] Slyomovics (1998: 201) writes about the commemoration of place names through naming daughters after lost Palestinian villages.

[5] Shaykh Izz al-Din al-Qassam (1882–1935) was an anti-Zionist and anti-British insurgent leader in Palestine. He was killed in a gun-battle against the British, and his death is thought to have been at least partially responsible for the 1936–1939 Arab revolt against Zionists and the British in Palestine. That he was a preacher, and an adherent of Salafi Islamism and pan-Islamic politics, has rendered him an acceptable ideological progenitor and mobilizing symbol for Hamas (Swedenburg 1995: 201). For a biography of Qassam, see Schleifer 1993.

organs of nearly all Palestinian political organizations. The most remarkable aspect of this naming practice is that with the exception of the Martyrs' Cemetery (itself subject to occasional threats of destruction by various urban-planning schemes of the post-civil war Lebanese state), commemoration always names that which is ephemeral or mobile, bestowing the memory of martyrs upon a person or an institution, rather than fixed places named permanently. In their permanent state of temporary exile, Palestinians have projected the practices of commemoration onto that which can be carried from city to city and camp to camp or that which is intangible and can be protected from physical annihilation. These naming practices embody the martyrs in new persons, places, events, and institutions.

Martyrs' funerals

> But I will be
> A Bridegroom in my death, and run into't
> As to a lover's bed.
> William Shakespeare, *Anthony and Cleopatra*

From the funeral of the first Fatah guerrilla to die in action in Lebanon in 1968 until today, mass funeral processions have acted as both mobilizing and pedagogic tools. Large processions accompanying martyrs' bodies showcase the large constituencies of political organizations and imply the legitimacy of the movement. The demonstrations themselves create the necessary momentum for attracting new recruits and public support. The contentiousness of these events can be gleaned from a passage written by Kamal Junblat, a Druze leader in Lebanon and a sympathizer to and an ally of the Palestinian cause. Junblat (quoted in Brynen 1990: 136; emphasis added) wrote that the guerrillas

carelessly exposed themselves to criticism and even hatred ... Outsiders making law in Lebanon, *armed demonstrators and ceremonies, military funerals for martyrs of the revolution,* it all mounted up and began to alienate public opinion, especially conservative opinion, which was particularly concerned about security ... I never saw a less discreet, less cautious revolution.

Martyrs' funerals have also functioned as pedagogic tools, disseminating a unified nationalist narrative. Martyrs' funerals in the camps of Lebanon – as in the wider Palestinian context – include elements shared across the region and the world. Among them is the transformation of the funeral ceremony into a "wedding." The funeral-as-wedding reaffirms hope amidst death, and allows for transformation – however fleeting – of wasted youth and human loss into a meaningful and heroic death that can give dignity and honor. The factions' transformation of wedding/funeral commemorations into major political events was predicated on borrowing non-political ritual elements from quotidian Palestinian lives and transforming these elements into symbolically loaded political practices which resonated with a wide public. In pre-1948 Palestinian villages, the elision of weddings to deaths occurred in a twofold manner: bridegrooms were said to be fighters going into battle (al-Bakr 1994), while the death of a young unmarried man was mourned by transforming his funeral into a wedding celebration – thus recognizing his untimely death, and his becoming "death's bridegroom."[6] As early as the 1936–1939 revolt against the British, these rituals were politicized, as one elderly Palestinian (quoted in Soukarieh 2000: 80–81) recalled:

[b]oth a funeral and a wedding were simultaneously taking place in our house. The women's trilling cries of joy were mixed with their relatives' bitter crying, national songs, and young men's threats were heard ... They were singing wedding songs for my brother, the martyred groom. My mother and the village women were putting henna on the hands of my brother who was twenty years old. A groom in the real sense of the word, he was being treated like one, as they dressed him in his best clothes and sang for him: "Groom, oh Groom, we are happy for you."

In such "weddings," the grieving family of the martyr is expected to ululate while weeping, guests are served sweetened – rather than bitter – coffee, and the martyr's political comrades hold "wedding" processions from the house of the martyr to his putative grave (or symbolic "wedding chamber") while firing bullets in the air, the latter being a celebratory practice usually performed at weddings. The event's polyvalence calls for the "celebrations" to be accompanied by the bitter laments of female family members. As a political event targeted at national audiences, the funeral-as-wedding and the very act of martyrdom it celebrates give heroic life to the movement. When performed for a foreign audience, however, the tragic element of death in youth prevails.

In a number of instances, the martyrs – if they had willingly gone to their deaths – also prepare themselves as if for a wedding. Martyrdom mythology has it that many Palestinian martyrs – much like Christian martyrs of legend – foresaw their own deaths (Kanaana 1998: 127).

---

[6] Similar "wedding" ceremonies mourn the untimely death of young men in Iran and beyond the Middle East. In fact, in Iran, the accoutrements of a young man's funeral often contain a glass container with his photo and other sentimental objects and is called the *hijla* or the wedding chamber.

Recounting his time with the guerrillas, Jean Genet (1987: 79) describes the meticulous grooming of young men who expected to die:

The *fidaiyyin* who were leaving for battle in the Jordan Valley, who were eighteen – from what I could understand from them they had fear, but at the same time they had a taste for martyrdom, thus of glory, even if this glory would be known to only a very small number of people. They took particular care about how they dressed when they set out. They would wear a leather jacket, quite tight. They wore their uniform, a bracelet – it was a whole preparation that was almost formal. They knew they were probably going to die, but they also knew that they were enacting a ceremony that went beyond them ... a kind of ritual ... They went freely.

Upon martyrdom, the martyr's body is considered purified. Legends of martyrdom indicate that the body of the martyr does not decompose (Kanaana 1998: 129). The blood of the martyr is not polluting, martyrs' bodies are not washed, and their clothes are not changed. The un-washed bloodied body is a potent political symbol. It can be carried wrapped in blood-spattered sheets through the streets and depending on the context and audience it can be interpreted both as a symbol of injustice and as the promise of continuing resistance. The vulnerability of the human body – emphasized by the abundance of blood – under-lines the notion of heroic sacrifice, legitimating the cause and honoring the courage of the martyr. Collective mourning and ecstatic celebrations of martyrdom both create a sense of community among the mourners, and the dead body appeals to observers' emotions of sympathy and fury and act as potent instruments of political mobilization (Ben-Amos 2000: 39; Ramphele 1997: 107; Verdery 1999).

The procession of the bloodied body of the martyr through the camps has sometimes been accompanied by political speeches and often with angry demonstrations. When Jihad Jibril, the son of PFLP–GC's chair-man, Ahmad Jibril, was assassinated in Beirut on 20 May 2002,[7] his bloody and mangled body was carried from the site of the car bombing to the Burj al-Barajna camp, carried through its narrow streets to the PFLP–GC office, while the camp youth formed a procession firing shots in the air in Jibril's honor. Jibril's death became a moment which mended political fissures in the camp and allowed for a demonstration of political unity. The theatrical elements of the funeral, the speeches, the chanting,

[7] Most indications point to a car-bombing assassination directed by Israeli secret services, since the Lebanese suspect sought in relation with Jibril's assassination had been a collaborator during the Israeli occupation of southern Lebanon (*al-Sharq al-Awsat*, 21 May 2002: 1). Prior to his assassination, Jihad Jibril had been the PFLP–GC military liaison with Hizbullah for military operations against Israel (*al Hayat*, 23 May 2002: 6; *Daily Star*, 24 May 2002: 2).

the rituals, as well as the funerary objects such as photographs and banners– and indeed the very body of the martyr – were marshaled in order to inscribe the martyr into national history in such a way as to reaffirm the nation. Jibril's death defiantly denoted the continuation of resistance, reaffirmed by the very public condolence visit paid to his father Ahmad Jibril in Damascus by the Hizbullah chairman, Sayyid Hasan Nasrallah (whose own son had also been lost in conflict with Israel). In that meeting, both men indicated that the struggle against Israel was to continue especially now that such precious life was lost in the course of battle.

Funerary rituals serve a range of political functions: they legitimate and integrate organizations, reinforce group solidarities, and viscerally embed political beliefs (Kertzer 1991), but they are also ceremonies which widely appeal to and resonate with publics. They not only allow for expression of the refugees' grief, but also allow for expression of their political voice. Refugees choose to participate in some public funeral processions and not others in order to declare their solidarity with a particular political program or organization and not others. Moments of cross-party solidarity are signalled by factions' unified front during particular funeral processions. In contrast, the absence of great numbers at a particular funeral – more than anything else – denotes the displeasure of the public for the particular party or the political cause of which the martyr was a member.

Martyrs' mothers

The martyr warned me: Do not believe their ululations
Believe my father when, weeping, he looks at my photograph
How did we trade roles, my son, how did you precede me.
I first, I the first one!

Mahmud Darwish, "Under Siege"

An important iconic figure in commemorations of martyrs is the martyr's mother, an older Palestinian woman who encourages her son to fight at any cost, and who rejoices rather than mourns his death. As Peteet (1991: 51) writes,

[a]fter the 1930 execution of Muhammad Jamjum of Hebron, condemned to death for his participation in the 1929 riots, people gathered at his mother's house to pay condolences. She is reported to receive them, calling out from her home, "Why do you cry? I am proud of my son who achieved great honour through martyrdom."

The source of Peteet's narrative is a document published by the PLO's General Union of Palestinian Women. In the periodicals of various

PLO factions throughout the 1960s and 1970s, interviews with martyrs' mothers often referred to their "pride," "glory," and "honor."
Similarly, Intifada Communiqué no. 29 salutes "the mother of the
martyr and her celebratory ululation, for she has ululated twice, the day
her son went to fight and was martyred, and the day the state was
declared" (see Massad 1995: 474). The courageous self-sacrificing
mother thus becomes the emblem of the nation.[8] This trope is not only
reproduced by political factions, but is in fact propagated by mothers of
martyrs where such performative bravery is called for and expected.
The persistence of the trope is rooted not only in institutional support
for families of martyrs (visits from officials, some financial support
however meagre, and being featured in factional organs), but also in the
charged ideational content of the trope, which advances notions of
honor and dignity in self-sacrifice. The iconic figure of the "mother of
the martyr" appears again and again in Palestinian communities and
her brave performance is guaranteed through imperceptible everyday
acts of affirmation and discipline imparted by members of her community, through public funerary rituals commemorating martyrs, and
through the factional organs and mass media. I observed one such
moment of discipline, when at the funeral of Jihad Jibril, a weeping
young woman was rebuked for her act of mourning; she was told that
Jibril was alive and well, and that her mourning was not becoming or
appropriate. Such pressure can also be brought to bear on mothers of
martyrs, whose notions of propriety and honor indicate that
they should publicly perform a celebration of their heroic children's
martyrdom.

The story of the brave mother who gives up her son to the homeland
is almost always for public consumption, preferably performed in front
of cameras. The trope is intended to give meaning to an act, to embed it
within a larger narrative; strength in the face of loss is supposed to
dissolve the moment in the broad story of the nation. But the martyr's
mother is not simply a symbolic device deployed by the political elite.
The stoicism and joyful pride of the martyr's mother is intended to
convey defiance and a challenge to the enemy, and place an obligation
upon the elite. This defiance signals that the mother – like her martyred
child before her – has taken her fate into her own hands. During spring
2002, when the Israeli military had reoccupied much of the West Bank,
the Jenin refugee camp was under siege, and various Arabic-language

---

[8] Enloe (2000) discusses American and Israeli mothers who sacrifice sons for the nation.

satellite television stations graphically showed casualties of the Israeli attack, Umm Wakid said to me,

[e]verybody in our society is a hero. I saw an old mother [on the television] yesterday and she was encouraging her son to go and become a martyr. "God is with us, and we have faith in our hearts; and so do those men of al-Aqsa and al-Quds," and she told him, "I am waiting for you to become a martyr, to hear about your martyrdom." The hair on my skin stood on end! In fact, he went and he was martyred, and the mother she waited in a chair until she heard the news of his martyrdom. I mean, the Palestinian mother, has the patience of prophets. (Burj al-Barajna, 13 March 2002)

The 60-year-old woman thus speaking about a Palestinian woman in the OPT had herself lost her husband and a son during the siege of Tal al-Za'tar. Umm Wakid's narrative tone was, however, ambiguous. That her hair stood on end while listening to the son-sacrificing mother could have been a result of awe, or of sorrow. She saw in the act of offering a child to the homeland "the patience of prophets" and a heroism equivalent to that of the martyred son.

Where control over one's destiny signifies honor (Peteet 1994, 1997b), the celebratory stance of the mothers is an act of political wilfulness. Much like the martyrs who in *choosing* death affirm their political agency, the mother of the martyr, in celebrating her child's martyrdom, declares her own will and signals her considered engagement in national politics. Additionally, the martyr's mother is entitled – in the name of her fallen child – to call the political elite to account. She can cite her sacrifice in order to participate in the political life of the camp, and a child's martyrdom gives the mother immunity to criticize leaders or the elite who were previously beyond reach. Public performances in which the martyr's mother loudly decries the condition of her family and her community without opprobrium are *de rigeur*.

Not all ideological contexts accommodate the narrative of celebrated martyrdom. This trope is rarely – if ever – deployed in the newspapers of secular factions (e.g. the PFLP or DFLP), though all do honor the loss of martyrs; whereas the religious organizations (such as the Hamas or Jihad), or parties which instrumentally and situationally deploy religion (such as PFLP–GC or Abu Nidal's Fatah–RC), use the trope of the martyr's mother unabashedly, celebrating her son's martyrdom with varying degrees of intensity and rhetorical panache. For example, the PLO/Fatah's organ tends to make the connection between martyrdom and the honor it bestows on the mother of the martyr less explicit:

Question: You are Palestinian, your son was martyred because of the *Thawra*. You live alone between these four walls; you have to spend money drop by drop. Frankly and openly, tell me how do you feel about the *Thawra*?

Answer: The *Thawra* is our revolution. And it is our son, and our daughter and our family. If my eyesight wasn't failing, I would have participated myself. May god grant it victory. (*Filastin Al-Thawra* [PLO], 2 February 1978)

However, with the more militant Abu Nidal group, martyrs' mothers are explicitly celebrated: "I pride and glory in the martyrdom of my daughter and I used to ask god to honor us with martyrdom, and he has honored us. And our sons are redeeming Palestine with their sacrifice" (*Filastin Al-Thawra* [Fatah–RC], 19 March 1992).

Interestingly, this standard trope is not hegemonic and is sometimes subverted by the personal narratives of many Palestinian mothers about their loss. The polyvalence of martyrdom in fact complicates commemorative narratives about it. Some mothers of martyrs who speak of their pride in public, berate and curse the officials who have come to pay their respects. Sometimes the very same mother who at the beginning of the interview spoke of her pride and honor in the standard language of defiance, later voices her loss and grief in a more intimate vocabulary. Some even choose not to voluntarily mention the martyred child, as if cherishing martyrdom as something private and intimate, not to be shared in a political performance. After having been interviewed about her life in Lebanon and her experiences of suffering, and after her having recounted the deaths of her father and her husband, Umm Shadi, a 55-year-old nurse in Burj al-Barajna was questioned about her worst memory. Only then, she said:

[m]y worst memory is the death of my father and the death of my husband, but worst of all is the death of my son Umar. He was only 16 and he was applying for immigration papers to Denmark. At the time [nine years ago], there was a war going on between Amal and Hizbullah and Amal had the control of all the ticket offices, the airport, the Middle East Airlines, and the ports, and they didn't let him fly. So my son went down to Saida to take a ship from the port there, and while he was down there he was martyred in the war between Amal and Hizbullah (Burj al-Barajna, 30 January 2002).

She refused to elaborate any more on Umar's life, but later mentioned that for two months after the martyrdom of Hasan Hasanayn and Shadi Anas which she had witnessed, she had nightmares, and she added, "I don't like to talk about these memories, because they are too hard."

Another Palestinian woman, Umm Faruq, who had spoken about Palestinians' readiness to sacrifice themselves for the homeland, spoke quietly about her son:

[a]ny mother's worst memory is the loss of her young sons. When [my son] was killed, I had no time to be sad and I had to worry about my other three sons, but once the war was over, I felt the loss of my son. (Burj al-Barajna, 6 February 2002)

For her and for many of the other mothers of the camps, the immediacy of existing troubles had to outweigh the process of mourning. The loss of a son to martyrdom, while a matter of retrospective honor and pride, was a devastating blow to these mothers who tried their best to prevent it. Umm Nizar, who had lost three sons (all of them guerrillas) in the civil war, proudly displayed their photographs, and spoke of the *'izza* (glory) and *karama* (honor) of being martyrs' mother; but in the course of her narrative, she came to recount how hard she had tried to prevent her sons' conscription into the guerrilla forces so that they could continue their education. Umm Nizar's narrative of her life contained both the predominant heroic commemorative narrative and the counternarrative which subverted it.

The public mode of commemoration – rejoicing in the death of one's sons – is produced and reproduced in the practices of mothers who have given meaning to their losses, and these practices and narratives are in turn taken, streamlined, and rebroadcast via the official organs and mass media. This recycling of martyrdom tropes transforms individual martyr's mothers into a collective national allegory. The intimate narratives of loss, on the other hand, are not consolidated through appropriation and promulgation by the factional organs and as such each contains the residues of personal loss and grief that escapes the hegemonic grasp of collective commemorations.

Archetypal martyrs

> Now he passes on as a martyr
> And leaves us as refugees
>   Mahmud Darwish, "Returning to Jaffa"

Some martyrs "belong" to all factions, while others become irrevocably claimed and iconized by specific political factions. Commemorations of archetypal martyrs reveal the complexity of factional interrelation as well as the strategies, ideologies, and claims of political organizations. The hagiographies of archetypal martyrs reflect the ideologies of the parties to which they belonged and as such tend to vary in content and iconography on the basis of "ownership" of the martyr, though all parties invest the figure of the martyr with mythological and sometimes mystical characteristics.

Swedenburg writes about the resurrection of Izz al-Din al-Qassam, an anti-colonial leader in Palestine, as the precursor of the fighters of the Intifada (Swedenburg 1995: 105). In the 1960s, the Marxist DFLP chose to name their armed wing Qassam Forces, and "portrayed

[Qassam] an early organiser of an incipient Palestinian working class, and perhaps a forerunner of another notable exile, Che Guevara" (Budeiri 1997: 323 fn. 24). Qassam was later appropriated by the Islamist movements as the populist preacher and fighter who brought Islam into the Palestinian national struggle. In 1985, and during a time of great tension between Fatah and the Syrian state, the Syria-supported PFLP–GC commemorated Qassam for resisting the separation of Palestine from the united Arab lands (*Il al-Amam*, 30 November 1985: 30–32). Shortly after the Oslo Accords, Abu Nidal's rejectionist organ emphasized Qassam's uncompromising armed struggle (*Filastin al-Thawra* [Fatah–RC] 18 November 1993: 10–11). In all instances, the commemorators chose to remember the martyr as it befitted their agenda and their ideology, analogizing the martyr's strategies with those of the current period and drawing conclusions on the basis of this analogy. For all these factions, the audience of the commemoration was the Palestinian population, and by emphasizing particular characteristics of the martyr which resembled that of the population (exile for the Palestinians in the diaspora), or which legitimated the claims of the commemorating institution (the reintroduction of Islam in the national struggle, pan-Arabism, or unyielding support for armed resistance), the organizations instrumentalized the martyr and the practice of remembering him.

The archetypal martyr iconised by various Palestinian political parties speaks to the political positions of those parties. For example, in many offices affiliated with the PFLP, posters of Che Guevara are on display, as are photographs of Ghassan Kanafani. Che Guevara loomed large in the PFLP imagination, so much so that one PFLP commando, himself killed in an operation against Israel, had chosen Guevara Gaza as his *nom de guerre*. The death of Che Guevara, which occurred only four months after the 1967 war, had come to signify revolutionary guerrilla resistance, as opposed to participation in regular armies of "reactionary regimes" who had been so resoundingly defeated by Israel in 1967. Leila Khaled (1973: 94) of the PFLP writes about her devastation upon hearing the news of Che's death and adds,

[to] me, Che's martyrdom can be justified because of its value to world revolution: his life was a form of perpetual renewal; his behaviour was exemplary; his commitment was total – qualities the revolutionary movement needed to absorb. His 'adventurism and romanticism' are necessary reminders of the unconquerable power of the human spirit in a world where the fear of America cripples millions, deactivates superpowers, and paralyses professional revolutionaries. Che lived heroically and died heroically.

Ghassan Kanafani's assassination by a Mossad car bomb in Beirut in 1972, accompanied by rumors of the complicity of Beirut's security forces in the killing, was more immediately and viscerally tied to the fortunes of Palestinians in Lebanon. Kanafani was a novelist and a painter, as well as the PFLP spokesman. At his funeral in Beirut, attended by tens of thousands of Palestinians and sympathetic Lebanese, a PFLP official said that Kanafani's martyrdom "show[ed] the strength and efficacy of the resistance and the pains to which the enemy would go [to challenge it]; and the intense participation of the masses [at the funeral showed] their support for the struggle of the vanguard. This should encourage us to intensify our revolutionary struggle against the enemy" (*al-Hadaf*, 15 July 1972: 5). Thus the defeat inherent in the loss of a fighter was claimed as a sign of the strength of the revolution. Kanafani himself was chosen as the "factional martyr" because his sensitive literary treatment of the Palestinian *Nakba*, his production of many icons of Palestinian struggle, his coining of phrases that entered the Palestinian revolutionary vernacular, and his position as PFLP spokesman, all combined to project him as the ideal archetype of the nationalist intellectual, one who fought with a pen rather than a sword. The commemorative emphasis placed on Kanafani shifted in different circumstances between *fighting* and *virtuoso penmanship*; the PFLP – and other armed militant groups – emphasized Kanafani's writer/fighter characteristic, especially in those times when the PLO's accommodationist policies were being called to task by oppositionist factions. Kanafani's aesthetic representation of the Palestinians was emphasized when the existence or efficacy of Palestinian artistic creation as a *national* enterprise was called into question. Additionally, commemorating Kanafani often included implicit references to the manner of his assassination, in an Arab capital with the possible collusion of Lebanon's security forces, and at the hands of unknown Israeli agents; this commemorative narrative in turn acted as a metaphor of the Palestinian condition in exile.

The assassination of Naji al-Ali, the beloved and revered political cartoonist, who also created many of the enduring symbols and symbolic narratives associated with Palestinian nationalism, on the other hand, served not as a mnemonic of Israeli treachery, but as an emblem of the Palestinian national movement's internal fractiousness. Al-Ali was a fiercely independent Palestinian cartoonist, who was raised in the Ain al-Hilwa camp in Lebanon. Al-Ali was assassinated in London on 22 July 1987, and was buried there, instead of Shajara in Galilee where he was born and wished to be buried, or in Ain al-Hilwa where his parents were buried. There is evidence of involvement of both Mossad and Arafat's Force 17 in his assassination.[9] Arafat's potential involvement was attributed to his frustration with al-Ali's "acerbic lampooning" of him (Sayigh 1997: 603). Al-Ali's artistic work, death in double exile (both from his homeland and from Ain al-Hilwa), and his unfulfilled wish of burial in his homeland made him an archetype of exilic martyrdom: he was remembered with the cry "the people's heart shall be your tomb" (*qabrak qalb al-sha'ab*), thus metaphorically burying the dead artist in the heart of the nation.

Al-Ali has been commemorated primarily through the proliferation of his iconic cartoon character Hanzala (a barefoot child in rags with his back to the viewer and his hands behind his back) on camp walls, posters, and necklace charms, and as a doodle familiar to almost all Palestinians. In al-Ali's cartoons, Hanzala is always the quietly critical observer of the plight of Palestinians, appearing in the corner of the cartoon, at once a signature and the Greek chorus of the image. In death, al-Ali and his creation became one as other visual artists honored al-Ali by making him the Hanzala of *their* cartoons. Al-Ali as a *shahid* then became both martyr and witness. His posthumous political biographies highlighted Ghassan Kanafani discovering al-Ali's talents as a cartoonist (*al-Hurriya*, 27 December 1987: 41), thus constructing a community of sacrificed intellectuals felled at the hands of enemy *and* friend, witness to – and embodying – the collective narrative of Palestinians in Lebanon. Though al-Ali was fondly remembered by leftist political factions (*al-Hadaf*, 12 October 1987: 37), he was also honored by Arafat's nemesis, Abu Nidal, in the designation of his military base in Libya as the Naji al-Ali base (Seale 1992), and he was commemorated through the appearance of Hanzala on the masthead and margin of every page of Abu Nidal Faction's organ, *Filastin al-Thawra* (Fatah–RC). Abu Nidal's audience was determinedly Palestinian, and the commemoration of al-Ali was intended to challenge the hegemony and legitimacy of Fatah and the PLO.

In the drama of nationalism, archetypal martyrs become iconic protagonists. They embody their people's histories. They become nationally recognized heroes whose stories are also the story of the faction, the polity, and the nation.

---

[9] Britain tried and convicted a Palestinian Mossad agent, Ismail Sawwan, and expelled two Israeli diplomats in relation to al-Ali's assassination (Seale 1992: 5). However, Abd al-Rahman Mustafa, an officer in Arafat's security detail, Force 17, has also been implicated in the killing (Ibid.; Sayigh 1997: 603).

National cemeteries and memorials

> Where national memories are concerned, griefs are of more value than
> triumphs, for they impose duties and require a common effort.
>
> Ernest Renan, *What Is a Nation?*

Through claiming "exemplary suicides, poignant martyrdoms, assassinations, executions, wars, and holocausts" (Anderson 1991: 206) for
the nation, national cemeteries provide succinct histories of that nation.
The burial of the body in the soil of a place territorializes the person and
ties him or her to that soil, and if that soil belongs to the nation, then the
"man–land" relationship at the core of nationalist ideologies is reaffirmed in the burial. But military and national cemeteries function in
more profane and prosaic ways as well, by providing a place for
nationalist ceremonies and rituals.

In the absence of a state, Palestinian parastatal institutions have
attempted to create such a narrative of national-unity-in-struggle by
establishing two Martyrs' Cemeteries in Lebanon. Before the *Thawra*
began in the 1960s, in most instances, the Palestinian and Lebanese
deceased of the same faith were buried in the same cemeteries. Exceptions occurred when Palestinian refugees died in hostile localities (e.g. in
Maronite areas), or when the deceased had been politically active and
thus construed as threatening by the Lebanese state apparatus; but
generally, cemeteries were shared. After the *Thawra* began, the PLO's
Martyrs' Affairs Bureau bought or leased Lebanese lands for the express
purpose of establishing at least one "national" cemetery for Palestinians
and for providing necessary funding for the ceremonies held after the
death of the martyr. These cemeteries and ceremonies would "allow for
the perpetuation of the revolution" and afford Palestinians dignity in
death (Khurshid 1972: 106). Near the Shatila camp, which was spatially
and politically located at the "heart" of the movement, and in Ain al-
Hilwa, which was and continues to be the largest refugee camp in
Lebanon, the Bureau established national Martyrs' Cemeteries in the
late 1960s and 1981, respectively. The Bureau continues to support
these cemeteries, unlike cemeteries in other camps which are maintained by families of the deceased or the camps' popular committees.

Like national cemeteries elsewhere, Martyrs' Cemeteries are symbols
of national unity, but unlike any other cemeteries in Lebanon, and
perhaps the rest of the Middle East, Shatila Martyrs' Cemetery contains
bodies of Christians, Muslims, and Jews alike, and the criteria of burial –
and of belonging to the nation – is simply having struggled for the
Palestinian national cause. As such Shatila Martyrs' Cemetery also
holds the remains of Turkish, German, Irish, and Iranian guerrillas,

among others, as well as two symbolic gravestones for two Japanese Red Army guerrillas. The cemetery chronicles Palestinian history in its display of the graves of the Mufti of Jerusalem, Haj Amin al-Husayni, Ghassan Kanafani, PLO leaders Kamal Nasir, Abu Yusif al-Najjar, and Kamal Udwan (assassinated by an Israeli force led by Ehud Barak in 1973), and the forlorn cenotaphs dedicated to massacres at Sabra and Shatila and Tal al-Za'tar, the latter of which could not be memorialized at the site of the massacre itself.

Palestinian Martyrs' Cemeteries in Lebanon are the concrete manifestations of Palestinian national heroism. In the process of constructing this narrative, nationalist political institutions have appropriated private rituals of mourning and placed them in the service of the nation. For example, the practice of visiting the graves of lost loved ones on special holidays – and reading the *fatiha* prayer for the dead of Muslim confession – has been a central feature of Palestinian life both before and after their diaspora. Subhi Ghosheh remembers that in his youth, in Palestine, "women visited graveyards in the afternoon [of 'Id]. They went there carrying cakes which they distributed. I still do not know the secret of this tradition, which is now obsolete, although the visiting of graveyards is still faithfully carried on" (Ghosheh 1992: 654). This integration of the dead into the lives of the living and their religious celebrations was adopted by nationalist organizations, which incorporated a visit to Martyrs' Cemeteries into Palestinian *national* holidays and public demonstrations and transformed the religious ritual of visiting the graves into nationalist ones.[10] As Abu Jihad (Khalil Wazir), one of the founding members of Fatah, has said, "martyrs touched the hearts of people – it was the way we opened the gate" (Brynen 1990: 47) and mobilized support among the refugees. A solemn promise to a martyr was construed as something sacred. Mamduh Nawfal recounted, "before leaving Beirut [in 1982], many of us, including the leadership went to the Martyrs' Cemetery, and there, upon the earth of the cemetery, we promised that we would continue our struggle until our people reached those goals for which the martyrs had given their lives" (Al-'Umd 1983b: 38).

---

[10] This also held true in the OPT, where, for example, during the first Intifada, visits to martyrs' graves transformed into protests against Israeli occupation. Intifada Communiqué No. 22 (dated 21 July 1988) invites Palestinians to celebrate "the 'Id days by organizing mass processions to visit the martyrs' tombs and place wreaths of flowers and Palestinian flags on them, staging mammoth demonstrations and visiting the families of martyrs, wounded, detainees and deportees" (Lockman and Beinin 1989: 371). Also see Robinson (2003).

Today the Martyrs Cemeteries in Lebanon are sites of nationalist political demonstrations organized by various factions. When in spring 2002, the Palestinian community in Lebanon held daily demonstrations against the Israeli military's invasion of West Bank towns, the Cemetery was often the termination point of raucous protest processions. There, political factions waved their flags, commemorated their martyrs, and spoke about the heroic resistance of revolutionary days, now being repeated in the OPT. In a sense, the cemetery became a space where a larger narrative about the unity of resistant Palestinians across borders could be illustrated by the concrete example of sacrifices so assiduously accumulated over the decades.

Quotidian memory places

Palestinian martyrdom in the camps is also commemorated in quotidian memory places scattered throughout. These memory places are numerous and primarily – though not entirely – consist of everyday locations appropriated for burial of martyrs during sieges or battles. These memory places – nurseries, schools, hospitals, and mosques[11] – are often shown to camp visitors as evidence of either heroic resistance or Palestinian suffering. Though these spots became places of mourning, by and large, as a result of unfortunate accidents, they have been maintained and incorporated into broader Palestinian commemorative practices by political organizations.

In the Najda nursery in the Burj al-Shamali camp, a small memorial in the shape of a map of Palestine commemorates fourteen guerrillas affiliated with the DFLP who fell there during the Israeli invasion in June 1982. In the same camp, in the small courtyard of al-Hawla youth club, a memorial is erected on the mass grave of 125–130 men, women, and children who had taken shelter therein during the 1982 invasion, and who were buried alive when an Israeli missile hit the shelter (Suleiman 1997a). This memorial is a cenotaph shaded by a tall archway and it contains the slowly fading names of the victims.

The most notable and well-known quotidian memory place, however, is the mosque in Shatila, which was used as a burial place for hundreds of Palestinians during the long siege of the War of the Camps in the mid-1980s.[12] In his memoir of the siege, Dr Chris Giannou (1991: 115–16) who was volunteering in the camp clinic at the time writes:

---

[11] For a comprehensive list and history of these places, see Hajjaj (2000b, 2000c).
[12] See "Qissat al-Masjid" ("The Story of the Mosque"), *Filastin al-Thawra*, 25 January 1986: 30–31.

[t]he real cemetery was well outside the camp's boundaries, impossible to reach during a siege, so Shatila's inhabitants converted the mosque into a cemetery. Normally, the dead are never buried in a mosque, [but out of necessity] eventually, the inhabitants interred more than 500 corpses [in the mosque], and expropriated a house just next door when the number of dead spilled over the confines of the mosque building ... Families and friends garlanded the tombs and interior of the mosque with wreaths, flowers, and palm leaves and lined the walls with photographs of the dead, considered martyrs by one and all. The transformation of the mosque – a religious and living social institution – into a mass grave was symbolic of what happened to Shatila.

Giannou conveys some of the ways in which the camp residents honored their dead who were buried in the mosque at a time when the state of siege made official or institutional commemoration impossible.

The significance of quotidian memory places such as the Shatila mosque rests in their incorporation into the daily lives of the Palestinians in the camp, as well as their multivalent representations by various political actors. Ordinary residents of the camp do not cordon off these places and do not transform them into hallowed ground. These places are used in the daily routines of those who inhabit and utilise them. On the day I visited the Najda nursery in Burj al-Shamali, the sunlit memorial was being used as a convenient drying rack for laundered children's clothing. The courtyard of Ain al-Hilwa's primary school, where the graves of four youths killed by the Lebanese military in 1958 lie, becomes a joyful and boisterously noisy playground at recess. The mosque in Shatila also remains a place of worship, where the conjunction of piety and pity for the dead results in startling instances of community co-operation. As a 67-year-old Shatila man, Husayn Mahmud Hasan recounts:

there is not a single family in this camp that doesn't have at least one martyr. But where is the blood of the martyrs? The camp mosque is an immense common grave, and our popular committee had to construct a floor so that we could pray. That's where, every Friday, we try to organise a modest collection for the families. What can we say to our martyrs when over their graves we collect these humble donations for their children and families? (Aql 1995: 59)

This weaving of death into the everyday places and practices of the refugees, on the one hand, reinforces the nationalist narrative of Palestinian history through its cartography of martyrdom and resistance superimposed upon the camps and, on the other hand, allows for popular appropriation of memory places in the narratives and practices of the refugees themselves. That the burial places hold the dead – most of them Palestinian – is not in dispute, but the *interpretation* of these deaths as an example of heroism, or alternatively as an embodiment of Palestinian suffering is contested. These deaths are sometimes taken as the private losses of families – ultimately abandoned by its leadership – and at other times as the public deaths claimed by the nation. Sometimes, family members who come to lay flowers or clean the common graves are joined by other Palestinians, some only acquaintances, others total strangers, who relate to them on the basis of a shared history. In these rites of private mourning, a dead kinsman or kinswoman is stolen back from the nation briefly, and a martyr becomes once again a lost son or husband or sister.

At other times, the ceremonies held in and around these places are the routinized rites of politics. For example, the route of many demonstrations held inside Shatila includes a symbolic pilgrimage to the mosque where martyrs therein are celebrated as heroic resisters in the cause of the nation. Palestinians often include the Shatila mosque and its mass grave (as well as other such quotidian memory places) in the narratives they tell of and about themselves to their foreign audiences of researchers, diplomats, journalists, and activists. NGO-sponsored tours of Shatila almost always include a pilgrimage to the mosque, where the martyrs' mass burial is explained as part and parcel of the narrative of Palestinian pain and suffering. These tragic narratives, as mentioned before, appeal to an international audience by capitalizing on sympathies reserved for victims in the discourse of human rights. Thus, the wasteful loss of young lives, the indignity of burial in unsuitable places, and the very continuation of the state of siege in other guises, all become the bases of appeals for recognition of Palestinian refugees' political claims. Quotidian memory places, then, are not interpreted or represented by Palestinians in a monolithic way. The polyvalence of these sites reveals itself in the range of meanings attributed to them in different settings, by different narrators, and for different audiences.

Martyrs as heroes, martyrs as victims

There is a gloomy existential allure about the idea of going down fighting, which is the final refutation of utilitarianism. Utilitarianism calculates the consequences, whereas ... the act performed at the point of death will quite literally have no consequences for oneself, and so is peculiarly privileged.

Terry Eagleton, *Sweet Violence*

The audience for the act of self-sacrifice embodied in martyrdom and for its commemoration are not always one and the same, and the allegiances of the martyr and those who honor him can also differ widely. Because martyrdom speaks to different audiences, the act of self-sacrifice is polyvalent and commemorations of the martyr are likewise complex and even internally contradictory. A close reading of different commemorative practices reveals the myriad meanings of *shahid* (witness, one who testifies, the person who sacrifices himself or herself). These multiple meanings lend it flexibility of usage, and the substantive imprecision and inter- pretative capaciousness of the concept render it effective as a rhetorical device of mobilization. The *shahid* in everyday Palestinian usage is not only the active dissident dying in the act of resistance, but also the innocent bystander, not necessarily armed and engaged in the act of fighting, who is however killed at the hands of the unjust oppressor. The inclusion of those passively sacrificed not only egalitarianizes commemorations, but also creates an equivalency between the death of bystanders and the active political engagement of armed guerrillas.

The common denominator of commemorated Palestinian martyrdom across the ideological spectrum is death at the hand of the enemy. In the 1970s, the militants made no religious distinctions between martyrs of different faiths: "Shahid is a man who dies in battle, in revolution ... It was a word in religion, but now it means only a *fida'i* who is killed. We don't use it as Muslims or as Christians because there is no difference – we are all Palestinians" (quoted in Johnson 1982: 79). Islamists, how- ever, exclude non-believers from the domain of martyrdom. An Islamist tract on Palestinian martyrdom states, "Our martyrs in Palestine are those who fell at the hand of the Romans, the Crusaders, the Tartar, the English, the Jew, and at the hands of all handmaidens and students of Colonialism," but excludes non-believers such as "Patrice Lumumba, John Jamal [?], Indira Gandhi, the infidel Communist and the idolater, etc." from martyrdom (Abu Faris 1990: 35). Both Islamists and secu- larists emphasize the act of injustice which results in martyrdom, such that any activity of the oppressor or enemy which results in the death of a Palestinian, transforms that potentially senseless death into a redemptive self-sacrifice for the nation. By defining martyrdom as any death delivered at the hand of the oppressor, the nation's collectivity is reaffirmed *vis-à-vis* the oppressor.

The qualitative transformation of the martyr in death from a mortal and flawed member of the community to an imperishable embodiment of the nation's abstract values makes them worthy of commemoration. Because they perpetuate the nation, interpretations of their death also feed the political strategies of achieving nationhood. At a rally to com- memorate the death of three PFLP commandos in a raid against Israel on 24 March 1973, George Habash told his audience of PFLP members:

[B]rothers, what is our duty to our heroic martyr, the Guevara of Gaza; what is our duty to his martyred comrades Kamal and al-Hadi? What are our duties and responsibilities to our martyrs Abu Ali Iyad and Ghassan Kanafani, Mahmoud al-Hamshari and all the martyrs of the Palestinian revolution?[13] What are our duties to their relatives, their fathers and mothers, their wives and children? ... Our duties to these martyrs are that we should see things clearly; that we should see our problems clearly. Our duty to them is that we should declare, resolve and act in the light of a clear view of things, that our revolution is continuing and will always continue, and that there is not and never will be on the face of the earth a force that can conquer the masses of our Palestinian people and our Arab people.[14]

In Habash's speech, martyrdom obliges survivors to persevere in resistance. The speech was given shortly before Arafat gave his "Gun and Olive Branch" speech at the UN which implicitly contemplated the idea of a two-state solution, an idea rejected by the PFLP among others. Again and again in a long speech, Habash emphasizes the clarity that the mourners and commemorators need to maintain – this clarity is the uncompromising moral steadfastness of a dissident faction in the face of possible compromise. Memory prevents compromise. The litany of invoked names paints a picture of Palestinian history and asserts implicitly that such sacrifices preclude capitulation.

Others commemorate the martyr differently. An example of the polyvalence of commemoration can be found in the exhibition discussed at the opening of this chapter. While the spectators from the camps recognized themselves and their lives in the articles belonging to the first 100 *martyrs* of the al-Aqsa Intifada, exhibition organizers had also their foreign audience of NGO workers, journalists, and academics in mind. Instead of using the word "martyr" with all the (perhaps religious) images and connotations it invokes, the original Arabic language *shahid* was employed to convey not only martyrdom but also bearing "faithful witness"(Laidi 2001: 204). In fact, the program for the event, which was an independently published book with the same title, also steadfastly refuses to use the English word "martyr" in favor of *shahid*. The appeal to an audience that may be squeamish about overt commemoration of bloody self-sacrifice is thus couched within a more familiar story of victimhood. The discourse of martyr as victim also overshadows the narrative of willing self-sacrifice and focuses instead on "innocent" or "unintentional" martyrdom. By doing so, it depoliticizes the act of dying for a cause, while highlighting the brutality of an enemy who

[13] Guevara Gaza, Kamal, and Hadi were the *noms de guerre* of PFLP commandos killed in a raid against Israel. Walid Nimr (Abu Ali Iyad) was a high-ranking Fatah military commander who was executed by the Jordanian military after being captured in the Jordanian–Palestinian conflict in 1971. Mahmoud al-Hamshari was the Fatah spokesman in Paris who was assassinated in 1973 by Mossad.

[14] From "Documents and Source Materials," *Journal of Palestine Studies* 2(4), 1973: 172.

inflicts death upon those who have nothing to do with politics. "They were going about their days, cooking or reading, or ... " becomes a catchphrase elucidating the guiltlessness of the political actor, implicitly making a moral judgment against a death emerging out of agential political resistance.

Fida'iyyin as iconic national heroes

> The [anti-colonial] rebels were laughed at because of their insistence on wearing khaki uniforms. Obviously, they hoped to be considered soldiers and treated in accordance with the rules of war. There is profound meaning to this emphatic desire, as it was by this tactic that they laid claim to and wore the dress of history.
>
> Albert Memmi, *The Colonizer and the Colonized*

The roots of the commemoration of martyrdom, the elevation of the figure of the martyr to national hero, and the standardized set of narratives that are told about the hero (including that of the brave mother who sends her fighting son to battle) are neither immutable "cultural" characteristics of Palestinians, nor solely a consequence of Islamic or Islamist teachings. Palestinian narratives valorizing martyrs and their journey to death have transformed over time and through necessary adaptations not only to local conditions and institutional changes, but also to transformations in available transnational discourses and systems of representations. In fact, the figure of the martyr in early Palestinian iconography is inseparable from the figure of the *fida'yi*, whose heyday was in the 1960s and 1970s.

The (re)emergence of the figure of *fida'yi* as the romantic hero (Jallul 1994: 35) of Palestinian national iconography dates back to the 1960s, when the national movement began actively to recruit in Palestinian refugee camps throughout the Arab world.[15] The success of the recruitment effort depended on the degree to which political organizations were willing to deploy violence to achieve their ends. Fatah's Khalid al-Hassan recalls that "the real increase, the real support that comes from the people, and permanently, started in '65 when we started our military action. Then the people realised that we were not

---

[15] In Ottoman times, *fida'iyyin* were specially trained soldiers who undertook dangerous missions and in discourses about them "the element of martyrdom and suicide was not at all predominant" (Norton 2003). The irregular combatants who fought against the British and Zionists in Palestine in the mid-1930s were also called *fida'iyyin*. Deploying the iconography of the past insurrections, however, does not necessarily mean that the Palestinian national symbols in the 1960s and in pre-1948 Palestine are one and the same. Picaudou, for example, does not see the *fida'yi* as a continuation of historic identity, but as a reborn and newly constructed one (1989: 113).

just another movement, talking like the others" (Cobban 1984: 25).[16]
The nascent Palestinian movement rooted itself in a history of Arab/
Palestinian insurrection, identified itself in solidarity with other anti-
colonial and anti-imperial revolutionary movements, and chose guerrilla
warfare as the primary strategy of its *thawra* (revolution), which was
intended to "increase Palestinian 'self-awareness'" (Abu Jihad quoted
in Sayigh 1997: 82) and be the catalyst for a mass movement, with the
aim of "liberation of the homeland" (Abu Iyad 1981: 36–37).[17] The
guerrilla embodied ideas of armed resistance and revolution, and the
iconography surrounding the guerrillas was reproduced in daily usage
and social and ritual interactions in the camps. This iconography
included postcard images of guerrillas running over hills with their guns
in hand, and factional newspaper photographs celebrating them. The
keffiyeh as the sartorial emblem of resistance became part of this iconography, as did the celebration of such figures as Leila Khaled, whose
aeroplane hijackings were much admired. The *fida'iyyin* were celebrated
in songs and in plays. They were feted at factional parties and political
festivals. They were even objects of European admiration: Gerard
Chaliand and Jean Genet both wrote long essays about the *fida'iyyin*,
with the latter – *Un captif amoureux* – reading like a love-letter to strong
and manly men whose every motion was meaningful and whose every
action decisive.

Even before the Cairo Accord of 1969, which granted Palestinians
autonomy in managing the camps and sanctioned their strategy of
armed resistance in southern Lebanon, guerrillas had begun to appear
in the camps, and refugees who had resented the interference and

---

[16] Yezid Sayigh (1997: 681) records jumps in Fatah recruitment after every *fida'yi*
operation.

[17] Palestinians chose armed struggle as their strategy of resistance because of (a) the
experience of violent expulsion by Zionist forces in 1948, and the desire to emulate the
victory of the Zionist forces; (b) the dispersion of Palestinians across several borders
preventing mass mobilization; (c) the experience of protest and political activism
against Israel as part of the Muslim Brotherhood or other local organizations (Sayigh
1997: 83); (d) the combat experience of many cadres of future guerrilla organizations
as officers in various Arab armies (Sayigh 1997); (e) the desire for independence from
Arab powers and their military decision-making apparatus (Sayigh 1997: 87–92); (e)
repressive Arab regimes preventing mass mobilization of any other sort (Sayigh 1997:
86); and (g) a desire to express an "independent will, a proof of existence" (Sayigh
1997: 91; Cobban 1984: 95). "In fact, from the perspective of over twenty years,
armed struggle can be seen to have had far more impact on the Palestinians themselves
than on its intended target, Israel, where the effect has been at best mixed. At an early
stage, armed struggle turned the Palestinian nearly overnight into the vanguard of the
post-1967 Arab struggle against Israel. It thus helped restore a sense of dignity to a
people whose self-respect had been cruelly eroded by their expulsion by Israel and
subsequent suppression by the Arab regimes" (Khalidi 1989: 119; also see Cobban
1984: 245, 253).

harassment of the *Deuxième Bureau* in their lives supported the armed *shabab*. Umm Shakir recalls:

[In 1965] I was five years old and I had just stepped outside when I saw two *fida'yi* guerrillas and they had their faces covered with *keffiyehs* and only their eyes could be seen. I became frightened and started crying and one of them picked me up, and tried to quieten me. My mother came out of the house, took me from him and told them "go, run, go son, go hide!" Then she said to me "if someone asks you why you are crying say that you saw a dog." Then the Lebanese secret police came up and they asked my mother "why is your daughter crying?" My mother said, "she saw a dog" and the security men looked at me and said "why are you crying?" I said "I saw a dog." They went away and I asked my mother "but you have told us not to lie," and my mother said "this kind of lying was necessary to protect the *fida'iyyin.*" I remember that must have been my first political memory. Maybe even because of that memory I decided to become active. (Beirut, 1 December 2001)

The emergence of the Palestinian armed resistance, however, was met with some ambivalence even in the camps: political factions undermined the traditional hierarchies imported from the villages into the camps, though village elders adapted to the situation by taking on the role of mediators between rival factions (Sayigh 1994: 98). The armed presence of PLO factions in the camps and their often arrogant and undisciplined behavior towards both camp Palestinians (Sayigh 1994: 94) and their Lebanese neighbors (Khalidi 1979: 115–116; Sayigh 1997: 512) often provoked resentment towards the organization and its leadership. But despite these shortcomings, the political organizations changed the face of the camps, and the guerrillas in particular came to be not only iconic figures, but also concrete embodiments of social mobilization.

Joining armed factions entitled the young men and women to privileges henceforth unknown: they were taught reading and writing (Peteet 1991: 194) and organizational skills, they were provided with a communal environment in which some of the more restrictive social norms such as the interaction of women and men were circumspectly loosened (Peteet 1991: 134) and where men and women were paid a monthly salary that would allow them to moderately upgrade their families' standard of living. Taking up arms and joining one of the political factions was considered not only a matter of national pride but also a much-needed vocation, when even low-paying jobs were nearly unattainable for Palestinians. While prosaically the guerrilla would also be a bread-earner, he (or increasingly she) also became the warrior of the family, a source of familial pride and prestige (Sayigh 1994: 97), perceived as restoring the lost honor of the community through a mythico-heroic presence. A former guerrilla, who at the time of our interview had laid down arms for two years and owned a shop, remembered his military tour with nostalgic fondness:

As a civilian, you don't do anything. You are lazy; you sit around, drink coffee and visit with people. But as a military person ... First of all, military life is respected, it teaches you discipline, bravery, pride of your dignity, ethics, how to treat people. Which is why I prefer military life. Even, with the arrests, the torture, the fighting. You know the *sabra* (prickly pear) cactus? It hurts when you pick it, but when you eat it, you enjoy it. [Being a *fida'yi*] was the same for me. It was my aim in life to fight, so when I was wounded I was happy to get better and fight some more. My main idea was to give something to my homeland and I was happy with that. When you stop doing that, you are useless. (Abu Husayn, Burj al Barajna, 14 February 2002)

The figure of the guerrilla was significant in other ways: the armed groups to some extent undermined ascriptive class designations. First, the founders and leaders of the new Palestinian political organizations were not the former scions of notable land-owning families who were taught to have caused the failure of the pre-1948 Palestinian national project, but rather educated sons of middle-class families, almost all of them refugees (Khalidi 1997: 180; Sayigh 1997: 87). More important, the institutional modes associated with the training of the *fida'iyyin* (rather than the bureaucratic management of the political factions) also reinforced a perceived egalitarianism and promoted the myth of the guerrilla as new proto-citizens overcoming both modern and traditional social categories. The trainees in the camps traversed many class (and national) barriers and not only included Palestinian students, camp residents, and members of the professional and middle classes, but also Arabs and non-Arabs who had come to fight alongside the Palestinians (Çandar 2000; Sayigh 1997: 511). That the nascent national movements of Palestine in the 1950s and 1960s chose *fida'yi* (redeemer) rather than *mujahid* (holy warrior) as the moniker for their fighters, subtly points to a religion-neutral, even secular, notion of self-sacrifice. During the time that the *fida'yi* was the primary national symbol of Palestinians, references to martyrdom persisted in the narratives and practices valorizing the guerrilla, but these references were secondary to guerrilla warfare and the *fida'yi* was considered to be the primary iconic figure.

From *fida'yi* to martyr

Transformations in commemorating Palestinian heroic figures – from the *fida'yi* to the *shahid* – came about as a result of local, regional, and international changes. The 1982 evacuation of PLO guerrillas from

Lebanon – being "cast out of the Revolution's paradise" ('Ayid 1984: 180) – and the defeat of Palestinians and their partners against Israel and its allies in Lebanon were perhaps the most decisive local factors in the gradual disappearance of the *fida'yi* from the camps' ranks of celebrated icons, lore, and practices. The departure of guerrilla fighters – one of whose first rules of engagement according to Che Guevara is preservation of the guerrilla's life (Guevara 1961: 25; 46) – downgraded the importance of self-preservation as a fundamental element of resistance, at least in the domain of revolutionary rhetoric. The proliferation of violent death and martyrdom as a result of successive massacres, sieges of Beirut more generally and the camps more specifically, and massive and indiscriminate Israeli bombing of Palestinian camps in Lebanon also contributed to the demise of the elite heroic figure of the fighter and generalization of martyrdom among the unwilling martyrs. Locally, the emergence of Hizbullah – whose ideology of resistance relied on martyrdom as both a means to an end and as an end in itself – also influenced the practices of hero-commemoration.

Regionally, the start of the first Intifada in the OPT, where tactics of resistance included mass mobilization, general strikes, demonstrations, stone-throwing, and not guerrilla or commando operations contributed to the fading away of the figure of the *fida'yi*. The rhetorical changes can be seen in the way in which various PLO organs shifted their attention from the Children of RPG – the Palestinian teen agers who took up rocket-propelled grenades to fight the Israeli military during its invasion of Lebanon – to the Children of Stone – the stone-throwing children of the OPT. The PLO's open acknowledgment of its statist project and its relinquishing of "terror" at the end of 1988 reduced its reliance on guerrillas, at the very same time that Hamas – joining Islamist discourse with nationalism – extensively promulgated symbols of martyrdom in the OPT. In return, secular groups tried to ride Hamas's coat-tails: "[m]indful of growing Islamic influence and the rising role of Islam as an effective factor in mobilising the masses, the nationalists ... resorted to the frequent use of Islamic references" (Abu Amr 1994: 86). Israel's deportation of over 400 Islamist militants to southern Lebanon at the end of 1992 helped export a Palestinian version of Islamism to Lebanon's Palestinian communities, while at the same time inculcated the deportees with Hizbullah's tactics, strategies, and symbolic language. After the Oslo Accords, the refugees in Lebanon, Jordan, and Syria feared that their right of return would be bargained away in return for a Palestinian state, and the Islamist organizations that were not party to negotiations with Israel, found much more sympathy in the Palestinian camps in Lebanon.

Internationally, the failure of the Soviet Union resulted in the termination of ideological and financial support for Marxist insurrectionary groups, among them Palestinian organizations, leading to shifts in the ideological underpinning of many such groups, and the receding of secularist notions of armed resistance; to be replaced in the Middle East with the Islamist version which had proved triumphant during the Iranian revolution of 1978/1979. Logistically and practically, mosques could act as safe havens and foci of meetings and gatherings under the watchful eyes of the Lebanese army and hostile militants, and Friday prayers were useful as starting points for demonstrations, both contributing to the increasing predominance of Islam-centered narratives in Palestinian commemorations (Budeiri 1997: 201).

The consequence of these political transformations over the last two decades of the twentieth century was a lessening of celebration of the secular, actively resistant guerrilla fighter, and the replacement of his heroic figure with that of the martyr, whose death and iconography accommodated religious narratives of self-sacrifice. As guerrilla warfare receded, martyrdom was given a privileged position in heroic commemorations. For example, in 1978, *Il al-Imam*, the organ of the PFLP–GC, called a guerrilla operation which had resulted in the death of the *fida'iyyin*, a suicide operation, (*'amaliyya intihariyya*) (14 April 1978: 4–5). In commemorating the same operation in 1996, *Il al-Imam* had begun referring to it as a martyrdom operation (*'amaliyya istishhadiyya*) (30 November 1996: 18–19). Furthermore, a wider variety of deaths can be construed as martyrdom, including deaths during bombings and accidental shootings, thus egalitarianizing martyrdom. This egalitarianization means that activist *shabab* or assassinated leaders are no longer the only people who would be known as heroes of self-sacrifice, and further it means that intentionality in seeking martyrdom is no longer required in order to acquire the honor and prestige that goes with it. More poignantly, mundane and accidental deaths of bystanders can acquire a meaning that they otherwise would not have had.

These symbolic and rhetorical changes were also reflected in institutional ones: theatre and music education in the summer schools established by various political factions in the camps that used to glorify the figure of the guerrilla, now paid homage to martyrs. During the 1960s and 1970s, group dances and skits included children who wore fatigues and carried toy guns; when the camps became habitable again after the end of the Lebanese civil war in the 1990s, children's performances began to include martyred child figures, shot by Israeli soldiers during stone-throwing. The shooting of 12-year-old Muhammad Al-Durra in September 2000 created an archetypal figure of commemoration for

Palestinian children in the camp, and several dance groups renamed themselves "Muhammad Al-Durra Folk Group." These institutional changes did not happen as a result of centralized orders (which in the fragmented and fractious atmosphere of post-civil war Palestinian camps would be impossible), but rather were propagated center by center, performance by performance and through the extant networks of social workers, theatre teachers and NGO activists interacting with one another at various commemorative events.

Conclusions

In this chapter, I have written about commemorations of martyrs in the Palestinian camps in Lebanon. Through a close reading of commemorative practices valorizing martyrs and contextualising these practices in historical and institutional processes, I have shown the unstable and changing meaning of martyrdom and guerrilla warfare in Palestinian national narratives. I have shown that interpretations of the act of self-sacrifice may in fact differ from the intent of the act for the martyr and that a single act of martyrdom can be represented in multivalent ways. In institutional commemorative practices performed for audiences of refugees and potential nationalist activists, the martyr concretizes Palestinian nationalist history, celebrates self-sacrifice, and reminds those left behind of a community shared by the dead and the living whose boundaries are defined by the nation. When performed for foreign audiences, the martyr reveals the suffering of the Palestinians, legitimating their demands, and calling upon the outsiders' sympathy and solidarity.

In earlier decades of Palestinian armed resistance, the tragic narrative of self-sacrifice was subsumed to the ideology of active resistance, which was itself bolstered through the intricate and complex network of social relations and institutions emerging around the guerrillas and the armed organizations. The image of the *fida'yi* emerged when, taking inspiration from other anti-colonial and nationalist movements, an ethos of armed resistance led to the upsurge in guerrilla activism among the refugees. Later, however, the defeat and exodus of militant Palestinian organisations from Lebanon, the proliferation of civilian deaths during the Lebanese civil war and Israeli invasion of Lebanon, and the emergence of NGOs whose audiences included foreign institutions and communities, all contributed to the commemoration of martyrdom as a symbol of collective suffering. Discourses of martyrdom are polyvalent and marry transnational heroism, Islamism, and a vocabulary of suffering.

With the proliferation of martyrs for the cause, commemorative practices, rituals, and narratives not only mobilize the refugees around a national cause, but also give meaning to daily violent deaths. The nearly universal experience of loss and communal remembrances of martyrs create an imagined community of resistance or suffering and translate the private losses of Palestinians into a national narrative of meaningful and purposive self-sacrifice.

7   Between battles and massacres:
commemorating violent events

Grief is a white bird
That does not come near the battlefields.
Soldiers sin who grieve.
Over there I was a machine, spitting out fire and death,
Turning space into a black bird.

Mahmud Darwish, "A Soldier Dreams of White Lilies"

We could not find a thing to show our own identity except our blood in
stains upon the wall.

Mahmud Darwish, "Beirut"

In the aftermath of the first bloody siege of Shatila by the Amal militia in
1985, Umm Muhammad, resident of Shatila, declared that the siege
wasn't "the first massacre that has been committed against us. Since
1947 our lives have been affected by them. My four children and husband were killed at the hand of the Israelis and the *Kata'ib* in the Sabra
and Shatila massacres – even those Lebanese who were married to
Palestinians were killed there" (*al-Hurriyya*, 8 Feb. 1985: 14). For
Umm Muhammad, the siege was unambiguously one in a long chain of
massacres committed against Palestinians. It was the historic persistence
of massacres that created an "us" against whom atrocities were committed. This "us" was the Palestinian refugee, whose political identity
was so dangerous that even Lebanese citizens *married* to Palestinians
were targets of violence. While Umm Muhammad considered the War
of the Camps – as the successive sieges of the camp by Amal came to be
known – as one massacre in a chain of massacres, the conflict has also
been described as a heroic battle, *and* as an example of quotidian
steadfastness. Battles and massacres are the iconic events at the very
center of Palestinian nationalist commemoration.

This chapter is about the story of the nation as refracted through
commemoration of iconic events. More specifically, this chapter
examines how battles and massacres can be commemorated as heroic or
tragic, depending on circumstances and audiences. Here, I first show

150

historical shifts in narratives of commemoration by interrogating the iconization of heroic battles during the *Thawra* and their later replacement by tragic commemorations of massacres. This transformation meant that battles which were so crucial to Palestinian national narrative in the 1960s and 1970s later receded to the background of the national imaginary, at least in Lebanon, and massacres came to the forefront of nationalist commemoration. These historical shifts can also be traced in the variable commemorations of different massacres. I argue that the layering of one massacre or battle (and its story and commemoration) over another – and the persistence of some narratives at times and their oblivion at others – indicate that not only are stories of nations habitually crafted and retold, but that the choice of events made into coherent commemorative narratives reveals the complexities and contours of changing politics (Trouillot 1995).

Second, I argue that the coherence of a singular national narrative can be subverted by the polyvalence of particular commemorated events. This polyvalence prevails especially in transitional periods, where the institutional infrastructure which reproduces national narratives is damaged or inconsequential. By analyzing the War of the Camps of which Umm Muhammad speaks, I show the ambiguity and multivalence of nationalist commemoration.

Battles as icons of militant nationalism

Each army has its poets and its historians.
Mahmud Darwish, "On a Canaanite Stone at the Dead Sea"

In 1968, on the threshold of the *Thawra*, a Fatah spokesman explained the organization's use of violence as a tactic of struggle by stating, "we waited and waited for justice from the United Nations, for the justice of the world ... but nothing happened ... the only way to return to our homes and land is [by] armed struggle" (quoted in Sharabi 1969: 198). By 1993, however, Fatah and the PLO leaders had declared their willingness to shift from armed to political struggle, and recognized Israel and the UN resolutions pertaining to the conflict (Abbas 1995; Al-Hassan 1992). Like many concurrent anti-colonial and liberationist struggles, throughout the *Thawra*, the most important elements of Palestinian nationalism "alongside national dress and national dances" (*al-Hadaf*, 29 August 1981: 14–15) was *bunduqiyya* – the "culture of the gun" – but by the 1990s, valorization of battle and guerrillas had lost its primacy as the symbolic representation of Palestinian national struggle. This transformation came about because from the very outset the "culture of the gun" was not an autonomous cultural construct stemming from some essential propensity of Palestinians to violence, but rather it was a tactic associated with distinct political institutions and nationalist agendas as well as an authorized transnational discourse of resistance. The "battle" was portrayed as a concrete means of achieving a Palestinian state, as battles had been waged to liberate Algeria, for example. But symbolically, the representation of the "battle" in Palestinian commemorative iconography encapsulated and encouraged such nationalist virtues as self-sacrifice for the nation and the "heroic" defense of national identities. A significant element of this heroic narrative was the valorization and militarization of masculinity (Sharoni 1996:111; Collins 2000: 103). Dispossession of Palestinians of their land and properties, eviction from their homeland, and the defeat of 1948 and 1967 were considered to have been blights on Palestinian honor (Amireh 2003: 751; Humphries and Khalili forthcoming), which only a "reclaiming of their manhood" (Fanon 1986) through battle could remedy.[1]

At the height of the *Thawra*, battles were considered not only as the continuation of politics by other means, but also as fulfillment of Palestinian destinies. Various political factions argued that battles were transformative events occasioning changes not only in the political arena, but also in the very "Palestinian personality" (*Filastin al-Thawra*, 19 March 1978: 6). In fact, the *commemoration* of the battles – rather than the events themselves – was the most transformative element about them, since commemoration articulated and promulgated particular national narratives; and because most battles against unequally powerful adversaries ended in military defeats anyway. That battles were represented as constitutive of identities could be seen in the way modern battles were made heir to ancient wars. In these commemorative narratives the pivotal battle of Karama, which marked the beginning of full-scale armed struggle, was placed alongside the battles of "Dhu Qar, Yarmuk, Qadisiyah, and Hittin" which were "critical points in Arab and Islamic conquests" (Johnson 1982: 91).[2] Creating this unbroken chain of heroism appropriated the past as part of the nationalist present, and naturalized an ancient history as the essential story of the emergence of the nation.

---

[1] Ashish Nandy similarly argues that colonization in India had the effect of "feminising" Indian men, and the anti-colonial discourse was imbued with masculinity (Nandy 1983).

[2] At Dhu Qar (604) the Arabs defeated the Persians. At Yarmuk (636) the Arabs defeated the Byzantine Empire and captured Damascus. At Qadisiyah (637) the Arabs defeated the Persians and captured Persia. At Hittin (1187), the forces of Salah al-Din defeated the Crusaders and captured Jerusalem.

The battle was also an unsurpassable site of recovery of dignity (Massad 1995: 477–8). Despite relatively numerous Palestinian casualties in most decisive battles, most former fighters I interviewed continued to commemorate the fighting in glowing terms. One man recalled the resistance against Israeli invasion by sweeping aside the possibility that the fighting could have been a source of suffering or loss:

My memories of [the invasion] are not like those of the other people who suffered, because I was moving from one place to another, fighting. (Abu Ahmad, Burj al-Barajna, 6 February 2002)

Another former guerrilla recounted a particularly bloody episode in defense of Beirut against incessant Israeli bombardment during the summer of 1982, recalling by name and village of origin the fallen and the injured, and yet his manners were nostalgic, almost dreamy, and he ended his story by aesthetizing the battle:

The condition was very bad in Hayy Sallum. The fighting was individual because there were no orders to fight. Only the group of Colonel Sayil, God rest his soul, were fighting against the Israelis, and many of them were killed there. Just one person survived and he was injured. Syrian helicopters came to fight in the Khalda area with the guys from Fatah, and even there people were killed in large numbers. One guy lost his legs right in front of us. The fighting was very hard and very beautiful. (Abu Husayn, Burj al Barajna, 14 February 2002)

The idea of a common fate, camaraderie and rituals bring fighters closer, and in commemorations of battles they are tropes which represent the battle as dangerous – thus worthy of men – but gratifying endeavors (Bourke 1999: 141–146). Retrospective celebration of camaraderie casts the rosy glow of courage upon bloody wars, capturing honor from death. As one former Turkish guerrilla fighting with Fatah would later recount:

Israeli mortars and gunfire were whistling above our heads, and helicopters were hovering over us, illuminating our defensive lines. We started to sing the Resistance song, "The Martyr's Testimony" and even put on our bayonets. We were convinced we were going to die. (Çandar 2000: 81)

Courage in the face of death is a central element of the battle mystique and a necessary trope in iconizing battles. Iconization transforms a concrete event, object, or being into a symbol. It is the process by which an event is decontextualized, shorn of its concrete details and transformed into an abstract symbol, often empty, which can then be instrumentalized as a mobilizing tool by being "filled" with necessary ideological rhetoric. Thus, in the process of iconization, social and political events are wrapped in the cloak of national piety, sacralized, and made worthy of sacrifice (Anderson 1991: 144; Sayigh 1997: 208).

Fighting in the battle for the nation then gains the kind of legitimacy that is usually reserved for fighting for God, and the grace of such sacrifice is reinforced through commemorative artefacts, rituals, and monuments.

With the adoption of armed struggle as the primary – if not sole – means of nationalist resistance in the 1960s and early 1970s, militant political factions began commemorating "battles" in visual artefacts and ceremonies. Armed resistance was celebrated as a vanguard of "the masses" arising from refugee tents. Photographs of guerrillas at battle throughout the years of the *Thawra* (1969–1982) in Lebanon contain a great deal of heroic markers in them: young and virile men, sometimes with the shoulder-length hair fashionable at the time, laughingly prepare to enter conflict. The posters for the Battle of Karama in particular display these iconic elements. One Fatah poster celebrates the guerrillas arm-in-arm with Jordanian military men and other "Liberation Forces," with ammunition belts criss-crossing their chests, and their *keffiyehs* slung across their shoulders or on their heads, while DFLP posters show young guerrillas (a Japanese recruit among them) running across the hills into battle (Ridhwan 1992). During the War of the Camps – whose status as both battle and massacre lends itself to multiple interpretations – the PFLP's *al-Hadaf* (10 June 1985: 27) illustrated with a photograph an article en-titled "Diaries of *Sumud* and Heroism" about the siege of the camp. In the photograph a young injured fighter sits upon a chair, legs spread wide in a masculine pose and his Kalashnikov is at the ready in his arms. The man's shirt is open to the waist giving the image a perceptible air of heroic masculinity, if not outright sexual virility. The man may be wearing bandages around his injured chest, but his con-fident hand resting upon the gun, his manly posture, and his open shirt all bespeak a jaunty heroism.

This valorization of the national heroic was present in all the factions' combination of "nationalism, quasi-Marxism, and Tier-Mondism [*sic*]," and was representative of the wave of anti-colonialist movements then sweeping Africa, Asia, and Latin America (Çandar 2000: 68). "Battles" in which the newly trained guerrillas' – and by extension, the "new" Palestinians' – mettle was tested and where camaraderie was forged in practice, were celebrated as the seedbed of the new *Thawra* and the site of its reproduction and renewal. Fighting in battle was considered a virtue, as it recuperated lost honor, transformed "passive" refugees into active fighters, and as some leftist political organizations claimed subverted social hierarchies such that "traditional" Palestinians became "modern" through their taking up arms. Commemoration of battle also allowed for judicious re-interpretation and re-membering of events such that even defeats in battle could be portrayed as political victories, helping to bring the organizations' political aims closer.

Heroic defeats

> You remember those days – women and tears and rice and shots fired into the air. . . . A defeated army withdrawing like victors! . . . Mothers filled the place, and young men were eating and weeping. Food and tears, that was the farewell. Mothers opening food wrapped in cloths and young men eating, and ululations and bullets.
>
> Elias Khoury, *Gate of the Sun*

A significant feature of the heroicization of battles has been the transformation of defeats into victories in subsequent commemoration. The Battles of Karama and Beirut as iconic symbols of Palestinian armed struggle share one prominent trait: they were both military failures that official institutions have commemorated and reinterpreted as political victories.[3] Rashid Khalidi (1997: 195–6) traces narratives of "failures as triumphs" to the Mandate years, and explains that "such a portrayal draws on the Palestinians' perception that throughout their modern history, they have faced a constellation of enemies so formidable as to be nearly insuperable" and that survival in the face of such insurmountable odds is a form of victory. Even a total catastrophe such as the defeat of Palestinian factions by the Jordanian military in September 1970, which was followed by a massacre of Palestinian civilians in the camps, was feted in internal Fatah documents as the "miraculous achievements" in Jordan, where Fatah had "triumphed politically even as we retreated militarily" (quoted in Sayigh 1997: 286). Accounts of the Battles of Karama and Beirut demonstrate the reinterpretation processes at work in subsequent commemoration of these battles.

On 21 March 1968, in retaliation for cross-border guerrilla operations, about 15,000 Israeli troops, supported by helicopters and armored vehicles attacked the village of Karama on the east bank of the Jordan River. Fatah, which had been alerted to the possibility of the attack decided to defend the village. Around 300 Fatah guerrillas who were eventually supported by Jordanian artillery stayed in the village to fight. The guerrillas, exhibiting what Abu Iyad (1981: 59) later commemorated as "suicidal heroism," killed 28 Israeli soldiers and captured

---

[3] Defining defeats as victories is not limited to Palestinians. Yael Zerubavel (1995: 220–1) describes the Israeli popularization of the Bar Kokhba revolt as a victory, and explains that "offering armed resistance to the enemy is commemorated as a symbolic victory in itself, above and beyond the historical outcome of that act."

12 tanks, while Fatah lost 120–200 guerrillas. Because of the losses suffered by the Israeli military, the battle was cast as a victory and celebrated throughout the Arab world. Even King Husayn of Jordan had declared: "We shall all be *fida'iyyin* soon" (Cobban 1948: 48). Although in military terms, Karama had resulted in massive losses for Fatah's fledgling forces, "by the thousands, by the tens of thousands, young and old flocked to join Fatah" (Abu Iyad 1981: 60). For a while, the battle became the central battle of the revolution, serving to bolster the heroic version of Palestinian nationalism (Terrill 2001). Karama made Arafat the unchallenged leader of Fatah and gave Palestinians a foothold in Jordan for their cross-border military operations (Sayigh 1997: 681). Only four months after Karama (which coincidentally means "dignity" in Arabic), the Fourth Palestinian National Council amended the Palestinian National Charter to reflect a shift in strategy towards armed struggle (Cobban 1983: 43).

Commemorating Karama six years later, and in the throes of the *Thawra* in Lebanon, Fatah's *Filastin al-Thawra* wrote that "the Karama battle was the greatest test of all, and for the first time, Palestinian training camps graduated fighters on this blessed day, this dawn of hope. ... And the army that could not be defeated was defeated ... and the gun was raised upon the shoulder of the Palestinian fighter to continue the long and fierce battle" towards the nation-state (*Filastin al-Thawra*, 15 December 1974: 8). In his biography of Arafat, Alan Hart (1989: 246) counts other reasons why Karama could be considered a political victory: armed struggle was intended "to keep the idea of struggle alive" and to ensure the persistence of the nationalist ideology. It also aimed "to teach the Israelis a lesson and to give the Arab nation an example" (1989: 261). He adds that Karama "did not take away the burden of shame that all Arabs had carried since 1948, and to which a great weight was added in 1967; but [it] did make the burden lighter and more easy to bear" (1989: 263). Karama had become that moment of victory necessary for nationalist self-imagining.[4] Abu Iyad (1981: 60) saw it as the clarion call of liberation and the turning point for "the Palestinian masses [who were] jeered and humiliated for decades" and now felt pride and hope. Ceremonies commemorating the Battle of

---

[4] Though in subsequent commemorations, Karama was remembered as a victory, there are some indications that internal dissent challenged this view. For example, in his introduction to a series of eyewitness testimonies on the Karama battle, Hadi Abu Aswan wrote that there had been much critique of the Karama battle, but that the testimonies he was prefacing were not supposed to address these critiques (1972: 197). In effect, this brief sentence pointed to perhaps extensive internal debates surrounding the strategies and consequences of Karama, but none of these debates seem to have been documented.

Karama were held frequently and were often used to comment upon contemporary political events. On 25 March 1976, on the eve of the Sinai negotiations between Egypt and Israel and after heavy fighting in the first bloody round of the Lebanese Civil War, Abu Mahir Yamani, one of the leaders of the PFLP, used his speech at a Karama memorial ceremony to refer to the treachery of Arab regimes and insist that the Battle of Karama has "taught Palestinians that the only thing they could depend on were themselves, *bunduqiyya* (the gun), bullets, *sumud*, and martyrdom" (*Filastin al-Thawra*, 11 April 1976).

Karama continued its hold over the Palestinian national imagination until it ceded its place as the most decisive battle of the Israeli–Palestinian conflict to the "Battle of Beirut," which was by any measure bigger, longer, and more devastating. The "Battle of Beirut" was the name given to the bloody resistance of Palestinian guerrillas alongside a coalition of Lebanese nationalist forces against a large-scale assault by the Israeli military on the city of Beirut in the summer of 1982. The two-month-long battle culminated in a month-long siege of the city where West Beirut's electricity and water were severed by the Israeli military and their allies, the city's residential neighborhoods and civilian infrastructure (including hospitals and shelters) were heavily bombarded, and several Palestinian refugee camps in the occupied areas were totally destroyed.

Throughout the Battle of Beirut, "seemingly small things like the shooting down of an A-4 Skyhawk and capture of a pilot, Captain Aharon Ihyaz, near Beaufort on June 6, or the initial failures of Israeli amphibious landings at Rashidiyeh and in the Zahrani area on the same day, *had an encouraging effect out of all proportion to their actual importance*, even as reverses elsewhere were being admitted" (Khalidi 1986: 74; emphasis added). The Battle of Beirut ended in August when after intense negotiations, the PLO was evacuated aboard tens of ships from the port of Beirut to other Arab and European capitals. On the morning of the scheduled departure of thousands of Palestinian guerrillas into their second or third exile, "thousands of sons of people gathered [at the Municipal Stadium] since sunrise, and there were sounds of applause and songs and ululation and dabke circles and sloganeering" (*Filastin al-Thawra*, 2 October 1982: 12). When the ships carrying the guerrillas set sail, the *fida'iyyin* were very visibly still "*carrying their personal arms* to signify that the evacuation was not the surrender Sharon had demanded" (Cobban 1984: 124; emphasis added). The defeat was already – somewhat ambiguously – being celebrated as a victory.

The fall of Beirut to Israel and its allies and proxy armies was followed by the massacres in Sabra and Shatila and by a long reign of terror over the camps by the state of Lebanon and various hostile militias which forcefully dismantled the social infrastructures the PLO had put into place over the previous decades. Successive waves of hostilities targeting the camps were followed by grassroots efforts at reconstruction inside the camps, while the Palestinian political leadership in exile was largely ineffective in influencing the lives of the refugees in Lebanon positively. Nevertheless, the Battle of Beirut was – in its immediate aftermath – cast as a victory in official political narratives.[5] Though Arafat bitterly complained that some of their Lebanese allies hadn't even lasted fifteen hours, much less fifteen days (quoted in Al-'Umd 1983c: 20), he nevertheless tallied the battle as something of a victory in which failure in fighting was offset by victories in provisioning of food, water, medicine, and telecommunications (1983c: 25). Others went even further. Fatah's Colonel Abu Musa – who shortly thereafter led a rebellion against Arafat – claimed:

It is incorrect to call what Beirut underwent "the siege of Beirut." There is nothing called "the siege of Beirut." What we have is the "*sumud* of Beirut." There is a difference between siege and *sumud*. Siege means that the besieged is waiting for his destiny to be determined by the encircling side. But *sumud* is something else entirely. The *sumud* of Beirut didn't mean that Israel could dictate the conditions of peace or exit or defeat ... It was only after the *Thawra* left Beirut that the Israeli military was able to invade it; not before then. (Abu Musa in Al-'Umd 1983a: 63)

Arafat variously labelled the Battle of Beirut as another Masada, which he defined as "defence of one's position and life to the point of martyrdom" (Arafat in Al-'Umd 1983c: 21), as the resistance of a David against a Goliath (Khalidi 1986: 90), as a "political victory snatched from the jaws of military defeat" (Brynen 1990: 179), and as a "legend of *sumud*" that "planted the seeds of great change for our people and our nation" (*Filastin al Thawra*, 2 October 1982: 12). In their subsequent assessment of the Battle of Beirut, the PFLP leaders declared that "the leadership of the Palestinian revolution led the process of military confrontation with courage and heroism, [and] also conducted the process of negotiation with proficiency" (Sayigh 1997: 542). Self-congratulatory assessments of the battle did not critically examine the political efficacy of militancy in the long-term, or the dangers of institutionalizing violence at the expense of alternative solutions, or the very apparent fact that

---

[5] The only exceptions to the glorification of the Battle of Beirut in its immediate aftermath seem to have come from Isam Sartawi and Shafiq al-Hut. At the PNC meeting in November 1982, Shafiq al-Hut, the PLO representative in Lebanon, denounced "those who would portray what had just happened in Lebanon as a victory, and accus[ed] them of lying to the Palestinian people." He was enthusiastically applauded (Khalidi 1997: 198–9).

successive Israeli governments feared a political solution far more than a military one (Morris 1997; Sayigh 1997:508; Shlaim 2000).

Popular commemorations of the Battle of Beirut, however, were more ambiguous. While the survival of the forces and their departures *with their armament* was acknowledged as something of a situational victory, uncertainties about the refugees' fate complicated the picture. Subsequent massacres in Sabra and Shatila reinforced this uncertainty and the circumstances following the massacres overwrote the narrative of the battle in the coming years. In a lament following the massacres of Sabra and Shatila, only shortly after the end of the Battle of Beirut, a woman wept:

Oh people, tell the world about what happened to the Palestinian people. Describe what happened to us.
Oh boat waiting in the port, on your return tell our beloved ones.
The days and the years glided away with the departure of my loved ones. It is a departure without return from exile, oh Palestinians!
Oh mother, my tears flow down my cheeks. Oh mother, where shall I go? I am already homeless in the land of the Arabs. I went to the sea, oh mother, to cast my net. And in the sea, I found that the net was lost. (Anonymous 1987: 2)

The lament contains not only ritual elements (grief for the departed, calling upon a mother, the evocation of being lost at sea), but also direct accusations against the host country which failed to protect the refugees ("I am already homeless in the land of the Arabs") and a world which stands by apathetically. As in other recorded laments of that time (Ang 1989: 6–8), standard refrains in the laments were here transformed into specific references to the devastation of the Battle of Beirut and what followed. The political victory of Palestinian political leaders was at some distance from the quotidian experience of the war for the hundreds of thousands of Palestinian refugees and Lebanese citizens. Where Arafat could define the "revolution as the succession of temporary setbacks until final victory" (quoted in Sayigh 1997: 286), those "temporary setbacks" were often devastating losses to the refugees whose uncertain lives in their repeatedly destroyed and reconstructed slums were to be made ever more catastrophic by the succession of massacres that followed defeats in battle.

Shifting between battles and massacres

My country, reiterated in massacres and songs.
Mahmud Darwish, "Psalm 2"

By the late 1980s, the center of Palestinian nationalist mobilization had shifted from the diaspora to the OPT, and the "Children of RPGs" had been replaced in Palestinian nationalist iconography by the "Children of Stones." Where during the *Thawra*, battles were considered the originary moments in which the nation's future was forged, by the time I conducted my research in the camps, the "battle" had lost much of its patina of nationalist glory. A 38-year-old Palestinian man responded to my query about his worst memories by saying:

I didn't have a childhood. My whole childhood was wars. As one war would end, another one would start. And even when there was no war, we never had any security, because we thought there could be a war tomorrow, and if not tomorrow, the day after tomorrow, and if not then, in a month. (Abu Said, Burj al-Barajna, 10 February 2002)

Abu Said and many others like him no longer regarded war as a constitutive component of Palestinian nationalism. War had lost its abstract heroism and had become a viscerally experienced lack of security and the ultimate symbol of uncertainty. "The battle" was no longer what made heroes out of children, but had rather become an affliction obliterating their childhood. Despite the fact that the Battle of Karama was still on the calendar of events to be commemorated at the offices of Fatah, none of the children in an after-school tutoring program run by an NGO in Shatila could tell me any concrete historical details about the battle itself. Some associated it with the Intifada and others with the Israeli invasion and occupation of Lebanon in the 1980s. This shift in knowledge about "the battle" as the central symbol of Palestinian resistance is significant, especially since "the battle" was such a pivotal construct of Palestinian national semiotics in the 1970s.

What had displaced "the battle" in the Palestinian nationalist narrative was the "massacre." During the *Thawra*, "the battle" as the focus of Palestinian nationalist commemoration was so significant that militant organizations defined even massacres as battles. For example, *Filastin al-Thawra* (15 December 1974: 9–10) described massacres as a form of battle in which revolutionary consciousness was forged. In 1975, *Filastin al-Thawra* wrote that "every body that fell in Dayr Yasin helped the *Thawra* towards victory" (*Filastin al-Thawra*, 13 April 1975). During the *Thawra* years, militant organisations described the massacre at Dayr Yasin as either a moment of failed resistance or another devastating loss in the Battle of Qastal (*Filastin al-Thawra*, 13 April 1975; *al-Hadaf*, 7 April 1990).[6]

---

[6] For a description of the Dayr Yasin massacre please see further below in the chapter. The Battle of Qastal in early April 1948 is notable for the death of the charismatic Palestinian military leader, Abd al-Qadir al-Husayni who fell during fighting on 9 April

During the *Thawra*, if an event included both violent clashes between armed units *and* the slaughter of civilians, the factions defined the event as a battle rather than a massacre. In the immediate aftermath of Tal al-Za'tar, all political organizations saw it as an instance of heroic struggle, "the symbol of Palestinian revolutionary existence, the evidence of reactionary fascism and of Syrian intervention, the symbol of power of *sumud*, the symbol of the cause" (*Filastin al-Thawra*, 8 August 1976: 6–7). Three years later, at the height of the Fakihani Republic, commemorating the "martyrdom and heroism" of Tal al-Za'tar, *Filastin al-Thawra* wrote, "after Karama, the Battle of Tal al-Za'tar was the first of its kind ... During the struggle, we learned new methods of confrontation and we made up for the shortage of supplies by finding new ways of using explosives and missiles. We came to depend on the expertise and creativity of our fighters, and of course, we gave many martyrs" (13 August 1979: 30–33). No mention was made of the hundreds of children who died of dehydration during the siege. Even where Tal al-Za'tar was not seen solely as an instance of armed struggle, it was considered to be transformative, changing women into fighters:

They take everything from us. Marriage, children, homes, stories, old people ... everything. So, all of the time, we defend ourselves as though we were not women, but [fighters] standing in the trenches. (Badr 1994: 260)

It was only after the evacuation of the guerrillas from Beirut and following the seismic shifts of the 1980s, that narratives of Tal al-Za'tar began to commemorate the suffering of civilians, rather than the glories of battle. After 1982, the primary organizations representing Palestinians in Lebanon were those advocacy and humanitarian organizations whose audiences were as much foreigners as local Palestinians. In their advocacy, presenting Palestinians as suffering victims could better mobilize sympathy in a world that many refugees said "had forgotten them." The shift in the representation of violent events from moments of resistance to instances of victimhood was repeated with other massacres as well. Forty days after the Fakihani bombing in 1981, the DFLP's *al-Hurriyya* attacked Begin, Reagan, and the silence of "American Arabs," and wrote of Fakihani as a glorious instance of heroism. The article did not appeal to the international community and repeatedly invoked the liberation of Palestine and the resistance of the *fida'iyyin*, rather than a claim to justice on the basis of the suffering of civilians (31 August 1981: 27–29). Twenty years later, and when tragic

1948. Qastal itself was close to Dayr Yasin and was a strategic point overlooking the road to Jerusalem (Shlaim 2000: 86).

narratives had come to the fore, the very same *al-Hurriyya* commemorated the event by quoting testimony from the international media (*Herald Tribune*, *New York Times*, etc.), called the bombing "terrorism" as defined by international law, and wrote of the victimhood of ordinary people and their suffering (28 July 2001: 22). The shift from heroism to tragedy was apparent. By 2001, the authorized discourse was one that at once appealed to international laws and international sympathies.

These transformations occurred not only because of militant factions losing power in camp politics, but also because of the fragmentation of the heroic narrative. After Oslo, commemoration of iconic massacres becomes a way of staking positions for or against Oslo, and by extension, for a nation-statist discourse or a liberationist one. To make matters more complicated, NGOs also had a hand in the act of representation, and even when affiliated with political factions, they constantly had to keep their international audiences in mind. This is apparent in the commemorative calendars of Fatah-related NGOs in Lebanon and Fatah in the OPT. In 2002 a Fatah-affiliated NGO in the Burj al-Shamali camp in southern Lebanon – which was considered a "model" NGO and was thus visited frequently by foreigners – carried a handwritten calendar commemorating significant days in Palestinian history. This calendar commemorated the Dayr Yasin Massacre (9 April 1948), the *Nakba* (15 May 1948), the beginning of the Palestinian *Thawra* (the first Fatah military raid on 1 January 1965), Martyrs' Day (7 January 1965),[7] the Karama Battle (21 March 1968), Land Day (30 March 1976),[8] the Fall of Tal al-Za'tar (16 August 1976), the Sabra and Shatila Massacres (17 September 1982), the beginning of the Intifada (9 December 1987), the massacre at the Ibrahimi Mosque (25 February 1994),[9] as well as the Balfour Declaration (2 November 1917)[10] and the Partition of Palestine (29 November 1947).[11] Of the twelve

---

[7] Fatah's Martyrs' Day which differs from the other organizations' commemorative day for martyrs marks the martyrdom of Ahmad Musa, the first Fatah martyr. Fatah has also celebrated 10 April – in 1973, the date of assassination of Kamal Udwan, Kamal Nasir and Yusif Najjar by Israeli commandos – as Martyrs' Day.

[8] To protest the Israeli state's seizures of lands owned by its Palestinian citizens, Palestinian residents of Galilee held demonstrations on 30 March 1976. Israeli police opened fire on the demonstrators and six Palestinians were killed and more than fifty were injured. The day became an important commemorative holiday celebrated by Palestinians everywhere.

[9] On 25 February 1994, an American settler in Hebron entered the Ibrahimi mosque and opened fire on those at prayer in the mosque. More than 20 men were killed.

[10] Balfour Declaration – issued by the British Foreign Secretary, Arthur Balfour, in November 1917 – marks the formal commitment of the British Empire to a Jewish state in Palestine.

[11] On 29 November 1947, on the basis of a Zionist plan endorsed by the United States, the UN General Assembly partitioned Palestine into an Arab and a Jewish state.

events commemorated, one-third (Dayr Yasin, Tal al-Zaʿtar, Sabra and Shatila, the Ibrahimi Mosque) were massacres. By contrast, calendars published by the Fatah political organization in the OPT – now firmly ensconced in the seat of PA power – overwhelmingly emphazise events which commemorate the emergence of the nascent state, such as peace accords, legislative elections, and Arafat's "homecoming" (Lindholm-Schulz 1999: 66–67). A Fatah-related NGO in Lebanon emphasizes a Palestinian history of suffering, whereas a Fatah party calendar in the OPT celebrates the triumphs of state-building. Each organization appeals directly to its local constituency, but the NGO is also aware of its foreign audience, and as such emphasizes the massacres.

Factional politics can be similarly gleaned from an editorial in the PFLP's *al-Hadaf* after the Ibrahimi Mosque (1994):

The Palestinian cause does not awaken the world conscience despite the [ongoing] murder of the *heroic* and *suffering* Palestinian people. Only massacres arouse the slumbering world conscience to recognise the cataract of Palestinian blood. They recognised Dayr Yasin and this recognition took the form of sympathy. They recognised Kafr Qasim and it took the form of compassion. When [Black] September [1970] came, the recognition was equivocal. Tal al-Zaʿtar arrived and the recognition came due to the world opinion. World conscience stood angry after Sabra and Shatila, but the anger blew over just as earth blew over the victims. In every instance, there was anger or pity or sympathy and yet the Palestinian suffering remains ... In the end, the matter is not about constant massacres, but related to the dreadful rhythm of suffering. This suffering is renewed and grows such that it defines the future of the Palestinian people. The massacre at Dayr Yasin pushes Palestinians out of their land. Massacres reach Palestinians who live in the camps of Jordan, and they slaughter those in Tal al-Zaʿtar, because Palestinians *refuse to be defenceless victims*; and massacres occur after Palestinians are *disarmed*. They go to the Palestinians of Sabra and Shatila at night and target them with gunships and car-bombs and mortars. (6 March 1994: 10–11; emphases added)

The passage is significant for several reasons. It emphasises massacres as the only means by which Palestinians can rouse an international audience. Celebration of heroic or liberationist nationalism does not appeal to the "world conscience" in the way suffering does. Thus far, this discourse is familiarly one espoused by NGOs. In 1994, when the editorial was written, the PFLP had lost much backing with the fall of the Soviet Union, was striving to be relevant, and in its struggle to find a legitimate discourse for Palestinian claim-making, it appealed to what had by then already become a familiar language of suffering. However, though the passage emphasizes Palestinian suffering, it rejects victimhood ("Palestinians refuse to be defenceless victims") and explains that disarmament can lead to victimhood. At the time the PFLP editors wrote this passage, the organization was actively opposing the concessions Arafat had made in Oslo and subsequent accords. This becomes even more apparent in the last paragraph, where the author of the editorial (Faisal Darraj) claims that the leaders (namely Arafat) who have announced that the "massacre will not stop the peace process" in fact "help the continuation of the massacre" (6 March 1994).

Where the above passage refuses victimhood and still tries to tie suffering and resistance together, other representations of massacres commemorate it as unalloyed pain and suffering. For example, on the twentieth anniversary of the Sabra and Shatila massacre, one of the central commemorative events was an exhibit of photographs of the massacre taken by Ryuichi Hirokawa. The exhibit was organized by the Palestinian NGO Forum – a body representing most major Palestinian NGOs in Lebanon, and Hirokawa's Sabra and Shatila photographs were shown alongside photographs of the re-invasion of Jenin by the Israeli military taken only months before the exhibit (*Daily Star*, 19 September 2002: 10). The photographs showed the bloated bodies of the massacred Palestinian men, women, and children; and those with invitations and access to the exhibition were mostly foreign NGO activists, visitors, scholars and journalists. The exhibition established a continuous line from one massacre to the next, with Sharon standing as the story's villain, constant through time.

Today, with the prevalence of NGOs in the camps, chronicles of atrocity – the narrative of successive massacres linked together through the Palestinian identity of their victims and their linkage across borders and calendar pages – are a crucial focus of Palestinian commemorations and a critical element of nationalist construction of Palestinian history. Almost all refugees in Lebanon have had a kin, friend, or acquaintance who has been a victim or survivor of a massacre over successive decades, and as such these narratives resonate with them. But interestingly, massacres are commemorated not only as important or constitutive events, but also as metaphors for the Palestinian predicament. Below, I examine massacres both as metaphor and as remembered event.

Massacre as a metaphor for the Palestinian predicament

Mass slaughter in the colonies at a certain stage of the embryonic development of consciousness increases that consciousness, for the hecatombs are an indication that between oppressors and oppressed everything can be solved by force.

Franz Fanon, *Wretched of the Earth*

Since the end of the *Thawra*, massacres have become a central motif of institutional Palestinian history. For example, the Palestinian Declaration of Independence issued by the 19th Session of the PNC in 1988 stated that "occupation, massacres, and dispersion had not deterred Palestinians from achieving their political goals" (quoted in Lockman and Beinin 1989: 396). The PNC thus placed massacres on the same footing as the occupation of Palestinian lands and the displacement of the refugees, both of which are determinative moments in twentieth-century Palestinian history. In the camps of Lebanon, this emphasis bears out: many of the "1948 generation" had personally witnessed or survived massacres in their villages. For others, the fear of impending massacres – about which they had heard through rumors and "whispering campaigns" (Masalha 1992: 179) – motivated their decision to abandon their villages until a safer time:

> There were [rumors] about Jewish gangs out to butcher the Arabs. This belief along with the ignorance of the Arabs at the time, and the people's fear for their honour, made them run away from the face of the shooting. (67-year-old Palestinian quoted in Yahya 1999: 27)

Utilization of massacres by extremist Zionist organizations and the Haganah, as tactics for evicting Arabs from Palestine between 1947 and 1949, is well documented though still the subject of intense controversy in Israel.[12] The massacre at Dayr Yasin is the best-known of these atrocities (Kana'ana and Zaytawi 1987; Khalidi 1999; McGowan and Ellis 1998). On 9 April 1948, Zionist guerrillas from Irgun and Lehi, with the aid and authorization of the Haganah, captured the village of Dayr Yasin, which had signed a non-aggression pact with neighboring Jewish settlements, and slaughtered "family after family" (Morris 1987: 113). Altogether some 100 civilians were murdered and others were raped and mutilated (Khalidi 1999; Morris 1987: 113). Dayr Yasin precipitated the exodus of many Palestinians (Morris 1987: 97; Kimmerling and Migdal 1993: 152). In a Knesset debate in 1949, Yaakov Meridor, the Herut representative claimed that "thanks to Deir Yassin [Israel] won the war" (Segev 1986: 89). The centrality of the Dayr Yasin massacre in the history of 1948 has given it a special place in Palestinian commemorations.

---

[12] Massacres recorded in scholarly literature include Dayr Yasin (Morris 1987: 114–116); al-Duwayma (Morris 1987: 222–223); Eilabun (Morris 1987: 229); Safsaf (Morris 1987: 230; Nazzal 1978: 95); Jish, Sa'sa, and Saliha (Morris 1987: 230); Majd al-Kurum (Morris 1987: 228; Nazzal 1978: 107); Ilut (Morris 2004: 253, fn. 57); Ain al-Zaytun, and Nasr al-Din (Nazzal 1978: 106–8). In his recently revised book, Morris cites "dozens" of massacres (2004). See the controversy surrounding the Tantura massacre (Pappé 2001).

After the establishment of the state of Israel, the Israeli military raided
villages both inside and outside the Green Line as a form of collective
punishment for guerrilla operations targeting both civilians and military
installations. These raids figure heavily in Palestinian commemorative
narratives and are usually categorized as massacres.[13] In October of
1972, in an article commemorating the massacres of Qibya and Kafr
Qasim – both of which had occurred in the month of October in the
1950s – *Filastin al-Thawra* (4 October 1972: 8) catalogues the attacks of
the IDF and its pre-1948 predecessors and adds that massacres have
become "part of Israeli policy which began with the slaughters of Dayr
Yasin and Lydda in 1949 [*sic*] and continued with the murder of civilians in the village of Kafr Qasim and al-Sumu', Tulkarm and Nahhalin
in the 1950s and terminated with the missile attacks against Jordanian
and Lebanese villages."

The massacres at Dayr Yasin, Qibya and Kafr Qasim have been
iconized as part of the Palestinian national narrative, and commemorating them has become routine. Neighborhoods in certain camps
(for example in the Yarmuk camp in Syria) have been named after Dayr
Yasin and Kafr Qasim massacres (Khaled 1998).[14] Each of these three
massacres stands as a symbol for a different category of aggression by the
Israeli military and its pre-state precursors: the massacre at Dayr Yasin
symbolizes violence against Palestinians leading to the establishment of
Israel, the massacre at Qibya stands for violence against the Palestinian
populations of the West Bank, and the massacre at Kafr Qasim as violence against the Palestinian citizens of Israel. Qibya came to have even
more significance to Palestinians in Lebanon after 1982. The officer in
charge of Unit 101 which committed the Qibya atrocities was Ariel
Sharon, who as the Israeli defence minister was held responsible by the
Kahan Commission (1982) for the massacres at Sabra and Shatila.

Interestingly, the iconization of the Dayr Yasin, Kafr Qasim and
Qibya massacres has been concurrent with the lack of commemoration,
acknowledgment and sometimes even knowledge of other massacres,

---

[13] The following massacres of civilians occurred in the 1950s and in response to guerrilla
attacks: the raids against Tulkarm on 20 May 1952 (Morris 1997: 222) and Nahhalin
on 22 April 1954 (Morris 1997: 315) left several civilians, including women and
children dead; Bureij (43 civilians killed on 29 August 1953) (Morris 1993: 255); and
Qibya (69 or 70 civilians killed on 14/15 October 1953) (Morris 1993: 257–265). The
massacre at Kafr Qasim (48 civilians killed on 29 October 1956) occurred on the eve of
the Suez war and was unprovoked (Robinson 2003; Morris 1993: 433, fn. 3). Morris
(1993: 259) writes that "most of the retaliatory strikes carried out – on Ben Gurion's
orders – before Qibya between 1949 and 1953 were explicitly designed to kill civilians
and their operational orders did not forbid harming women and children."

[14] In the same camp, there are neighborhoods named after the Battle of Karama and the
Battle of Qastal (Khaled 1998).

especially those occurring during the 1948 war. A survivor of the Safsaf massacre spoke of this neglect:[15]

I mean all these people talk about Deir Yassin, but the number of people killed in Deir Yassin is only a quarter of those who died in Safsaf, believe it by God. And they made a big deal about it, while in Safsaf 60 young men were killed after thirteen hours of resistance. So it wasn't by flight that people left Safsaf. (Jaber Yunis, 1997, Sidon, quoted in ARCPA 1998: 28)

Like all those who use their suffering to make claims, Jaber Yunis considers his own suffering paramount and unsurpassed. He is also vehement about the neglect of the memory of atrocities committed in 1948 by the Israeli military. This neglect can perhaps be attributed to the streamlined quality of commemorative practices of factions and NGOs, where proliferation of details can detract from the simplicity, narrative coherence, or visceral impact of a particular national narrative. Thus, while Dayr Yasin comes to stand – often in the abstract – as the generalized atrocity of the *Nakba*, Safsaf is forgotten by all but its survivors. The predominance of iconized massacres is bolstered by the unavailability of centralized resources for the kind of oral history projects that could have recorded the stories of similar massacres. Though during the *Thawra*, factional and independent publications commemorated Dayr Yasin, Qibya and Kafr Qasim on their pages, and though as early as 1974, Nafez Nazzal's groundbreaking oral history project (1974, 1978) documented the violence used to evict Palestinians from their villages in 1948, neither political factions nor the PLO itself expended the necessary resources for systematically recording and documenting the extant oral history accounts from the refugees in Lebanon who had been witnesses to the atrocities.

Dispersion, dispossession, fear, and uncertainty have affected the ability of many survivors of atrocities to speak about them. But also, statelessness, with its attendant absence of material resources necessary for making comprehensive histories, a perpetual state of conflict which has often been accompanied by deliberate Israeli appropriation or destruction of Palestinian archives, and partiality towards elite histories which often exclude oral accounts and testimonies of large-scale violence, have all shaped Palestinian commemorations.

---

[15] One Safsaf massacre survivor recounted the massacre to Nafez Nazzal (1978: 95): "As we lined up, a few Jewish soldiers ordered four girls to accompany them to carry water for the soldiers. Instead, they took them to our empty houses and raped them. About 70 of our men were blindfolded and shot to death, one after the other, in front of us." This account has been confirmed by Israel Galili, the head of the Haganah National Command: "52 men [in Safsaf] were tied with a rope and dropped into a well and shot. 10 were killed. Women pleaded for mercy. [There were 3 cases of rape] ... A girl aged 14 was raped. Another 4 were killed" (Morris 1987: 230).

Commemorating Tal al-Za'tar and Sabra/Shatila

Between 1975 and 1976, the Lebanese Forces (LF) planned and executed sieges, mass expulsions, and massacres of the residents of the mixed-nationality slum of Maslakh-Karantina and the Palestinian camps of Dbaya, Tal al-Za'tar and Jisr al-Basha, and the subsequent razing of the living quarters in those camps and neighborhoods. Since the LF had asked for Hafiz al-Asad's intervention, the Syrian military is thought to be culpable at least in the siege and massacre at Tal al-Za'tar where the camp was under siege for fifty-five days and where at least 4,280 Palestinian and Lebanese camp residents perished (Sayigh 1997: 401).[16] Shortly after the Tal al-Za'tar massacre, the refugees composed bitterly humorous songs and narratives to recount the horrors they had experienced. These popular stories were neither entirely heroic, nor wholly suffused with suffering. They portrayed daily life under siege, and reproduced the sheer resilience needed to survive weeks of hunger, thirst, sniper fire, and mortar attacks. Most men chose to commemorate instances of armed resistance against the siege, celebrating for example "the Syrian people who lived in the camp and took up arms alongside us" (Mandas 1977: 38). Women, on the other hand, had to carry the multiple burdens of food provisioning, gathering water at the communal tap, caring for the injured, and burying the dead – under the stairway of the bomb shelter, as Umm Wakid was forced to do with her child who died of hunger and dehydration during the siege.[17] As such, in local settings, and for local audiences, women also became the primary tellers of the "fragmented prose of daily life" (Elias Khoury quoted in Baily 2000: 11). One of a handful of books produced about any of the massacres which rely solely on the testimonies of the refugees themselves, Hani Mandas's remarkable *Tariq al-Tal al-Za'tar* (*The Way of Tal al-Za'tar*) contains many such stories, among which the "lentil tales" are prominent. Bushra 'Adil recalls: "Everybody in the camp was rationed lentils. People had little provisions, and if it weren't for lentils, we would die of hunger. Lentils in the morning, lentils at noon, and lentils at night" (Mandas 1977: 22). Hamda Muhsin's narrative similarly commemorates the days of lentils: "It was all lentils and lentils. Nothing else. For two months they harassed us. There was no gas, and no coal; all we had was wood from the destroyed houses [to cook with]" (Mandas 1977: 22). During the siege, ordinary routines of daily

---

[16] On the Tal al-Za'tar massacre, also see Badr 1994; Fayid 1977; Khalaf 1977; Mandas 1976, 1977; Sharif 1977.
[17] Nearly 300 newborns and toddlers died of malnutrition under the siege (Sayigh 1997: 401).

life became deadly: even to gather water was dangerous as LF snipers fired upon the queue of women at the communal water well at the edge of the camp: "women were killed doing this night after night" (Fatmeh quoted in Antonius 1979: 33). A song written weeks after the massacre similarly remembered the travails of daily life under siege alongside its more macabre elements:

Tal al-Za'tar, light of my eyes
They envy your steadfastness
In the Burj al-'Ali quarter
They attacked the refugees
In the Miya quarter
Steadfastly resisted the Fida'iyyin
When they occupied Talat al-Mir
We had to drink from the wells
We ate lentils without any appetite
We drank water full of blood
Our daughters were in the trucks
Or in the hospitals being examined
We have no sons left who can be concealed
For their shelters were destroyed. (*al-Hadaf*, 27 November 1976: 18)

The song refers specifically to the geography of the siege and the camp quarters in which fighting occurred. It also catalogues the hardships civilians had to endure, from the endless diet of lentils (which many of the surviving women claimed dried their breast milk) to well-waters that were bloodied by fallen corpses of murdered women. The song also describes women who had to be trucked by the ICRC through the Green Line from East Beirut to West Beirut, after having survived beatings, attacks, and rapes subsequent to the fall of the camp. The final line of the song points to the despair of mothers who could not hide their sons from the militiamen who executed all males over the age of twelve in the procession of refugees leaving the camp.

In the years after the massacre, the presence of militant factions – which despite their failure to protect the refugees of the camp and despite infighting nevertheless supported the survivors – left room for hope and for a more multi-faceted commemoration. At the time, many survivors could even seek redemption and social transformation in the narratives of suffering, and where in the immediate aftermath of the massacre, "lentil" stories were prevalent, in the ensuing nationalist period, positive emphasis on the transformative effects of the suffering appeared frequently:

Due to what we've seen in Tal al-Za'tar, no mother would tell her daughter, "You're not allowed to go to the clinic." She would tell her to go and not to stay in the shelter – "You have to go to the clinic and work, to see if there are wounded, help them, check if people need food, cook for them." Even older women started to go to clinic. They would go and check if they were needed. (Haifa, interviewed in 1981, quoted in Peteet 1995: 74)

With a more general shift towards tragic commemorations and an actual increase in hardship and devastation, narratives of the siege shift in emphasis again and other elements of it – already delineated in that subtle and multifaceted song – come to the fore:

Even when we surrendered they killed some of us at the church, even women and children. . . . Anyone who was on the streets, they were killing . . . My husband ran away and until today I don't know where he is. [The men] weren't killed then, but we don't know where they are. They loaded all the women on a truck at the church and brought us to the Museum [crossing] and there, the *fida'iyyin* came and took us and brought us to the camp. Some women were lucky, they were hiding the children, covering them with blankets, but the rest were taken away, left at the church and we don't know what happened to them. Since then, my life in the camp has been full of suffering . . . We women had to get jobs here. I had five daughters and three sons. One of my sons was paralysed by a bullet and he is in Germany [to get treatment] and the other son has a problem with his blood and he is getting treatment there also . . . There is something wrong with his red and white cells. When we came here, we worked [as maids] in people's houses. Now, we talk about our memories to other people who have lost their children, but we just can't cry. If we cried for everything, we would die. If we started crying, where would we stop? My mother died last year, and I have problems in my kidneys, but what can I do? (Umm Husayn, Burj al-Barajna, 29 January 2002)

Umm Husayn had undoubtedly suffered during the siege and the subsequent massacre. She lost her husband and had two disabled sons, both of whom lived far away. Her story, so similar to the narratives of other female survivors, had acquired particular thematic consistencies with other Tal al-Za'tar narratives, among them the notion of being left unprotected after the massacre. The murder of male children, the forced dispersion of families, and the disappearance of men left women vulnerable not only to the violence of militias but also to the vagaries of the economy. These elements are all enframed by an overall narrative of suffering, substantiated by the evidence of corporeal pain, and addressed to a wider audience whose attention, intervention, and most importantly, moral judgment is sought.

Similarly, in the following narrative about the Israeli invasion of Lebanon, the Sabra and Shatila massacre in 1982, and the War of the Camps in 1987, certain events are iconized. A young Palestinian from

Burj al-Barajna who was seven years old in 1982 tells this story not only to this researcher, but also to her classroom of ten-year-old children receiving after-school tutoring at an independent NGO:

When the air-raids started, I was outside. We heard aeroplanes over the camps, and all the kids ran in different directions. I lost my parents and I was trying to find them and I couldn't. Then I remembered my cousins. But they had run away and they couldn't help me ... So I found some other people and I told them who I was and some man remembered my name and remembered where my father's shop was and took me there. I saw a woman with her head decapitated which was horrible. During the Israeli occupation, there were *fida'iyyin* hiding on the roofs and families were hiding in the shelters and Israelis were bombing with big missiles that went through the shelters. A shell fell inside the shelter and a woman was injured when it fell on her: she was totally burnt and her hair had gone completely white.

During the Sabra and Shatila massacres, I was small. We heard about it. We used to hide our identifications in our shoes, because we had heard what had happened there. Our Lebanese cousins didn't want to have anything to do with us, because after Sabra and Shatila they were afraid that they would also be killed. But we [kids] didn't know what was going on, and it was a terrifying time for all of us, because we thought the same thing was going to happen to us.

During the siege of the camps, we were afraid that the same thing as Tal al-Za'tar was going to happen to us. We were very hungry and we spent a week without eating – just drinking water, we were looking for cats, because people were eating cats and donkeys but couldn't even find cats to eat. So my brother went to look for grass for us to eat, because my mother could make a salad for us. And this grass made us all feel very sleepy; it must have had some sort of narcotic in it. We slept for three days. (Fatin, Burj al-Barajna, 22 January 2002)

Several elements of Fatin's narrative are suggestive: she wove together the story of one atrocity after another. The shifts from the Battle of Beirut to the subsequent massacre at Sabra and Shatila, and from that to the War of the Camps five years later occurred quite naturally, as did the inter-linking of massacres and sieges. The sense of vulnerability and uncertainty, the deadliness of air-raid shelters and the Palestinian iden-tity (card) which were at once protective and dangerous, the betrayal of Lebanese cousins, the search for cats to be eaten during the sieges (also a recurring motif of the siege of Tal al-Za'tar) are now elements of a story which recur with great frequency. Their recurrence shows how commemorative narratives are formalized and shaped.

The Sabra and Shatila massacres are perhaps the most widely known atrocity committed against Palestinians. Only weeks after the massacres, commemoration of the events by foreign nurses who had been present in camp hospitals on the day of the massacre was considered dangerously *political*:

On the fortieth day after the massacre, the international health-care workers wanted to walk, in our white coats, from the hospital to the mass graves which is down at the end of the street in Shatila. This is a big area, the largest of several mass graves dug up by bulldozers, where the camp residents buried massacre victims. We wanted to place a wreath on the grave, but the Red Crescent asked us not to. It would be seen as a political, not a humanitarian act, and the Red Crescent was working out a relationship with the Lebanese government and it didn't want any problems. Over the next two days we went near the grave and saw women and children. The children were placing the Palestinian flag on the grave. (Siegel 1983: 69)

There were, however, commemorative demonstrations and sit-ins in Ba'albak, the Shuf Mountains (the stronghold of the Druze), Tripoli, and the camps of Tyre (Anonymous 1983: 122). On the fortieth day after the massacre, settlers in the West Bank opened fire on Palestinian demonstrators commemorating the massacres (Anonymous 1983: 123; al-Az'ar 1991: 53). On the same day in Lebanon, Palestinian women and children attended demonstrations – men feared harassment and arrest by the Lebanese army or Maronite militias – where the following slogans were given: "With our soul and blood, we honour you, O martyrs," "Sabra and Shatila were destroyed with the departure of the revolutionaries," "Palestine is Arabic," "Abu Ammar, where are you? Where are you? Borders have come between you and me" and "The blood of the children won't melt away futilely, General Sharon" (Anonymous 1983: 124). Around the same time, the Palestinian news agency, Wafa, called for installation of a memorial for the martyrs of the massacre (Anonymous 1983: 124). A small cenotaph was erected in the Martyrs' Cemetery in Beirut, though the mass graves remained off-limits to Palestinians. In the years after the end of the Civil War, the anniversary of the Sabra and Shatila massacres has seen marches by Palestinians around the Shatila camp, on routes which pass "places of memory" such as the Gaza and Acre Hospitals and end at the Martyrs' Cemetery, or in more recent years at the site of the massacre itself. The massacre at Sabra and Shatila has been commemorated in ceremonies held to honor other atrocities. For example, a demonstration on 18 April 2002 protesting the Israeli military's re-occupation of the West Bank towns was terminated at a UN building in Beirut, and the demonstrators carried placards painted with the slogan: "From Dayr Yasin to Sabra, Qana, and Jenin."

Aside from tributes to massacres in ceremonies and history-telling, monuments at massacre sites are some of the most significant commemorative forms. Most Palestinian massacre sites are devoid of monuments. The site of the Tal al-Za'tar massacre is today an anonymous plot of land. The lack of commemorative signs, plaques, or monuments there is startling. The land upon which the ruins of the camp rest is now being slowly developed by its owners. On one corner of the site, a chemical factory has been erected, during whose construction "dead houses" were excavated from the debris and the ruins (Nasri Hajjaj, Beirut, 5 May 2002). The rest of the site is a field, wherein the only sign of former habitation are forlorn olive trees once belonging to Palestinian households, and rubbish-strewn entryways to burnt-out bomb shelters. There are immediately apparent reasons for the neglect of the site and absence of any monuments therein: the camp-site remains in the majority-Maronite East Beirut and is owned by the Maronite Patriarchate. As post-war reconstruction drives up real estate prices, the owners are reluctant to cede any land for purposes which may not generate revenue.

Among all Palestinian memory-places, two massacre sites stand out from others by virtue of the existence of memorials of sorts therein. The first is the site of the massacre in the Maslakh-Karantina shantytown, where, by designing a macabre nightclub, the radical Lebanese architect Bernard Khoury comments deliberately not only on the massacre, but on the predicament of post-civil war Lebanon. The second memory-place is the Sabra and Shatila massacre site, whose history of becoming a memorial and its adoption by the Hizbullah in recent years as an emblematic space expose the complexities of commemoration in Lebanon. What distinguishes both these locales from other un-commemorated massacre sites is that only by being championed by *Lebanese* actors could these sites have become consciously memorialized, especially given post-civil war Lebanon's open hostility towards the Palestinian refugees and the negation of their claims, rights, and memories.

Maslakh–Karantina began its life as a quarantine camp for survivors of the Armenian genocide in 1915, later becoming a slaughterhouse and tannery, and yet later a shantytown housing Palestinian refugees, and Lebanese, Kurdish, and Syrian poor families. On 18 January 1976, LF militiamen, who considered the shantytown strategically important, razed it, killing hundreds of its inhabitants and expelling the remaining thousands to West Beirut (Sayigh 1997: 376). The razed site was then used as the headquarters for the LF throughout the Civil War. After the war, the site lay unused and rubble-strewn, surrounded by dense urban neighborhoods until 1998, when Khoury was asked to design a nightclub on that tract. Khoury himself says that the site was one "which I did not choose, but had to confront" (Khoury 2002). The nightclub, BO18, is situated three-and-a-half meters underground "to make it invisible, paralleling how the shantytown was made invisible" to the rest of the city by a high wall, and the building itself is shaped like a bunker or coffin (Khoury 2002). Inside, the entry vestibule is divided from the rest of the club by a wall punctuated with small "sniper windows" that allow a one-sided voyeurism by the club clientele. The tables in the seating area are tombstone-shaped, with pictures of jazz singers on them as if commemorating the dead, and all have a small vase with wilted flowers in front of the photograph. The seats around the tables are arranged to evoke seating at a wake. The BO18 design is intended as a conversation with the public, as a controversial argument about memory and war, because "there are no public institutions for materializing this debate in architecture, and so one has to resort to 'vulgar' buildings such as bars or restaurants to speak about things that are being silenced" (Beirut, 13 May 2002). Khoury uses the Palestinian place of memory as the backdrop for his own critical commentary on the political amnesia that has beset Lebanon and which prevents the country from addressing the social fissures that lay at the roots of the civil war. The ambiguity of using private architecture to deal with public issues of political and moral accountability, not to mention the incongruity of using a pleasure palace to memorialize a massacre, all complicate the meaning and role of commemoration on the Maslakh–Karantina massacre site.

The story of the memorial on the Sabra and Shatila massacre site also elucidates the complex social relations which shape commemorations. The number of massacre victims buried at this site is difficult to ascertain, but the most painstakingly researched estimates place it at 1,200 (al-Hut 2003). Many bodies were removed from the scene; others were interned in mass graves (MacBride *et al.*: 1983: 176). Yet other bodies were buried alive in the rubble of houses demolished atop their inhabitants by Israeli military bulldozers driven by LF militiamen. During the War of the Camps, Shatila's perimeter contracted and eventually came to exclude the massacre site. The site was then made inaccessible to camp residents for years, and was unavoidably neglected. In 1998, as part of the fiftieth anniversary ceremonies commemorating the *Nakba*, a group of Palestinian and Lebanese intellectuals organized a march to the site. As the Lebanese novelist Elias Khoury recalls, "It had become a garbage dump. We turned it once again into a cemetery. It is not an accident that it had become a garbage dump. This is the way the Palestinians are treated in Lebanon" (Mejcher 2001: 47). Because after the end of the civil war plans had been discussed to remove all Palestinian refugees from Beirut and raze the camps, the indignities visited upon the massacre site were considered to be part and parcel of this larger plan (*al-Safir*, 6 April 1998: 1).

In 1999, the Hizbullah-controlled Ghubayri municipality, which neighbors the camp, enclosed the mass grave, marked its entrance and planted white roses and trees on its margins. The key to the site was given to a groundskeeper, himself related to many of the massacre victims. Hizbullah has often festooned the desolate and empty space with banners bearing anti-Zionist slogans in English, questioning the role of the United States in the atrocities. More recently, large photographs of bloated bodies and mutilated corpses have been added to the site, among which one particular poster stands out; it commemorates a family of *Shi'a* (rather than Palestinian) massacre victims. The slogans surrounding the images are more accusatory than sorrowful. Nothing indicates that the site is central to Palestinian refugees' recent history. Rather, the site is presented as a concrete exhibit of Israeli brutality. Hizbullah has used the site as a mobilising space and holds anti-Zionist and anti-imperialist demonstrations there. Speeches given at the site, and the slogans and banners all refer to the massacre as a persuasive justification for militancy. As such, whereas Palestinian NGOs refer to Sabra and Shatila as evidence of suffering and victimization, the massacres in Hizbullah's militant narrative are the originary moments of heroic resistance. Heroic and tragic commemorations are most starkly contrasted at the site of the Sabra and Shatila massacres.

Finally, one of the more significant ways in which the Sabra and Shatila massacres have been commemorated is through appeals to international law. On 18 June 2001, eight Lebanese and fifteen Palestinian survivors of the Sabra and Shatila massacres lodged a complaint with a Belgian court against Ariel Sharon, Amos Yaron, and Rafael Eitan "and other Israelis and Lebanese responsible for the massacre, killing, rape, and disappearance of civilians" under Belgium's universal jurisdiction war crimes law (Anonymous 2001). The text of the complaint contained testimonies of the twenty-three survivors, all of whom had lost at least one family member in the massacres. The complaint aimed to establish the victims' version of what happened to the refugees on 16–19 September 1982 and offer an alternative to the Israeli Kahan Commission version where of 221 witnesses, only a handful were non-Israelis, and the testimonies of Palestinian and Lebanese survivors were completely neglected (Kapeliouk 1983: 81). Bringing a case about atrocities to a court of law is a claim to justice, a means of transforming everyday memories of atrocities into collective memories, and a method of *authorizing* a uniform and coherent version of the victims' narrative.[18]

---

[18] On the use of memories in courts, see Campbell 2002; Esmair 2003; Felman 1992: 166; Mamdani 2000: 177; Mertus 2000: 148–150; Osiel 1997: 239.

The court case acts as a commemorative practice insofar as it performs a version of the massacre's history for a much wider international audience, attempting to make that version the predominant one, while at the same time the case mobilizes international support with the aim of establishing rights for refugees that are otherwise unprotected. This appeal to international human rights on the one hand demands a moral accounting, and on the other hand, emphasizes Palestinian victimhood. The painful spectacle of survivors having to recount their stories over and over again in order to garner sympathy and support lays open the predicaments associated with tragic representations of pasts. On the one hand, establishing that a crime was committed against Palestinians is a decidedly *political* act; on the other hand, it requires the intervention of an international audience, and even more problematically, the assumption of abjection and victimhood by the survivors of the crime. That the case *has* to emphasize the "innocence" of the victims (i.e. they were not militants or political agents) in order to establish their legitimacy elucidates the difficulty of this dilemma.

In any event, the case did not proceed. Elie Hobeika, the LF officer who oversaw the carnage at Sabra and Shatila was assassinated in Beirut on 24 January 2002. Only two days before his assassination – likely at the hands of Syrian agents – he confirmed to Belgian senators his willingness to testify in court against Ariel Sharon, now the Israeli Prime Minister. Despite the significant setback to the case that his assassination was, the court case was to go on. However, on 1 August 2003, despite the best efforts of the plaintiffs and the NGO formed to support them, under heavy pressure from the United States and Israel, the Belgian Senate approved an overhaul of the nation's war crimes law, dropped the universal jurisdiction provision, limited the applicability of the law to those cases where the victim or the suspect are Belgian citizens or long-term residents at the time of the crime, and granted diplomatic immunity from prosecution to heads of state and other government officials, thus in effect throwing out the Sabra and Shatila case.

A palimpsest of massacres

> To "palimpsest" is to layer and to efface ineffectively because the underlying picture seeps through, but the result may be to collide violently by superimposition.
>
> Susan Slyomovics, *The Object of Memory*

Following the Gulf War, and during attacks against Palestinians in response to Arafat's support of the Iraqi invasion of Kuwait, "Kuwaiti vigilantes wrote the following graffiti on the walls of Palestinian camps: 'Amman 1970, Beirut 1982, Kuwait 1991'" (Siddiq 1995: 99). The vigilantes self-consciously declared the massacres of Palestinians in Jordan during the Black September of 1970 and the Sabra and Shatila massacres of 1982 as the predecessors for their acts of violence. The macabre palimpsest of massacres was significant not only for the layering of one atrocity upon the other, but also because past events never seem to disappear entirely and are cited as progenitors for subsequent massacres.

The layering of massacres of Palestinians one upon the other during the Lebanese civil war, and the layering of their commemoration one upon the other throughout the war and afterwards have not necessarily erased individual experiences of those massacres. However, significantly, dissimilar commemoration leads to some events occluding those before it. In the official history of the civil war, the massacre at Ain al-Rummana is overlain with that at Maslakh–Karantina. The atrocities at Jisr al-Basha are layered over by the greater carnage at Tal al-Za'tar, and the death of more than 160 civilians during the bombing of the Fakihani building is layered over by the vacuum bomb dropped on the residential flats near Sanaya' Gardens in 1982, resulting in another 250 civilian deaths.[19] The Sabra and Shatila massacres inscribe their mark over all that came before them.

The palimpsest of massacres also appears in the commemorative calendars of political organizations. After the Fakihani bombing, the DFLP's *al-Hurriyya* ties that event to Tal al-Za'tar and Dayr Yasin, and to Guernica and My Lai further afield (17 August 1981). In the immediate aftermath of the Sabra and Shatila massacres, Fatah's *Filastin al-Thawra* (2 October 1982: 19–25) reminded the readers that Menachem Begin, then Prime Minister of Israel, had, as an Irgun commander, been responsible for Dayr Yasin, and that Ariel Sharon was guilty of the massacres at Qibya. The chain of atrocities was cited as the reason needed for the establishment of a Palestinian state: "they attacked us when the fighters had left, and we were left unarmed. They confronted us and butchered us, and our blood flows river after river, generation after generation. This is not justice. We die and so do our children. ... It is necessary for us to teach our children that the Arabs, despite all their great slogans about their responsibility to liberate Palestine, never did a thing to support Palestinian people during battles or massacres." The

---

[19] During the 17 July 1981 Israeli bombing of the Fakihani district, six buildings were destroyed, thirty-two others were damaged, 166 persons – mostly civilians – were killed and 586 were injured (*Filastin al-Thawra* 27 July 1981; also Cobban 1984: 111; Badr 1993). On 6 August 1982, the Israeli military used a vacuum bomb to destroy buildings near the Sanaya' Gardens, where they erroneously thought PLO officials were hiding (MacBride *et al.* 1983: 47, 86).

conclusion the editorial drew – in those days of uncertainty and transition which followed the evacuation of the PLO from Lebanon – was that the only remedy for this palimpsest of massacres was "to build a Palestinian state on Palestinian land."

In all publications, commemorative articles wrote of the bloody Aprils which saw both Dayr Yasin and Ain al-Rummana, black Septembers in Jordan in 1970 and in Beirut in 1982 (and for some, of the Oslo Accords in 1993),[20] of the catastrophes that were the June War of 1967 and the June War of 1982, and so on. The calendar itself became the point of connection between successive layers of massacres. Though on the one hand, the calendar established a cyclical structure for the narrative of Palestinian suffering, its sparseness of narration in fact unmoored the events from their horrific and human details, abstracted the massacres from their particular social and historical contexts, and iconized some in the service of a coherent nationalist narrative. This meant that the massacres of Tal al-Za'tar and to a far greater extent – and for a far wider audience – the massacres at Sabra and Shatila came to dominate Palestinian national history. Much less frequently commemorated and mourned have been the deaths of nearly a hundred civilians in the civilian bomb-shelters at the Burj al-Shamali camp (Suleiman 1997a), and the indiscriminate bombings of Ain al-Hilwa and Nahr al-Barid camps leading to large but uncounted numbers of civilian deaths during the 1982 Israeli invasion of Lebanon and in subsequent years.

In the decades that have passed, the massacres at Sabra and Shatila have become a far more commemorated event than Tal al-Za'tar, though the fall of the latter camp in 1976 still appears on official calendars. Several factors can account for why Sabra and Shatila loom so much larger than Tal al-Za'tar. The physical annihilation of Tal al-Za'tar as a place of human habitation certainly has something to do with the absence of ceremonies focusing on it, as does the extensive dispersion of the inhabitants of the camps, many of whom were displaced again and again in subsequent years, and many of whom did not manage to survive the Israeli invasion of 1982, or the Sabra and Shatila massacres, or the carnage of the War of the Camps between 1985 and 1988. There are no central locales where the survivors of Tal al-Za'tar can gather and exchange stories about the massacre. The absence of a locus of common commiseration partially accounts for the dearth of

---

[20] PFLP–GC's *Il al-Amam* called the Oslo Accords "another massacre against the homeland" and tied it to Black September and Shatila (16–22 September 1994: 18). Interestingly, commemorations of the 1970 massacres in Jordan disappeared from Fatah's calendars and documents with the signing of Oslo Accords and the separate peace treaty between Jordan and Israel in 1993/1994.

systematic commemorations of the massacre there, but specific political considerations and conflicts which still affect the Palestinian community in Lebanon are also responsible for the latter.

Only weeks after the massacre, some Palestinian factions implied that the reason the camp was allowed to fall was the lack of interest of the Fatah leadership in saving a camp where most of the resident families were affiliated with the DFLP, PFLP and PFLP–GC, rather than Fatah. Furthermore, commemorating Tal al-Za'tar requires recognition of the complicity of Syrian forces in the atrocities (Cobban 1984: 73). When I conducted my interviews, the Syrian military and security services still had a very visible presence in Lebanon. In conversation, though most Palestinian refugees remembered Tal al-Za'tar, many were wary and frightened of doing so openly. During one of my interviews, my interlocutor stood up, closed the window of the room, and indicated that the Syrian *Mukhabirat* was the reason she didn't want to talk about Tal al-Za'tar. Although acknowledging the complicity of a "nationalist" Arab regime in the slaughter of "fellow Arabs" was not politically expedient for the representatives of dominant PLO factions in Lebanon, the experience of the Syrian state's complicity was still a searing and present memory for the refugees, whose sense of vulnerability was exacerbated by the Syrian clampdown on the camps after 1983 (in northern Lebanon) and especially in the late 1980s (in and around Beirut). Additionally, most of the survivors of the massacre, though still blaming the Syrian state for the massacre, also held Israel culpable. Some saw the roots of Tal al-Za'tar in their original expulsion from Palestine and as such found Israel indirectly responsible for that atrocity (al-Hut 2003: 483). Others pointed to the fact that the Israeli military armed and trained the militiamen who committed the massacres at Tal al-Za'tar (Ron 2003: 184).

The more intense commemoration of the massacres at Sabra and Shatila also owe something to the specificities of that atrocity. The unambiguous nature of the massacre is certainly one aspect contributing to the horror associated with this massacre: whereas there had been fighting before the massacres of Black September and gun battles prior to the assault on the civilians at Tal al-Za'tar and Jisr al-Basha, the Sabra and Shatila inhabitants were entirely unprotected, defenseless, and unarmed. Today, Shatila and Sabra are still inhabited (though squalid), and much of Shatila's population – though suffering multiple displacements – has not dispersed to the same extent as Tal al-Za'tar residents, allowing for the spatial concentration of commemoration. Commemorative ceremonies can occur more easily in a place where survivors can gather conveniently; Shatila is the most well-known camp internationally, and a regular "stop" on the circuit of those interested in the history of the civil war and the Palestinian predicament. The unambiguous "victimhood" of the Sabra and Shatila victims – in comparison, Tal al-Za'tar had resisted its annihilation by the force of arms – makes Sabra and Shatila a better representative of unalloyed Palestinian suffering.

The Israeli military and cabinet's culpability in the carnage at Sabra and Shatila more easily locates these events in the terrain of violent conflict between Israel and Palestinian nationalists, and as such the massacre at Sabra and Shatila better encapsulates Palestinian nationalist claims in that conflict. The liability of Israel in the massacre and using foreigners as scapegoats in Lebanese politics have overshadowed the responsibility of Lebanese parties to the massacre. For example, on the twentieth anniversary of the massacres, demonstrators commemorating the massacre carried placards containing slogans such as "Sharon and Bush: Criminals." The placards were carried not only by Lebanese political organizations, who, preferring national "reconciliation," had papered over the role of local militiamen in the massacres, but also by Palestinians for whom the continuing conflict with the Israeli state justified the focus solely on Israel. Observing these demonstrations, Ellen Siegel – an American witness of the massacres who testified to the Kahan Commission – asked "What about the Phalangists? Aren't they criminal too?" (*Daily Star* 17 September 2002: 1). On the one hand, the Palestinians' vulnerability in Lebanon has led to their reluctant silence on the guilt of LF militiamen. On the other hand, the incorporation of the Sabra and Shatila massacre in the nationalist narrative has meant that the memory of the massacre is now simplified, stripped of its historical complexity, and transformed into an iconized event that can be narrated, commemorated and instrumentalized politically. The simplification of the narrative of Sabra and Shatila by political organizations allows for national boundaries to be drawn in a reified manner, and excludes the transgressions of other Arabs from the story of the nation, while also providing the massacre as a proof of the suffering of innocent Palestinians for an international public.

Polyvalent events: War(s) of the Camps

He came back to live under the siege – three years of siege and destruction, and the camp became more and more crowded with its demolished houses until it became something like a handful of houses, the one holding up the debris of the other.

Elias Khoury, *The Kingdom of Strangers*

The shift from the commemoration of battles to commemoration of massacres indicates a diachronic transformation in the national narrative, with one narrative replacing the other in the Lebanese context. Some events, however, are polyvalent and their commemoration has never privileged a stable narrative.[21] The War of the Camps – as experienced and commemorated by the residents of Shatila and Burj al-Barajna in particular – is one such event.

Between 1985 and 1988 the Shi'a militias of Amal – allied to Syria and consolidating its power in southern Lebanon – placed the camps of Beirut and southern Lebanon under intermittent sieges and exposed them to intensive mortar attacks and sniper fire, killing women at communal water-taps in a macabre replay of Tal al-Za'tar. In response, male residents of the camps – and many women as well – organized the camps, took over the rationing of food, fuel, and medicine and put up fierce resistance with whatever armament they had left.[22] The dual nature of the event – both armed resistance and relentless siege – permits the event to be commemorated as both battle and massacre, both a moment of intense suffering and of great heroism – and more often than not as an instance of *sumud*. Because of the absence of a political and organizational infrastructure, unlike the siege and massacre of Tal al-Za'tar, one particular narrative about the War of the Camps is not privileged. The dearth of a dominant official narrative has in turn left some interpretative space for the polyvalent narration of the event. Syria's role as the sponsor of the Amal militia and the complexity of internal Palestinian politics during the War of the Camps add further dimensions to the way the event is remembered. The transitional nature of politics at that point has also affected the commemoration of the War of the Camps. By the end of the wars of the camps, the *Intifada* had begun and the terrain of national struggle had shifted from Lebanon to the OPT and nationalist strategies had changed from guerrilla warfare to mass mobilization. This transition was even clear in the proclamations of the PLO's Executive Committee, which stated:

After six years of *sumud* by the heroic Shatila camp, defending the rights of our people to maintain freedom and right of return, after six years of legendary *sumud* against the Zionist enemy, and repeated massacres, and long sieges imposed upon it by diverse plotters and traitors, Shatila has been transformed into a luminous symbol among the symbols of our long national struggle, which has matured into the great popular Intifada in our occupied land. We wish to

---

[21] The *Oxford English Dictionary* defines polyvalent as "having or open to many different applications, interpretations, meanings, or values."

[22] On the War of the Camps see Cutting 1988; Giannou 1991; Hagopian 1985; and especially Sayigh 1994.

focus on the Intifada and its revolutionary movement at a time when Syria's side-shows distracts us from the primary locus of struggle in the Occupied Territories and a time when we expect Syria with its capabilities and resources to be in the trenches of the nationalist struggle whose horizons the Intifada has opened wide. (*Filastin al-Thawra*, 3 July 1988: 12)

In its statement, the leadership no longer spoke of the *Thawra* and its battles. The War of the Camps was now another instance of *sumud* among others, a continuation of the Palestinian steadfastness in the face of massacres. Shatila was no longer the center of resistance. It was now "a luminous symbol" whose trials and travails supposedly distracted from the central battle of the *Intifada* in the OPT but in reality gave a boost to the PLO there (Khalidi 1989: 121). A Fatah fighter conveyed the refugees' disillusionment in a letter to Arafat: "our [political] credit with the masses is below zero. There is anger and regret at the return of the revolution's forces, and if things stay as they are the forces and everyone else will be expelled by the people of the camp" (Sayigh 1997: 592). The intense disagreements over political alliances and strategies between different factions of the PLO were also reflected in the commemorations of the events. While Arafat was becoming closer to King Husayn of Jordan, oppositionist factions within the PLO resisted this rapprochement and edged closer to Syria. Many residents of Burj al-Barajna affiliated with the DFLP and PFLP told me over and over again, "Arafat didn't care about us. He used us for his own purposes." In the months following successive sieges, Fatah periodicals carried articles containing interviews "with the masses" intended to convince Palestinians that – as one elderly woman had said – "no, dear, it is not Abu Ammar's fault" (*Filastin al-Thawra*, 23 March 1985), or "we are with Arafat, because we want to remain independent" (*Filastin al-Thawra*, 30 March 1985).

Factional periodicals throughout the War of the Camps consistently celebrated the refugees' *sumud*, rather than their *batula* (heroism) or *muqawama* (resistance). *Sumud* brought together the OPT and the camps of Lebanon and allowed the political activity in one place to directly influence politics in the other place. Where under Israeli Occupation, *sumud* meant "to stay put, to cling to our homes and land by all means available" (Shehadeh 1982: vii; Lindholm-Schulz 1999: 55), in Lebanon, *sumud* had come to mean surviving against all odds in the camps. Where once the heroes of the *Thawra* were commemorated, now the "leaders of *sumud*" received the kudos of the factional periodicals (*Filastin al-Thawra*, 28 February 1987). This emphasis on *sumud* itself allowed a spectrum of interpretative and strategic frameworks to emerge in the camps. To withstand hunger, thirst and lack of cigarettes became an act of *sumud* as did the women's job of sneaking in food past Amal checkpoints:

Once I had a fight with an Amal fighter ... He was mixing all the stuff we were buying, the lentil, rice, and sugar. I told him, if you want to take these things, take it, but don't mix them together! They used to take everything they wanted and mixed everything else. Then we couldn't use them, so I argued with him. After that, whenever I went outside the camp, he would threaten me: "I told you several times not to leave the camp!" I said, "I am leaving the camp because I need to buy food for my family." He said, "If you come out, I will kill you." I said, "You can do whatever you want." So when I was going back inside the camp, he shot at me, but he missed me. (Umm Walid, Burj al-Barajna, 19 January 2002)

A former fighter who had been involved in the defense of the Burj al-Barajna camp had written his memoirs of the siege, though he was hesitant about showing it to me and certainly about publishing it. He feared not only retaliation by the Syrian secret police which at the time had a heavy presence in the camps, but also from members of rival political factions. He nevertheless recounted what he found of immense importance, and what he chose to record in his memoirs of the siege:

I wrote about good and bad things, I wrote about the massacres during that war and how thirteen people were injured when a shelter collapsed, and how they lost their legs, and how in the hospital, we had no equipment, or bandage or fuel. We didn't have fuel to do any operations on the injured people. I wrote about people who shared their bread and those who were stealing others' bread. I talk about children who were brave, and adults who were cowards. I talk about women who were sewing sandbags out of their bed linens. I talk about the volunteer girls at the hospital who were fighting ... I talk about the good and bad. I talk about women who were making bread and food and delivering them to the fighters. I talk about some guys who were giving blood far more than once in six months, and about how a general doctor became a surgeon, and about how people died without knowing why they died. (Abu Mustafa, Burj al-Barajna, 6 February 2002)

Many particular aspects of the narratives of the War of the Camps have become formalized, most significant among them stories about the ingenuity of the women in sneaking in necessities, the mixing of the foodstuff by vengeful Amal soldiers,[23] women sewing sandbags and provisioning the fighters, and of course the mortal dangers of gathering water at the communal tap. However, I found that the manner in which the War of the Camps was remembered was far more varied, and far more diverse than other events. Abu Mustafa could speak of *both*

---

[23] Interestingly, this method of cruelty seems to have been exercised by British soldiers in Mandate Palestine as well (Swedenburg 1995: 131, 180).

heroism and cowardice, attesting to the non-hegemonic nature of a narrative of heroism. Young women who had been active in provisioning activities could look back to those days and see their very activity as redemptive of any suffering (and there *was* much hunger, human loss, and devastation), because victimhood was not how they interpreted their experience. *Sumud* opened up a mobilizing space for women who may have been nudged out of the masculinizing forms of "heroic" armed resistance (Peteet 1991: 153). Steadfastness against the siege mobilized those skills and reserves of local knowledge more readily available to the women of the camps. The multiplicity of stories emerging out of the experience of the War of the Camps partially speaks to the centrality of women's role in the defense and survival of the camps against the onslaughts. The polyvalence also emerges out of the absence of an active and hierarchical political structure. While on the one hand, the absence of PLO fighters on a large scale left the camps unprotected, on the other hand, it allowed for some measure of community mobilization at grassroots (Giannou 1991: 80–1; Sayigh 1994: 236–241). Significantly for my thesis, it also left the discursive arena open to simultaneous and competing commemorative narratives.

In the spring of 2002, when the Israeli military re-invaded the cities of West Bank and besieged Jenin, Ramallah and Bethlehem, the siege of the Jenin refugee camp in particular evoked memories of the War of the Camps among Palestinians of Burj al-Barajna and Shatila. Time and again, in the homes of my interlocutors and friends in the camps, I saw Palestinians from those two camps – who voraciously and unstoppably consumed news about Palestine – turn off their television sets in despair in the middle of a report on what was happening in Jenin and tell me that the combination of armed resistance by Palestinians in Jenin and the heavy curfews and "closures" placed on that camp by the Israeli military reminded them too much of the War of the Camps. But in various public commemorations, Palestinian political actors drew different parallels and invoked events differently depending on the context. For example, in a ceremony held on 4 May 2003 in the UNESCO Palace to commemorate the *Nakba*, an NGO activist from Burj al-Barajna spoke of the resistance of Jenin and of the way it invoked the War of the Camps. The audience was almost entirely Palestinian and the events were being held in Arabic. The commemorative narrative of heroic (armed) resistance by "our *shabab* (young men)" fit the celebration of battles in the cause of the nation. This narrative, however, was not appropriate for a wider international audience to whom an appeal was to be made on the basis of principles of human rights and international conventions. During demonstrations that were being held almost daily in the camps or on the streets of Beirut, the same activist was questioned by a reporter from a foreign news agency about "the reaction of Palestinian refugees in Lebanon to the events in Jenin." She immediately drew parallels between Sabra and Shatila (rather than the War of the Camps) and Jenin, spoke of the unalloyed suffering of Palestinian refugees everywhere, and insisted on the culpability of Ariel Sharon in both atrocities (later in the conversation, she also brought up the massacre at Qibya in 1953). In turn, after the siege of Jenin was lifted, the residents of Jenin referred to the massacres at Sabra and Shatila when explaining why the *shabab* chose to defend the camp (Baroud 2003: 31). The palimpsest of massacres and battles was again on display in both the event and its commemoration.

The absence of a hegemonic narrative about the War of the Camps and the occurrence of that event during a massive transition in the terrain of Palestinian politics distinguishes it from the events at Tal al-Zaʿtar. Where both events included a brutal siege, the complicity of the Syrian state, and a combination of "battles" and "massacres," Tal al-Zaʿtar is now commemorated as a massacre alone, even though at the time of its occurrence, it was interpreted as a momentous battle. The absence of militant factions or humanitarian NGOs capable of propagating a monolithic narrative about the War of the Camps has allowed for the event to remain polyvalent, lending itself to strategically variant invocations, commemorations and interpretations. This has in turn allowed for the event to be less a mobilizing instrument and more a standard for judging and understanding similar events.

Conclusions

In this chapter I have discussed the ways in which commemorative narratives enframe violent events as moments of heroism, tragedy, or steadfastness, and transform them into elements of a coherent national narrative. The actual experiences of battle or massacre have shaped Palestinian lives in the camps of Lebanon. However, the commemoration of heroism in battle or the suffering of massacres, and the relative weight given to particular battles or massacres are of great importance. While militant Palestinian factions were still a significant part of the Palestinian community and daily life in Lebanon, nationalist battle and armed resistance were celebrated not only as a path to forging the nation, but also as a way of constructing members of the national polity. The shift from the battle to the massacre as the central motif of Palestinian existence occurred with the evacuation of the PLO fighters and leadership from Lebanon and with the Sabra and Shatila massacres. Though *sumud* was predominant in the uncertain transition years between 1982 and the end of the war and up to the signing of the Oslo Accords, tragedy began to make its appearance as the primary mode of understanding present events and commemorating past ones. This was partly due to the ascendancy of humanitarian and advocacy NGOs, but also because in the absence of factions, narratives of suffering best resonated with the refugees experiencing violence firsthand. The polyvalence of the War of the Camps and its variable commemoration speak to the ability of multiple narratives to emerge in the absence of political institutions whose resources can help establish the predominance of particular narratives.

I have also shown that even when either battles or massacres become the central motif of commemoration, not all massacres or battles are commemorated equally. Certain events have become iconized as the primary symbolic event within a particular category. The massacre at Dayr Yasin has come to stand as a metaphor for the Palestinian predicament, while other 1948 massacres have receded to the background. It is not, however, simply the effect of time which has resulted in the selective process of iconization. Social and political factors, such as fear of Syrian surveillance, the spatial dispersion of massacre survivors, and emphasis on the Israeli–Palestinian conflict sometimes concurrent with de-emphasizing the Arab regimes' guilt have all led to the ebbing of Tal al-Za'tar as an iconized massacre. Conversely, the culpability of the Israeli military in the massacres at Sabra and Shatila, the unambiguous nature of the event as a case of violence against civilians, and the absence of reconciliation or retribution for those responsible have all kept the Sabra and Shatila massacres present in the nationalist commemorative practices.

8   Commemoration in the Occupied Palestinian Territories

Yasser Arafat's *keffiyeh*, folded and fixed in place with symbolic and folkloric importance, became the moral and political guide to Palestine ... Yet, surprises were brewing elsewhere. When venturing back from the heights of Hellenic hermeneutics, the symbolic being had to shed some of the burden of his epic stature. A country had to be built and administered and new means were needed to end the occupation. He was now exposed and vulnerable; he could be touched, whispered about, brought to account. It was also the hero's misfortune to have to conquer his enemies in uneven battles and, simultaneously, to safeguard his image in the public imagination from festering protuberances.

Mahmud Darwish, "Farewell Arafat"

Arafat's funeral in Cairo and Ramallah, on 12 November 2004, exemplified the distinction between two sorts of heroic commemorative narratives: the first, an official ceremony mourning a founding father and head of state, and the other, that of a liberationist-nationalist movement burying a "martyred" icon of armed resistance. The entire spectacle was inflected through the lens of Israeli military occupation, which had made itself "invisible" for three days but which had ultimately set the parameters of the ceremony and subsequent burial (*Jerusalem Post*, 16 November 2004). In Cairo, attendance at the funeral organized by President Husni Mubarak was limited to dignitaries and was strictly closed to the public. Arafat's flag-draped coffin was loaded onto a golden horse-drawn carriage, and led a procession of heads of state and other public figures down an eerily deserted boulevard to a military airfield, where it was transferred to helicopters for its final journey to Ramallah. Though Arafat had wished to be buried on the grounds of the Haram al-Sharif in Jerusalem, the Israeli state had expressly prevented the fulfillment of this wish. Hence, Arafat's body was to be laid to rest in a "temporary" grave in the Muqata'a compound, where the Old Man had lived under an intermittent state of siege for two and a half years prior to his death.[1] The Egyptian helicopters which brought Arafat's body to Ramallah were greeted with a sea of mourners and with symbols of official nationalism even more numerous than in Cairo: flags, marching bands, red carpets, soil from Jerusalem within which Arafat's body was to be entombed. Around 1,000 security men interspersed the crowd. The security men had been "permitted" by Israel to carry guns for three days surrounding the funeral to keep order (*Jerusalem Post*, 15 November 2004). While Palestinian officials wanted a "stately" funeral, the popular grief of tens of thousands of mourners could not be so easily channeled by the officials. The crowds, many of whom had come to Ramallah from those villages not sealed off by the Israeli military, converged on the Muqata'a, tore down the barbed wire around the compound, and climbed over the ruins and rubble left behind by the Israeli military gunships and bulldozers. Militants fired volleys of bullets in the air to salute the dead leader. Wave after wave of mourners lifted the flag-draped coffin, and when the flag slipped off, they swathed the coffin in a *keffiyeh*, that universally recognizable symbol of Palestinian struggle which Arafat had worn folded and draped in such a way as to resemble the map of Palestine. The crowds attempted to break through the cordon of security officers and carry Arafat's body to Jerusalem, where on the same day, the Israeli military had clashed with Palestinian youths who had been among thousands of men under the age of 45 prevented by the military from praying for Arafat at the al-Aqsa mosque.

The Palestinian Authority's meticulous plans for a stately and sombre ceremony – where bereaved officials were to lay wreaths on the grave in full view of the world's camera lenses – was scuttled by crowds of ordinary Palestinians and militants who chanted Arafat's name, fired thousands of bullets into the air, and exuberantly defied the officials by trying to carry Arafat's body to Jerusalem. In fact, in press speculations leading to the funeral, the Israeli military was said to be most concerned about such a popular procession towards Jerusalem. In the end, the security forces, with senior members clambering atop the coffin, managed to reroute the coffin to the designated place within the compound and bury it with what seemed indecent haste, so as to forestall a clash with the Israeli military. The bereaved and forlorn crowd, stymied in its radical attempt to transform the commemoration into an uprising,

---

[1] Beginning in December 2001, the Israeli military placed the Muqata'a under intermittent siege, culminating in two climactic moments in April and September 2002, when the IDF shelled and bulldozed most of the compound, leaving Arafat the sovereign of only two rooms.

milled around the compound for a few more hours, and dispersed by the early evening.

Where the officials had wanted to tell the story of the Palestinian nation as a narrative ending inevitably in the creation of the state – with its recognized and recognizable trappings of flags, solemn official ceremonies, and national tomb-cum-shrines, militant Palestinians had wanted to commemorate a man who was in their view not so much a founding statesman but an icon of nationalist resistance. The officials had wanted the ceremony to be yet another affirmation of the legitimacy of the state: an event that showed the PA's organizational abilities, links to foreign dignitaries, and accoutrements of governance. Commemorating Arafat was to legitimate the PA. Two things had put paid to this desire. First had been the visible and invisible signs of a military occupation: the PA's security men needed the permission of the foreign military to carry their weapons, and the ground of the Muqata'a was strewn with the rubble resulting from the Israeli military invasion. As significant, the enthusiastic and undomesticated action of the militants had shown the difficulties the PA had had in consolidating its power and legitimacy among the population. The militants themselves had wanted the commemoration, and more specifically, the burial of Arafat in Jerusalem, to be the ember that sparked a new uprising.

The contentious encounter between the militants and PA officialdom – with its statesmen and security apparatus – reflects the complexities of nationalist mobilization in the OPT. The militants are mostly youth born and raised in the OPT, and their political activism – even within Fatah, which until January 2006 was the party of the officialdom – is clearly bound up with their armed resistance to Israeli occupation. The PA elite, on the other hand, in trying to legitimate their rule, still refer to their militant past, but in their current policy, they counter and discipline the militants' insistence on armed struggle, preferring a focus on "negotiations" alone. Militants outside Fatah – and especially those belonging to Islamist organizations such as Hamas or Jihad – were not at the time constrained by the ruling state in this way, and as such could be oppositional, armed, and combative. This bifurcation of nationalist sentiment into an official nation-statist discourse and a militant ethos of armed struggle has in a sense resulted from the failure of the nation-statist project in the OPT.

In this chapter, I write about these two distinct heroic narratives, as well as, the narratives of suffering and *sumud* that constitute national commemoration in the OPT. With the expulsion of the PLO from Lebanon in 1982, and the beginning of the Intifada in 1987, the center of gravity of the Palestinian nationalist movement shifted to Gaza, the

West Bank, and East Jerusalem. In this chapter, I argue that given the similarities of institutional forms and transnational discourses, heroic and tragic narratives have also framed commemoration and contention in the OPT. However, the politics and semiotics of nationalist commemoration has been performed in a wholly different arena in the OPT, as military occupation, insider/outsider contention, fissures of class, and camp/refugee differences profoundly affect politics therein.

The State's biography of the nation

In 1970, Abu Ali Iyad, another Fatah hero from bygone years, coined a slogan days before he was killed: "We will die standing, but never kneel." It inspired generations of Fatah militants, seeing them through for more than two decades. One is hard-pressed today to imagine a possible equivalent: "Let us build institutions for a democratic state" somehow does not have quite the same ring.

Hussein Agha and Robert Malley, "The Lost Palestinians"

We live in [an] amazing, shameful time, but you should know that every revolution has its fighters, thinkers and profiteers. Our fighters have been killed, our thinkers assassinated, and all we have left are the profiteers. These don't think even primarily of the cause, they don't think of it at all. They know that they are just transients here, as they were in Tunis, and, as with any regime whose end is near, they think only of profiting from it while they can.

Former Fatah Cadre[2]

The final transformation of the PLO from a liberationist movement in diaspora into a quasi-state institution in the OPT – which had been in the making in Beirut – entailed a shift not only in the charter, institutional organization, and character of the PLO, but also in its nationalist discourse and practices manifested through commemoration. By signing the Oslo Accords in September 1993, the PLO elite guaranteed their continued political relevance and ensured a foothold – and much more – in the OPT (Jamal 2005). When in 1994, Arafat and other PLO officials returned to the OPT, they brought with them the militant infrastructure and political institutions they had so painstakingly established on the "outside." The institutional character of the OPT was slowly transformed. Extant and new local civil organizations quickly established connections to an emerging, resource-rich, and powerful system of non-governmental organizations and their donors who were willing to spend millions of dollars to build states, civil society, and political "capacity" (Brynen 2000). Grassroots organizations which under direct Israeli military occupation had combined resistance with NGO work were

---

[2] Quoted in Brynen 2000: 142.

replaced under the PA with professionalized development or humanitarian or human rights NGOs, and many abdicated activities associated with direct resistance or mass mobilization (Hanafi and Tabar 2005). Many militant youth whose struggles during the Intifada had brought the uprising to the world's attention were co-opted into the massive security apparatus which cropped up around the Palestinian Authority. Billions of dollars in "state-building" aid funded the establishment of a number of ministries (Brynen 2000). The colors of the Palestinian flag, for so long banned by the Israeli military, flew over official buildings – first in Gaza and Jericho, and later in Ramallah and other cities of the OPT. The Israeli military continued its visible presence throughout, settlement-building accelerated, and the state of Israel continued its control over the borders, airspace, inter-city transportation, customs, the economic infrastructure, and water sources of the OPT. Meanwhile, the PA was quick to build prisons, expand its overlapping police and security forces, launch a whole host of governmental organizations, print stamps, and raise its flags and banners over public buildings. To monopolize political power in the body of the Palestinian Authority, the PLO elite pushed to backstage local grassroots resistance and co-opted the militants of the OPT (Jamal 2005; Robinson 1997); but alongside institutional changes, symbolic ones occurred as well.

If the PLO's liberationist discourse had used the commemoration of heroism as the catalyst to transform torpor and inaction into political mobilization, the PA's biography of the nation, and the commemorative practices it deployed began to cast all struggle as the necessary precursor to the sanctified *telos*: the state itself. The linear narratives in which all past activity, sacrifices, heroism, and even defeats and setbacks are predetermined stages in the emergence and evolution of the state became "self-legitimating tales" which perpetually vindicated its existence, and tried to fix its institutions in time, place, and the public's sympathies and memories (Malley 1996: 109). But the necessary monopolization of coercion in the state's security apparatus required that stories of past armed struggle be tamed and commemorations of present political violence be neutralized. Thus, hyper-masculine heroes of the revolution gave way to founding fathers, the visual markers of the state – the flag, the stamp, the bureaucratic offices of the state – pushed the more militant symbols of armed struggle to the background, and instead of martyrs' funerals or militant festivals, more stately rituals were adopted to celebrate and affirm the founding and reproduction of the state.

While Arafat led the PA, he awkwardly straddled the divide between liberationist heroism and nation-statist statesmanship. He was a much more familiar figure in his military uniforms; he never forsook that ultimate symbol of his militant past: the *keffiyeh* worn to look like the map of Palestine. Other PLO officials, however, quickly donned suit and tie, rarely if ever again appearing in khaki combat gear. When addressing his foreign audience, Arafat was a conciliatory statesman; in speaking to his Palestinian audience, he still spoke the language of heroism, even declaring his readiness for martyrdom – *"shahidan shahidan shahidan"* – when the Muqata'a was placed under Israeli military siege in 2002. He sat at the negotiating table with Israeli prime ministers, shaking their hands for photo-ops, and yet, managed to rally many young militants of the refugee camps around him. When his popularity was plummeting, Israeli military attacks on his compound and verbal threats against him only served once again to transform him into a popular figure and a symbol of Palestinian resistance. Nevertheless, Arafat and other political elite of the PLO and the OPT were instrumental in transforming the revolutionary movement into a nation-statist project of institution-building, however malfunctioning those institutions may have been (Jamal 2005; Brown 2003).

If the security apparatus was both the symbolic representation and institutional manifestation of Palestinian nation-statism, the PA's nascent education system had become the most important media for disseminating the proto-state's history, "national memory," com-memorative discourse and rituals, and the primary domain for the "assertion of a once incomplete and suppressed but finally restored identity" (Said 1994: 267). The schools flew flags and celebrated nationalist holidays which emphasized the birth of the state. Nationalist icons were inserted throughout the schoolbooks. "A grammatic point was illustrated with a quotation from the 1988 declaration of independence ... In learning calligraphy, second-grade students copied, 'Jerusalem is in the heart of every Arab' ... The students read nationalist writings when studying Arabic and counted Palestinian flags while studying arithmetic" (Brown 2003: 222). In these texts, the Palestinian nation was traced back to the Canaanites, was made timeless and eternal, and a seamless elision was made between the Palestinian identity and an Islamic one (2003: 223). More significantly, the state of Palestine was represented as "neither problematic, nor contested in any way" (2003: 224). The state was envisioned as whole and sovereign, not only with its own flag and declaration of independence, but also with clear borders, political institutions, and Jerusalem as its capital. In this celebration of the stately institutions, commemoration of those central icons of Palestinian nationalism, armed revolution, guerrilla struggle, and self-sacrifice, barely appeared (Brown 2003: 224). The heroes celebrated were literary ones, discussion of maps was left to the discretion of teachers, and "closures, checkpoints, and identity cards ... home demolitions, continued detention of prisoners, and settlement expansion" were all erased (2003: 225). This symbolic work did a number of things: it depoliticized the state and erased the conflict with Israel, willfully ignoring the still extant occupation. The education system in effect naturalized the state and "inculcat[ed] new forms of authority" (Said 1994: 267), instilling in the students a visceral acquiescence to a centralized and hegemonic state, as well as to "God, nation, family, ... school, and other social institutions" (Brown 2003: 218).

Alongside concrete state institutions, the PA adopted familiar commemorative forms in which the inevitable linear ascent to statehood was celebrated and the concentration of coercion and violence within the body of the state were commemorated. Among these rituals were military marches through city streets, where the state's security forces, in dress uniform and carrying weapons, memorialized revolutionary struggle (tamed in the service of the state) using slogans and banners that, though reminiscent of past heroic moments of revolution, nevertheless had a decidedly stately character: it was now the Palestinian state, its putative capital in Jerusalem, its flag, and its leader that were object of celebration, not the heroic young men running over the hills with their Kalashnikovs. The gun or *bunduqiyya* was no longer celebrated as the liberator of the captive nation, but rather as instruments of order, as the security forces with their elaborate logos, uniforms, and slogans "potently" represented state power (Lindholm-Schulz 1995: 10). And the martyrs remembered and valorized – among them the three PLO leaders assassinated in 1973 in Beirut – were no longer portrayed as men of revolution, but as founding fathers of the nation-state cut down in their prime. As revolutionaries, they subverted established orders, transformed worlds, and their self-sacrifice regenerated resistance. As founding fathers, their martyrdom affirmed the legitimacy of the nation-state and celebrated the order enforced by the state. Death in the cause of the nation was no longer a moment of raucous popular mobilization, but rather the basis of commemoration of dead statesmen. On the first anniversary of Arafat's death, the PA announced that his burial place would become a museum and mausoleum. Heroic myths of self-sacrifice and national mobilization were thus fixed through stately forms used to celebrate national histories (Anderson 1991; Ben-Amos 2000) and transformed into at once concretized commemorations of the nation and the object of tourists' gaze.

Less obviously, elections have taken the place of honor as rituals of commemoration where the campaign media, the narratives told, and the pasts recapitulated eerily parallel the liberationist heroic discourse (also see Malley 1996: 109). The replacement of martyrs' posters with campaign images and militant gatherings with electioneering rallies are not coincidental. In the aftermath of his coming to power in January 2005, Mahmud Abbas (Abu Mazin) ordered that the walls of Ramallah, the seat of the Palestinian Authority, be purged of martyrs' posters. When I visited the OPT in September 2005, after having become habituated to the commemorative markers of the refugee camps, I found the absence of such posters in Ramallah city streets disorientating. The same was not true of any other city I visited. The walls of Abu Dis, Nablus, Hebron, Bethlehem, Birzeit, and East Jerusalem were all covered with commemorative martyrs' posters and murals familiar to me from the refugee camps in Lebanon. But in Ramallah, where the Fatah-led PA demonstrated its stateliness to the world, such posters were only to be found in less visible alleyways or forgotten corners such as the dark depths of the bus station. In their place, large banners and posters showed the somber faces of candidates for the local elections scheduled to be held in late September 2005. The election posters still deployed the familiar and iconic images: the flag, the colors associated with the Palestinian nation, and images of the Dome of the Rock. But unlike martyrs' posters, they did not commemorate martyrdom, self-sacrifice, or armed struggle. Indeed, if martyrs were invoked at all, they were portrayed as benign, smiling forces appearing through heavenly clouds, bestowing their blessings on the elections – as the images of Shaykh Ahmad Yasin and, surprisingly, Arafat, on Hamas election posters in spring 2006 attested. The astonishing incorporation of Arafat on Hamas elections posters intended to show that a more "mature" and "statesmanlike" Hamas was willing to compromise with their hitherto bitter political rivals. Election rallies similarly celebrated the emergence and persistence of the state via officially sanctioned images and vocabulary of the state, and advancing a story about the state which buttresses its hegemony and supports its quest for popular legitimacy. Though the music played at these rallies is the rousing music in which the nation and its heroes are valorized, the order of the day is no longer a fundamental transformation of the society, but the everyday bureaucracy of its maintenance.

What perhaps makes the nation-statist gesture of the PA an awkward one is that despite its pretension to state-ness and the concurrent visible elimination of militancy in its discourse and practice, its commemorative practices have not been made safe from the Israeli state's violent attempts at silencing them, and its nascent institutions have been subjected to wanton destruction by the Israeli military. When in spring 2002, the Israeli military invaded the West Bank, its primary targets in

Ramallah seemed to be the records, computer files, archives, and libraries of Palestinian Authority ministries, schools, universities, mass media, and cultural centers, as well various NGOs. The extent of damage to the raw matter of national history-making – especially at the Ministries of Culture and Education – was astonishing (Hammami *et al.* 2002; Twiss 2003). Expensive electronic equipment, transmitters, computers, video recorders and various other archiving paraphernalia were looted or destroyed, hard drives of computers were removed, and irreplaceable contents of archives, libraries, and filing cabinets were packed up and taken away. Records, films, books, journals, statistics, and raw data accumulated over years – and sometimes decades – were either damaged or confiscated. The comprehensive theft of the archives was accompanied by symbolic violence on an unprecedented scale: even when doors could be opened with keys, the soldiers destroyed them using explosives. They opened fire on the plaques of buildings and left bullet holes and rocket damage throughout. They wrote insulting graffiti on all the walls, and defecated on floors, inside desk drawers, and on chairs. In the aftermath of the invasion, not only was the PA infrastructure devastated, but also the very image of the Authority's sovereignty and legitimacy was undermined. The concrete brutality of the occupation showed that the triumphant Palestinian state at the core of nationalist commemoration was still a fragile thing, subject to the policies of Israel. The narratives of the nation told to foreign audiences after that invasion, thus, framed the events as suffering and victimization.

Oppositional heroic narratives

> To throw a stone is to be "one of the guys"; to hit an Israeli car is to become a hero; and to be arrested and not confess to having done anything is to be a man.
>
> Daoud Kuttab, "A Profile of the Stonethrowers"

In the diaspora, Palestinian political factions and militant organizations advanced the nationalist-liberationist discourse which celebrates a heroic rise from stupor and silence and which is addressed squarely at a national audience they aim to mobilize. The heroic discourse, which in the heyday of the *Thawra* was fervently embraced by diasporan Palestinians, found its most concrete and sustained manifestations in the refugee camps. Militancy in the OPT also arose primarily from the nineteen camps that house some 650,000 registered refugees (out of a total of nearly 1,700,000 refugees in the OPT), but the complexion of Palestinian heroic militancy in the OPT has transformed over time. The leaders and participants of the first Intifada (1987–1991) had decisively broken with the PLO's strategy of armed struggle, and advanced mass mobilization as the primary strategy of resistance. *Bunduqiyya* as the principal mode of struggle emerged again during the al-Aqsa Intifada which began in 2000. By then, the presence of the PA and its security apparatus, the increasing impoverishment of the OPT, ever-increasing numbers of violent settlers, and the intransigency of the Israeli military occupation had all led to the re-emergence of armed struggle (Hammami and Tamari 2001). However, significantly, even when armed struggle was not the chief strategy of resistance, militants in the OPT used the heroic discourse of nationalist/liberationist resistance to rally their Palestinian constituencies.

The commemorative practices of the first Intifada still contained a notion of progressive emergence from the miasma of inaction, a valorization of martyrdom and self-sacrifice for the nation, and a celebration of defiance. However, the discourse and practices of the first Intifada also indicated a rhetorical rupture with the PLO: heroism no longer lay in the *bunduqiyya*, in battlefields, or in "the children of the RPGs," but rather the mantle of resistance had passed to the "children of stones." Thus, the iconic figure of a young guerrilla, armed and ready to do battle, was replaced with the equally iconic stonethrower, his face covered in the *keffiyeh*, sometimes carrying a "sling and stone, like David" (Makhul 1988: 97; Kuttab 1988).

In recollections of the first Intifada, the period between 1967 and 1987 is seen as a time of humiliation, stupor, and silence. Many participants insist that "the economic situation" immediately prior to the Intifada was good, and therefore the basic cause of the Intifada was the "injustice" which they suffered (Collins 2004: 173) and which they bore in silence, with "resignation (perhaps even self-pity)" (Farsoun and Landis 1991: 28). Conventionally, the period between 1982 (the expulsion of the PLO from Lebanon) and 1987 (the beginning of the Intifada) in the OPT is known as the period of *sumud*, of a stubborn "hanging on." However, while *sumud* in Lebanon had been an acceptable strategy of survival, in the OPT, it came to be an official policy of political organizations. In order to guarantee the survival of Palestinians in the OPT, and for the PLO to remain relevant, the organization had to focus on the Palestinians in the OPT. Thus, the PLO with the help of Gulf states and Jordan established *sumud* funds to underwrite agriculture, education, housing, and municipal services. However, on the one hand, these *sumud* funds went astray, funding the "building [of] middle class villas, subsidies to non-productive industrial firms, and ... patronage moneys to nationalist institutions and personalities," and on the other hand, these funds alleviated pressures on the Israeli

Civil Administration's budgets, and the Israeli military saw them as a means of support for "more moderate" elements within the Palestinian polity (Tamari 1991: 63). As such, *sumud* in the OPT came to have a more pejorative connotation, associated on the one hand with nepotism and elitism, and on the other hand with a fatalistic passive resistance or (even "aggressive non-resistance") to military occupation (Tamari 1991: 61; al-Wazir 1985: 8–9). The heroism of the *jil-al-Intifada* (the Intifada Generation) intended to negate the torpor of the *sumud* era.

A significant feature of the first Intifada was the emergence of popular committees that reached out to and mobilized social segments previously excluded from politics. Women, youth, workers, and refugees were all mobilized through these institutions which had emerged out of (and sometimes fronting) political factions affiliated with the PLO (Hiltermann 1991). When after the spontaneous uprising of the first few weeks of the Intifada, these organizations began to channel and consolidate popular resistance, their mass base and the constraints of operating under a brutal military regime meant that they had to break with past strategies. Thus, the focus on armed struggle as the sole strategy of resistance against the occupation was diluted, but the nationalist appeal to the *jil al-Intifada* espoused just as fervent a discourse of heroic liberation as the one advanced in exile. Where once the *Thawra* had been sanctified, now the Intifada was considered "triumphant," "glorious," and "sacred" (Communiqué No. 28 quoted in Lockman and Beinin 1989: 387; also Lindholm-Schulz 1999: 65).

Intifada communiqués came to be one of the key media through which nationalist commemorative practices were advertised, discursive parameters of the revolt were established, and the vocabulary of resistance was fashioned. Commemoration of heroism was the central element of the communiqués' mobilizing language (Collins 2004: 42). Communiqués issued by the Unified National Leadership (UNL), Hamas, and Islamic Jihad all outlined tactics of resistance and used commemorative languages to reinforce collective mobilization. The very first communiqué of the Intifada (dated 8 January 1988), called for a general strike in order to "reaffirm the need to achieve further cohesion with our revolution and our heroic masses" and asked the workers to abide by the strike in order to show their "real support for the glorious uprising and a sanctioning of the pure blood of our martyrs" (quoted in Lockman and Beinin 1989: 328). Hamas's first communiqué promised that "the blood of our martyrs shall not be forgotten. Every drop of blood shall become a Molotov Cocktail, a time bomb, and a roadside charge that will rip out the intestines of the Jews" (quoted in Mishal and Aharoni 1994: 202). In the transformation of blood into weapons, commemoration became the basis of political action. The first communiqué of the Islamic Jihad saluted the heroic resisters:

> Bravo to the passionate, bravo to the men of freedom, bravo to the honourable, bravo to the defenders of the homeland and our people, bravo to those in whose veins the blood of rejection and revolution pulsates. (Quoted in Lindholm-Schulz 1999: 78)

The second UNL communiqué (dated 13 January 1988) called upon the "people of martyrs, grandsons of al-Qassam, … brothers and comrades of Abu Sharar, Khalid Nazzal and Kanafani" to commemorate 15 January 1988 as "a day of unity and solidarity in commemoration of the martyrs of the uprising."[3] By invoking the names of archetypal martyrs, their mantle of heroism – and the burden of resistance that it brought – was bestowed on the national audience of the communiqués, and by choosing one martyr from each major faction the communiqué recognized different PLO actors. This communiqué invited the Palestinians of the OPT to hold symbolic funerals for the martyrs, and to use these symbolic funerals as the focus of political demonstrations, stone throwing, general strikes and mass mobilization (quoted in Lockman and Beinin 1989: 329–330). Real funerals, however, were also moments around which dissent crystallized, and through which the public unified, showed their support for resistance, valorized self-sacrifice for the nation, and became political agents (Allen 2005, chapter 5). The Israeli military was well aware of this, as a leader of the Intifada attested:

> The occupation authorities think that if someone dies and they take the body and permit the burial only during the night, then there will not be any disturbance. But our thinking has already passed this barrier. The new system is that we snatch the body from the hospital and bury it and turn this into a sort of spontaneous demonstration. (Quoted in Makhul 1988: 93)

Heroic commemorations during the first Intifada transformed into "ritual[s] of sheer bravura. Masking the face with a *keffieh*, scrawling political slogans on walls, flying Palestinian flags, escaping the army's vigilance during curfews, distributing and reading [UNL] communiqués: all these things were strictly prohibited on pain of arrest" (Bucaille 2004: 17). Symbols – the *keffiyeh*, photographs of archetypal martyrs, the forbidden colors of the flag worn in defiance, the image of Hanzala spray-painted on walls, martyrs' commemorative posters – all

---

[3] Majid Abu Sharar, a leftist Fatah activist was assassinated by Mossad [or possibly Abu Nidal] in Rome in 1981. Khalid Nazzal of the DFLP was assassinated by Mossad in Athens in 1986. For Kanafani, see chapter 5.

played a pivotal role in the everyday acts of resistance whose accumulation shaped the contours of the Intifada alongside more visible acts of collective mobilization such as demonstrations or strikes. In the second Intifada, martyrs' posters and funerals became iconized markers of oppositionist politics.

Other commemorative practices were intended to create a coherent narrative and strategy of resistance across temporal and spatial boundaries. The Intifada was again and again tied to the 1936–1939 revolt through invocations of Izz al-Din al-Qassam's name and the uncanny similarities between the two events (Stein 1990; Swedenburg 1995: 171–2), and local histories were located as episodes of longer narratives where heroic resistance connected a series of revolts throughout history (Bowman 2001: 52). Place names were changed to commemorate the transnational Palestinian polity's struggles. The people of Bayt Sahur in the West Bank named streets and neighborhoods after Shqif (or Beaufort) Castle in Lebanon, or Tal al-Za'tar or Shatila camps.[4] Interestingly, the latter two camps were remembered as places of resistance or battle, rather than as massacre sites (Bowman 2001: 52). During the second Intifada, the Ibda' Youth Centre in the Dheisheh Refugee camp commemorated the massacres at Sabra and Shatila by showing a documentary about the atrocity (Allen 2005, chapter 2). The naming of places after recognizable mnemonic markers of past resistances and remembrance of past atrocities emplaced the local histories of the OPT within a larger Palestinian commemorative geography and shored up the claims to transnationality of the Palestinian public. Some activist *shabab* even saw their uprising as part of a larger anti-colonial struggle (Collins 2004: 182).

The intent to construct a transnational Palestine is also obvious in the UNL communiqué 25 in which Black September and Sabra and Shatila are remembered as massacres intended "to finish off what was begun at Deir Yassin, Qibya, Duweima, and Kafr Qassim, with the aim of obliterating our people's distinctive national identity" (Mishal and Aharoni 1994: 125). But the communiqué, which draws the map of Palestine using the geography of massacres, continues "we have always emerged from your massacres and your slaughterhouses with head upright, standing erect despite our wounds and continuing on the road on which our forefathers embarked, headed by the warrior Sheykh al-Qassam and Abd al-Qadir al-Husseini" (1994). Massacres are thus transformed into moments in which the warrior ethos can overcome

---

[4] Beaufort Castle, which fell to the Israeli military in 1982, had been a primary military base of the PLO forces in southern Lebanon.

humiliation and oppression. Recollecting archetypal martyrs Qassam and Husseini connects the aforementioned massacres to the heroism of both Islamist and nationalist leaders.

In the OPT, the figure of the prisoner has also been valorized alongside heroic *fida'iyyin* and martyrs. Since 1967, the Israeli state and military have recorded nearly *one million* arrests or "administrative detentions" (without charge or trial) of Palestinians. Out of a population of 3.6 million Palestinians, an estimated *half a million* Palestinians have been prosecuted since 1967 (Hajjar 2005: 185–6). During this period, young men's beating and detention have been transformed into rites of passage into manhood, and prisoners have become important – and iconic – figures in nationalist practice (Peteet 1994; Rosenfeld 2004: 211–237). Prisoners and prison experiences are commemorated by both the prisoners themselves and by families and political groups. When confronted with a foreign audience, former prisoners often recount their prison experience of torture, abuse, and humiliation in order for the memory of their prison suffering to be "used," and re-told to the world (Hajjar 2005: 201). Their sophisticated utilization of the human rights discourse frames their suffering as prisoners and gives it meaning and purpose; and they deploy the discourse of suffering in order to appeal to a wider international audience. In a national setting, however, "a determined act of collective hermeneutic reversal" transforms the squalid confines of the prison into a place of education, resistance, and growth (Collins 2004: 125; Allen 1998; Thornhill 1992). Narratives of organized and collective struggle within and outside the prison form part of the larger heroic narrative of national resistance (Rosenfeld 2004: 238–265). The commemoration of the prisoner in militant discourse sees them as captive heroes, whose incarceration is "regarded as a respectable and admirable sacrifice for the national cause" (Hajjar 2005: 209). The UNL communiqué no. 24 addresses the prisoners in Ansar and other detention centres:[5]

Glory is yours. You are raising defiance armed with nothing expect your faith in your people and their just cause. Glory to the martyrs of the uprising behind bars ... Your people in the occupied homeland – that large prison – and in the diaspora are firmly convinced that you will pursue confrontation of the plans of liquidation and humiliation being practiced against yours. Yours is part of your people's struggle for their legitimate rights and national independence. (Quoted in Lockman and Beinin 1989: 377)

---

[5] Ansar III or Ketziot prison camp is a large outdoor tent prison operated by the Israeli military. Located in the Negev desert and first opened during the first Intifada, the camp holds thousands of administrative detainees without charge or trial (Cook *et al.* 2005: 85–6).

The prison experience is seen as another node of resistance, and commemoration of prisoners has become another exhortation to mobilization. The polyvalence of the prison experience – being at once a marker of heroic nationalism and social trauma – shows the complexity of and overlap between different commemorative discourses, and the importance of understanding to which audience they are expected to appeal.

In the aftermath of the Oslo Accords, emerging and semi-independent militant factions were either subsumed by the Fatah/PLO/Palestinian Authority nexus, or found themselves in opposition to it, even when the militant organization was an offshoot of Fatah, as happened later with al-Aqsa Martyrs' Brigade (AMB). The PA's unreciprocated compromises made during the negotiations, the subsequent failure of the PA to hold the Israeli state to its Oslo promises, as well as the Authority's prominent role in disciplining and detaining militants, all resulted in the disillusionment of the *jil al-Intifada* and in their radicalization. When the al-Aqsa Intifada began in 2000, the oppositional pole of politics was occupied by the young radical cadres of the AMB and the Islamist organizations, Hamas and Islamic Jihad.[6] Like the guerrilla organizations of the *Thawra* era, these militant organizations also utilized the vocabulary of heroic resistance, armed struggle, self-sacrifice for the cause, and redemption through violence. In 1993, Hamas began to use a violent political tactic utilized in Sri Lanka, Turkey, and Lebanon: suicide bombings. In 1994, and in response to settler Baruch Goldstein's massacre of dozens of Palestinians in the Ibrahimi Mosque in Hebron, Hamas deployed the tactic inside Israel for the first time. The commemorative practices which appeared around suicide bombings not only bolstered the heroic language of the militant movements, but also introduced elements borrowed through direct contact with groups such as the Lebanese Hizbullah.

Valorization of martyrs contains historical layers of practice and mythology, and sedimentations of both nationalist and religious ideologies. For example, the suicide-bombers' recording of videos prior to their operations was a particular characteristic of Lebanese suicide operations committed by both secular and Islamist groups (Nasrallah 1985) which some claim Palestinian Islamist organizations acquired from Lebanese militants when Israel forcibly deported over 400 Islamist militants to a no-man's-land in southern Lebanon in the winter of 1992 (Mishal and Sela 2000: 66). In these martyrdom videos, militants preparing for their suicide missions give their reasons for self-sacrifice, say

---

[6] Leftist oppositionist organizations such as the PFLP were rapidly overtaken by their radical brethren in Hamas or the AMB in number and importance.

their goodbyes, and exhort their audience to rejoice and mobilize. Although the symbolic elements present in the videos are Palestinian nationalist symbols (the flag, the *keffiyeh*, the familiar poses of young men with their Kalashnikovs), the format itself and other elements therein remind the viewer of other martyrdom videos elsewhere. The headbands worn by the soon-to-be-martyr recall the headbands of Iranian martyrdom-seekers during the Iran–Iraq war or the militants of Hizbullah; they contain slogans or Qur'anic verses. The language of masculine bravery is also familiar from the same context. Martyrs' videos, as macabre as they may seem, are also a forum for the martyr-in-waiting to articulate his or her own reasons for seeking martyrdom, and in a sense to commemorate his or her own impending self-sacrifice. These videos often attribute the occupation to pre-nationalist weakness and decay: "We are a nation living in disgrace and under Jewish occupation ... because we didn't fight them" (quoted in Reuter 2002: 91). The statements of martyrs-in-waiting laud martyrdom not as an instance of seeking death, but as a force for the regeneration of life-as-resistance: "I reject this terrible and dark situation which I know and experience and I have decided to become a shining light, illuminating the way for all Muslims" (quoted in Reuter 2002: 91). Thus the exhortation of the martyrs-in-waiting for their families and putative audiences to celebrate their martyrdom repeats the equivalences made during the *Thawra* era between martyrs and bridegrooms or between funerals of martyrs and weddings of youths.

This performance of heroism on public videos, however, is often accompanied with private wills in which martyrs apologise to their parents for not fulfilling their wishes and recognize the hardship they may cause their parents. Yet even here, the masculine heroism of nationalism seeps through as children address their fathers, "You are the one who taught me to be a man in every situation. You are the one who raised a lion in his house" (Reuter 2002: 92). The gendered language of heroism imbues the thoughts of young men and women who commemorate their own self-sacrifice as redemption of past inaction and illumination of the route to future mobilization of others. Interestingly, the discourse of martyrdom as an affirmation of masculine warrior virtue is confirmed in a roundabout way by female suicide-bombers. In her fascinating study of the discourses of martyrdom deployed about and by Palestinian female suicide-bombers, Frances Hasso (2005: 29) tells us that women's self-destructive acts of agency shame (in the words of a female suicide bomber) "Arab armies who are sitting and watching the girls of Palestine fighting while they are asleep" and calls "upon Arab men leaders to fulfil their masculine duties of protecting and defending the community and its women."

But gender also plays another role. Rema Hammami (1994) argues that Hamas used pressure on women to wear the hijab by appealing to the martyrs: in mourning for martyrs, hair should be covered, so uncovered female heads would be construed as frivolous and anti-revolutionary (also see Swedenburg 1995: 189–191). Hamas was also the very last militant group reluctantly to allow women to become suicide-bombers. Indeed, in a direct challenge to the Hamas leadership's pronouncements, Daryan Abu Aysh, who was sympathetic to Hamas but was prepared by the AMB for her suicide operation, declared in her videoed last will and testament, that women's roles "will not only be confined to weeping over a son, brother or husband" (quoted in Hasso 2005: 31). Interestingly, in the 2006 Legislative Council elections, one of the most prominent Hamas candidates was Maryam Farahat who while affirming her gendered position as the mother of three Hamas martyrs, nevertheless actively campaigned and was among the six Hamas women who were elected to the Council.

Videos of martyrs' funerals also attempt to extend the reach of commemoration beyond the actual event. These videos resemble martyrs' commemorative posters as vehicles for conveying a message for the public long after a young man or woman has chosen self-sacrifice for the cause (Allen 2005: chapter 2). Commemorative videos and posters are composed and edited to contain references to blood (Allen 2005: chapter 3), flags, keffiyehs, doves, stones, the Dome of the Rock, Kalashnikovs, and other iconic images. If produced by the Islamist organizations or the AMB, they often contain the famed reference to the Qur'anic verse which declares that the martyrs are not dead, but that martyrdom has guaranteed them life. Though this Qur'anic verse and other Islamic slogans are prominent in the posters, even in the commemorative discourse of the Islamist movement, the nation is the intended object of sacrifice and heroic resistance. Hamas considers dying *for the nation* as a religiously sanctified act and insists that the organization is a "distinct Palestinian movement" (Article 6 of Charter in Hroub 2000: 270) as opposed to a pan-Islamic one. Their charter declares that "the nationalism of the Islamic Resistance Movement is part of its religion; it educates its members on this, and they perform Jihad to raise the banner of God over their nation" (Article 13 in Hroub 2000: 274). In another Article of the Hamas charter, the organization asserts: "Nationalism from the point of view of the Islamic Resistance Movement (Hamas) is part and parcel of religious ideology. Nothing is loftier in nationalism or deeper in devotion than this: If an enemy invades Muslim territories, then Jihad and fighting the enemy becomes an individual duty on every Muslim" (Article 12 in Hroub 2000: 274).

The semiotic and historical richness of Jerusalem as the third most important site of Islam encourages this elision between religion and the nation, but the elision also shows the mutual imbrication of Islamist and nationalist discourses of heroism and self-sacrifice worldwide.

The primary spectators of the commemoration of a funeral or the primary consumer of martyrdom videos are in fact the youth which these commemorative practices act to mobilize. That is why the semiotic vocabulary used in these commemorations is so replete with recognizable icons. Although these commemorative artefacts are meant for a domestic audience, they are sometimes witnessed by foreign observers. When performed for a foreigner, the funeral of a martyr is held under the sign of suffering and claims are made on the moral legitimacy that is acquired through self-sacrifice (Allen 2005).

Victims in NGO and solidarity discourses

In the OPT, the performance of victimhood for an international audience whose sympathy and solidarity is mobilized by the spectacle of suffering has been especially taken up by two groups of actors: solidarity activists and (some) NGOs. Although discourses of suffering have always been deployed where misery, dispossession, impoverishment, and powerlessness have framed people's lives, what distinguishes more recent tragic commemorative narratives is their performance for international audiences and the claims they make on these foreign publics. Where local actors are aware of an international audience whose solidarity or resources can be mobilized, the passive victimhood of Palestinians, and especially of children, is emphasized (Collins 2004: 45). Although the discourse of suffering places a great deal of emphasis on the injustice of the occupation, it also makes resistance to occupation incumbent upon external actors, thus sometimes tacitly delegitimizing local resistances. By privileging victimhood over resistance, international sympathy over local mobilization, and alleviation of suffering over addressing root causes, the larger conflict is depoliticized.

In order to appeal to the larger international audience, often the subjecthood of Palestinians, their struggle, and their militancy are veiled, and in order to present Palestinians as worthy and "innocent" recipients of aid or sympathy, they are constructed as abject victims. Children often take center stage in discourses of victimhood. In speaking on behalf of victimized children, a wholly "innocent" object of empathy is projected and Palestinian childhood becomes "an arena of struggle linking occupier, occupied, and a host of experts (lawyers, psychologists, case workers) in a highly charged contest over who is the true defender of the rights of children and who merely 'uses' children for political ends, a contest whose audience is global" (Collins 2004: 44). The moral reckoning takes the form of a performance of suffering and appeal to universal laws and rights and a discourse of progressive economic and political development.

Whereas in Lebanon, the bulk of NGOs are human rights or humanitarian organizations serving a population in a state of emergency, in the OPT, these are outnumbered by development-related NGOs that do work in the fields of education, reconstruction, agriculture and industry, and environmental services (Hanafi and Tabar 2005: 74–5).[7] In the OPT, a number of local NGOs existed before the post-Oslo flow of "state-building" aid from the outside. Among them, human rights NGOs directly engaged and challenged the state of Israel over its policies in the OPT. They advocated for the rights of prisoners, spoke out against Israel's "iron fist" policy in the OPT, and brought to light the brutality of the occupation regime (Hajjar 2005: 58–75). Though these NGOs offered legal – rather than ostensibly political – critiques of the occupation, in their representation of the lives of Palestinians under occupation, they in fact engaged in the politics of resistance to the occupation (Hanafi and Tabar 2005: 149–156). Alongside these NGOs, organizations loosely affiliated with political factions provided social services and humanitarian relief to their constituencies. As long as these NGOs received funding from and maintained their relations with the factions, their work was quietly political, extending the mandate and reach of the political factions into the communities they served, and garnering the loyalty of the Palestinians assisted (Robinson 1997: 38–65).

The emergence of one humanitarian NGO in particular was very much influenced by the violence in Lebanon. The Welfare Association (*Muassasat al-Ta'awun*), whose mandate was to serve Palestinians everywhere, was established in the latter months of 1982 and as a direct response to the routing of the PLO from Lebanon, and the Sabra and Shatila massacres (Nakhleh 2004: 42). It sought to realize the aspiration of the Palestinian people "especially in the social, cultural and intellectual domains, in addition to safeguarding the identity of the Palestinian people and its Arab and humanistic tradition, ... [d]eepening the

---

[7] Both the PA and the Israeli state are dependent on economic aid provided by foreign donors and administered through both the government and the NGOs. The former needs the foreign aid not only to bolster the production and reproduction of quasi-state institutions, but also to relieve some of the symptoms of economic and political devastation. The Israeli state, on the other hand, depends on the aid to alleviate the costs associated with its ongoing occupation and the attendant circumscription and destruction of Palestinian economic and political infrastructure (Shearer and Meyer 2005).

connection between [the different parts] of the Palestinian people, and safeguarding [the Palestinian's] holistic entity and solidifying his presence on his land" (Nakhleh 2004: 44). Deploying the language of nationalism, the NGO declared that its "most urgent task ... is to arrest the insidious forces of social disintegration and retrogression in the occupied areas of Palestine ... and to assist in nurturing the positive forces of growth and development" (Nakhleh 2004: 45–6). Already, the commemoration of massacres had become the platform for the emergence of political organizations.

The extraordinary mushrooming and professionalization of NGOs after Oslo, however, accelerated their depoliticization and their dependence on foreign funding (Hammami 1995). Because so few local NGOs have core funding, they have had to apply to foreign donors for resources on a project by project basis (Hanafi and Tabar 2005: 189). This has meant that NGO agendas and priorities, rather than being necessarily dictated by local needs, are increasingly shaped by donor priorities and development fashions (Brynen 2000: 188; Hanafi and Tabar 2005: 158–200). To the extent that NGOs are enmeshed in transnational matrices of discourse, practice, and resource allocation, their own representations of the Palestinian past and present has become increasingly framed by discourses of suffering and victimhood. On the other hand, those NGOs which did not necessarily depend on foreign donors for their survival, or which already had an articulated mobilizing discourse, had more complex approaches and did not – or did not solely – present Palestinians as abject victims. Among the latter, for example, are NGOs dealing with violation of the rights of prisoners or Islamic NGOs providing services to their constituencies, especially in Gaza (Roy 2000; Hanafi and Tabar 2005: 242–244). Where the performance of suffering for an international audience was needed, however, NGOs provided the "innocent" subjects upon whom the occupation had wreaked havoc.

NGOs use a number of different venues for "memorializing" suffering. Within these venues, an implicit discourse of commemoration and remembrance frames representations of suffering. Witnessing tours organized by various NGOs – in which they can display the suffering of Palestinians – is a significant part of their advocacy work. In addition to these local visits, NGOs also present the Palestinian case to the world, and represent Palestinians at foreign conferences. In doing so, they highlight Palestinian anguish and misery, often to the exclusion of their efforts to challenge or resist. Lori Allen (2005) describes how Defence for Children International / Palestine Section (DCI/PS) asked an eleven-year-old girl from Jenin to represent the collective suffering of

Palestinians at the UN in Geneva. A local activist justified their choice thus:

Why we chose a girl: first of all, she saw the facts ... The crime by itself, and the pictures that came out of what happened in Jenin, nobody could possibly see them without getting goose bumps. Nobody could see them without becoming sad ... You send numbers and facts about these crimes, and then a child comes along, eleven years old. She has seen crimes, lived through crimes. Her father was killed. She saw her father killed before her eyes. And she says, "I saw these crimes with my eyes." (Quoted in Allen 2005)

In the NGO officers' opinion, a small girl's female-ness, youth, and "innocence" best represent the suffering of Palestine, not only because she has been an eyewitness to atrocities, but also because as a vulnerable youth, she cannot be a political agent, and as such better embodies the kind of abjection that secures international sympathy and support.

What is interesting is that even when they are depoliticized, NGOs nevertheless do political work in cities, camps, and villages, and here they find themselves in competition with militant political factions who focus on heroic armed struggle. This competition to (re)present the Palestinian polity as resolute in its defiance or as abject in its suffering has frequently taken centre stage in the domain of politics, where complex positioning *vis-à-vis* foreign and local audiences, and rival commemorations of acts of resistance in the past also influence strategies of resistance in the present. When in December 2002, after hundreds of Palestinians had been killed by the Israeli military, and following a series of retaliatory suicide bombings, a number of political actors – some of whom were NGO leaders – signed a widely publicized petition critiquing suicide bombings, they were met with derision or criticism by militants (Allen 2002). In a sense, "[b]y critiquing armed resistance without a sustained critique or strategic analysis of the occupation," the NGO officials had delegitimized their own agendas and approaches in the eyes of not only the opposition activists but also large swathes of the population who support a whole range of strategies of resistance to occupation (Hanafi and Tabar 2005: 18). That many NGO activists also represent a nascent elite, with ready access to transnational resources and audiences, also adds to the tensions that had emerged into the open during this episode. The PFLP called NGO activists who had signed the petition "a cocktail of 'civilized intellectuals' who have nothing in common except opening the flow of funds from donor countries to their increasingly cramped pockets" (quoted in Allen 2002), and young militants not only decried the class provenance of these activists, but also pointed to their performance as tailored for foreign audiences (which it may have been, as the petition was published in a prominent Palestinian newspaper monitored by foreign news agencies).

But the NGOs have also found themselves in competition against the PA over scarce resources, priorities, operational issues, and last but not least the (re)presentation of the Palestinian condition to the outside world (Brynen 2000: 187). Both NGOs and the PA have accused one another of corruption, bad faith, and misrepresenting the interests of their constituency. The PA claims to represent all Palestinians, whereas most NGOs inevitably serve smaller sectoral constituencies. In speaking for the nation, the PA projects Palestinians as a nation on the march of progress, whereas the NGOs have portrayed Palestinians as victims in need of support. In both instances, however, the fact of military occupation has moved to the backstage, and the funding is used to alleviate its symptoms, rather than address the military occupation at the core of it.

In this competition, NGO activists have used the discussion of suffering to criticize the power of the PA. If radical militants criticize the NGOs for appropriating foreign funds, NGO activists criticize PA officials for their conspicuous consumption. By contrasting the villas of the PA "returnees" from Tunis to the poverty and deprivation on the ground, the legitimacy of the former is questioned. In 1994, an NGO activist from Gaza interrogated the ease with which the PA had established its power there, "They are the Fatah fat cats ... What do they know of our suffering? They come from Tunis, they buy up all the villas in Gaza, and we are still in the camps. Nothing has changed" (quoted in Ditmars 2000: 19). Only after the al-Aqsa Intifada began and its first few months saw much carnage, did the NGOs present a united front with the PA and address the occupation directly. In the later months of 2000, the network of Palestinian NGOs published a report in which they declared that Palestinian capabilities could be enhanced by "arranging our internal front to enhance our steadfastness, and by continuing the uprising in its mass shape, until the defeat of the occupation and the establishment of our forthcoming independent state" (PNGO 2000: 6). The moment of confrontation had resulted in a discursive shift, where the nationalist discourse of the al-Aqsa Intifada had become more prominent, but where resistance was not militant or armed but had a "mass shape."

The same discursive shifts and utilisation of the polyvalent symbols can also been seen in the manner in which iconic events and persons were commemorated. The martyrs' exhibit I discussed at the beginning of Chapter 6, in which martyrdom was portrayed as an instance of injustice and suffering visited upon helpless and innocent bodies, is one such moment. Produced by a sophisticated Ramallah-based NGO, the exhibit intends to show the suffering of the Palestinian polity to an international audience; it does so through evoking memories and mnemonic artefacts recalling unintentional martyrs. The performance of martyrdom here is devoid of heroism and redemption lies not in the mobilization of militancy, but in the garnering of the sympathies of the audience. Martyrs' funerals also lend themselves to this polyvalence. Where addressed to a domestic audience, they are exhortations to militancy, but when observed by a foreign audience and mediated through the language of advocacy NGOs, they are stories of suffering (Allen 2005). In visits with foreign activists, bodily wounds often displayed as corporeal evidence of suffering could have in fact been acquired during stone-throwing or street clashes (Collins 2004: 86). The wound as a marker of heroism and manliness in a domestic context becomes a sign of suffering for a foreign audience.

An important instance of multiplying an interpreted iconic moment is the destruction of the Jenin camp in April 2002. After a series of suicide bombings, the Israeli military attacked the Jenin refugee camp – known as a node of militant resistance – using tanks, fighter jets, Apache and Cobra helicopters, and infantry. After placing the camp under a week-long siege, the military destroyed the camp's electricity generators and bulldozed hundreds of homes, sometimes without warning their occupants. Militant descriptions of the siege and struggle of Jenin emphasized the heroic resistance of the *shabab* in the camp and the infliction of casualties – 23 dead soldiers – on the Israeli military. NGOs and solidarity activists emphasized the wanton destruction of the civilian infrastructure in the camp and the suffering of the civilians. Jenin-as-battle and Jenin-as-massacre are not contradictory. Of the 63 confirmed Palestinian deaths, over twenty were civilians, some of whom were killed execution style, while most were shot dead by Israeli snipers (Baroud 2003; HRW 2003). A year later, in the wake of the US invasion of Iraq, many residents of Jenin invoked the narrative of heroic battle in solidarity: "In 1948, the Iraqis liberated Jenin from the Israeli army. Today we are marching for Iraq and in memory of *the battle* in Jenin refugee camp. There is a big connection between Iraq and Jenin – they can learn from what we did here a year ago" an Al-Aqsa Martyrs' Brigade fighter explained to reporters, one of whom was Palestinian (War and Abu Bakr 2003). By contrast, local advocacy NGOs, whether working in relief, human rights, or development, were crucial in disseminating the narrative of Jenin's suffering to the world, and in doing so, they forestaged the losses of the civilians, rather than the battle waged by the *shabab*.

In addition to NGOs, solidarity organizations are also active agents in representing the Palestinian condition through a framework of suffering. Witnessing Palestinian misery and disseminating information about it to the world had occurred long before the first Intifada, intensified during the first Intifada, and grained a more concrete organizational form during the al-Aqsa Intifada. In 2001, the International Solidarity Movement (ISM) was established in the OPT, drawing activists – including Palestinians and Israelis holding other passports – from overseas (Seitz 2003). ISM activists have used their technological savvy to present Palestinian suffering to the world through their websites and web-logs. Two of their rank, American Rachel Corrie and British Tom Hurndall, have been killed by the Israeli military, while many others have been beaten and deported. The Palestinian-led ISM declares as its mandate not only the protection of civilians, but also and especially witnessing and providing information to the mainstream media (ISM 2005). The ISM activists' web writings and books (Stohlman and Aladin 2003; Sandercock et al. 2004) take their job of witnessing seriously. They attest to the suffering of Palestinians, and appeal to their international audiences' sympathies and feelings by detailed descriptions of how universally recognizable elements of Palestinian lives – their children, their grandmothers, their homes, their olive-tree farms, and even their furniture – have been attacked and destroyed by the Israeli military.

Palestinians themselves have become accustomed to representing their suffering to these foreign witnesses who are conduits to "the world." Adoption of the language of suffering has greatly bifurcated Palestinian discourse between the heroism of violent struggle and the tragic helplessness of suffering. What is ironic, however, is that after the first intifada, when not performing to an international audience, a quieter discourse of hope belied the landscape of hopelessness projected in discourses of suffering. In the face of privation, oppression, and everyday difficulties of negotiating checkpoints, house demolitions, curfews, closures, and firefights, a tenderly tended belief in a glorious tomorrow flourished and all hardship and sacrifice were seen eventually – one day, however distant – to bear fruit. As Lønning (1994: 166–167) observed:

For most of the people you speak to, even the poorest of the poor, even people who have been beaten or jailed and exposed to torture, when you ask them how they see their future, their stories – highly realistic in their description of the contemporary tragic situation both on the internal, regional and international front – generally end with some vision of better days and justice ahead. Behind all this oppression and misery there is a peculiar kind of optimism ... Hope may be put on, for example, internal strength, on divine intervention, on Arab or

European interference, or on a US change of policy. In short, on virtually anything.

Since the second Intifada, the hopes nurtured during and after the first Intifada do not have a counterpart in the OPT. This persistent hopefulness (or *sumud*) has given way either to the bravura of violent self-sacrifice or to the pathos of helplessness. Many Palestinians, who are conscious of their large international audience, often "perform examples of what the visitors view as the essence of 'Palestinianness' – namely, stories of suffering and victimization. The visitor, in turn, is expected to observe and record (in writing, on tape or film, in his or her memory) the 'evidence' of suffering" (Collins 2004: 86). The visitors are often activists who then bear the news of suffering to their respective audiences.

Where the Movement finds itself in contention with militants in the OPT – some of whom publicly voice some gratitude for the ISM's solidarity – is over the issue of armed struggle. In its primary documentation, the Movement states that it hopes to achieve its aims "using only non-violent, direct-action methods, strategies and principles" (ISM 2005). One of the leaders of the ISM, Ghassan Andoni, actively encourages non-violent mobilization, because "rallying large numbers to this form of protest would greatly augment the Palestinian struggle, especially since only a tiny percentage of Palestinians is actively engaged, with the others 'suffering and 'steadfasting'" (quoted in Seitz 2003: 60). However, rejecting militancy has had contentious side-effects. When in 2001, Marwan Barghouthi, the celebrated head of Fatah in the West Bank, showed up at an ISM rally in Ramallah, some ISM leaders asked him to leave (Seitz 2003: 54), resulting in great anger within the Movement's ranks. Furthermore, local militant activists consider the ISM's insistence on non-violence to be a negative judgment of their own militancy. Their response is akin to one given by local militants to another set of solidarity activists in another time and place: "Foreigners come here, they take a quick look around, and they judge us!" (quoted in Jean-Klein 2002: 68). In her analysis of "political audit tourism" Jean-Klein carefully criticizes this tendency by describing how on occasion solidarity organizations pressure the local activists "to contrive, in appearance at least, organizational forms which complied with outsiders' expectations of what it means to be modern and progressive" (Jean-Klein 2002: 49).

Conclusions

In the Occupied Palestinian Territories, as in the refugee camps of Lebanon, commemoration is contentious and shaped by the confluence of local institutional forms and transnational mobilizing discourses. What distinguishes the OPT from the Lebanese camps is the substantial role played by quasi-state bodies and the significance of nation-statist commemorative practices in competition with militant heroism and the NGOs' narratives of suffering. Although germs of this nation-statist heroism were present even in the *Thawra*-era refugee camps, this commemorative narrative – celebrating the state, its coercive machinery, and its founding fathers – was most fully realized in the OPT. However, because the Palestinian state has had only nominal control over its institutions, or indeed even the territory ostensibly under its rule, commemorations have been largely limited to symbolic assertions of a non-existent sovereignty on the one hand, and an unrestrained celebration of the quasi-state's security apparatus on the other.

The bifurcation of the heroic narrative in the OPT has meant that while the militants still celebrate heroic resistance embodied in armed struggle and self-sacrifice for the nation, nation-statist heroism valorizes the state itself. The iconic figures of the former are the fighter, the prisoner, and the martyr, and of the latter, the statesman and founding father. In the former, the commemorative events which fix a heroic national narrative in the public's mind are the martyrs' funerals, while in the latter, they are the elections. Celebration of armed struggle in the oppositionist discourse gives way to valorization of security men of the state. Flags, red carpets, government buildings, museums, and national uniforms all come to embody the nation and tell its story, while at the same time, they act as the portentous symbolic furniture of nation-statehood. In the case of Palestine, this bifurcation was complicated by the figure of Arafat who was, throughout his rule in the OPT, at once the symbol of nationalist/liberationist struggle and the concrete embodiment of ruling power. His funeral brought to the fore this seeming contradiction, and after his death, the fissure between the ruling elite and the younger militant *shabab* was further crystallized.

While this largely internal struggle over the parameters of heroic commemoration and militant mobilization goes on between the quasi-state and oppositionist militants, a third discourse which portrays Palestinians as victims in need of external assistance largely addresses a foreign audience, not only to garner their sympathy or solidarity, but also to secure funding through them. This latter task guarantees the continuation of the provision of services to the Palestinian population – though constrained by international priorities and agendas. It also serves to reproduce and strengthen these NGOs, or what Hanafi and Tabar (2005) rightfully call a "new globalised elite" with extensive connections to international organizations, access to their discourses, and the ability to act as conduits for the dissemination of their practices at local levels. What distinguishes NGOs operating in the OPT from their cohorts in the camps in Lebanon are their ostensibly different functions. If the former are in the business of "development," the latter focus on "humanitarian" aid. The discourse of human rights is deployed in both contexts, but because of the direct encounter between OPT human rights activists and the military/juridical apparatus of the Israeli state, this discourse has far more bite in the OPT. Nevertheless, NGOs in both the OPT and the camps in Lebanon are conduits of funds and the ethos of suffering. These allocative and distributive institutional functions, however, are challenged by the quasi-state institutions of the PA which are in direct competition over funds with the NGOs. In this competition, then, the PA officials on occasion co-opt the discourse and commemoration of suffering and frequently perform this discourse for international audiences.

The discourses and practices promoted by the NGOs and solidarity organizations are also contested by oppositionist organizations. Militant oppositionists see in the promotion of a Palestinian victim subject, robust endorsement of non-violent tactics of resistance, and appeal to international audiences, a crowding out of local agency and depoliticization of the Palestinian struggles. Furthermore, the shift to a discourse of liberal rights, legal enforcement, and international sympathy throws the focus of claim-making on symptoms of foreign military occupation, rather than the occupation itself. As such, many militant organizations find whatever political space may have opened up through appealing to international rights and solidarity to be restrictive spaces where foreign actors and powers, rather than local ones, define the shape of a Palestinian polity. This contestation over whether the Palestinian condition in the OPT is best seen as an instance of resistance, or a tragedy of victimhood then has direct relevance to the particular strategies of mobilization used by political organizations there.

9   Conclusions

> But where are facts if not embedded in history, and then reconstituted
> and recovered by human agents stirred by some perceived or desired or
> hoped-for historical narrative whose future aim is to restore justice to
> the dispossessed?
>
> Edward Said, "Permission to Narrate"

> We travel like other people,
> but we return to nowhere
> We have a country of words;
> speak speak so I can put my road on the stone of a stone.
> We have a country of words.
> Speak speak so we may know the end of this travel.
>
> Mahmud Darwish, "We travel like other people"

This book has been about the struggles, failures and triumphs of a
nationalist movement in imagining the nation. I have argued that a
fundamental practice in the constellation of Palestinian nationalist
practices is commemoration, and that narratives contained within
commemorative practices are crucial in shaping the stories of Palestinian
peoplehood. These commemorative practices – ceremonies, rituals,
memorials, and history-telling – all represent, reinterpret, and remember
the national past in an ongoing and dynamic way and in so doing, set the
stage for crafting future strategies. In trying to better understand
nationalism, in earlier pages I have examined Palestinian commemorative forms and the narratives of heroism, suffering and *sumud* they
contain, the emergence of these narratives at the intersection of available
transnational discourses and local political institutions, and the diverse
and dynamic performances of these narratives for different audiences.

Form and content of commemorations

This study shows that commemorative practices have forms and contents. Commemorative forms include texts and images produced in
books, magazines, and newspapers, on posters and websites, in murals

and music. Place and human names, museums, memorials, and cemeteries can all concretize "memories" of the past. Commemoration can
happen through school books, holiday cycles, calendars, ceremonies, and
gatherings. People can commemorate by history-telling. These forms are
easily adopted and adapted across borders and have been associated with
nationalist practice in general. Some forms of commemoration are borrowed from everyday social and cultural lives of a people and are then
transformed into political events. Funeral ceremonies for martyrs, for
example, transform grief for human losses into an affirmation of the
nation through sacrifice and a basis of political sympathy, solidarity, or
mobilization. By eliding everyday rituals with political theatre, the weight
of extant social practice legitimates the politics, while the performance of
politics transforms the rituals into a public event that binds the commemorating nationals. Some forms of commemoration, like history-
telling, require scant resources, while the maintenance of others, such as
museums, at the very least necessitates the efforts of a curator in
acquiring materials and objects of memory. Most spatial forms of commemoration require control over place and an institutional infrastructure
to construct and maintain monuments, cemeteries, memory-places, and
the like. However painstakingly established, such places are never
immune from the ravages of political conflict, as for example, the
destroyed and rebuilt Palestinian "national" cemetery at the Ain al-
Hilwa refugee camp, or the threatened Shatila cemetery in Beirut attest.
Yet other commemorative forms, such as holiday cycles, can only be
implemented through institutional channels, as they require the participation of large swathes of a commemorating public with ties to that
institution. However, institutions such as UNRWA will not necessarily
introduce such holiday cycles in their schools without pressure from
activists within the organization or political factions outside it. Nor is the
introduction of these holiday cycles a guarantee that the narrative they
contain is disseminated or absorbed. While a particular holiday with a
symbolically significant name – such as Land Day or Martyrs' Day – may
be commemorated widely and fervently, commemorators can as easily be
paying homage to the iconized symbols of land or martyrdom rather
than the historical narratives behind these commemorative events. While
the details of the narrative are not absorbed, its iconic element and its
general mood of celebratory heroism or plaintive victimhood are.
Other forms of commemoration show the profound personal and emotional investment of the commemorator: parents who name their
daughters after the Jenin camp, or their son after Ghassan Kanfani are in
effect inscribing an object of commemoration upon the bodies of their
children.

All these commemorative forms – whether explicitly as in history-telling, or implicitly as in monuments – contain narratives which transform inchoate events into coherent stories with protagonists, adversaries, plots, and putative endings. These commemorative narratives adhere to particular moods: they can be about heroism, suffering, or *sumud*. Over the last half century, Palestinian commemoration in Lebanon has shifted from heroic narratives valorizing the *fida'iyyin* and battles for the nation to tragic narratives which lament victims and grieve massacres, while transitional *sumud* (steadfastness) narratives have focused on the adaptive resilience of the refugees at times of utmost uncertainty. In the OPT, nation-statist versions of the heroic narrative have appropriated many of the liberationist tropes in the service of the state. Militant heroic narratives have nevertheless endured and because of the conditions of life under occupation diverged to include non-violent variants, valorizing prisoners and celebrating the Intifada resistance, and acquired Islamist tinges. The heroic narratives of the OPT persist alongside narratives of suffering most prominently advanced by the NGOs and solidarity activists but also by the PA and Palestinians themselves when addressing an international audience.

In the refugee camps of Lebanon, the massive upheavals following the Israeli invasion of Lebanon and the ouster of the PLO from that country resulted in seismic changes in the manner of mobilization and memorialization. During the *Thawra* period (1969–1982), when the PLO finally wrested the control of the camps from the Lebanese security forces, militant organizations came to the fore. They mobilized the refugees, transformed the camps into militant spaces, renamed camp quarters after political factions and archetypal martyrs, and made over camp aesthetics by introducing commemorative posters, nationalist icons, murals, and graffiti. In this period, not only the militant organizations, but most refugees, and indeed most Lebanese and Palestinians celebrated the masculine virtues of young warriors, and the past and present were cast in the heroic mold. These heroic narratives see an ancient past of glory, a direct progenitor of today's nation, dishonored by a subsequent period of decay and torpor, and they perceive militant mobilization as the present-day moment of recuperation of that past glory. Nation-statist variants of the heroic narrative prevalent in the OPT domesticate militancy and heroism into the manifold representations of security forces. The young and virile male warriors give way to solemn and stately founding fathers in nation-statist heroism, and the ephemeral ceremonies celebrating the nation are replaced by the pomp and circumstance of red carpets and state museums. In both variants of the heroic narrative, the iconic, literal, and figurative force of *bunduqiyya* resides in what is seen as the regenerative quality of violent resistance. Manhood and honor lost in the humiliation of defeat to the adversary are recuperated through militant mobilization, and a new man – with all the sublimated gender discourse this term implies – is created in the act of resistance.

If the central figure of the heroic narrative is a *fida'yi*, armed, beautiful and confident running on the crest of hills, the tragic narrative throws the spotlight upon the victimized woman or child, shorn of power and protection, left exposed to the cruelty of adversaries and the betrayal of allies. The narrative of suffering sees the past as a series of unqualified defeats, where the massacre comes to stand as a metaphor for the Palestinian condition. The horror of history is crystallized in the sequence of atrocities committed against innocent Palestinian victims, and successive massacres crowd out histories of resistance. In history-telling, descriptions of bodily pain act as the opening into the litany of injustice and suffering the refugee has endured. Two elements make the tragic narrative more than simply a lamentation of victimhood. First, there is the implicit claim within the tragic narrative that: "I have suffered, therefore I deserve recognition of my claims and restoration of my rights." Whether these rights are articulated within the framework of citizenship ("The PA cannot forget me, even if I am in Lebanon, for I have suffered for Palestine") or that of the universal human rights ("How can the world community stand and watch my suffering?") tragic discourses demand inclusion in a larger polity and the protections that affords. Second, no suffering is seen as eternal. All suffering is seen to be redeemed one day by the justice acquired as a result of so much suffering, "if not for me, then for my son, or for my grandson." The redemptive quality of the tragic narrative thus implies that suffering is not a passive act, but rather the basis of contentious claim-making.

Somewhere outside these two familiar moods stands the narrative of *sumud*. Steadfastness in the face of ongoing assault is a sort of infra-politics of the powerless. It neither demands self-sacrifice, nor valorizes suffering. At its core is the quiet dignity of "hanging on," no matter how battered, assailed, and embattled one becomes. It is the inconspicuous act of resistance required to rebuild your house even after it has been destroyed for the fifth time, to once again have children even after your sons were butchered in front of you, to remain in the camp or on the land even after the perimeter of those spaces were invaded by militaries, mortars, and tanks.

Each of these stories not only frames the past in a particular way, but it also gives meaning to present conditions. Violence and powerlessness are explained through their narrative force, and they resonate with the commemorating public because in their familiarity and reiterations, they encapsulate not just a particular genre but also the particular times in which these stories have been told. The anti-colonial struggle, the Cold War, creation and movement of millions of refugees, five Israel–Arab wars, the rise of NGOs, and several revolutions have all affected the narratives' plots and turning points. History and biography are often conjoined in these narratives. The predominance of a particular narrative is acutely affected not only by their performative setting but, crucially, by authorized transnational discourses and the resources of local institutions.

Available transnational discourses and local political institutions

One of the ironies of nationalist mobilization in the twentieth century has been the frequency with which nationalist movements have cloaked themselves in transnational discourses whose very local legitimacy often rests on their widespread resonance across borders and the perception that they transcend the national community in appealing to and bringing together large publics. The best-known transnational discourse of course is one which authorizes the nation-state as the most legitimate unit of global politics. What Robert Malley (1996) has called nation-statism, a kind of nationalism which venerates the state as the repository of national sovereignty and sentiment, has of course emerged and flourished alongside modern nation-states, but it has found a particularly potent variant in the post-colonial states of the twentieth century. Another variant of nationalism, a more radical one that finds sanction in the radical liberationist movements of the anti-colonial era, is the militant version which valorizes armed struggle and foresees not only self-determination and sovereignty, but also a deep-seated transformation of the social sphere, the creation of a "new man" and the negation of colonial/neo-colonial/imperialist exploitation and humiliation. Yet a third transnational discourse celebrating the nation in a Third World context appeals to Islamic symbols and ideas in order to recuperate lost dignity, restore self-rule, and revitalize a local culture contaminated by colonial or imperial intervention. In all these discourses, a heroic ethos prevails which demands not only the imagination of a tautly interconnected community, but also works to mobilize this community against adversaries of the nation and does not shy away from violence. In fact, violence is seen not only as a legitimate tactic of struggle, but also as a regenerative conflagration which guarantees the birth of a new man and a new society.

Tectonic political shifts worldwide have meant that those transnational discourses which use heroic frames to reinterpret the past, give meaning to the present, and mobilize publics have been joined by discourses of universal human rights and the ethos of international (military or economic) intervention. The latter had emerged in the wake of the Second World War, but it was only with the end of the Cold War and the dizzying rise of NGOs that it moved to center stage. Largely liberal in its pedigree, this discourse has been used both by anti-establishment activists looking for an authorized discourse and instrument of transnational mobilization and by the sole hyperpower, the United States, which has wielded the language of rights as one weapon among many in its arsenal of tools used to make the new world order. If nationalist and nation-statist discourses privileged heroic – and sometimes militant – appeals to more bounded communities of nationals, the discourse of suffering uses a history of victimization and a language of nation-transcending rights to appeal to a large transnational community. If a fierce pride structures feelings in heroic nationalisms, a plea for sympathy shapes tragic claims to rights. In its weaker variants, concrete demands for locally enforceable and accountable governance give way to vague calls for recognition of universal humanities ultimately derived from "natural" rights. When backed by political force, this language of rights nevertheless has to struggle against far more powerful and better-equipped actors, such as states.

Although these discourses ultimately have many of the same referents, it is instructive to examine the role of the United Nations in nation-statist and universal rights discourses. In the former, the UN is an organization which certifies membership of a new nation as an ostensibly equal member of the community of nations. In the discourse of rights, the UN becomes the supposed ultimate arbiter and audience for the claims to human rights. So, when Arafat refers to his acceptance by the General Assembly as a badge of pride and mark of international legitimacy, he perceives the UN as a mechanism of certification of the nation, the majority of whose members are in fact themselves post-colonial states. On the other hand, more recent appeals made to the UN on the basis of universal human rights imagine it not as such a certifying agency or as a community of sovereign nations, but as the home of universal human rights, and as such, an interventionist body that in advancing human rights must and should challenge national sovereignties. This shift is decisive in how heroic or tragic discourses imagine the relevant political actors and significant transnational values: once nations and national sovereignty, today the international community and universal rights.

Significantly, the maintenance and dissemination of these discourses require, among other things, institutions which command necessary resources and technologies. At the local level, in the Palestinian case, these institutions have included political factions, UNRWA and NGOs, and ultimately, the quasi-state structure of the Palestinian Authority. Commemorative practices – iconization of places, memorialization of holidays, naming of objects, places and persons to honor what is lost or dead, ceremonial gatherings which through their ritual elements tell a story, and electronic media, textbooks, and publications which tell histories – all require the kinds of resources that often only institutions can muster, and which are rarely available to individual refugees. Institutional control over commemoration, in turn, has meant that the forms, contents, and referents of commemoration have been those which the institutions have considered relevant or legitimate, and the audiences for whom commemoration is performed are those with whom the institutions interact: for example, because of the international connections and relations of NGOs, it is inevitable that the audience of the NGOs would be the international community.

The changing character of Palestinian political institutions in Lebanon and beyond has been crucially important in the transformation of Palestinian commemoration. As the primacy of militant Palestinian factions and guerrilla groups was eclipsed by the non-governmental organizations, the aims, audiences, and available discourses used by these organizations were similarly transformed.

While political institutions focused primarily on mobilizing refugee youth, the NGOs concentrated on providing relief and services to the refugee camps. The former aimed to forge "new" Palestinians in the crucible of revolutionary wars of liberation; the latter made claims on behalf of the refugees, demanding recognition and acknowledgment of their suffering. Intense struggles have occurred over the form and content of commemoration – and over the history of the nation. Yet, because political institutions have access to material and symbolic resources – to financial assets, pedagogic institutions, electronic media, the press and the like – they have been successful in promulgating their version of nationalist histories. Their success is indicated not only by the ordinary refugees adopting commemorative forms generated by the institutions, but also by the polyvalence of commemorated events in the absence of dominating institutional narratives. For example, whereas in Lebanon, *sumud* became the narrative of resilience in the face of overwhelming violence, propelled simply by the everyday acts of obstinacy by the refugees, *sumud* in the OPT was eventually institutionalized and transformed directly into a strategy of political mobilization with a vast budget and networks of influence. Such a transformation meant that for the period where *sumud* was the order of the day, past histories were viewed and commemorated solely through its lens. But also such institutionalized dominance also meant that in the subsequent period, an inevitable backlash in the OPT came to view *sumud* as the very condition of corruption and decay that heroic mobilization was trying to overcome.

Although commemorative narratives borrow much from authorised transnational discourses, a whole range of contextual conditions influence the actual shape of these commemorations. The contestation between different factions, as I have shown, has resulted in commemoration of some martyrs as archetypal ones, some events as special to a particular group, as some places more relevant to some factions. For example, cartoonist Naji al-Ali is remembered as a victim of Arafat's megalomania as much as he is a victim of multiple exiles. Asymmetries of power between the refugees and other actors have also affected the contours of commemoration. The Tal al-Za'tar massacre is not commemorated with the same intensity as the massacre at Sabra and Shatila, not only because the site of the former is within a Maronite-controlled area of Beirut and thus inaccessible to Palestinians, but also because of the complex calculus of power persisting in the region. Commemorating Tal al-Za'tar requires that the culpability of Syria be recognized when Syria has for so long controlled politics in Lebanon with an iron fist. Furthermore, factional rivalries and the dispersion of the survivors of the massacre have made the commemoration of Tal al-Za'tar nearly impossible.

Struggling against direct military occupation in the OPT has meant that Palestinian NGOs in the OPT did not always deploy the language of abjection, or that during the first Intifada armed struggle was not as valorized as it had been during the *Thawra* in Lebanon. The concurrence of heroic and suffering discourses in the OPT, furthermore, speaks to the contemporaneous existence of both militant factions and NGOs there. In Lebanon, by contrast, the tragic commemorative narrative has followed in the heels of narratives of heroism and *sumud*, reflecting the sequential prominence of, first, factions and then NGOs, with an interregnum where few institutions could operate, much less predominate.

Therefore, although authorized transnational discourses legitimate local narratives and practices and empower local institutions, contextual conditions are also of great importance. Asymmetries of power, alliances, rivalries, and enmities all have molded the contours of commemoration; among the most important local conditions affecting commemoration has been its performative context.

Commemoration as performance

Despite the relative power of local institutions in reproducing particular national commemorations and narratives, commemoration has not emerged solely out of elite agency. The very performative nature of commemoration – that it fundamentally requires an audience – has meant that commemorations have to draw on that audience's values, experiences, memories, sympathies, and beliefs. For commemoration to be popular, for it to resonate with and mobilize Palestinians, it has to say something about *their* past, make some meaning of *their* present lives, offer something about *their* future.

In the actual practice of commemoration, ordinary Palestinians become not only the audience for these institutional performances, but also actors within them, leaving their mark on the practices and narratives. Sometimes, Palestinians emphasize those symbols whose relative abstraction allow them to be filled with meaning drawn from the Palestinians' intimate lives. Thus, a heroic battle celebrated becomes a generic stand-in for all heroic battles, the Land Day a commemoration of all lost land, Martyrs' Day an homage to all martyrs. In other instances, institutionally advocated commemorations are subverted by their audience through their lack of participation in it. That Palestinian refugee youths cannot tell the story of the battle of Karama – indeed cannot even say where Karama might be – says something of the precipitous fall of that icon in the wake of the PLO's withdrawal from Lebanon. Sometimes, persons or events are commemorated because they embodied an era, a belief, a hope. Ghassan Kanafani, for example, to many Palestinians is not simply an assassinated martyr; he is also the original chronicler of dispossession and exile. Many of those who venerate him see in his stories an articulation of their own lives and words and images that crystallize their histories. Even more important, those words and images are recognizable and beloved because Kanafani was himself inspired by the lives of the refugees who read his stories. In the mutual borrowing of Palestinians' experiences from commemorative narratives and of commemorations from Palestinians' lives, commemoration is thus dialogically crafted.

Furthermore, institutions can go "off-script" when performing for an unusual audience. For example, the dependence of the PA on foreign donations has meant that quasi-state institutions have adopted the language of suffering familiar from NGOs alongside their more usual deployment of heroic nation-statism. Prior to 1993 and before becoming the recipient of international donations and scrutiny, local NGOs in the OPT primarily appealed to local audiences, and as such, suffering took a backstage to discourses of heroic resistance or *sumud*. When caught in the international media spotlight, those militant factions that are more media-savvy can deploy the language of suffering in such a way as to appeal to an international audience that may be wary of violent or militant resistance.

But audiences are also important in determining the very meaning of heroism or suffering, or the categorization of a particular object of memory as heroic or tragic. For example, NGOs have had two audiences for their performance of Palestinian suffering. Commemoration of suffering is intended to move an international donor community to better fund programs to alleviate local hardships. Here, suffering implies helplessness. Performed for an audience of scholars, activists, or journalists who are thought to wield influence in the fate of the refugees, suffering is intended as a call for sympathy, solidarity, and support. On the other hand, Palestinians have also performed their commemoration of suffering for their political leadership in the OPT. In this case, suffering legitimates a demand for inclusion in the Palestinian polity. A refugee in Lebanon, in this instance, displays her suffering as a proof that she has sacrificed much for the nation, and as such has to be included as part of that larger polity. Where faced with exclusion from political participation in the Palestinian community, suffering comes to be a certificate of membership. Martyrdom similarly can be considered tragic when the martyrs are women, children, or unintentional victims of conflict, but especially when martyrdom is commemorated for an international audience. Commemoration of intentional martyrs for local audiences, however, bears all the marks of heroism and pay homage to nationalist militancy.

The performativity of commemoration, then, complicates the mapping of certain discourses to particular institutions, and introduces nuances and complexities that become apparent when one examines the specificities of a particular time and place more attentively.

Evaluating tragic, heroic, and *sumud* narratives

Across national borders, tragic, heroic and *sumud* narratives have had a profound influence on how Palestinians imagine their past, how they envision their nation, and plan their future strategies. In order to better understand the significance of different commemorative narratives, their impact and efficacy as mobilizing discourses have to be evaluated.

The primary merit of Palestinian heroic narratives has been their celebration of ordinary refugees' agency. The heroic narrative which posits a negation of apathy and abjection challenges passive acqui-escence or fatalism, demands action in the face of dispossession and defiantly claims a place at the table of nations for communities long excluded from self-determination. A primary instrument in forging nations, the heroic narrative provides the basis of community, encourages pride and dignity in the face of subjugation, and inspires resistance. But heroic commemorations which valorize violent resistance across generations – even centuries – are quite costly. The self-perpetuating dynamics of heroic militancy antagonizes potential allies – as it did with the Shi'a in southern Lebanon – and through the force and appeal of its rhetoric subverts alternative solutions. Honoring militants and militancy reproduces the "culture of the gun," prioritizes political violence, and sometimes forecloses the possibility of finding political solutions to conflicts. Internally, the heroic narrative encoura-ges the development of an armed vanguard at the expense of mass political mobilization.

The tragic narrative by contrast, egalitarianizes the role of the public in the cause of the nation. Through its recognition of the suffering of refugees and ordinary people, it acknowledges their day-to-day sacrifices alongside activist mobilization. It opens a space in national discourse for the ordinary, often silent – though not always passive – majority who are usually overshadowed in the self-congratulatory glare of heroic com-memorations. It pulls back the curtain concealing the costs of nationalist mobilization for the dispossessed, and demands the world to see and to act. But in doing so, it shifts the onus of action onto the international community, makes suffering itself a virtue, and denies the possibility of agency, mobilization or collective action. The tragic discourse insists that the suffering of the past suffices as a necessary condition for acquiring rights in the future, and sometimes subverts the possibility of internal organization and mobilization.

Finally, narratives of *sumud* are the most complex of the three nar-ratives, perhaps because they came to mean such differing things in the OPT and in the diaspora. Steadfastness provides a framework for ordinary refugees' struggles to survive in conditions of extreme duress. Although only in the OPT did *sumud* become a deliberate strategy of resistance, it was never a revolutionary ideology. Since *sumud* is an invitation to stubbornly "hang on," come what may, it allows for the ordinary members of the community to find a solution – however ephemeral and ineffective it may prove in the long term – which fits the constraints of *their* lives and does not demand of them further sacrifices. It neither requires collective mobilization, nor adherence to a larger ideology, but in its everydayness, it acknowledges the oft-ignored role of marginalized actors, foremost among them women, in holding the community together in desperate times. Emblematic of the *infrapolitics* of the dispossessed and the disempowered, the efficacy of *sumud* is not in its ability to beget political cataclysms, but rather in its cumulative force over decades resulting in incremental changes, which may not substantially alter societies, but which provide a breathing space for those who are most often trampled in the stampede of history.

Palestinians themselves evaluate the efficacy of these narratives depending on their institutional ties and subjective positions. A former guerrilla and current political activist, for example, told me that he detested narratives of suffering and wanted more attention to be paid to daily moments of resistance. He believed that tragic narratives were the route to creating a passive population which begged for charity from the rich and political assistance from the powerful. A local NGO activist, on the other hand, insisted that displays of resistance were counterproductive, as they could frighten off international donors and sympathizers. She insisted that it was only through the performance of Palestinian suffering that international intervention on behalf of the refugees could be guaranteed.

I believe that while each narrative has had its merits and shortcomings, cumulatively, Palestinian narratives of heroism, suffering, and *sumud* have all been broadly effective in achieving a great many of their goals: keeping the Palestinian conflict and the predicament of Palestinian refugees at the forefront of the international stage (even if in the last instance, remedies to the problems are difficult to find) and ensuring that the voice of the refugees would not be ignored at their leadership's negotiating tables. Most importantly, in all their variety, stories perpetuated via Palestinian commemorative practices have been irreplaceable in forging a nation out of communities of dispersed and disparate Palestinians across national boundaries throughout the world.

The enduring resonance of national biographies

Thou Shalt Not is soon forgotten, but Once Upon A Time lasts forever.
Philip Pullman

In these pages, I have tried to show the centrality of narratives about the past in the nationalist crafting of imagined communities. If there is one universal cultural practice shared across time and space, that is storytelling. We tell stories about journeys, transformations, redemptions, losses, and triumphs. The news about events in the world do come to us as stories; we mold disparate historical events into coherent narratives;

we make excuses, give explanations, mobilize, and are moved to action by telling stories. We tell stories because it is through the structure of a story that we tame time, map space, and understand character and motive. What makes stories such powerful media of communication, explanation, and mobilization is their performative nature; story-tellers shape and perform their stories in response to a particular audience. In this performance, they take cues from their audiences, respond to their reaction, implore them to engage with the substance of the performance and craft their stories in ongoing, iterative, and dialogic ways. From other political actors, story-tellers borrow tropes, symbols, icons, and discursive frames proven useful or resonant in other settings. What allows for these elements of story-telling to be transportable across boundaries is not only the similarity of social context or ideological solidarities, but the possibility of human sympathy with another's story.

As I have shown, national commemorations also tell stories about the nation, and in so doing, they anthropomorphize the nation, telling its history as if it were a collective biography for all members of the nation. Though few would dare to claim full understanding of the causes for the pervasive ability of nationalism to move people to great – almost transcendental – acts of self-sacrifice, here I have suggested that understanding nationalist commemoration can also aid us in understanding the power of nationalism. As I have shown, nationalist commemoration draws a great deal of its authority from its conflation of the history of the nation with the life-stories of the nationals. In the absence of a monolithic or universal way of understanding what binds the nation together – shared culture, language, religion, or common origins? – these heroic or tragic narratives map the experiences of the nationals within the imaginary space of the nation. The power of the story of the nation, its special resonance, is that it allows us to locate ourselves within this mapped space. Because we can locate ourselves alongside so many others within this space, this narrative – the story of peoplehood – gives our lives meaning.

Furthermore, nationalist commemoration bestows honor and glory upon the dead, redeems losses, and transforms what can be otherwise wasted lives and ruined futures into noble self-sacrifice in a larger cause. Nationalist commemoration borrows and politicizes a great many rituals and quotidian practices, thus utilizing the familiarity of known forms (for example funerals) and incorporating them as irretrievable parts of the nation. In turn, nationalist commemoration proffers durable and powerful forms of remembering that can be borrowed and appropriated by the dispossessed. Commemoration provides a medium through which those who are often silenced and marginalized can at least express

that they exist. In appealing to global audiences, nationalist commemoration provides a stage on which the heroism, resilience, or suffering of the dispossessed is honored and made meaningful. Like religion,
and perhaps unlike any other ideology, by making the memories of
individuals an inseparable part of the memory of a larger community,
commemoration firmly establishes ordinary persons as the central protagonists of the heroic or tragic drama that is nationalist struggle.

Bibliography

Newspapers, Periodicals and Factional Organs (dates indicate years reviewed)

Daily Star. 1999–2005

Filastin (Supplement to *Al-Muharrir*). 1964–1966.

Filastin al-Muslima (Organ of Hamas). 1991–2004.

Filastin al-Thawra (Organ of Fatah–Revolutionary Council, Abu Nidal). Intermittently between 1974 and 1991.

Filastin al-Thawra (Organ of PLO). 1972–1994.

Filastinuna (Organ of Fatah). 1959–1972.

Al-Hadaf (Organ of PFLP). 1969–2005.

Al-Hayat. 1993–2005

Al-Hurriyya (Organ of Arab Nationalist Movement) 1960–1969. (Organ of DFLP). 1969–2005.

Il al-Amam (Organ of PFLP–GC). 1972–2002.

Al-Jana The periodical published by the Arab Resource Centre for Popular Arts. (1994–2002).

Jerusalem Post. 2005.

Journal of Palestine Studies – Various Special Documents, Source Materials, and Daily Reports and Chronologies.

Al-Nahar. 1973–2005.

Al-Safir. 1973–2005.

Samid (Organ of PLO Welfare and Social Services). 1979–1995.

Al-Sharq al-Awsat. 2000–2005.

Shu'un al-Filastiniyya (Organ of PLO). 1971–1993.

Primary and Secondary Sources

Abbas, Mahmoud (Abu Mazen). 1995. *Through Secret Channels. The Road to Oslo: Senior PLO Leader Abu Mazen's Revealing Story of Negotiations with Israel*. Reading: Garnet Publishing.

Abbas, Mahmoud, Hussein Shaaban, Bassem Sirhan and Ali Hassan. 1997. "The Socio-economic Conditions of the Palestinians in Lebanon" in *Journal of Refugee Studies* 10(3): 378–396.

Abrahamian, Ervand. 1988. " 'Ali Shari'ati: Ideologue of the Iranian Revolution" in Edmund Burke III and Ira M. Lapidus (eds.), *Islam, Politics, and Social Movements*. Berkeley CA: University of California Press: 289–297.

Abrahamian, Ervand. 1993. *Khomeinism*. London: I. B. Tauris.

Abu Amr, Ziad. 1994. *Islamic Fundamentalism in the West Bank and Gaza: Muslim Brotherhood and Islamic Jihad*. Bloomington IN: Indiana University Press.

Abu Amr, Ziad. 1997. "Shaykh Ahmad Yasin and the Origins of Hamas" in R. Scott Appleby (ed.), *Spokesmen for the Despised: Fundamentalist Leaders of the Middle East*. Chicago IL: University of Chicago Press: 225–256.

Abu Aswan, Hadi (ed.). 1972. "Shihadat min Ma'raka al-Karama" ("Testimonies from the Battle of Karama"), *Shu'un Filastiniyya* 8: 197–210.

Abu El-Haj, Nadia. 2001. *Facts on the Ground: Archaeological Practice and Territorial Self-Fashioning in Israeli Society*. Chicago IL: University of Chicago Press.

Abu Faris, Muhammad Abd al-Qadir. 1990. *Shuhada' al-Filastin* (Palestinian Martyrs). Amman: Dar al-Firqan.

Abu Iyad with Eric Rouleau. 1981. *My Home, My Land: A Narrative of the Palestinian Struggle*. Translated by Linda Butler Koseoglu. New York: New York Times Books.

Abu Jihad. N. D. *'Amaliat al-Shaheed Kamal 'Udwan* (*Operation Martyr Kamal 'Udwan*) in Muhammad Isma'il (ed.), *Awraq Shakhsiyah Dalal Mughrabi*. (*The Personal Papers of Dalal Mughrabi*). Beirut: n.p.

AbuKhalil, As'ad. 1992. "A New Arab Ideology? The Rejuvenation of Arab Nationalism," *The Middle East Journal* 46(1): 22–37.

Abu Shawar, Rashad. 1992. Excerpts from *O Beirut*, in Salma Khadra Jayyusi (ed.), *Anthology of Modern Palestinian Literature*. New York: Columbia University: 609–621.

Aghaie, Kamran Scot. 2004. *The Martyrs of Karbala: Shi'i Symbolism and Rituals in Modern Iran*. Seattle WA: University of Washington Press.

Ajami, Fouad. 1978/1979. "The End of Pan-Arabism," *Foreign Affairs* 57(2): 355–373.

Alexander, Jeffrey C. 2002. "On the Social Construction of Moral Universals: The 'Holocaust' from War Crime to Trauma Drama," *European Journal of Social Theory* 5(1): 5–85.

Al-Ali, Mahmud. 1999. "Atfal al-Filastiniyyun fi Madaris al-UNRUA fi Lubnan bayn al-Irth wa-al-Warith" ("Palestinian Children in Lebanon's UNRWA Schools between Inheritance and Inheritor"), *Majalla Dirasat al-Filastiniyya* 37: 127–147.

Allen, Lori A. 1998. "Discipline, Punish, and Position Abuse: The Torture of Palestinians in the West Bank and Gaza." Chicago IL: University of Chicago Masters thesis.

Allen, Lori A. 2002. "Palestinians Debate 'Polite' Resistance to Occupation," *Middle East Report* 225: 38–43.

Allen, Lori A. 2005. "Suffering through a National Uprising: The Cultural Politics of Violence, Victimization and Human Rights in Palestine." Chicago IL: University of Chicago Ph.D. dissertation.

230   Bibliography

Al-'Az' ar, Muhammad Khalid. 1991. *Al Muqawamat al Filastiniyya Bayn Ghazw Lubnan wa al-Intifadha (The Palestinian Resistance between the War on Lebanon and the Intifada)*. Beirut: Markaz al-Dirasat al-Wahdat al-Arabiyyah.

Amadiume, Ifi and Abdullahi An-Na'im (eds.). 2000. *The Politics of Memory: Truth, Healing & Social Justice*. London: Zed Books.

Amin, Shahid. 1995. *Event, Metaphor, Memory: Chauri Chaura, 1922–1992*. Berkeley CA: University of California Press.

Amireh, Amal. 2003. "Between Complicity and Subversion: Boyd Politics in Palestinian National Narrative," *South Atlantic Quarterly* 102(4) : 747–772.

Anderson, Benedict. 1991. *Imagined Communities: Reflections on the Origin and Spread of Nationalism*. London: Verso.

Ang, Swee Chai. 1989. *From Beirut to Jerusalem*. London: Grafton.

Anonymous. 1982. "Shihadat al-Najin min al-Majzara" ("The Testimonies of Survivors of the Massacre"), *Shu'un Filastiniyya* 132–133: 41–58.

Anonymous. 1983. "Majzara Mukhayyami Sabra wa-Shatila: Nata'ij Bahht Midani" ("The Massacre in the Sabra and Shatila Camps: Results of Field Research"), *Shu'un Filastiniyya* 138: 97–136.

Anonymous. 1987. "Sabra and Shatila: In Memoriam," *Journal of Palestine Studies* 16(4): 2.

Anonymous. 1988. "Refugee Interviews," *Journal of Palestine Studies* 18(1): 158–171.

Anonymous. 1995. "Palestinian Refugees of Lebanon Speak," *Journal of Palestine Studies* 25(1): 54–60.

Anonymous. 2001. *Complaint against Ariel Sharon, Lodged in Belgium on 18 June 2001*. International Campaign for Justice for the Victims of Sabra and Shatila; www.indictsharon.net.

Antonius, Soraya. 1979. "Fighting on Two Fronts: Conversations with Palestinian Women," *Journal of Palestine Studies* 8(3): 26–45.

Aql, Abd al-Salam. 1995. "Palestinian Refugees of Lebanon Speak," *Journal of Palestine Studies* 25(1): 54–60.

ARCPA. 1998. " 'This Illiterate Woman . . . She Talked to Us': Participants' Responses to ARCPA's 1948 Uprooting Oral History Project," *al-Jana* (the Journal of the Arab Resource Centre for Popular Arts), May 1998: 26–49.

ARCPA. 2002. "Bibliography," *al-Jana* (the Journal of the Arab Resource Centre for Popular Arts): 67–74.

Arendt, Hannah. 1968[1951]. *Imperialism: Part Two of The Origins of Totalitarianism*. New York: Harcourt Brace Jovanovich.

Aruri, Naseer (ed.). 2001. *Palestinian Refugees: The Right of Return*. London: Pluto Press.

Asad, Talal. 2000. "What Do Human Rights Do? An Anthropological Enquiry," *Theory and Event* 4(4).

Axel, Brian Keith. 2001. *The Nation's Tortured Body: Violence, Representation, and the Formation of a Sikh "Diaspora."* Durham: Duke University Press.

'Ayid, Khaled. 1984. *Qitar al-Mawt: Ma'raka Beirut fi Siyaq al-Irhab wa-al-Tawassa' al-Sahyouni (The Train of Death: Beirut Battle in the Context of Zionist Terror and Expansionism)*. Beirut: Dar al-Sharq al-Awsat.

Azaryahu, Maoz and Rebecca Kook. 2002. "Mapping the Nation: Street Names and Arab-Palestinian Identity: Three Case Studies," *Nations and Nationalism* 8(2): 195–213.

al-'Azm, Muhammad Hisham. 1974. "Suqut al-Safad" ("The Fall of Safad"), *Shu'un al-Filastiniyya* 33: 122–132.

Badr, Liana. 1994. *The Eye of the Mirror*. Translated by Samira Kawar. Reading UK: Garnet Publishing.

Baily, Alison. 2000. "The Dissolution of Community: Visions of Beirut in the Novels of Elias Khoury, 1975–1991." Hilary College, Oxford University BA dissertation.

Al-Bakr, Mahmud Muflih. 1994. "Al-'Aris al-Muharib" ("The Warrior Bridegroom"), *al-Jana* 2: 8–10.

Bardenstein, Carol B. 1998. "Threads of Memory and Discourses of Rootedness: of Trees, Oranges, and Prickly Pear Cactus in Israel/Palestine," *Edebiyat* 8(1): 1–36.

Bardenstein, Carol B. 1999. "Trees, Forests, and the Shaping of Palestinian and Israeli Collective Memory" in Mieke Bal, Jonathan Crewe and Leo Spitzer (eds.), *Acts of Memory: Cultural Recall in the Present*. Hanover: Dartmouth College: 148–168.

Barghouti, As'ad Muhammad. 1973. "Risala Min Qari' hawl Maqal 'Soquot al-Safad'" ("Reader's Letter Regarding 'The Fall of Safad'"), *Shu'un al-Filastiniyya* 24: 161–165.

Barghouti, Mourid. 2000. *I Saw Ramallah*. Translated by Ahdaf Soueif. Cairo: American University Press.

Baron, Beth. 2005. *Egypt as a Woman: Nationalism, Gender, and Politics*. Berkeley CA: University of California Press.

Baroud, Ramzy (ed.). 2003. *Searching Jenin: Eyewitness Accounts of the Israeli Invasion*. Seattle WA: Cune Press.

Bashur, Najla' Nasir. 1971. "Changes to the Curricula in the West Bank of the River Jordan After 1967," *Shu'un Filastiniyya* 3: 229–241.

Baumel, Judith Tydor. 1995. "'In Everlasting Memory': Individual and Communal Holocaust Commemoration in Israel" in Robert Wistrich and David Ohana (eds.), *The Shaping of Israeli Identity: Myth, Memory and Trauma*. London: Frank Cass: 146–170.

Baumel, Judith Tydor. 2002. "Founding Myths and Heroic Icons: Reflections on the Funerals of Theodor Herzl and Hannah Szenes," *Women's Studies International Forum* 25(6): 679–695.

Bellah, Robert N. 1967. "Civil Religion in America," *Daedalus* 96: 1–21.

Ben-Amos, Avner and Ilana Bet-El. 1999. "Holocaust Day and Memorial Day in Israeli Schools: Ceremonies, Education and History," *Israel Studies* 4(1): 258–284.

Ben-Amos, Avner. 2000. *Funerals, Politics, and Memory in Modern France 1789–1996*. Oxford: Oxford University Press.

Billig, Michael, 1995. *Banal Nationalism*. London: Sage Publishers.

Bilu, Yoram and Eliezer Witztum. 2000. "War-Related Loss and Suffering in Israeli Society: An Historical Perspective," *Israel Studies* 5(2): 1–32.

Bob, Clifford. 2002. "Merchants of Morality," *Foreign Policy*, March/April 2002: 35–45.

Bolatnski, Luc. 1999. *Distant Suffering: Morality, Media and Politics*. Trans. Graham Burchell. Cambridge: Cambridge University Press.

Bommes, Michael and Patrick Wright. 1982. "'Charms of Residence': the Public and the Past" in Johnson *et al.* (eds.): 253–302.

Bookmiller, Kirsten N. and Robert J. Bookmiller. 1990. "Palestinian Radio and the Intifada," *Journal of Palestine Studies* 19(4): 96–105.

Bourdieu, Pierre. 1999. "Understanding" in Pierre Bourdieu *et al.* (eds.), *The Weight of the World: Social Suffering in Contemporary Society.* Translated by Priscilla Parkhurst Ferguson *et al.* Cambridge: Polity Press: 607–626.

Bourke, Joanna. 1999. *An Intimate History of Killing: Face-to-Face Killing in Twentieth-Century Warfare.* London: Granta Books.

Bowker, Robert. 2003. *Palestinian Refugees: Mythology, Identity, and the Search for Peace.* Boulder: Lynne Rienner Publishers.

Bowman, Glenn. 1993. "Nationalizing the Sacred: Shrines and Shifting Identities in the Israeli-Occupied Territories," *Man* 28(3): 431–460.

Bowman, Glenn. 1994. "'A Country of Words': Conceiving the Palestinian Nation from the Position of Exile" in Ernesto Laclau (ed.), *The Making of Political Identities.* London: Verso: 138–170.

Braidotti, Rosi. 1997. "In the Sign of the Feminine: Reading Diana," *Theory and Event* 1(4).

Brand, Laurie A. 1988. *Palestinians in the Arab World: Institution Building and the Search for State.* New York: Columbia University Press.

Brog, Mooli. 2003. "Victim and Victor: Holocaust and Military Commemoration in Israel Collective Memory," *Israel Studies* 8(3): 65–99.

Brown, Nathan J. 2003. *Palestinian Politics after the Oslo Accords: Resuming Arab Palestine.* Berkeley CA: University of California Press.

Browne, Donald R. 1975. "The Voices of Palestine: A Broadcasting House Divided," *Middle East Journal* 29(2): 133–150.

Brubaker, Rogers and Margit Feischmidt. 2002. "1848 in 1998: The Politics of Commemoration in Hungary, Romania, and Slovakia," *Comparative Studies in Society and History* 44(4): 700–744.

Bruner, Edward M. 1984. "Opening up Anthropology" in Edward M. Bruner (ed.), *Text, Play and Story: The Construction and Reconstruction of Self and Society.* Prospect Heights IL: Waveland Press: 1–16.

Bruner, Edward M. and Phyllis Gorfain. 1984. "Dialogic Narration and the Paradoxes of Masada" in Edward M. Bruner (ed.), *Text, Play and Story: The Construction and Reconstruction of Self and Society.* Prospect Heights, IL: Waveland Press: 56–79.

Brynen, Rex. 1990. *Sanctuary and Survival: The PLO in Lebanon.* Boulder CO: Westview Press.

Brynen, Rex. 2000. *A Very Political Economy: Peacebuilding and Foreign Aid in the West Bank and Gaza.* Washington DC: US Institute of Peace Press.

Boullata, Kamal. 2003. "Artists Re-member Beirut," *Journal of Palestine Studies* 32(4): 22–38.

Bucaille, Laetitia. 2004. *Growing Up Palestinian: Israeli Occupation and the Intifada Generation.* Trans. Anthony Roberts. Princeton NJ: Princeton University Press.

Budeiri, Musa 1997. "The Palestinians: Tensions between Nationalist and Religious Identities" in James Jankowski and Israel Gershoni (eds.),

Rethinking Nationalism in the Arab Middle East. New York: Columbia University Press: 191–206.

Buehrig, Edward H. 1971. *The UN and the Palestinian Refugees: A Study in Nonterritorial Administration.* Bloomington IN: Indiana University Press.

Cabral, Amilcar. 1969. *Revolution in Guinea: An African People's Struggle.* Translated by Richard Handyside. London: Stage 1.

Cabral, Amilcar. 1973. *Return to the Source: Selected Speeches by Amilcar Cabral.* Edited by Africa Information Service. New York: Monthly Review Press.

Cabral, Amilcar. 1974. *Our People Are Our Mountains: On The Guinean Revolution.* London: Committee for Freedom in Mozambique, Angola and Guine.

Campbell, Kirsten. 2002. "Legal Memories: Sexual Assault, Memory, and International Humanitarian Law," *Signs* 28(1): 149–178.

Çandar, Cengiz. 2000. "A Turk in the Palestinian Resistance," *Journal of Palestine Studies* 30(1): 68–82.

Carapico, Sheila. 2000. "NGOs, INGOs, GO-NGOs and DO-NGOs: Making Sense of Non-Governmental Organizations," *Middle East Report* 214: 12–15.

Chaliand, Gérard. 1977. *Revolution in the Third World.* Trans. Diana Johnstone. New York: Penguin Books.

Chaliand, Gérard. 1989. *Revolution in the Third World.* Trans. Diana Johnstone. New York: Viking Press.

Cobban, Helena. 1984. *The Palestinian Liberation Organization: People, Power, and Politics.* Cambridge: Cambridge University Press.

Collins, John Martin. 2000. "Children of the Stones: The Intifada, Popular Memory, and 'Generation' of Palestinian Nationalism." Minneapolis MN: University of Minnesota. Ph.D. Dissertation.

Collins, John. 2004. *Occupied by Memory: The Intifada Generation and the Palestinian State of Emergency.* New York: New York University Press.

Colvin, Christopher. 2004. "Ambivalent Narrations: Pursuing the Political through Traumatic Storytelling," *Political and Legal Anthropological Review* 27(1): 72–89.

Connell, Dan. 2002. *Rethinking Revolution: New Strategies for Democracy and Social Justice: The Experiences of Eritrea, South Africa, Palestine and Nicaragua.* Lawrenceville NI: The Red Sea Press.

Connerton, Paul. 1989. *How Societies Remember.* Cambridge: Cambridge University Press.

Cook, Catherine, Adam Hanieh and Adah Key. 2004. *Stolen Youth: The Politics of Israel's Detention of Palestinian Children.* London: Pluto Books.

Cooley, Alexander and James Ron. 2002. "The NGO Scramble: Organizational Insecurity and the Political Economy of Transnational Action," *International Security* 27(1): 5–39.

Cooley, John K. 1973. *Green March, Black September: The Story of the Palestinian Arabs.* London: Frank Cass.

Cutting, Pauline. 1988. *Children of the Siege.* London: Pan Books.

Dabashi, Hamid. 1993. *Theology of Discontent: The Ideological Foundations of the Islamic Revolution in Iran.* New York: New York University Press.

Daniel, E. Valentine and John Chr. Knudsen (eds.). 1995. *Mistrusting Refugees*. Berkeley CA: University of California Press.

Darraj, Faisal. 1994. "'An 'Alaqat al-Ardh wa-al-Watan wa-al-Zakira" ("On the Relations between Land, Homeland, and Memory"), *Al-Hadaf* 1183 (3 April 1994): 8–9.

Darwish, Mahmoud. 1995. *Memory for Forgetfulness: August, Beirut, 1982*. Trans. Ibrahim Muhawi. Berkeley CA: University of California Press.

Davidson, Basil. 1969. *The Liberation of Guiné: Aspects of an African Revolution with a Foreword by Amilcar Cabral*. London: Penguin Books.

Davidson, Basil. 1978. *Africa in Modern History: The Search for a New Society*. London: Penguin Books.

Davidson, Basil. 1981. *The People's Cause: A History of Guerrillas in Africa*. Essex: Longman Group.

Davis, Rochelle. 2002. "The Attar of History: Palestinian Narratives of Life before 1948." Ann Arbor MI: University of Michigan Ph.D. dissertation.

Davis, Rochelle. Forthcoming. "Mapping the Past, Recreating the Homeland" in Lila Abu-Lughod and Ahmad Sa'di (eds.), *The Claims of Memory: Palestine 1948*. New York: Columbia University Press.

Ditmars, Hadani. 2000. "Gaza Dispatch," *Middle East Report* 214: 18–19.

Donnelly, Jack. 1998. "Human Rights: A New Standard of Civilization," *International Affairs* 74(1): 1–24.

Ebtekar, Massoumeh. 2000. *Takeover in Tehran: The Inside Story of the 1979 US Embassy Capture*. As told to Fred Reed. Vancouver WA: Talon Books.

Elyachar, Julia. 2002. "Empowerment Money: the World Bank, Non-Governmental Organizations, and the Value of Culture in Egypt," *Public Culture* 14(3): 493–513.

Enloe, Cynthia. 2000. *Maneuvers: The International Politics of Militarizing Women's Lives*. Berkeley CA: University of California Press.

Esmair, Samera. 2003. "1948: Law, History, Memory," *Social Text* 21(2): 25–48.

Fanon, Frantz. 1963. *The Wretched of the Earth*. Trans. Constance Farrington. New York: Grove Press.

Farah, Randa. 1997. "Crossing Boundaries: Reconstruction of Palestinian Identities in al-Baq'a Camp, Jordan" in Riccardo Bocco, Blandine Detremau and Jean Hannoyer (eds.), *Palestine, Palestiniens: Territoire National, Espaces Communautaires*. Beirut: CERMOC: 259–298.

Farah, Randa Rafiq. 1999. "Popular Memory and Reconstructions of Palestinian Identity: Al-Baq'a Refugee Camp, Jordan." Toronto University of Toronto. Ph.D. Dissertation.

Farmer, Sarah. 1999. *Martyred Village: Commemorating the 1944 Massacre at Oradour-sur-Glen*. Berkeley CA: University of California Press.

Farsoun, Samih K. and Jean M. Landis. 1991. "The Sociology of an Uprising" in Nassar and Heacock (eds.): 15–35.

Fayid, Layla. 1977. *Al Shihada wa-al-Hilm: Hiwarat Wathaq'iyya 'an Tajraba Atfal Tal al-Za'tar (The Testimony and the Dream: Documentary Texts on the Experiences of Children of Tal Za'tar)*. Beirut: PLO Research Centre.

Feldman, Allen. 1991. *Formations of Violence: The Narrative of the Body and Political Terror in Northern Ireland*. Chicago IL: University of Chicago Press.

Felman, Shoshana. 1992. "The Return of the Voice: Claude Lanzman's *Shoah*" in Shoshana Felman and Dori Laub (eds.), *Testimony: Crises of Witnessing in Literature, Psychoanalysis, and History*. New York: Routledge: 204–83.

Ferguson, James. 1990. *The Anti-politics Machine: 'Development,' Depoliticization, and Bureaucratic Power in Lesotho*. Cambridge: Cambridge University Press.

Finkelstein, Norman G. 1995. *Image and Reality of the Israel–Palestine Conflict*. London: Verso.

Fischer, Michael M. J. 1980. *Iran: From Religious Dispute to Revolution*. Cambridge, MA: Harvard University Press.

Fleischmann, Ellen L. 2003. *The Nation and Its "New" Women: the Palestinian Women's Movement 1920–1948*. Berkeley CA: University of California Press.

Foucault, Michel. 1977. *Language, Counter-Memory, Practice: Selected Essays and Interviews*. Trans. Donald Bouchard and Sherry Simon. Oxford: Blackwell Publishers.

Garfield, Mark. 1984. "Recent Books," *Journal of Palestine Studies* 13(3): 97–104.

Gellner, Ernest. 1983. *Nations and Nationalism*. Ithaca NY: Cornell University Press.

Gelvin, James. 1999. "Modernity *and* Its Discontents: On the Durability of Nationalism in the Arab Middle East," *Nations and Nationalism* 5(1): 71–89.

General Union of Palestinian Women (GUPW). 1977. *Tal al-Za'tar: Al-Shaheed wa-al-Shâhid (Tal Zaatar: Martyr and Witness)*. Beirut: General Union of Palestinian Women (GUPW).

Genet, Jean. 1983. "Four Hours in Shatila," *Journal of Palestine Studies* 12(3): 3–22.

Genet, Jean. 1987. "Affirmation of Existence through Rebellion," *Journal of Palestine Studies* 16(2): 64–84.

Genet, Jean. 1989. *Prisoner of Love*. Trans. Barbara Bray. Hanover: Wesleyan University Press.

Ghosheh, Subhi. 1992. Excerpts from *Our Sun Will Never Set* in Salma Khadra Jayyusi (ed.), *Anthology of Modern Palestinian Literature*. New York: Columbia University: 650–657.

Giannou, Chris. 1991. *Besieged: A Doctor's Story of Life and Death in Beirut*. London: Bloomsbury.

Gillis, John R. (ed.). 1994. *Commemorations: The Politics of National Identity*. Princeton, NJ: Princeton University Press.

Global Ideas Bank. N. D. "International Human Suffering Index" http://www.globalideasbank.org/site/bank/idea.php?ideaId=775 accessed on 5 Dec. 2005.

Graham-Brown, Sarah. 1984. *Education, Repression, and Liberation: Palestinians*. London: World University Service.

Guevara, Ernesto "Che." 1961. *Guerrilla Warfare*. New York: Monthly Review Press.

Guevara, Ernesto "Che." 1968. *Venceremos! The Speeches and Writings of Ernesto Che Guevara.* Edited by John Gerassi. London: Weidenfield and Nicolson.

Gupta, Akhil. 1992. "The Song of the Nonaligned World: Transnational Identities and the Reinscription of Space in Late Capitalism," *Cultural Anthropology* 7(1): 63–79.

Gur-Ze'ev, Ilan. 2001. "The Production of the Self and the Destruction of the Other's Memory and Identity: Israeli/Palestinian Education on the Holocaust/Nakbah," *Studies in Philosophy and Education* 20(3): 255–266.

Gusmão, Xanana. 2005. "View from a Small Country," *Le Monde Diplomatique* (September) at http://mondediplo.com/2005/09/09timor accessed on 12 October 2005.

Hadawi, Sami. 1989. *Bitter Harvest: A Modern History of Palestine.* Essex: Scorpion Publishing.

Hafez, Mohammed M. 2003. *Why Muslims Rebel: Repression and Resistance in the Islamic World.* Boulder CO: Lynne Rienner Publishers.

Hagopian, Elaine C. (ed.). 1985. *Amal and the Palestinians: Understanding the Battle of the Camps.* Belmont, MA: Association of Arab-American University Graduates Inc.

Hajjaj, Nasri. 2000a. *Al-Laji'un al-Filastiniyyun fi Lubnan: Ila Mata? (Palestinian Refugees in Lebanon: To Where?).* Cairo: Shaml–Palestinian Diaspora and Refugee Center.

Hajjaj, Nasri. 2000b. "Qobur al-Filastiniyyin fi Lubnan: Laji'un Ahia'an … Laji'un Amwatan–1" ("Palestinian Gravesites in Lebanon: Living and Deceased Refugees, Part I"), *Al-Quds al-Arabi*, 2 November 2000: 13.

Hajjaj, Nasri. 2000c. "Qobur al-Filastiniyyin fi Lubnan: Laji'un Ahia'an … Laji'un Amwatan–2" ("Palestinian Gravesites in Lebanon: Living and Deceased Refugees, Part II"), *Al-Quds al-Arabi*, 3 November 2000: 13.

Hajjar, Lisa. 2000. "Problems of Dependecy: Human Rights Organizations in the Arab World; an Interview with Abdullah An-Na'im," *Middle East Report* 214: 20–23; 46–47.

Hajjar, Lisa. 2005. *Courting Conflict: The Israeli Military Court System in the West Bank and Gaza.* Berkeley CA: University of California Press.

Halbwachs, Maurice. 1992. *On Collective Memory.* Trans. Lewis A. Coser. Chicago IL: The University of Chicago Press.

Hammami, Rema. 1990. "Women, the Hijab and the Intifada," *Middle East Report* 164/165: 24–28, 71, 78.

Hammami, Rema. 1995. "NGOs: The Professionalisation of Politics," *Race & Class* 37(2): 51–63.

Hammami, Rema. 1997. "From Immodesty to Collaboration: Hamas, the Women's Movement, and National Identity in the Intifada," in Joel Beinin and Joe Stork (eds.), *Political Islam: Essays from Middle East Report.* Berkeley CA: University of California Press: 195–210.

Hammami, Rema. 2000. "Palestinian NGOs since Oslo: From NGO Politics to Social Movements?" *Middle East Report* 214: 16–19; 27.

Hammami, Rema. 2003. "Gender, *Nakbe* and Nation: Palestinian Women's Presence and Absence in the Narration of 1948 Memories" in Ron Robin and Bo Stråth (eds.), *Homelands: Poetic Power and the Politics of Space*. Brussels: PIE Peter Lang: 35–60.

Hammami, Rema and Salim Tamari. 2001. "The Second Uprising: End or New Beginning?" *Journal of Palestine Studies* 30(2): 5–25.

Hammami, Rema, Sari Hanafi and Elizabeth Taylor. 2002. "Destruction of Palestinian Public Institutions." Report of Palestine Emergency Committee. http://www.jmcc.org/new/02/apr/destruction.htm accessed on 31 October 2005.

Hanafi, Sari and Linda Tabar. 2005. *The Emergence of a Palestinian Globalized Elite: Donors, International Organizations and Local NGOs*. Jerusalem: Institute of Jerusalem Studies.

Hart, Alan. 1989. *Arafat: A Political Biography*. Bloomington IN: Indiana University Press.

Hart, Alan. 1994. *Arafat: A Political Biography*. London: Sidgwick and Jackson.

Hass, Amira. 2002. "Operation Destroy Data," *Ha'aretz* 24 April 2002.

Al-Hassan, Khaled. 1992. *Grasping the Nettle of Peace: A Senior Palestinian Figure Speaks Out*. London: Saqi Books.

Hasso, Frances. 2000. "Modernity and Gender in the 1948 and 1967 Defeats," *International Journal of Middle East Studies* 32: 491–510.

Hasso, Frances. 2005. "Discursive and Political Deployments by/of the 2002 Palestinian Women Suicide Bombers/Martyrs," *Feminist Review* 81: 23–51.

Hiltermann, Joost R. 1991. *Behind the Intifada: Labor and Women's Movements in the Occupied Territories*. Princeton NJ: Princeton niversity Press.

Al-Hout, Bayan. 1998. "Oral History: Continuous, Permanent Connection," *al Jana* (the Journal of the Arab Resource Centre for Popular Arts), May 1998: 10–12.

Hroub, Khaled. 2000. *Hamas: Political Thought and Practice*. Washington DC: Institute for Palestine Studies.

Human Rights Watch (HRW). 2003. *World Report: Israel, the Occupied West Bank and Gaza Strip, and Palestinian Authority Territories*. New York: Human Rights Watch.

Humphries, Isabelle and Laleh Khalili. Forthcoming. "The Gender of Nakba Memory" in Lila Abu-Lughod and Ahmad Sa'di (eds.), *The Claims of Memory: Palestine 1948*. New York: Columbia University Press.

Hunter, F. Robert. 1993. *The Palestinian Uprising: A War by Other Means*. Berkeley CA: University of California Press.

Al-Husseini, Jalal. 2000. "UNRWA and the Palestinian Nation-Building Process," *Journal of Palestine Studies* 29(2): 51–64.

Al-Hut, Bayan Nuayhad. 2003. *Sabra wa-Shatila: Aylul 1982 (Sabra and Shatila: September 1982)*. Beirut: Institute for Palestine Studies.

Al-Hut, Shafiq. 1986. *'Ashrun 'Aman fi Munazzamat al-Tahrir al-Filastiniyya 1964–1984 (20 Years in the Palestine Liberation Organization 1964–1984)*. Beirut: Dar al-Istiqlal.

ISM. 2005. *The Website of the International Solidarity Movement*. http://www.palsolidarity.org/main/about-ism/ accessed on 31 October 2005.

Isma'il, Muhammad (ed.). N.D. *Awraq Shakhsiyah Dalal Mughrabi*. (The Personal Papers of Dalal Mughrabi), Beirut: n.p.

Ismail, Salwa. 2003. *Rethinking Islamist Politics: Culture, the State and Islamism*. London: I. B. Tauris.

Jallul, Faisal. 1994. *Naqd al-Silah al-Filastini; Burj al-Barajneh: Ahlan wa-Thawratan wa-Mukhayyaman (Critique of Palestinian Armed Resistance; Burj al-Brajneh: Its People, Revolution and Refugee Camp)*. Beirut: Dar al-Jadid.

Jamal, Amal. 2005. *The Palestinian National Movement: Politics of Contention, 1967–2005*. Bloomington IN: Indiana University Press.

Jean-Klein, Iris. 2002. "Alternative Modernities, or Accountable Modernities? The Palestinian Movement(s) and Political (Audit) Tourism during the First Intifada," *Journal of Mediterranean Studies* 12 (1): 43–80.

Johnson, Nels. 1982. *Islam and the Politics of Meaning in Palestinian Nationalism*. London: KPI Limited.

Johnson, Richard, Gregor McLennan, Bill Schwartz, and David Sutton (eds.). 1982. *Making Histories: Studies in History-Writing and Politics*. London: Hutchinson.

Juergensmeyer, Mark. 2000. *Terror in the Mind of God: The Global Rise of Religious Violence*. Berkeley CA: University of California Press.

Al-Jundi, Muhammad. 1989. "Al-Majzara wa-al-Majazir" ("The Massacre and Massacres"), *Shu'un Filastiniyya* 200: 3–14.

Kahin, George McTurnan. 1956. *The Asian–African Conference, Bandung, Indonesia, April 1955*. Port Washington: Kennikat Press.

Kallam, Mahmoud Abdallah. 2001. *Kamil al-Turab al-Filastini: Min Ajal Haza Qatalooni*. Beirut: Bissan.

Kanaana, Sharif. 1998. "Women in the Legends of the Intifada" in Suha Sabbagh (ed.), *Palestinian Women of Gaza and the West Bank*. Bloomington IN: Indiana University Press: 114–135.

Kana'ana, Sharif and Nihad Zaytawi. 1987. *Dayr Yasin*. Monograph No. 4, Palestinian Destroyed Villages Series. Bir Zeit: Center for Documentation and Research.

Kanaaneh, Rhoda. 2002. *Birthing the Nation: Strategies of Palestinian Women in Israel*. Berkeley CA: University of California Press.

Kanafani, Anni. 1973. *Ghassan Kanafani*. Beirut: Near East Ecumenical Bureau for Information and Interpretation.

Kanafani, Ghassan. 1978. *Men in the Sun*. Trans. Hilary Kilpatrick. London: Heinemann.

Kanafani, Ghassan. 2000 [1967]. "The Child Discovers that the Key Looks Like an Axe" in Ghassan Kanafani, *Palestine's Children: Returning to Haifa and Other Stories*. Trans. Barbara Harlow and Karen E. Riley. Boulder CO: Lynne Rienner Publishers: 107–113.

Kapeliouk, Amnon. 1983. *Sabra and Shatila: Inquiry into a Massacre*. Belmont, MA: Association of Arab-American University Graduates Inc.

Kapur, Ratna. 2002. "The Tragedy of Victimization Rhetoric: Resurrecting the 'Native' Subject in International/Post-Colonial Feminist Legal Politics," *Harvard Human Rights Journal* 15: 1–38.

Karmi, Ghada. 2002. "Israel's Cultural Massacre," *Dialogue* (May): 2.

Karner, Christian and Alan Aldridge. 2004. "Theorizing Religion in a Globalizing World," *International Journal of Politics, Culture, and Society* 18 (1/2): 5–32.

Keddie, Nikki. 1988. "Iranian Revolutions in Comparative Perspective" in Edmund Burke III and Ira M. Lapidus (eds.), *Islam, Politics, and Social Movements*. Berkeley CA: University of California Press: 298–313.

Keddie, Nikki. 1998. "The New Religious Politics: Where, When, and Why Do 'Fundamentalisms' Appear?" *Comparative Studies in Society and History* 40(4): 696–723.

Kennedy, David. 2004. *The Dark Sides of Virtue: Reassessing International Humanitarianism*. Princeton NJ: Princeton University Press.

Kerr, Malcolm. 1971. *The Arab Cold War: Gamal Abd el-Nasir and His Rivals 1958–1970*. London: Oxford University Press.

Kertzer, David I. 1991. "The Role of Ritual in State Formation" in Eric R. Wolf (ed.), *Religious Regimes and State-Formation: Perspectives from European Ethnology*. Albany: State University of New York Press: 85–104.

Khalaf, Ali Husayn. 1977. *Al-Nahwadh Marra Ukhra: Shihadat Waqi'iyya min Tal al-Za'tar (Another Insurrection: Testimonies from Tal al-Za'tar)*. Beirut: Central Public Relations Office of DFLP.

Khaled, Ghassan. 1998. "Le camp de réfugies Palestiniens du Yarmok à Damas: précarité attenué dans l'attente de l'application du droit au retour." Paris: Universite Francois Rabelais. Ph.D. dissertation.

Khaled, Leila. 1973. *My People Shall Live: The Autobiography of a Revolutionary*. George Hajjar (ed.). London: Hodder and Stoughton.

Khalidi, Rashid. 1986. *Under Siege: PLO Decisionmaking During the 1982 War*. New York: Columbia University Press.

Khalidi, Rashid. 1989. "The Palestinian People: Twenty-two Years After 1967" in Lockman and Beinin (eds.): 113–126.

Khalidi, Rashid. 1997. *Palestinian Identity: The Construction of Modern National Consciousness*. New York: Columbia University Press.

Khalidi, Rashid. 2001. "The Palestinians and 1948: The Underlying Causes of Failure" in Rogan and Shlaim (eds.): 12–36.

Al-Khalidi, Salah. 1993. "Al-Ardh al-Muqadaddasa fi al-Qur'an" ("The Holy Land in the Qur'an"), *Filastin al-Muslima* (July 1993): 44–45.

Khalidi, Walid (ed.). 1971. *From Haven to Conquest: Readings in Zionism and on the Palestine Problem Until 1948*. Beirut: Institute for Palestine Studies.

Khalidi, Walid. 1979. *Conflict and Violence in Lebanon: Confrontation in the Middle East*. Cambridge, MA: Center of International Studies, Harvard University.

Khalidi, Walid. 1988. "Plan Dalet: Master Plan for the Conquest of Palestine," *Journal of Palestine Studies* 18: 4–20.

Khalidi, Walid *et al.* 1992. *All That Remains: The Palestinian Villages Occupied and Depopulated by Israel in 1948*. Washington DC: Institute for Palestine Studies.

Khalidi, Walid. 1999. *Dayr Yasin: Al-Jum'a, 9–4–1948 (Dayr Yasin: Friday, 9 April 1948)*. Beirut: Institute for Palestine Studies.

Khalili, Laleh. 2004. "Grassroots Commemorations: Remembering the Land in the Camps of Lebanon," *Journal of Palestine Studies* 34(1): 5–22.

Khalili, Laleh. 2005a. "Landscapes of Uncertainty: Palestinians in Lebanon," *Middle East Report* 236: 34–39.

Khalili, Laleh. 2005b. "Palestinian Refugees in Lebanon and the Right of Return" in Ian Lustick and Ann Lesch (eds.), *Exile and Return: Predicaments of Palestinians and Jews*. Palo Alto: Stanford University Press: 19–40.

Khalili, Laleh. 2005c. "Places of Mourning and Memory: Palestinian Commemoration in the Refugee Camps of Lebanon," *Comparative Studies of South Asia, Africa and the Middle East* 25(1): 30–45.

Khalili, Laleh. 2005d. "Virtual Nation: Palestinian Cyberculture in Lebanese Camps" in Stein and Swedenburg (eds.): 126–149.

Khomeini, Ruhallah. 1981. *Islam and Revolution*. Trans. and annotated by Hamid Algar. Berkeley CA: Mizan Press.

Khoury, Bernard. 2002. "Urban or Artefact." Talk given at American University of Beirut, 8 May 2002.

Khoury, Elias. 1973. "Jadal al-Shi'r wa-al-Waqi': Qira'a fi al-Shi'r al-Filastini al-Mu'asir" ("The Intertwining of Poetry and Reality: A Reading of Modern Palestinian Poetry"), *Shu'un Filastiniyya* 19: 142–160.

Khoury, Elias. 2005. *Gate of the Sun*. Trans. Humphrey Davies. London: Harveill-Secker.

Khurshid, Ghazi. 1972. "Al-Muqawam al-Filastinyya wa-al-'Amal al-Ijtima'i" ("Palestinian Resistance and Social Services"), *Shu'un Filastinyya* 6: 104–122.

Kimmerling, Baruch. 1983. *Zionism and Territory*. Berkeley CA: Institute of International Studies.

King-Irani, Laurie. 2000. "Land, Identity and the Limits of Resistance in the Galilee," *Middle East Report* 216: 40–44.

Klausner, Samuel Z. 1987. "Martyrdom" in Mircea Eliade (ed.), *Encyclopedia of Religion* vol. 9. New York: Macmillan.

Kleib, Fathi. 2001. *Da'ere al-Hirman* (*The Circle of Deprivation: A View on the Services of UNRWA to the Palestinian Refugees in Lebanon*). Beirut: Sherkat al-Taqaddom al-Arabi.

Kleinman, Arthur, Veena Das, and Margaret Lock (eds.). 1997. *Social Suffering*. Berkeley CA: University of California Press.

Kramer, Martin. 1997. "The Oracle of Hizbullah: Sayyid Muhammad Husayn Fadlallah" in R. Scott Appleby (ed.), *Spokesmen for the Despised: Fundamentalist Leaders of the Middle East*. Chicago IL: University of Chicago Press: 83–181.

Kurayyam, Muhammad. 1995. "Sahafa al-Muqawama al-Filastiniyya fi al-Shitat" ("The Publications of the Palestinian Resistance in Diaspora"), *Samid* 102: 123–153.

Kuttab, Daoud. 1988. "A Profile of Stonethrowers," *Journal of Palestine Studies* 17(3): 14–23.

Laidi, Adila. 2001. "Notes on the Exhibit" and "Afterwords" in Sakakini Cultural Centre: 203–206.

Lambek, Michael. 1996. "The Past Imperfect: Remembering as Moral Practice" in Paul Antze and Michael Lambek (eds.), *Tense Past: Cultural Essays in Trauma and Memory*. London: Routledge: 235–255.

Le Goff, Jacques. 1992. *History and Memory*. Trans. Steven Randall. New York: Columbia University Press.

Leys, Colin and John S. Saul (ed.). 1995. *Namibia's Liberation Struggle: The Two-Edged Sword*. London: James Currey.

Lieven, Anatol. 2004. *America Right or Wrong: An Anatomy of American Nationalism*. Oxford: Oxford University Press.

Lindholm-Schulz, Helena. 1995. *One Year into Self-Government: Perceptions of Palestinian Political Elite*. Jerusalem: PASSIA.

Lindholm-Schulz, Helena. 1999. *The Reconstruction of Palestinian Nationalism: Between Revolution and Statehood*. Manchester: Manchester University Press.

Lockman, Zachary and Joel Beinin (eds.). 1989. *Intifada: The Palestinian Uprising Against Israeli Occupation*. Boston MA: South End Press.

Lønning, Dag Jørund. 1998. "Vision and Reality Diverging: Palestinian Survival strategies in the Post-Oslo Era" in George Giacaman and Dag Lønning (eds.), *After Oslo: New Realities, Old Problems*. London: Pluto Press: 162–188.

MacBride, Seán et al (eds.). 1983. *Israel in Lebanon: The Report of the International Commission to enquire into reported violations of International Law by Israel during its invasion of the Lebanon*. London: The International Commission.

Makhul, Akram Khouri. 1988. "This Is Not a Revolt – This Is a War," *Journal of Palestine Studies* 17(3): 91–99.

Malkki, Liisa. 1995. *Purity and Exile: Violence, Memory and National Cosmology among Hutu Refugees in Tanzania*. Chicago IL: University of Chicago Press.

Mallat, Chibli. 1993. *The Renewal of Islamic Law: Muhammad Baqer as-Sadr, Najaf and the Shi'i International*. Cambridge: Cambridge University Press.

Malley, Robert. 1996. *The Call from Algeria: Third Worldism, Revolution, and the Turn to Islam*. Berkeley CA: University of California Press.

Mamdani, Mahmood. 2000. "The Truth According to the TRC" in Amadiume and An-Na'im (eds.): 176–183.

Mamdani, Mahmood. 2004. *Good Muslim, Bad Muslim: America, the Cold War, and the Roots of Terror*. New York: Pantheon Books.

Mandas, Hani. 1974. *Al-'Amal wa-al-'Ummal fi al-Mukhayyam al-Filastini (Work and Workers in a Palestinian Refugee Camp: Field Research in Tal al-Za'tar Refugee Camp)*. Beirut: PLO Research Centre.

Mandas, Hani. 1976. "Tariq ila Tal al-Za'tar" ("The Road to Tal al-Za'tar"), *Shu'un Filastiniyya* 59: 6–30.

Mandas, Hani. 1977. *Tariq Tal al-Za'tar (The Way of Tal al-Za'tar)*. Beirut: PLO Research Centre.

Marvin, Carolyn and David W. Ingle. 1999. *Blood Sacrifice and the Nation: Totem Rituals and the American Flag*. Cambridge: Cambridge University Press.

Masalha, Nur. 1992. *Expulsion of the Palestinians: The Concept of 'Transfer' in Zionist Political Thought, 1882–1948*. Washington DC: Institute for Palestine Studies.

Masalha, Nur. 2003. *The Politics of Denial: Israel and the Palestinian Refugee Problem*. London: Pluto Press.

Massad, Joseph. 1995. "Conceiving the Masculine: Gender and Palestinian Nationalism," *Middle East Journal* 49(3): 467–483.

Massad, Joseph. 2003. "Liberating Songs: Palestine Put to Music," *Journal of Palestine Studies* 32(3): 21–38.

Mbembe, Achille. 2002. "African Modes of Self-Writing." Trans. Steven Randall. *Public Culture* 14(1): 239–273.

McGowan, Daniel and Marc H. Ellis. 1998. *Remembering Deir Yassin: The Future of Israel and Palestine*. New York: Olive Branch Press.

Meister, Robert. 2002. "Human Rights and the Politics of Victimhood," *Ethics & International Affairs* 16(2): 91–110.

Mejcher, Sonja. 2001. *Geschichten über Geschichten: Erinnerung in Romanwerk von Ilyas Huri*. Wiesbaden: Reichert Verlag.

Mertus, Julie. 2000. "Truth in a Box: The Limits of Justice through Judicial Mechanisms" in Amadiume and An-Na'im (eds.): 142–161.

Mishal, Shaul and Reuben Aharoni. 1994. *Speaking Stones: Communiqués from the Intifada Underground*. Syracuse NY: Syracuse University Press.

Mishal, Shaul and Avraham Sela. 2000. *The Palestinian Hamas: Vision, Violence and Coexistence*. New York: Columbia University Press.

Morris, Benny. 1987. *The Birth of the Palestinian Refugee Problem, 1947–1949*. Cambridge: Cambridge University Press.

Morris, Benny. 1997. *Israel's Border Wars 1949–1956*. Oxford: Clarendon Press.

Morris, Benny. 2004. *The Birth of the Palestinian Refugee Problem Revisited*. Cambridge: Cambridge University Press.

Morris, David. 1997. "Voice, Genre, and Moral Community" in Kleinman, Das, and Lock (eds.): 25–47.

Mosse, George. 1985. *Nationalism and Sexuality, Respectability and Abnormal Sexuality in Modern Europe*. New York: Howard Fertig.

Mosse, George L. 1990. *Fallen Soldiers: Reshaping the Memory of the World Wars*. Oxford: Oxford University Press.

Mouassali, Ahmad S. 1999. *Moderate and Radical Islamic Fundamentalism: The Quest for Modernity, Legitimacy, and the Islamic State*. Gainesville FL: University Press of Florida.

Mustafa, Abd al-Tawab. 2003. *Al-Amaliyyat al-Istishhadiyya: Taraf am Mamarr Ijbari? (Martyrdom Operations: Self Indulgence of Imperative Way?)*. Cairo: Dar El-Kalema.

An-Naim, Abdullahi. 2000. "Problems of Dependency: Human Rights Organizations in the Arab World," *Middle East Report* 214: 22–23; 46–48.

Nakhleh, Khalil. 2004. *The Myth of Palestinian Development: Political Aid and Sustainable Deceit*. Jerusalem: PASSIA.

Nandy, Ashish. 1983. *The Intimate Enemy: Loss and Recovery of Self under Colonialism*. Oxford: Oxford University Press.

Nasrallah, Rafiq (ed.). 1985. *Al Muqawama al–Wataniyya al-Lubnaniyya 1982– 1985: Al-Amaliyyat al-Istishhadiyya – Wathai'q wa Suwar (Lebanese National*

Resistance 1982–1985: Martyrdom Operations – Documents and Images). Beirut: al-Markaz al-Arabi lil-Ma'lumat.

Nassar, Jamal E. and Roger Heacock (eds.). 1991. *Intifada: Palestine at the Crossroads.* Birzeit: Birzeit University and Praeger Publishers.

Al-Natour, Souheil Mahmoud. 1993. *Awdha' al-Sha'ab al-Filastini fi Lubnan (The Situation of Palestinian People in Lebanon).* Beirut: Dar al-Taqaddum al-Arabi.

Al-Natour, Souheil. 1997. "The Legal Status of Palestinians in Lebanon," *Journal of Refugee Studies* 10(3): 360–378.

Al-Natour, Souheil. 2001. "Al-Filastiniyyun wa Ta'dil Qanun al-Mulkiyya al-'Aqariyya" ("Palestinians and the Passage of Property Ownership Law"). Beirut: Unpublished MS.

Nazzal, Nafez. 1974. "The Zionist Occupation of Western Galilee, 1948," *Journal of Palestine Studies* 3(3): 58–76.

Nazzal, Nafez. 1978. *The Palestinian Exodus from Galilee, 1948.* Washington DC: The Institute for Palestine Studies.

Newton, Huey P. 1995. *Revolutionary Suicide.* New York: Writers and Readers Publishing Inc.

Nkrumah, Kwame. 1973. *The Struggle Continues; 6 Panaf Pamphlets.* London: Panaf Books Ltd.

Nora, Pierre. 1996. "General Introduction: Between Memory and History" in Nora (ed.), *Realms of Memory,* 1996: 1–20.

Nora, Pierre (ed.). 1996. *Realms of Memory – Volume I: Conflicts and Divisions.* Trans. Arthur Goldhammer. New York: Columbia University Press.

Nora, Pierre (ed.). 1997. *Realms of Memory – Volume II: Traditions.* Trans. Arthur Goldhammer. New York: Columbia University Press.

Nora, Pierre (ed.). 1998. *Realms of Memory – Volume III: Symbols.* Trans. Arthur Goldhammer. New York: Columbia University Press.

Norton, Ann. 1993. "Ruling Memory," *Political Theory* 21(3): 453–463.

Norton, Augustus Richard. 1987. *Amal and the Shi'a: Struggle for the Soul of Lebanon.* Austin TX: University of Texas Press.

Norton, Claire. 2003. "Marines versus *Fedayeen*: Interpretive Naming and Constructing the 'Other,'" *Bad Subjects* 63: http://eserver.org/bs/63/norton.html

Olick, Jeffrey K. 2003. *States of Memory: Continuities, Conflicts, and Transformations in National Retrospection.* Durham NC: Duke University Press.

Olick, Jeffrey K. and Joyce Robbins. 1998. "Social Memory Studies: From 'Collective Memory' to the Historical Sociology of Mnemonic Practices," *Annual Review of Sociology* 24:105–40.

Osiel, Mark. 1997. *Mass Atrocity, Collective Memory, and the Law.* New Brunswick NJ: Transaction Publishers.

Paknejad, Shokrollah. 1971. *The "Palestine Group" Defends Itself in Military Tribunal (Text of Defence Speech of S. Paknejad in Military Tribunal No 3 of Teheran).* Firenze: Confederation of Iranian Students – National Union.

Palestinian National Council (PNC). 1988. *Proclamation of the Independent Palestinian State: Issued by the Nineteenth Session of the Palestine National Council, held in Algiers, November 15, 1988* in Lockman and Beinin (eds.): 395–399.

Palestinian Non-Governmental Organizations Network (PNGO). 2000. *Annual Report*. Ramallah: PNGO.

Pappé, Ilan. 1992. *The Making of the Arab–Israeli Conflict 1947–1951*. London: I. B. Tauris.

Pappé, Ilan. 2001. "The Tantura Case in Israel: The Katz Research and Trial," *Journal of Palestine Studies* 30(3): 19–39.

Peteet, Julie. 1991. *Gender in Crisis: Women and the Palestinian Resistance Movement*. New York: Columbia University Press.

Peteet, Julie. 1994. "Male Gender and Rituals of Resistance in the Palestinian 'Intifada': A Cultural Politics of Violence," *the American Ethnologist* 21(1): 31–49.

Peteet, Julie. 1995. "Transforming Trust: Dispossession and Empowerment among Palestinian Refugees" in Daniel and Knudsen (eds.): 168–186.

Peteet, Julie. 1996. "From Refugees to Minority: Palestinians in Post-War Lebanon," *Middle East Report* 200: 27–30.

Peteet, Julie. 1997. "Icons and Militants: Mothering in the Danger Zone," *Signs* 23(1): 103–129.

Peteet, Julie. 2000. "Refugees, Resistance and Identity" in John A Guidry, Michael D. Kennedy and Mayer N. Zald (eds.), *Globalization and Social Movements: Culture, Power, and the Transnational Public Sphere*. Ann Arbor MI: University of Michigan Press: 183–209.

Peteet, Julie. 2005. *Landscape of Hope and Despair: Palestinian Refugee Camps*. Philadelphia PA: University of Pennsylvania Press.

Picard, Elizabeth. 2002. *Lebanon: A Shattered Country*. Trans. Franklin Philip. New York: Holmes and Meier.

Picaudou, Nadine. 1989. "Pouvoir, société et espace dans l'imaginaire politique palestinien," *Maghreb-Machrek* (123): 108–115.

Polletta, Francesca. 1998a. "Contending Stories: Narrative in Social Movements," *Qualitative Sociology* 21(4): 419–446.

Polletta, Francesca. 1998b. " 'It Was Like a Fever': Narrative and Identity in Social Protest," *Social Problems* 45(2): 136–157.

Popular Memory Group. 1982. "Popular Memory: Theory, Politics, Method" in R. Johnson *et al.* (eds.): 205–252.

Portelli, Alessandro. 1997. *The Battle of Valle Giulia: Oral History and the Art of Dialogue*. Madison WI: The University of Wisconsin Press.

Portelli, Alessandro. 1998 [1981]. "What Makes Oral History Different" in Robert Perks and Alistair Thomson (eds.), *The Oral History Reader*. London: Routledge: 63–74.

Qutb, Sayyid. 1990. *Milestones*. Trans. Ahmad Zaki Hammad. Indianapolis IN: American Trust Publications.

Rackley, Edward Barnes. 2002. "Solidarity and the Limits of Humanitarianism: A Critique of Humanitarian Reason". New York: The New School for Social Research Ph.D. dissertation.

Rahimi, Babak. 2003. "Social Death and War: US Media Representations of Sacrifice in the Iraq War," *Bad Subjects* 63: http://eserver.org/bs/63/rahimi. html accessed on 22 December 2005.

Rahnema, Ali. 1998. *An Islamic Utopian: A Political Biography of Ali Shari'ati*. London: I. B. Tauris.

Ramphele, Mamphela. 1997. "Political Widowhood in South Africa: The Embodiment of Ambiguity" in Kleinman, Das, and Lock (eds.): 99–118.

Resnik, Julia. 2003. "'Sites of Memory' of the Holocaust: shaping national memory in the education system in Israel," *Nations and Nationalism* 9(2): 297–317.

Reuter, Christopher. 2002. *My Life Is a Weapon: A Modern History of Suicide Bombing*. Trans. Helena Ragg-Kirkby. Princeton NJ: Princeton University Press.

Ridhwan, Shafiq. 1992. *Al-Mulsaq al-Filastini: Mashakel al-Nishat wa-al-Tatawwar (The Palestinian Posters: Problems of Gensiş and Development)*. Damascus: Da'eret al-Thaqafah, Munazzamat al-Tahrir al-Filastini.

Rieff, David. 2002. *A Bed for the Night: Humanitarianism in Crisis*. New York: Simon and Schuster.

Roberts, Rebecca. 1999. "Bourj al Barahneh: The Significance of Village Origin in a Palestinian Refugee Camp". Durham NC: University of Durham MA dissertation.

Robin, Ron. 2003. "The Necropolitics of Homeland: The Role of Tombs and Village Cemeteries in the Middle East Conflict" in Ron Robin and Bo Stråth (eds.), *Homelands: Poetic Power and the Politics of Space*. Brussels: P.I. E. Peter Lang: 209–219.

Robinson, Glenn. 1997. *Building a Palestinian State: The Incomplete Revolution*. Bloomington IN: Indiana University Press.

Robinson, Shira. 2003. "Local Struggle, National Struggle: Palestinian Responses to the Kafr Qasim Massacre and Its Aftermath, 1956–1966," *International Journal of Middle East Studies* 35: 393–415.

Rogan, Eugene L. and Avi Shlaim (eds.). 2001. *The War for Palestine: Rewriting the History of 1948*. Cambridge: Cambridge University of Press.

Ron, James. 2003. *Frontiers and Ghettos: State Violence in Serbia and Israel*. Berkeley CA: University of California Press.

Rosenfeld, Maya. 2004. *Confronting the Occupation: Work, Education, and Political Activism of Palestinian Families in a Refugee Camp*. Berkeley CA: University of California Press.

Roy, Olivier. 2004. *Globalised Islam: The Search for a New Ummah*. London: Hurst and Company.

Roy, Sara. 2000. "The Transformation of Islamic NGOs in Palestine," *Middle East Report* 214: 24–26.

Saad-Ghorayeb, Amal. 2002. *Hizbu'llah: Politics, Religion*. London: Pluto Press.

Said, Edward W. 1984. "Permission to Narrate," *Journal of Palestine Studies* 8(3): 27–48.

Said, Edward W. 1994. *Culture and Imperialism*. New York: Vintage Books.

Said, Edward W. and Jean Mohr, 1986. *After the Last Sky: Palestinian Lives*. London: Vintage.

Sakakini Cultural Centre. 2001. *100 Shaheed, 100 Lives*. Ramallah: Khalil Sakakini Cultural Centre.

Salaita, Steven. 2001. "Liyana Badr: To Write and Remember," *Al-Jadid* 35: 10–11, 21.

Salman, Talal. 1969. *Ma' Fatah wa-al-Fida'iyyin (With Fatah and the Fida'iyyin)*. Beirut: Dar al-Awda.

Sandercock, Josie *et al.* (eds.). 2004. *Peace Under Fire: Israel, Palestine, and the International Solidarity Movement*. London: Verso Books.

Sarhan, Basim. 1973. "Al-Tarbiya al-Thawriyya al-Filastiniyya" ("Palestinian Revolutionary Education"), *Shu'un Filastiniyya* 25: 102–109.

Sayigh, Mai. 1992. Excerpts from *The Siege* in Salma Khadra Jayyusi (ed.), *Anthology of Modern Palestinian Literature*. New York: Columbia University: 685–695.

Sayigh, Rosemary. 1979. *Palestinians: From Peasants to Revolutionaries*. London: Zed Books.

Sayigh, Rosemary. 1985. "The *Mukhabarat* State: A Palestinian Woman's Testimony," *Journal of Palestine Studies* 24(3): 18–31.

Sayigh, Rosemary. 1994. *Too Many Enemies: The Palestinian Experience in Lebanon*. London: Zed Books.

Sayigh, Rosemary. 1995. "Palestinians in Lebanon: Harsh Present, Uncertain Future," *Journal of Palestine Studies* 25(1): 37–53.

Sayigh, Rosemary. 1996a. "Palestinian Refugees in Lebanon." Presentation to North American Coordinating Committee of NGOs on the Question of Palestine, New York.

Sayigh, Rosemary. 1996b. "Researching Gender in a Palestinian Camp: Political, Theoretical and Methodological Issues" in Deniz Kandiyoti (ed.), *Gendering the Middle East: Emerging Perspectives*. London: I. B. Tauris: 145–167.

Sayigh, Rosemary. 1998a. "Dis/Solving the 'Refugee Problem,'" *Middle East Report* 207: 19–23.

Sayigh, Rosemary. 1998b. "Palestinian Camp Women as Tellers of History," *Journal of Palestine Studies* 27(2): 42–258.

Sayigh, Rosemary. 2001. "Palestinian Refugees in Lebanon: Implantations, Transfer, or Return?" *Middle East Policy* 8(1): 94–105.

Sayigh, Rosemary. 2002. "Bibliography," *al-Jana*: 67–73.

Sayigh, Yezid Y. 1983. "Palestinian Military Performance in the 1982 War," *Journal of Palestine Studies* 12(4): 3–24.

Sayigh, Yezid Y. 1997. *Armed Struggle and the Search for State: The Palestinian National Movement, 1949–1993*. Oxford: Oxford University Press.

Sayigh, Yusif A. 1952. "Economic Implications of UNRWA Operations in Jordan, Syria and Lebanon". Beirut: American University of Beirut Ph.D. dissertation.

Schiff, Ze'ev and Ehud Ya'ari. 1984. *Israel's Lebanon War*. New York: Simon and Schuster.

Schleifer, Abdullah. 1995. "Izz al-Din al-Qassam: Preacher and *Mujahid*" in Edmund Burke III (ed.), *Struggle and Survival in the Modern Middle East*. Berkeley CA: University of California Press: 164–178.

Scott, James C. 1990. *Domination and the Arts of Resistance: Hidden Transcripts*. New Haven CT: Yale University Press.

Seale, Patrick. 1992. *Abu Nidal: A Gun for Hire.* New York: Random House.

Segev, Tom. 1986. *1949: The First Israelis.* New York: Owl Books.

Seitz, Charmaine. 2003. "ISM at the Crossroads: the Evolution of the International Solidarity Movement," *Journal of Palestine Studies* 32(4): 50–67.

Seitz, Charmaine. 2004. "A New Kind of Killing," *Middle East Report Online* (30 March 2004). http://www.merip.org/mero/mero033004.html

Shafiq, Munir. 1994. *Shuhada' wa-Masira: Abu Hassan wa-Hamdi wa-Ikhwanuhuma (Martyrs and the March: Abu Hassan, Hamdi and Their Brothers).* Beirut: Wafa' Institute.

Shafir, Gershon and Yoav Peled. 2002. *Being Israel: The Dynamics of Multiple Citizenship.* Cambridge: Cambridge University Press.

Shahid, Leila. 2002. "The Sabra and Shatila Massacres: Eye-Witness Reports" with an introduction by Linda Butler, *Journal of Palestine Studies* 32(1): 36–58.

al-Shaikh, Zakaria. 1984. "Sabra and Shatila 1982: Resisting the Massacre," *Journal of Palestine Studies* 14(1): 57–90.

Shamgar-Handelman, Lea. 1986. *Israeli War Widows: Beyond the Glory of Heroism.* Boston MA: Bergin and Garvey Publishers.

Sharabi, Hisham. 1969. *Palestine and Israel: The Lethal Dilemma.* New York: Pegasus.

Shari'ati, Ali. 1981. *Martyrdom: Arise and Bear Witness.* Trans. Ali Asghar Ghassemy. Tehran: The Ministry of Islamic Guidance.

Shari'ati, Ali. N. D. *Ali: Osture-yi dar tarikh (Ali: A Legend in History).* Tehran: n.p.

Sharif, 'Adnan (ed.). 1977. *Tal al-Za'tar: Al-Shahid wa-al-Shahid (Tal al-Za'tar: The Martyr and the Witness).* Beirut: General Union of Palestinian Women.

Sharoni, Simona. 1996. "Gender and the Israeli-Palestinian Accord: Feminist Approaches to International Relations" in Deniz Kandiyoti (ed.), *Gendering the Middle East: Emerging Perspectives.* London: I. B. Tauris: 107–126.

Shearer, Daniel and Anuschka Meyer. 2005. "The Dilemma of Aid Under Occupation" in Michael Keating, Anne Le More, and Robert Lowe (eds.), *Aid, Diplomacy and Facts on the Ground: the Case of Palestine.* London: Royal Institute of International Affairs: 165–176.

Sheffi, Na'ama. 2002. "Israeli Education System in Search of a Pantheon of Heroes, 1948–1967," *Israeli Studies* 7(2): 62–83.

Shehadeh, Raja. 1982. *The Third Way: A Journal of Life in the West Bank.* London: Quartet Books.

Shehadeh, Raja. 1992. *The Sealed Room: Selections from the Diary of a Palestinian Living Under Israeli Occupation: September 1990–August 1991.* London: Quartet Books.

Shepard, William A. 1996. *Sayyid Qutb and Islamic Activism: A Translation and Critical Analysis of Social Justice in Islam.* Leiden: E. J. Brill.

Shlaim, Avi. 1998. *The Politics of Partition: King Abdullah, the Zionists, and Palestine 1921–1951.* Oxford: Oxford University Press.

Shlaim, Avi. 2000. *The Iron Wall: Israel and the Arab World.* London: Penguin Books.

Shlaim, Avi. 2001. "Israel and the Arab Coalition in 1948" in Rogan and Shlaim (eds.): 79–103.

Short, Ramsay. 2003. "Struggling to create a future for women," *Daily Star* 18 March 2003.

Shoufani, Elias. 1972. "The Fall of a Village," *Journal of Palestine Studies* 1(4): 108–121.

Siddiq, Muhammad. 1984. *Man is a Cause: Political Consciousness and the Fiction of Ghassan Kanafani*. Seattle WA: University of Washington Press.

Siddiq, Muhammad. 1995. "On Ropes of Memory: Narrating the Palestinian Refugees" in Daniel and Knudsen (eds.): 87–101.

Siegel, Ellen. 1983. "Inside and Outside the Hospital, People Were Screaming: 'Haddad, *Kataeb*, Israel – Massacre,'" *Journal of Palestine Studies* 12(2): 61–71.

Siegel, Ellen. 2001. "After Nineteen Years: Sabra and Shatila Remembered," *Middle East Policy* 8(4): 86–101.

Slyomovics, Susan. 1998. *The Objects of Memory: Arab and Jew Narrate the Palestinian Village*. Philadelphia PA: University of Pennsylvania Press.

Smith, Anthony D. 1986. *The Ethic Origin of Nations*. London: Blackwell Publishers.

Smith, Rogers. 2003. *Stories of Peoplehood: The Politics and Morals of Political Membership*. Cambridge: Cambridge University Press.

Somers, Margaret. 1992. "Narrativity, Narrative Identity, and Social Action: Rethinking English Working-Class Formation," *Social Science History* 16(4): 591–630.

Soukarieh, Mayssoun Faden. 2000. "For the Sake of Remembrance: A Reader in English for 9th Graders in the Palestinian Camps in Lebanon." Beirut: American University of Beirut MA. Thesis.

Stein, Kenneth W. 1990. "The Intifada and the 1936–39 Uprising: A Comparison," *Journal of Palestine Studies* 19(4): 64–85.

Stein, Rebecca and Ted Swedenburg (eds.). 2005. *Palestine/Israel and the Politics of Popular Culture*. Durham, NC: Duke University Press.

Stohlman, Nancy and Laurieann Aladin. 2003. *Live from Palestine: International and Palestinian Direct Action Against the Occupation*. Boston MA: Southend Press.

Sukarieh, Mayssoun. 1999. "Through Children's Eyes: Children's Rights in Shatila Camp," *Journal of Palestine Studies* 29(1): 50–57.

Sukarieh, Mayssoun. 2001a. "Documenting Silences in Interviews: Remembering (and Forgetting) the Nakba in Palestinian Refugees' Social Memory." Unpublished Manuscript.

Sukarieh, Mayssoun. 2001b. "Life in the Camps" in Roane Carey (ed.), *The New Intifada: Resisting Israel's Apartheid*. London: Verso: 287–292.

Suleiman, Jabir. 1997a. "15 'Aman 'ala Huzayran/Yuniu 1982: Shihadat 'an Ma'raka 'Burj al-Shamali' wa-Majazar al-Qusuf al-Israili" ("15 Years after June 1982: Testimonies about the Battle of Burj al-Shamali and the Massacre by Israeli Missiles"), *Majalla Dirasat al-Filastiniyya* 32: 67–97.

Suleiman, Jabir. 1997b. "Palestinians in Lebanon and the Role of Non-governmental Organizations," *Journal of Refugee Studies* 10(3): 397–410.

Suleiman, Jabir. 1999. "The Current Political, Organizational, and Security Situation in the Palestinian Refugee Camps of Lebanon," *Journal of Palestine Studies* 29(1): 66–80.

Sundstrom, Elisabet. 2003. "Welcome Way-Station for Backpackers' Trail Soon to Open in Shatila," *Daily Star* 16 July 2003: 10.

Swedenburg, Ted. 1990. "The Palestinian Peasant as National Signifier," *Anthropological Quarterly* 63: 18–30.

Swedenburg, Ted. 1995. *Memories of Revolt: The 1936–1939 Rebellion and the Palestinian National Past*. Minneapolis MN: University of Minnesota Press.

Talas, Mustafa. 1984. *Mazbaha Sabra wa-Shatila (Sabra and Shatila The Slaughterhouse)*. Damascus: Dar al-Talas.

Taleqani, Mahmud, Murtada Mutahhari and Ali Shari'ati. 1986. *Jihad and Shahadat: Struggle and Martyrdom in Islam*. Mehdi Abedi and Gary Legenhausen (eds.). Houston TX: The Institute for Research and Islamic Studies.

Tamari, Salim. 1991. "The Palestinian Movement in Transition: Historical Reversals and Uprisings," *Journal of Palestine Studies* 20(2): 57–70.

Tamari, Salim. 2002. "Narratives of Exile," *Palestine-Israel Journal* 9(4): 101–109.

Tamari, Salim. 2003. "Bourgeois Nostalgia and Exilic Narratives" in Ron Robin and Bo Stråth (eds.), *Homelands: Poetic Power and the Politics of Space*. Brussels: P.I.E. Peter Lang: 61–77.

Tamari, Salim (ed.). 2002. *Jerusalem 1948: the Arab Neighbourhoods and their Fate in the War*. Jerusalem: Institute of Jerusalem Studies and Badil Resource Center.

Terrill, W. Andrew. 2001. "The Political Mythology of the Battle of Karameh," *Middle East Journal* 55(1): 91–111.

Thornhill, Teresa. 1992. *Making Women Talk: The Interrogation of Palestinian Women Security Detainees by the Israeli General Security Services*. London: Lawyers for Palestinian Human Rights.

Tilly, Charles. 1994. "Afterword: Political Memories in Space and Time" in Jonathan Boyarin (ed.), *Remapping Memory: The Politics of TimeSpace*. Minneapolis MN: University of Minnesota Press: 241–256.

Tilly, Charles. 2003. *The Politics of Collective Violence*. Cambridge: Cambridge University Press.

Tonkin, Elizabeth. 1992. *Narrating Our Past: The Social Construction of Oral History*. Cambridge University Press.

Toufic, Jalal. 2002. "I Am the Martyr Sana Yusif Muhaydli," *Discourse* 24(1): 76–84.

Trouillot, Michel-Rolph. 1995. *Silencing the Past: Power and the Production of History*. Boston MA: Beacon Press.

Turki, Fawaz. 1972. *The Disinherited: Journal of a Palestinian Exile*. New York: Monthly Review Press.

Turki, Fawaz. 1988. *Soul in Exile: Lives of a Palestinian Revolutionary*. New York: Monthly Review Press.

Turki, Fawaz. 1994. *Exile's Return: The Making of a Palestinian American*. New York: The Free Press.

Turner, Victor. 1980. "Social Dramas and Stories about Them" in W. J. T. Mitchell (ed.), *On Narrative*. Chicago IL: University of Chicago Press: 137–164.

Twiss, Tom. 2003. "Damage to Palestinian Libraries and Archives during the Spring of 2002." Report of International Responsibilities Task Force of the American Library Association's Social Responsibilities Round Table. http://www.pitt.edu/~ttwiss/irtf/palestinlibsdmg.html accessed on 31 October 2005.

Tzahor, Ze'ev. 1995. "Ben-Gurion's Mythopolitics" in Robert Wistrich and David Ohana (eds.), *The Shaping of Israeli Identity: Myth, Memory and Trauma*. London: Frank Cass: 61–84.

Al-'Umd, Salwa (ed.). 1982. "Shihadat 'an al-Harb" ("Testimonies on the War"), *Shu'un Filastiniyya* 132–133: 8–16.

Al-'Umd, Salwa (ed.). 1983a. "Al-'Aqid Abu Musa: Lit al-Arab, Kul al-Arab, A'tu Nisf Ma A'tuhu Beirut" ("Colonel Abu Musa: The Arab [regimes], all of them, didn't give half of what Beirut gave"), *Shu'un Filastiniyya* 134: 53–70.

Al-'Umd, Salwa (ed.). 1983b. "Shihada Mamduh Nawfal 'an al-Harb: al-wahda wataniyya wa al-wahda 'askariyya" ("The Testimony of Mamduh Nawfal: National Unity and Military Unity"), *Shu'un Filastiniyya* 135: 27–39.

Al-'Umd, Salwa (ed.). 1983c. "Yasir Arafat yatahaddath 'an al-Harb: Ma'raka Beirut Shahdat al-Wilada al-Fi'liyya lil-Quwwat al-'Askariyya al-Filastiniyya" ("Yasir Arafat speaks on the war: the Battle of Beirut saw the operational birth of the Palestinian military forces"), *Shu'un Filastiniyya* 136–137: 21–30.

UN–General Assembly (UNGA). 2001a. *Report of the Commissioner-General of the United Nations Relief and Works Agency for Palestine Refugees in the Near East*. New York: United Nations General Assembly Official Records, 2 October 2001.

UN–General Assembly (UNGA). 2001b. *Report of the Commissioner-General of the United Nations Relief and Works Agency for Palestine Refugees in the Near East. Addendum: Programme Budget 2002–2003*. New York: United Nations General Assembly Official Records, 2 October 2001.

United Nations Relief and Works Agency (UNRWA). 2000. *UNRWA and the Palestinian Refugees: 50 Years*. Gaza: UNRWA Public Information Office.

Varon, Jeremy. 2004. *Bringing the War Home: The Weather Underground, the Red Army Faction, and Revolutionary Violence in the Sixties and Seventies*. Berkeley CA: University of California Press.

Verdery, Katherine. 1996. "Whither 'Nation' and 'Nationalism'?" in Gopal Balakrishnan (ed.), *Mapping the Nation*. London: Verso: 226–234.

Verdery, Katherine. 1999. *The Political Lives of Dead Bodies: Reburial and Postsocialist Change*. New York: Columbia University Press.

War, Hazel and Nasser Abu Bakr. 2003. "Palestinians urge Iraq to Learn from Jenin Battle," Agence France Press, 4 April 2003.

Warnock, Kitty. 1990. *Land before Honour: Palestinian Women in the Occupied Territories*. New York: Monthly Review Press.

Watson, Rubie S. (ed.). 1994. *Memory, History, and Opposition under State Socialism*. Santa Fe CA: School of American Research Advanced Seminar Series.

Al-Wazir, Khalil and Ghassan Bishara. 1985. "The 17th National Council," *Journal of Palestine Studies* 14(2): 3–12.

Weighill, Marie-Lousie. 1999. "Palestinians in Exile: Legal, Geographical and Statistical Aspects" in Ghada Karmi and Cotran, Eugene (eds.), *The Palestinian Exodus (1948–1998)*. Reading MA: Ithaca Press: 7–36.

Weitz, Yechiam. 1995. "Political Dimensions of Holocaust Memory in Israel during the 1950s" in Robert Wistrich and David Ohana (eds.), *The Shaping of Israeli Identity: Myth, Memory and Trauma*. London: Frank Cass.: 129–145.

Werbner, Pnina. 2002. *Imagined Diasporas among Manchester Muslims*. Oxford: James Currey.

Werbner, Richard. 1995. "Human Rights and Moral Knowledge: Arguments of Accountability in Zimbabwe" in Marilyn Strathern (ed.), *Shifting Contexts: Transformation in Anthropological Knowledge*. London: Routledge: 99–117.

White, Hayden. 1987. *The Content of the Form: Narrative Discourse and Historical Representation*. Baltimore MD: Johns Hopkins University Press.

Wiktorowicz, Quintan. 2005. *Radical Islam Rising: Muslim Extremism in the West*. New York: Rowman & Littlefield Publishers.

Willetts, Peter. 1978. *The Non-Aligned Movement: the Origins of a Third World Alliance*. London: Frances Pinter.

Williams, Raymond. 1985 [1973]. *The Country and the City*. London: Hogarth Press.

Winter, Jay. 1995. *Sites of Memory, Sites of Mourning: The Great War in European Cultural History*. Cambridge: Cambridge University Press.

Wright, Richard. 1995 [1956]. *The Color Curtain: A Report on the Bandung Conference*. Jackson: University Press of Mississippi.

Yahya, Adel H. 1999. *The Palestinian Refugees 1948–1998: An Oral History*. Ramallah: The Palestinian Association for Cultural Exchange (PACE).

Yoneyama, Lisa. 1999. *Hiroshima Traces: Time, Space, and the Dialectics of Memory*. Berkeley CA: University of California Press.

Young, James E. 1993. *The Texture of Memory: Holocaust Memorials and Meaning*. New Haven CT: Yale University Press.

Young, Robert J. C. 2001. *Postcolonialism: An Historical Introduction*. London: Blackwell Publishers.

Yunis, Ayman H. 2001. "Al-Muqabala: Al-Rawaiyya al-Filastiniyya Liyana Badr" ("Interview: Palestinian Writer, Liyana Badr"), *Al-Hasna'* 1708 (August): 51–53.

Yuval-Davis, Nira. 1997. *Gender and Nation*. London: Sage Publications.

Zaytun, Safa' Husayn. ND. *Sabra and Shatila: Al-Mazbaha (Sabra and Shatila: the Massacre)*. Cairo: Dar al-Fattah al-Arabi.

Zertal, Idith. 2005. *Israel's Holocaust and the Politics of Nationhood*. Trans. Chaya Galai. Cambridge: Cambridge University Press.

Zerubavel, Eviatar. 2003. "Calendars and History: A Comparative Study of the Social Organization of Memory" in Olick (ed.): 315–338.

Zerubavel, Yael. 1994. "The Death of Memory and the Memory of Death: Masada and the Holocaust as Historical Metaphors," *Representations* 45: 72–100.

Zerubavel, Yael. 1995. *Recovered Roots: Collective Memory and the Making of Israeli National Tradition*. Chicago IL: University of Chicago Press.

Zubaida, Sami. 2004. "Islam and Nationalism: Continuities and Contradictions," *Nations and Nationalism* 10(4): 407–420.

Zurayq, Qustantin. 1948. *Ma'na al-Nakba (The Meaning of the Catastrophe)*. Beirut: Dar al-'Ilm al-Malayin.

Index

Cambridge Middle East Studies 27

Printed in Great Britain
by Amazon